EXPERIMENTAL PSYCHOLOGY
An Active Learning Workbook

CHRISTOPHER LEGROW | APRIL FUGETT

Kendall Hunt
publishing company

Kendall Hunt
publishing company

www.kendallhunt.com
Send all inquiries to:
4050 Westmark Drive
Dubuque, IA 52004-1840

CONTENTS

MODULE

1

The Four Goals of Psychological Research

As a discipline, psychology is dedicated to the scientific study of human behavior and mental processes. Psychologists use a variety of research methods to acquire new knowledge, gain a more thorough understanding of the diversity of human behavior, develop solutions for individual, organizational, and social problems, and improve our quality of life. Psychologists are guided by four primary goals when designing and conducting psychological research. These goals are to describe, predict, explain, and modify behavior.[1,2,3,4]

Describing Behavior

One of the primary goals of psychological research is to provide a detailed and accurate description of the world we live in. Psychologists accomplish this goal through the process of systematic observation.[1,2,5,6] Observing behavior in a variety of situations allows psychologists to acquire knowledge that is sufficient to make sound predictions about future behavior, identify the underlying causes of behavior, and to ultimately control/modify behavior to improve society and peoples' lives. While psychology focuses mainly on human behavior and mental processes, psychologists are also interested in observing and describing the behavior of animals; especially when the knowledge gained from observing animal behavior generalizes to the study of human behavior.[1,4,6] Psychologists also observe human behavior and mental processes across multiple levels of analysis (e.g. individuals, groups, organizations, sub-cultures, cultures).

To describe the world accurately, psychologists must ensure the observations they make are objective and reliable.[2] To enhance objectivity and reliability, psychologists need to clearly define the behaviors and/or mental processes to be observed (i.e. "operational definitions"). An observer can then use these definitions to determine whether or not a specific behavior or mental process is observed. While most behaviors are visible and easily observed, psychologists often have to infer information about mental processes from observable behaviors (e.g. emotions may be inferred from an individual's observable body language).[5] Psychologists also develop coding systems to help observers describe the characteristics of the situation in which observations are occurring, record the types or frequency of behaviors observed, and document any unexpected or atypical behaviors that are observed.[1] When studying human and animal behavior, psychologists may use multiple observers. When multiple observers produce reliable observations of behavior, psychologists become more confident that their descriptions of behavior are accurate. Over time, as observations of behavior accumulate, psychologists may begin to see systematic relationships between the behaviors, mental processes, subject characteristics, and/or situational characteristics that they are observing.[1,2,5,6] When systematic relationships are observed, psychologists are then ready to pursue the second goal of psychological research: predicting behavior.

Predicting Behavior

When a systematic relationship is observed between two variables, psychologists will describe the variables as being "correlated." A correlation represents the degree of relationship between two variables. When examining the nature of the correlation between two variables, psychologists will evaluate the strength and direction of the correlation. Psychologists use a statistic known as a correlation coefficient to measure the strength of the relationship between two variables. Correlation coefficients range in value from .00 (i.e. indicating the absence of a systematic relationship between two variables) to 1.00 (i.e. indicating the presence of a perfect systematic relationship between two variables). The higher the correlation coefficient value, the stronger the relationship between the two variables. The direction of a correlation is described by psychologists as positive (+) or negative (−). A positive correlation indicates that as the value of variable A increases, the value of variable B also increases (e.g. as study time increases, exam scores increase). A negative correlation indicates that as the value of variable A increases, the value of variable B decreases (e.g. as class absences increase, exam scores decrease).[7]

Once the nature of the relationship between two variables is known, psychologists can use this information to make predictions about future behavior.[1,3,5] When two variables are correlated, if the value of variable A is known, psychologists can predict the likely value of variable B (e.g. if a student's mid-term exam score is known, a prediction can be made about the student's likely score on the final exam).[1,6,7] The level of confidence in the prediction would be determined by the strength of the correlation that exists between the two variables. The stronger the correlation, the greater the confidence in the accuracy of the prediction. Knowing variables are correlated allows psychologists to make predictions about future behavior; however, it does not allow psychologists to make statements of cause and effect. While there may be a systematic relationship between two variables (e.g. as the number of grandchildren increases, memory loss increases), there may not be a causal relationship between the variables (i.e. clearly, having more grandchildren does not cause someone to experience increased memory loss).[1,6] An unidentified 3rd variable (e.g. age) might be the true underlying cause of the systematic relationship between the two variables (e.g. as age increases, individuals are likely to have more grandchildren and to experience a decline in memory skills).[8,9] To make statements of cause and effect, psychologists need to pursue the third goal of psychological research: explaining behavior.

Explaining Behavior

To truly understand why events occur in the world around us and why people think, feel, and act the way they do, psychologists must identify the underlying cause (or causes) of behavior and/or mental processes.[1,2,3] Making a cause and effect statement, however, requires a higher standard of evidence than correlational evidence used by psychologists to make predictions about future behavior. For psychologists to acquire the evidence necessary to make a cause and effect statement, they must conduct controlled, systematic, and rigorous experimental research.

Psychologists begin by generating a hypothesis (i.e. a proposed explanation) about the cause of a behavior or mental process (e.g. seasonal affective disorder (SAD)[10] is caused by a reduction in sunlight during the fall and winter months).[1,2] The hypothesis is then tested under controlled conditions (often in a lab) where the proposed cause (i.e. reduced sunlight) can be isolated and its effects studied (e.g. Fifty people with SAD are brought to a laboratory. Twenty-five receive light therapy and 25 receive no light therapy. All other factors are kept constant across participants. The severity of SAD-related depression is compared across groups.). If the results fail to support the hypothesis (i.e. people who received light therapy did not have lower SAD-related depression than people who received no light therapy), psychologists will then have to propose and test new hypotheses to identify the cause of the behavior.[1,2] If the results support the hypothesis (i.e. people who received light therapy did have significantly lower SAD-related depression than people who received no light therapy), psychologists will conduct additional experiments in an effort to replicate the results. If the results can be replicated and alternative explanations can be eliminated, psychologists are now in a position to make a cause and effect statement.

Over time, as psychologists and other researchers conduct additional experiments and new knowledge emerges, psychologists develop a broader and more thorough understanding of a behavior or mental process (e.g. genetic, neurological, psychological, situational influences on SAD). Psychologists may then develop a theory that serves to organize the existing knowledge, specifies the conditions under which a behavior or mental process will or will not occur, and which can be used to generate additional research hypotheses.[1,2] A theory, however, is tentative and must be expanded, modified, or even abandoned as new research evidence emerges.[2,5] Once psychologists have identified the cause (or causes) of behaviors and mental processes, they are now in a position to pursue the fourth goal of psychological research: modifying behavior.

Modifying Behavior

Once the causes of behavior and mental processes have been identified, psychologists can use that knowledge to attempt to modify behavior.[2] By modifying behavior, psychologists can help solve problems faced by individuals, organizations, and society. They can also improve the quality of peoples' lives.[1,3,4] For individuals, psychologists can develop therapeutic, educational, and behavior modification programs designed to modify unhealthy behavior (e.g. addiction, self-injury, obesity), change unhealthy attitudes (e.g. prejudice, pessimism), develop important life skills (e.g. parenting, financial planning), and help people cope more effectively with problems of everyday life (e.g. divorce, unemployment). When working with organizations, psychologists can develop training programs to teach employees to be more safety conscious and to work more effectively in a team. They can also teach management how to implement programs designed to modify employee behavior and to reduce costly personnel problems (e.g. lateness, absenteeism). At the societal level, psychologists can work with community leaders to develop interventions designed to improve quality of life within the community through the modification of behavior. Such interventions could target community beautification (e.g. pollution, litter, graffiti), crime prevention (e.g. neighborhood watches, child abuse prevention programs), education (e.g. stay-in-school campaigns, after-school enrichment programs), as well as public health (e.g. alcohol and drug education, health/fitness education, health screenings, healthy school lunch programs, sex education). The success of these interventions and behavior modification programs will in large part be determined by the extent to which they are able to directly target the underlying cause (or causes) of the behavior that are desired to be changed.

EXERCISE 1A

Diverse Settings and Interests—Common Research Goals

To study the diversity of human behavior, psychologists conduct research across a variety of settings. Some psychologists can be found in clinical and counseling settings, evaluating the effectiveness of therapeutic interventions (e.g. therapy, medication, education). Others can be found working in laboratory settings studying human and animal behavior as well as conducting experiments on a wide range of mental processes (e.g. emotion, perception, motivation). Still others can be found in applied settings (e.g. schools, businesses, hospitals, military) conducting research and designing interventions to solve applied problems. Regardless of the settings in which they work, or the areas of interest that serve as the focus for their research, psychologists' research is designed to achieve one or more of the 4 primary goals of psychological research: to describe, predict, explain, or modify behavior. Below are 20 scenarios, each describing research being conducted by psychologists across a variety of clinical, laboratory, and/or applied settings. For each of the 20 scenarios, please determine if the primary goal of the psychologist's research is to describe, predict, explain, or modify behavior and write your answer in the space provided.

01. A School Psychologist develops an educational program for students designed to improve anger management and communication skills in an effort to reduce the number of verbal and physical altercations occurring at school.

> **Goal =** modifying

02. A Developmental Psychologist assesses students currently enrolled in kindergarten in the local school district and writes a report for the superintendent of schools summarizing the types of developmental disabilities present, prevalence of each type of disability, and the percentage of students who will require early intervention services from the school district.

> **Goal =** describing

03. A Clinical Psychologist who specializes in the treatment of depression treats half his patients with cognitive-behavioral therapy and the other half with humanistic therapy to determine if differences in treatment outcomes are due to differences in therapeutic approach.

> **Goal =** explaining

04. An Environmental Psychologist observes people walking their dogs in a local park and finds nearly 80% of dog owners are not picking up their dogs' poop. In response, he places free bags, pooper scoopers, and signs reading "Don't Be a Poop—Please Scoop" around the park to see if more dog owners will begin cleaning up after their dogs when walking in the park.

> **Goal =** modifying

05. A Physiological Psychologist measures the blood pressure, cholesterol level, triglyceride level, height, and weight of 100 adults, and she then uses these measurements to determine the likelihood that each of the 100 adults will suffer a heart attack before the age of 40.

> **Goal =** predicting

06. An Experimental Psychologist places 25 rats in a room filled with cigarette smoke and 25 rats in a smoke-free room for a year. At the end of the year, she examines all 50 rats for the presence of tumor growth to determine if exposure to second-hand smoke can cause cancer.

> **Goal =** explaining

07. A Social Psychologist disguises himself as an elderly man and pretends to fall and injure himself at various locations around a community. He then records the types of assistance he receives from people who pass by him (e.g. no assistance, provide first aid, call police, call ambulance) and the characteristics of those people who offer assistance (e.g. age, sex).

> **Goal =** describing

08. A Cognitive Psychologist develops a test assessing memory impairment and administers the test to 25 people who have suffered brain injuries. She uses the test scores to estimate the amount of rehabilitation each person will need to recover their memory abilities.

> **Goal =** predicting

09. An Industrial-Organizational psychologist develops a theory of job satisfaction to illustrate how work-related and non-work-related factors combine to determine whether individuals will be satisfied or dissatisfied with their current job positions.

> **Goal =** explaining

10. A Quantitative Psychologist analyzes physical measurements (e.g. height, weight, % body fat, arm length), 40-yard dash times, bench press weights, and agility test performances of 50 college football players. He uses the data to help professional football teams determine the likelihood that each of these college players will have a successful professional career.

> **Goal =** predicting

11. A Sports Psychologist trains 10 professional golfers to use techniques of relaxation and positive visual imagery in an effort to help these golfers hit more quality shots and to make more putts when playing under the pressure of a professional golf tournament.

> **Goal =** modifying

12. A Cross-Cultural Psychologist observed the cultural practices and rituals associated with birth, marriage, and death across several cultures. She then wrote a book in which she summarized the major similarities and differences she observed across cultures.

> **Goal =** describing

13. A Neuropsychologist conducts brain scans on individuals with a history of chronic alcohol abuse to show them the damaging effects alcohol is having on their brains. She believes by seeing visual images of the damage to their brains, these individuals will stop using alcohol and decide to enter rehabilitation facilities.

> **Goal =** modifying

14. A Consumer Psychologist places 10 products on the bottom shelves in a supermarket for a week. He then places the same 10 products on the middle shelves for a week. Finally, he places the 10 products on the top shelves for a week. He wants to determine whether the shelf placement of a product can cause significant differences in product sales.

> **Goal =** predicting

explaining

15. A Personality Psychologist administers a personality inventory to high school students to identify which personality traits are most strongly related to popularity in high school.

> **Goal =** describing

predicting

16. A Community Psychologist conducts a series of town hall meetings with residents of the local community to identify the most pressing problems and issues the community faces. He prepares a report for the Mayor summarizing the results of the town hall meetings.

> **Goal =** *describing*

17. An Educational Psychologist recruits 50 college students to take a statistics course. He has 25 students complete an online version of the course and 25 students complete an in-class, lecture-style version of the course. He then administers a test of statistical knowledge to the students to determine whether the different methods of instruction produced a difference in the level of statistical knowledge displayed by the students.

> **Goal =** *explaining*

18. A Health Psychologist convinces the CEO of a large organization to allow employees to take naps during the workday (with pay!) in an effort to increase employee production and reduce fatigue-related employee errors and accidents.

> **Goal =** *modifying*

19. A Forensic Psychologist conducts in-depth interviews and psychological assessments on prison inmates incarcerated for committing violent crimes. He uses the results of these interviews and assessments to provide the prison parole board with his opinions as to the likelihood each of the inmates would commit a violent crime if paroled.

> **Goal =** *predicting*

20. A Media Psychologist is hired by executives at a major television network to monitor web pages, blogs, social media, and tweets related to the network's top-rated show. Each week, he prepares a presentation for the network executives summarizing fan reactions to the most recent episode of the show, new story-lines, and characters introduced into the show.

> **Goal =** *describing*

EXERCISE 1B

Identifying Research Goals in Published Research

After designing, conducting, and analyzing the results of their research investigations, psychologists can share the results of their research with the scientific community by publishing their work in peer-reviewed psychology journals. The peer-review process helps to ensure that the research was well-designed, analyzed appropriately, based on sound scientific principles and theory, and conducted in an ethical manner. The peer-review process also ensures the research makes a valuable contribution to the field and that it achieves one or more of the 4 primary goals of psychological research; to describe, predict, explain, or modify behavior.

Below is a list of citations for journal articles that present the results of psychological research. Please select **three (3)** of the citations from the list and conduct an Internet or library search for a full-text version of the articles (*Note*: a full-text version for all of the articles on the list can be found through a Google Scholar search—www.googlescholar.com). After locating and reading each of your three articles, you will be asked to do the following:

For **each** of your three articles:

(a) Determine which of the 4 goals of psychological research the researcher(s) were attempting to achieve (Note: Researchers may attempt to achieve multiple goals).

(b) Provide a rationale for your determinations (i.e. What information in the articles illustrates an attempt to describe, predict, explain, or modify behavior?)

(c) Describe the main conclusion(s) that can be drawn from the research.

Article Citation List

Bator, R. J., Bryan, A. D., & Schultz, P. W. (2011). Who gives a hoot?: Intercept surveys of litterers and disposers. *Environment and Behavior, 43*(3), 295–315.

Bohrn, I., Carbon, C. C., & Hutzler, F. (2010). Mona Lisa's smile: Perception or deception? *Psychological Science, 21*(3), 378–380.

Clifasefi, S. L, Bernstein, D. M., Mantonakis, A., & Loftus, E. F. (2013). "Queasy does it": False alcohol beliefs and memories may lead to diminished alcohol preferences. *Acta Psychologica, 143*, 14–19.

Geier, A., Wansink, B., & Rozin, P. (2012). Red potato chips: Segmentation cues can substantially decrease food intake. *Health Psychology, 31*(3), 398–401.

Greitemeyer, T., & Osswald, S. (2010). Effects of prosocial video games on prosocial behavior. *Journal of Personality and Social Psychology, 98*(2), 211–221.

Hyman, I. E., Boss, S. M., Wise, B. M., McKenzie, K. E., & Caggiano, J. M. (2010). Did you see the uni-cycling clown? Inattentional blindness while walking and talking on a cell phone. *Applied Cognitive Psychology, 24,* 597–607.

Johnson, S. K., Podratz, K. E., Dipboye, R. L., & Gibbons, E. (2010). Physical attractiveness biases in ratings of employment suitability: Tracking down the "beauty is beastly" effect. *The Journal of Social Psychology, 150*(3), 301–318.

McConnell, A. R., Brown, C. M., Shoda, T. M., Stayton, L. E., & Martin, C. E. (2011). Friends with benefits: On the positive consequences of pet ownership. *Journal of Personality and Social Psychology, 101*(6), 1239–1252.

McFerran, B., Dahl, D. W., Fitzsimons, G. J., & Morales, A. C. (2010). Might an overweight waitress make you eat more?: How the body type of others is sufficient to alter our food consumption. *Journal of Consumer Psychology, 20*(2), 146–151.

Ridolfo, H., Baxter, A., & Lucas, J. W. (2010). Social influences on paranormal belief: Popular versus scien-tific support. *Current Research in Social Psychology, 15*(3), 33–41.

Saraglou, V., Lacour, C., & Demeure, M. E. (2010). Bad humor, bad marriage: Humor styles in divorced and married couples. *Europe's Journal of Psychology, 6*(3), 94–121.

Sorokowska, A. (2013). Assessing personality using body odor: Differences between children and adults. *Journal of Nonverbal Behavior, 37,* 153–163.

Wansink, B., Payne, C. R., & Shimizu, M. (2010). "Is this a meal or a snack?": Situational cues that drive perceptions. *Appetite, 54,* 214–216.

Welsh, A. (2010). On the perils of living dangerously in the slasher horror film: Gender differences in the association between sexual activity and survival. *Sex Roles, 62,* 762–773.

Wood, M. J., Douglas, K., & Sutton, R. M. (2012). Dead and alive: Beliefs in contradictory conspiracy theo-ries. *Social Psychological and Personality Science, 3*(6), 767–773.

Title of Article 1: _____

_____

Goal(s) of the Research (Circle All that Apply):

        Describe Behavior   Predict Behavior

        Explain Behavior   Modify Behavior

Rationale for the Goal(s) Selected:

Major Conclusion(s) of the Research:

Title of Article 2: _____

_____

Goal(s) of the Research (Circle All that Apply):

        Describe Behavior   Predict Behavior

        Explain Behavior   Modify Behavior

Rationale for the Goal(s) Selected:

Major Conclusion(s) of the Research:

Title of Article 3: _____

_____

Goal(s) of the Research (Circle All that Apply):

        Describe Behavior   Predict Behavior

        Explain Behavior   Modify Behavior

Rationale for the Goal(s) Selected:

Major Conclusion(s) of the Research

EXERCISE 1C

Designing Research to Achieve a Specific Goal

Psychologists are often given the task of designing a research study to achieve a specific research goal. Depending upon the nature of the project, psychologists may be asked to design a research study to describe, predict, explain, and/or modify behavior. Because they have diverse interests and work in diverse settings, psychologists need to have the ability to design research studies capable of achieving any of the 4 primary goals of psychological research.

Below you will find 4 scenarios. Each scenario describes a research study being designed by a psychologist to describe, predict, explain, or modify behavior. You will assume the role of the psychologist in each scenario. Each scenario will expose you to the types of design-related decisions psychologists have to make when designing a study to achieve a specific research goal. Read each of the scenarios, make the design-related decisions necessary to achieve the specific research goal, and write your rationale for your decisions in the spaces provided.

SCENARIO 1: *Describing Behavior*

Despite the fact married couples make a promise to love one another till death us do part, many marriages ultimately end in divorce. You are a Counseling Psychologist currently working with a couple experiencing marital difficulties. The couple wants your expert opinion as to whether their marriage is worth saving. You tell the couple in order for you to form an opinion, you will need to observe how they interact as a couple in a variety of settings. You will then meet with them to describe your observations and provide your opinion as to the viability of the marriage.

(a) Identify **three (3)** specific settings in which you would like to observe the behavior of the couple to help you assess the marriage.

Setting 1	
Setting 2	
Setting 3	

What is your rationale for selecting these 3 specific settings?

(b) Identify **<u>three (3)</u>** specific behaviors you would like to observe in the couple to help you assess the marriage. How would you define and code each of these behaviors to help you code them accurately and reliably?

Behavior 1	
Behavior 2	
Behavior 3	

	Definition	Coding Categories
Behavior 1		
Behavior 2		
Behavior 3		

How could you observe the couple without your presence causing them to alter their typical behavior (and potentially biasing your assessment)?

SCENARIO 2: *Predicting Behavior*

Every year, U.S. employees are victims of violence or threats of violence in the workplace. As a result, workplace violence is now the second-leading cause of occupational injury.[11] You are an Industrial-Organizational Psychologist who is currently working with several large organizations to prevent future incidences of workplace violence. Specifically, you are attempting to identify the work-related factors, non-work-related factors, and personal characteristics of employees that predict which employees will commit workplace violence.

(a) Identify **three (3)** work-related factors, **three (3)** non-work-related factors, and **three (3)** personal characteristics of employees you believe would enable organizations to predict which employees will commit workplace violence.

Work Factors	1. _____ 2. _____ 3. _____
Non-Work Factors	1. _____ 2. _____ 3. _____
Employee Factors	1. _____ 2. _____ 3. _____

What is your rationale for selecting these specific factors?

Which of the specific factors you selected would you hypothesize is most strongly correlated with workplace violence, and therefore the best predictor?

```
┌─────────────────────────────────┐
│                                 │
│                                 │
│                                 │
│                                 │
└─────────────────────────────────┘
```

(b) An employee scores high on all factors and characteristics you identified in **(a)**. You predict he will commit workplace violence within the next year. A year later, he has committed no violent acts. How would you explain the failure of your prediction?

```
┌─────────────────────────────────────────────────┐
│              Explanation:                        │
│                                                 │
│                                                 │
│                                                 │
│                                                 │
│                                                 │
│                                                 │
│                                                 │
│                                                 │
│                                                 │
└─────────────────────────────────────────────────┘
```

(c) An employee scores low on all factors and characteristics you identified in **(a)**. You predict he is not a risk for committing workplace violence. A year later, he comes to work and kills 5 coworkers. How would you explain the failure of your prediction?

```
┌─────────────────────────────────────────────────┐
│              Explanation:                        │
│                                                 │
│                                                 │
│                                                 │
│                                                 │
│                                                 │
│                                                 │
│                                                 │
│                                                 │
└─────────────────────────────────────────────────┘
```

SCENARIO 3: *Explaining Behavior*

Every day, people apply for jobs and are, unfortunately, not hired. A lack of work experience, a lack of essential job-related skills, and/or a poor interview performance are some of the reasons why applicants are not hired. Some applicants, however, claim that "age" was the real reason why they were not hired (i.e. they were perceived to be "too old for the job"). You are a Social Psychologist interested in age discrimination in the workplace.[12] You want to collect evidence that age truly does affect hiring outcomes. Specifically, you want to show that older applicants are less likely to be hired than younger applicants when applying for the same jobs.

Assume you have been asked to design a research study to test whether older applicants are less likely to be hired than younger applicants when applying for the same jobs.

(a) How would you define "older" and "younger" in your study?

Definition of an "older" applicant	Definition of a "younger" applicant

(b) What factors would you have to control in your research study to ensure applicant age is the "cause" of any observed differences in hiring outcomes?

Factors to control in the study would include:

(c) Assume that you personally want the evidence to show that age affects hiring outcomes. You also, however, want to conduct an objective and ethical research study. What would you do to ensure that your personal biases did not influence the outcome of the study?

Strategies to reduce potential biases would include:

(d) A researcher publishes an article which states that there is a strong positive correlation (+.86) between applicant age and the number of resumes sent out before getting hired (i.e. as applicant age increases, the number of resumes sent out before being hired also increases). Instead of conducting your experiment, could you use this correlation data to conclude that age is the reason why older applicants are less likely to get hired than younger applicants when applying for the same job positions? Explain.

Explanation:

SCENARIO 4: *Modifying Behavior*

Cell phone technology has had a dramatic impact on society. People are using their cell phones to accomplish many tasks including making calls, surfing the Internet, sending e-mail messages, sharing photographs, monitoring social media sites, and sending text messages. Unfortunately, people are now using their cell phones while driving their cars and putting their lives as well as the lives of others at risk.[13] You are a Health Psychologist interested in increasing public safety by reducing the number of people who use their cell phones while driving.

Assume you have been asked to develop an educational program designed to modify behavior and reduce the number of people using cell phones while driving.

(a) Who specifically would you target to be the first participants in your program? How would you recruit your target and get them to participate in the program?

Target Participants	
Method of Recruitment/ Incentives	

(b) What content would you want to include in your educational program? What methods of instruction would be most effective to present the program content?

Program Content	Methods of Instruction

(c) How would you assess whether your educational program was effective in reducing the number of people using cell phones while driving?

Methods of assessment would include:

(d) As a researcher, what actions would you take if you found your educational program was not effective in reducing the number of people using cell phones while driving?

My next course of action would be:

References

1. Passer, M. W. (2013). *Research methods: Concepts and connections.* New York, NY: Worth Publishers.

2. Beins, B. C. (2012). *Research methods: A tool for life* (3rd ed.). Boston, MA: Pearson Publishers.

3. Levy, P. E. (2012). *Industrial-organizational psychology: Understanding the workplace (*4th ed.). New York, NY: Worth Publishers.

4. Evans, A. N., & Rooney, B. F. (2007). *Methods in psychological research.* Thousand Oaks, CA: Sage Publications.

5. Cozby, P. C., & Bates, S. C. (2011). *Methods in behavioral research.* (11th ed.). New York, NY: McGraw-Hill Publishers.

6. Jackson, S. L. (2014). *Research methods: A modular approach* (3rd ed.). Stamford, CT: Cengage Learning.

7. Gravetter, F. J., & Wallnau, L. B. (2012). *Statistics for the behavioral sciences* (9th ed.). Belmont, CA: Wadsworth-Cengage Learning.

8. Kantowitz, B. H., Roediger, H. L., & Elmes, D. G. (2014). *Experimental psychology* (10th ed.). Stamford, CT: Cengage Learning.

9. Leary, M. R. (2007). *Introduction to behavioral research methods* (5th ed.). Boston, MA: Pearson/Allyn & Bacon.

10. American Psychiatric Association. (2013). *Diagnostic and statistical manual of mental disorders* (5th ed.—DSM-5). Washington, DC: American Psychiatric Publishing.

11. National Center for Victims of Crime. (2013). *NCVRW resource guide: New challenges. New solutions.* Retrieved from http://www.victimsofcrime.org/our-programs/national-crime-victims'-rights-week/previous-ncvrw-resource-guides

12. U.S. Equal Employment Opportunity Commission. (2008). *Facts about age discrimination.* Retrieved from http://www.eeoc.gov/facts/age.html

13. Steppa, N. (2013). Impactful distraction: Talking while driving poses dangers that people seem unable to see. *Science News, 184*(4), 20–24.

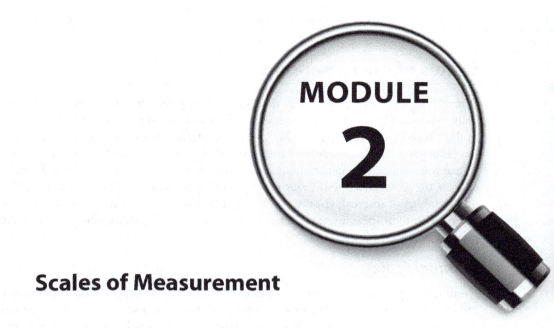

MODULE 2

Scales of Measurement

Once psychologists have established their research goal(s) and selected their variables of interest, they must decide how best to measure these variables. Measurement is the systematic process through which psychologists assign qualitative (e.g. category labels) or quantitative (e.g. numbers) values to the people, objects, or situations they observe in the world around them.[1,2,3] For psychologists, the measurement of behavior and mental processes in both laboratory and applied settings serves as the focus of psychological research.

In order for psychological research to produce results that contribute to our understanding of behavior and mental processes, the research must be built on a foundation of sound, scientific measurement. To meet the criteria for sound, scientific measurement, measurement instruments used by psychologists to conduct their research have to possess several essential characteristics. Most importantly, the measurement instruments must be valid.[1,2,4,5,6] Measurement instruments must measure what they claim to measure (e.g. a measure of self-esteem truly does measure an individual's evaluation of his/her self-worth). Measurement instruments must also be reliable. Reliable measurement instruments produce consistent outcomes (e.g. scores, ratings, amounts) across repeated measurements.[1,2,4,5,6] If a measurement instrument is reliable, multiple observers of the same behavior or mental process should all arrive at a similar measurement outcome (e.g. multiple observers of a couple on a blind date should report similar ratings for the amount of attraction and physical intimacy during the date). Measurement instruments must also possess precision sufficient to measure the subtle variability in the behavior or mental processes being studied by researchers[1,2,4,5] (e.g. video cameras are able to capture subtle facial gestures and/or body language that an observer might miss using only his or her eyes; an fMRI scan can reveal more detailed information about the brain than a CAT scan is capable of revealing).

The measurement instruments selected by researchers must also be appropriate for the research questions they are attempting to answer. Researchers have to ensure their measurement instruments are: (a) appropriate for use with the target participants (e.g. children, adults, animals) in their research,[4] (b) appropriate for use by members of the research team (e.g. observers, raters, test administrators, statisticians) given their levels of training/experience,[1,4] (c) accepted by the scientific community as appropriate measures of the behaviors or mental processes under study[4] (e.g. the Beck Depression Inventory (BDI)[7] is an accepted measure of the severity of depression in Clinical Psychology), and most importantly (d) capable of providing sufficient information to allow researchers to answer their research questions and to make informed decisions regarding the implications/applications of the results of their research.[4] Psychologists should also select measurement instruments that yield information that is applicable to real-world settings beyond the laboratory[4,5] and which can be understood by both scientific and non-scientific audiences. Finally, psychologists should select measurement instruments which: (a) are easy to administer, (b) can be scored and interpreted objectively, and (c) are cost effective (i.e. the costs associated with the use of an instrument are justified by the quantity and quality of information that the measurement instrument yields for researchers).[1,5]

Scales of Measurement

When designing their research studies and deciding how best to measure their variables of interest, psychologists must decide which level (or levels) of measurement provide sufficient information to achieve the goal(s) of their research. Among researchers, levels of measurement are often referred to as "scales of measurement." Psychologists use four scales of measurement in their research to measure behaviors and mental processes. These four scales of measurement are known as nominal, ordinal, interval, and ratio scales.[2,4,6,8] The scale(s) chosen by researchers will determine: (a) the type and amount of information researchers will learn about the variables of interest, (b) the types of mathematical operations and statistical analyses that researchers can perform on their measurement data, and (c) the types of conclusions that can be drawn based on the results of their research.

Nominal Scales

Nominal scales are qualitative in nature and involve a categorization (or naming) of the characteristics of individuals, objects, or situations.[1,2,6] Values on a nominal scale differ in name only. There are no quantitative differences implied between different values on a nominal scale (e.g. while college majors differ in name (psychology, special education), there are no quantitative differences implied between majors). There is also no implied order for values on a nominal scale.[4] In fact, the order of the values on a nominal scale is irrelevant (e.g. whether the category of Blonde precedes or follows the category of Brunette on a nominal scale measuring hair color is irrelevant). The categories on a nominal scale are "mutually exclusive."[1] Individuals, objects, and situations are coded into one, and only one, category based upon the characteristics they possess (e.g. when measuring "party affiliation" in politics, individuals can be categorized as a Democrat, Republican, or Independent and cannot be a member of multiple political parties). Researchers using nominal scales are limited to analyses of frequencies and/or percentages of observations across scale categories[1,2,4] (e.g. is there a significant difference in the percentage of individuals in a community who identify Catholic, Protestant, Mormon, or Baptist as their religious affiliation?).

Ordinal Scales

While there is no implied order or quantitative differences between the values on a nominal scale, the values on an ordinal scale are organized along a continuum with scale values reflecting differences in the quantity of a specific characteristic, behavior, or mental process being measured[2,4,8] (e.g. mild, moderate, severe test anxiety). There is no assumption, however, that quantitative differences between scale values are equivalent[4,6] (e.g. the difference between Mild and Moderate levels of test anxiety is not assumed to be equal to the difference between Moderate and Severe test anxiety). As a result, a researcher who uses an ordinal scale to measure a specific characteristic (e.g. personality trait) among a target group of individuals can determine which individuals possess more or less of the characteristic, but cannot determine how much more or less of the characteristic these individuals possess.[2,4] Similar conclusions can be drawn by researchers when using ordinal scales to measure specific behaviors and/or mental processes. Ranks are also considered an ordinal scale of measurement. Similar to categorical scale values, quantitative differences between consecutive rank ordered positions (e.g. 1st, 2nd, 3rd) are not assumed to be equivalent.[1,2,6] For example, a psychologist may rank individuals based on the order in which they complete a problem-solving task. While ranks would provide information about the order in which participants completed the task, they would not provide information about the actual differences in completion time between individuals at various rank ordered positions (e.g. the difference in completion time for the 1st and 2nd ranked individuals may be 5 minutes, while the completion times for the 2nd and 3rd ranked individuals may differ by only 1 second).

Interval Scales

Unlike ordinal scales of measurement, interval scales have equal units of measurement[2,6,8] (i.e. quantitative differences between consecutive values on an interval scale are equal). Celsius and Fahrenheit temperature scales are both examples of interval scales. On a Fahrenheit or Celsius temperature scale, each unit (or degree) measures an equivalent amount of temperature. Standardized tests of IQ and achievement are also examples of interval scales (i.e. each unit of measurement on standardized IQ tests and achievement tests measure an equal amount of intelligence or achievement). Researchers can, therefore, conclude that 10 point differences in temperature, IQ, or achievement scores are equal regardless of where the 10 point differences occur on the interval scales[2,4,6,8] (e.g. the amount of intelligence between IQ scores of 70–80 is equivalent to the amount of intelligence between IQ scores of 100–110). Interval scales do not, however, contain a true (or absolute) zero point.[4,6] A scale value of zero should represent a complete absence of the construct being measured (e.g. if no one is standing on a scale, there is a complete absence of weight and the scale should read 0). Some interval scales do not contain a zero value (e.g. many standardized tests of achievement, personality, and IQ produce minimum scores that are greater than 0). Other interval scales contain zero values that are arbitrary[4,6,8] and values on the scale below 0 (e.g. a Fahrenheit or Celsius thermometer that reads 0 degrees does not indicate a complete lack of temperature. There are also temperature values below 0). The absence of a true (or absolute) zero prevents researchers from making ratio comparisons[4,6] (e.g. when measuring temperature on a Fahrenheit or Celsius scale, researchers cannot conclude that a temperature of 90 degrees is three times as hot as a temperature of 30 degrees).

Ratio Scales

Ratio scales provide researchers with the greatest amount of information about their variables of interest. Like interval scales of measurement, ratio scales have equal units of measurement.[1,2,4,6,8] Unlike interval scales, ratio scales contain a true (or absolute) zero point.[1,2,4,6,8] The Kelvin temperature scale is an example of a ratio scale of measurement. Each unit (or degree) on the Kelvin temperature scale measures an equivalent amount of heat and a value of 0 Kelvin is the point at which there truly is a complete absence of heat.[1,4] Variables that are measured by counting the number of behavioral responses (e.g. the number of text messages sent in a day), the passage of time (e.g. the amount of time parents spend with their children per week), or physical attributes of individuals, objects, and/or situations (e.g. height, weight, length) are also examples of ratio scales.[4,6] All of these variables start at a value of zero and increase in value as the number of responses, amount of time, or amount of the physical attribute increases. Due to the equal units of measurement and presence of a true zero point, researchers using ratio scales can make ratio comparisons.[1,2,4,6,8] For instance, a child who has played video games for 8 hours can be said to have played 4 times as long as a child who has played video games for 2 hours. Likewise, a rat that pressed a bar in a Skinner box 100 times a minute can be said to have responded twice as fast as a rat that pressed the bar 50 times a minute.

Name: Kamdyn Curfman

Date:

EXERCISE 2A

Scales of Measurement in Psychological Research

Psychologists study a wide range of behaviors, mental processes, and psychological constructs (e.g. intelligence, creativity). These behaviors, mental processes, and psychological constructs can be measured in multiple ways (each with advantages and disadvantages). When psychologists design research, they must decide how best to measure their variables of interest. An important consideration in this decision is which scale(s) of measurement they will use to measure their variables. Below are 20 scenarios describing research conducted by psychologists across a variety of clinical, laboratory, and applied settings. For each scenario, please determine the scale of measurement (i.e. nominal, ordinal, interval, ratio) being used by the psychologist to measure his/her variable of interest and write your answer in the space provided.

01. A Social Psychologist interviews men who are members of an Internet dating service and asks them what their favorite thing to do on a first date would be using the scale below:

Go on a picnic ☐	Go out to dinner ☐
Go to the movies ☐	Go out dancing ☐

Scale = __Nominal__

02. An Industrial-Organizational Psychologist spends a week at a local hospital observing the job performance of physicians and measures their productivity using the scale below:

Total # of Patients Treated
Patients = _____
Total # of Surgeries Performed
Surgeries = _____

Scale = __Ratio__

03. A Consumer Psychologist approaches shoppers as they leave a large retail store and asks them to evaluate the quality of their customer service experiences using the scale below:

☐ THUMBS UP!	☐ THUMBS DOWN!

Scale = ~~nominal~~ ordinal

04. A Community Psychologist studying the influence of socioeconomic status (SES) on mental health measures the SES of each member of the local community using the scale below:

◯	High SES
◯	Middle SES
◯	Low SES

Scale = ordinal

05. An Environmental Psychologist studying the relationship between temperature and mood among construction workers in a large city measures temperature using the Fahrenheit thermometer scale below:

-30F -20F -10F 0F +10F +20F +30F +40F +50F +60F +70F +80F +90F +100F

Scale = interval

06. A Health Psychologist studying the potential relationship between soda consumption and obesity measures the soda consumption of 100 obese individuals using the scale below:

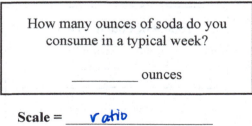

How many ounces of soda do you consume in a typical week?

_____ ounces

Scale = ratio

07. A Media Psychologist studying societies' current fascination with zombies asks individuals leaving a local theater to rank 5 of the top zombie films of all time using the scale below:

1 = Best Film; 5 = Worst Film

	Rank
A Taste for Brains	
Guts for Dinner	
Rotting Away	
Parade of Corpses	
Hungry for Life	

Scale = _Ordinal_

08. A Sports Psychologist studying the attitudes of professional athletes toward steroid usage measures the attitudes of 100 professional athletes using the scale below:

> "I would take steroids to improve my athletic performance
> if I knew I would not get caught."
>
> | −2 | −1 | 0 | +1 | +2 |
> |----|----|---|----|----|
> | Definitely Wouldn't | Probably Wouldn't | Unsure | Probably Would | Definitely Would |

Scale = _interval_

09. After meeting with each of his new patients, a Clinical Psychologist places each patient into a diagnostic category based on their symptoms using the scale below:

Mood Disorder	◯
Personality Disorder	◯
Anxiety Disorder	◯
Schizophrenia	◯

Scale = _nominal_

10. A Counseling Psychologist working with a client who was recently laid off by her employer, measures her client's motivation to find a new job using the scale below:

> How many jobs have you applied for since you lost your job?
>
> _____ jobs

Scale = _ratio_

11. A Military Psychologist studying the relationship between military rank and satisfaction with life in the military measures soldiers' military rank using the scale below:

Sergeant	Lieutenant	Captain	Major	Colonel	General
○	○	○	○	○	○

Scale = _nominal_ X _ordinal_

12. A Quantitative Psychologist studying the math skills of high school graduates measures math skills with a standardized test of mathematical reasoning using the scale below:

> Test of Mathematical Reasoning
> (Range = 50–200; Mean = 125; SD = 25)
>
> 50   75   100   125   150   175   200
> Minimum   Average   Maximum

Scale = _interval_

13. A Developmental Psychologist studying career ambitions in boys asks 25 teenage boys to tell her what they would like to be when they grow up using the scale below:

Fireman	Scientist	Rock Star	Soldier	Athlete
○	○	○	○	○

Scale = _nominal_

14. A Cognitive Psychologist studying the relationship between intelligence and memory skills measures intelligence with a standardized intelligence test using the scale below:

Intelligence Test
(Range = 10–130; Mean = 70; SD = 15)

10   25   40   55   70   85   100   115   130
Minimum   Average   Maximum

Scale = ___interval___

15. A Neuropsychologist studying migraine headaches asks individuals to indicate where they feel the most intense pain during a migraine headache using the scale below:

When you have a migraine, where do you feel the most intense pain?
In my neck   ☐
In my temples   ☐
In my forehead   ☐
In my eyes   ☐

Scale = ___Nominal___

16. A Parapsychologist studying reportedly "haunted" locations around the world measures the amount of paranormal activity present at these locations using the scale below:

Extreme Activity	BOO! BOO! BOO! BOO!
Strong Activity	BOO! BOO! BOO!
Moderate Activity	BOO! BOO!
Minimal Activity	BOO!

Scale = ~~interval~~ ordinal

17. A Cultural Psychologist studying access to health care in rural communities measures the distance from these communities to the nearest health care facility using the scale below:

> Distance to the Nearest Medical Facility
>
> |▮▮▮|
>
> 0 Miles   50 Miles   100 Miles

Scale = _ratio_

18. An Educational Psychologist studying student satisfaction with on-line college courses measures student satisfaction using the scale below:

1	2	3	4
Slightly Satisfied	Moderately Satisfied	Very Satisfied	Extremely Satisfied
☐	☐	☐	☐

Scale = _Ordinal_

19. A School Psychologist studying the effectiveness of a truancy-reduction program measures the number of unexcused absences since the start of the program using the scale below:

> How many unexcused absences have you had since the start of the *"Don't Be a Fool, Come to School"* program at our school?
>
> _____ absences

Scale = _ratio_

20. An Experimental Psychologist studying female body image asks women who currently wear size 12 dresses, to indicate what dress size they would prefer to wear using the scale below:

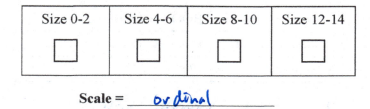

Size 0-2	Size 4-6	Size 8-10	Size 12-14
☐	☐	☐	☐

Scale = _ordinal_

EXERCISE 2B

What Scale of Measurement is That?

When designing their research studies, psychologists use nominal, ordinal, interval, and ratio scales of measurement to measure their variables of interest. Although each of these scales of measurement have clearly defined properties (e.g. categorization, order, equal measurement units, true (or absolute) zero), it's sometimes difficult to determine which scales of measurement are represented by the rating scales and measurements used in psychological research. Below are 8 scenarios describing rating scales used by psychologists in their research. For each of these 8 scenarios, please determine which scale of measurement (i.e. nominal, ordinal, interval, ratio) is represented (circle your choice) and provide a rationale for your choice in the space provided.

01. A Clinical Psychologist studying the relationship between the magnitude of a natural disaster and the severity of post-disaster mental health difficulties uses the enhanced Fujita Scale (F-Scale)[9] to assess the intensity of tornados.

Category	Wind Speed	Damage
F5	> 200 MPH	Incredible
F4	166–200 MPH	Devastating
F3	136–165 MPH	Severe
F2	111–135 MPH	Considerable
F1	86–110 MPH	Moderate
F0	65–85 MPH	Light

Scale of Measurement (Circle One)

NOMINAL   ORDINAL   INTERVAL   RATIO

Rationale:

02. An Industrial-Organizational Psychologist studying "presenteeism" (i.e. an employee being physically present at work but not fully engaged or productive due to illness and/or personal problems)[10] measures the level of "presenteeism" displayed by each of 100 customer service employees at a large call center using the scale below:

Question:

What percentage of the time are you physically present at work but not fully engaged and productive because you are sick or having personal problems?

0%	10%	20%	30%	40%	50%	60%	70%	80%	90%	100%

I am always engaged/productive at work	I am engaged/ productive at work half the time	I am never engaged/productive at work

Scale of Measurement (Circle One)

NOMINAL   ORDINAL   INTERVAL   RATIO

Rationale:

03. A Developmental Psychologist studying generational differences in parenting styles uses a combination of two factors to measure parenting style: (a) the level of support provided by a parent to his/her child(ren) and (b) the level of control exerted by a parent over the behavior of his/her child(ren)[11,12]. Based on these two factors, the psychologist classifies each parent in her study into one of the 4 styles of parenting shown in the model below:

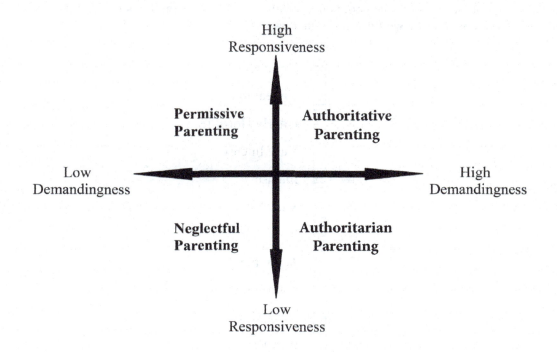

Scale of Measurement (Circle One)

NOMINAL   ORDINAL   INTERVAL   RATIO

Rationale:

04. A Health Psychologist studying the effectiveness of a new pain management program measures program participants' pain levels at the start of the program and then again at the completion of the program using the 10-point pain scale[13] below:

Question:

Please consider the intensity of the pain you are feeling at this moment. On a scale of 0 (Pain Free) to 10 (Unimaginable), how intense would you say that pain is?

10	Unimaginable
9	Unbearable
8	Utterly Horrible
7	Very Intense
6	Intense
5	Very Distressing
4	Distressing
3	Tolerable
2	Discomforting
1	Very Mild
0	Pain Free

Scale of Measurement (Circle One)

NOMINAL   ORDINAL   INTERVAL   RATIO

Rationale:

05. A Forensic Psychologist studying the childhood experiences of adult serial killers interviews 20 serial killers who are currently in prison for their crimes. Based on the motivation behind each of the killer's murders, the psychologist classifies each of the serial killers in his study into one of 5 serial killer "types"[14] using the scale below:

Visionary Killers

Voices in their heads compel them to kill

Power/Control Killers

Kill for the satisfaction that comes from having complete control over their victims

Thrill Killers

Kill for adrenalin rush that accompanies the act

Lust Killers

Kill for sexual arousal that accompanies the act

Mission Killers

Believe that it's their mission in life to kill a particular person or type of person

Scale of Measurement (Circle One)

NOMINAL   ORDINAL   INTERVAL   RATIO

Rationale:

06. A Clinical Psychologist studying the variability in human sexuality asks a sample of male college students to evaluate their sexuality using the Kinsey Heterosexual-Homosexual Rating Scale (1948)[15] below:

	Description
0	Exclusively heterosexual with no homosexual
1	Predominantly heterosexual, only incidentally homosexual
2	Predominantly heterosexual, more than incidental homosexual
3	Equally heterosexual and homosexual
4	Predominantly homosexual, more than incidentally heterosexual
5	Predominantly homosexual, only incidentally heterosexual
6	Exclusively homosexual

Scale of Measurement (Circle One)

NOMINAL   ORDINAL   INTERVAL   RATIO

Rationale:

07. A Physiological Psychologist studying the influence of altitude on the functioning of the human body measures the physiological functioning of people living different distances above and below sea level. The Physiological Psychologist measures the distance above or below sea level using the scale below:

Question:

When considering the location where you currently live, how far (in feet) do you live above or below sea level?

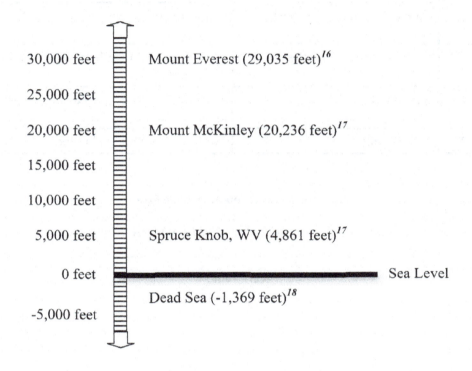

Scale of Measurement (Circle One)

NOMINAL   ORDINAL   INTERVAL   RATIO

Rationale:

08. A Media Psychologist studying parental perceptions of movie content (e.g. sexual content, violent content, mature language, adult themes), measures movie content using the Motion Picture Association of America (MPAA) rating system[19] below:

Rating	Definition	Restrictions
G	General Audiences	All ages admitted
PG	Parental Guidance Suggested	Some material may not be suitable for children
PG-13	Parents Strongly Cautioned	Some material may be inappropriate for children under 13
R	Restricted	Under 17 requires accompanying parent or adult guardian
NC-17	Adults Only	No one 17 or under admitted

Scale of Measurement (Circle One)

NOMINAL   ORDINAL   INTERVAL   RATIO

Rationale:

EXERCISE 2C

Which Scale of Measurement Best Answers My Research Question

When deciding how best to measure their variables of interest, psychologists must decide which scale of measurement will provide the type and amount of information necessary for them to answer their research question. Below are 4 scenarios describing psychological research. For each scenario, 4 different methods of measuring the variable of interest are presented. For each scenario, select 1 method of measurement that you feel would allow psychologists to best answer their research question (circle your choice), identify the scale of measurement represented, and provide a rationale for your choice of measurement method.

Scenario #1

A Counseling Psychologist is approached by a couple who want an answer to the question: "Should we get married?"

(A) The psychologist sends the couple on a weekend retreat with 9 other couples who are also considering marriage. Based on her observations of the couples at the retreat, the psychologist ranks the couples from 1 (Most Compatible) to 10 (Least Compatible).

(B) The psychologist has the male member of the couple who appears more uncertain about the decision to get married take the "Do I Really Want to Get Married?" test. The test assesses the "desire to be married" using the scale below.

−10	−8	−6	−4	−2	0	+2	+4	+6	+8	+10

I would rather be single   I have no preference   I would rather be married

(C) The psychologist interviews the couple for 1 hour and counts the number of positive comments made about marriage by each member of the couple.

(D) The psychologist interviews the couple for 1 hour and based on the interview tells the couple that in her opinion the marriage is likely to (a) Succeed or (b) Fail.

Method of Measurement (Circle One)

A   B   C   D

Scale of Measurement (Circle One)

NOMINAL   ORDINAL   INTERVAL   RATIO

Rationale:

Scenario #2

A Political Psychologist has been asked by a conservative candidate to answer the question: "Will I win my upcoming election against my liberal opponent?"

(A) The psychologist surveys registered voters and asks them how many conservative and liberal political candidates they have voted for in the past 10 years.

(B) The psychologist surveys registered voters and asks them how politically conservative they are using a 1 (Extremely Liberal) to 7 (Extremely Conservative) rating scale.

(C) The psychologist has a random sample of voters complete a "Conservative-Liberal Attitudes Scale" and then evaluates their scores using the scale below:

Very Liberal [|||||||||||||||||||||||||||||||||||||||||||] Very Conservative
$$-15 \quad -10 \quad -5 \quad 0 \quad +5 \quad +10 \quad +15$$
Neutral

(D) The psychologist surveys registered voters and asks them if they are registered as a: (a) Democrat, (b) Republican, (c) Independent, or (d) Other.

Method of Measurement (Circle One)

A   B   C   D

Scale of Measurement (Circle One)

NOMINAL   ORDINAL   INTERVAL   RATIO

Rationale:

Scenario #3

An Environmental Psychologist has been asked by the Mayor and members of the city council to answer the question: "How polluted is the river that flows through our city?"

(A) The psychologist measures the Ph level[20] of the water at several points along the river to determine if the Ph levels are higher or lower than normal (which would indicate the presence of pollutants) using the scale below:

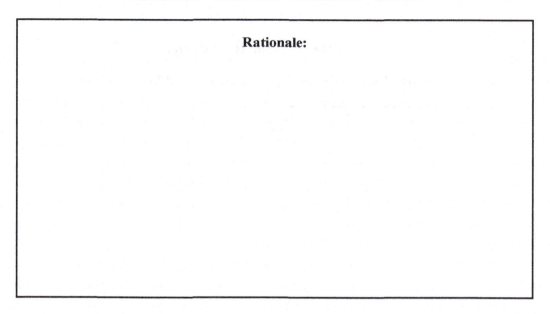

(B) The psychologist counts the number of pounds of garbage, sewage, medical waste, and industrial contaminants pulled out of the river in a one-hour time period.

(C) The psychologist asks fishermen fishing along the banks of the river whether they consider the river to be: (a) Polluted or (b) Clean.

(D) The psychologist asks people living along the river whether they think the health of their family members would be at risk if they swam in the river, drank water from the river, or ate fish caught in the river using a 1 (Definitely Not a Health Risk) to 7 (Definitely a Health Risk) rating scale.

Method of Measurement (Circle One)

A   B   C   D

Scale of Measurement (Circle One)

NOMINAL   ORDINAL   INTERVAL   RATIO

Rationale:

Scenario # 4

A Clinical Psychologist working with a female client having difficulty finding love and romance is asked by his client to answer the question: "Am I attractive?"

(A) The psychologist takes his client to a local nightclub and has her sit at the bar. The psychologist then counts the total number of people who approach her and ask her to dance over the course of the next hour.

(B) The psychologist takes a picture of his client to a local mall and asks shoppers to look at her picture and tell him whether they think she is: (a) Hot or (b) Not Hot.

(C) The psychologist posts his client's picture on several social media sites and asks people who visit the site to rate how attractive she is using the rating scale below:

Extremely Hot	HOT! HOT! HOT! HOT!
Very Hot	HOT! HOT! HOT!
Moderately Hot	HOT! HOT!
Slightly Hot	HOT!

(D) The psychologist shows his client's picture to people walking in the park and asks them to rate how attractive she is using the "Supermodel Scale of Attractiveness" below:

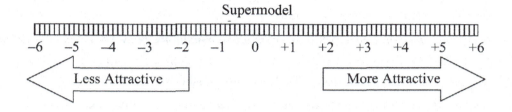

Method of Measurement (Circle One)

A   B   C   D

Scale of Measurement (Circle One)

NOMINAL   ORDINAL   INTERVAL   RATIO

Rationale:

References

1. Cascio, W. F., & Aguinis, H. (2005). *Applied psychology in human resource management* (6th ed.). Upper Saddle River, NJ: Pearson/Prentice Hall.

2. Passer, M. W. (2013). *Research methods: Concepts and connections.* New York, NY: Worth Publishers.

3. Smith, R. A., & Davis, S. F. (2012). *The psychologist as detective: An introduction to conducting research in psychology* (6th ed.). Boston, MA: Pearson Publishers.

4. Bordens, K. S., & Abbot, B. B. (2011). *Research design and methods: A process approach* (8th ed.). Boston, MA: McGraw-Hill Publishers.

5. Muchinsky, P. M. (2011). Psychology applied to work (10th ed.). Summerfield, NC: Hypergraphic Press.

6. Cozby, P. C., & Bates, S. C. (2011). *Methods in behavioral research.* (11th ed.). New York, NY: McGraw-Hill Publishers.

7. Beck, A. T., Steer, R. A., & Brown, G. K. (1996). *Manual for the Beck Depression Inventory* (BDI-II). San Antonio, TX: Psychological Corporation.

8. Ray, W. J. (2011). Methods: *Towards a science of behavior and experience* (10th ed.). Belmont, CA: Wadsworth/Cengage Learning.

9. What is the Enhanced Fujita Scale? (2013). *The Weather Channel.* Retrieved from http:// www.weather.com/news/enhanced-fujita-scale-20130206

10. Johns, G. (2010). Presenteeism in the workplace: A review and research agenda. *Journal of Organizational Behavior, 31*(4), 519–542.

11. Baumrind, D. (1967). Child care practices anteceding three patterns of preschool behavior. *Genetic Psychology Monographs, 75*(1), 43–88.

12. Pizarro, K. (2011). Baumrind's parenting style and Maccoby & Martin's parenting style typologies. *Scribd.Com.* Retrieved from http://www.scribd.com/doc/49300379/Baumrind-s-Parenting-style-and-Maccoby-Martin-s-Parenting-Style-Typologies

13. Whitworth, M. (n.d.). *A review of the evaluation of pain using a variety of pain scales.* Indiana Pain Society. Retrieved from http://indianapainsociety.org/index.php/member-tools?catid=144&id=151

14. Canter, D. V., & Wentink, N. (2004). An empirical test of Holmes and Holmes's serial murder typology. *Criminal Justice and Behavior, 31*(4), 489–515.

15. Kinsey, A. C., Pomeroy, W. B., & Martin, C. E. (1948). *Sexual behavior in the human male.* Bloomington, IN: Indiana University Press.

16. Rosenberg, M. (2014). Important facts about Mount Everest. *About.com Geography.* Retrieved from http://geography.about.com/od/specificplacesofinterest/a/mounteverest.htm

17. Briney, A. (n.d.). U.S. high points: List of the highest points in each of the 50 U.S. states. *About.com Geography.* Retrieved from http://geography.about.com/od/lists/a/ushighpoints.htm

18. Rosenberg, M. (2014). Lowest points on land. *About.com Geography.* Retrieved from http://geography.about.com/od/learnabouttheearth/a/extremes_2.htm

19. Understanding the film ratings. (2014). *Motion Picture Association of America.* Retrieved from http://www.mpaa.org/film-ratings/

20. What is pH? (2012). *Environmental Protection Agency.* Retrieved from http://www.epa.gov/acidrain/measure/ph.html

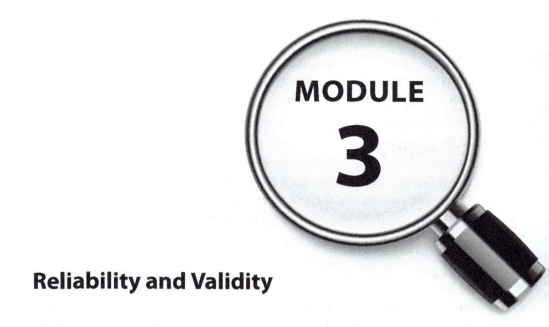

MODULE
3

Reliability and Validity

For the results of psychological research to be meaningful, applicable, and generalizable, psychologists must measure their variables of interest using measurement instruments (e.g. tests, scales, apparatus, raters) that meet two basic requirements. First, the measurement instruments must be reliable.[1,2] Reliable measurement instruments produce consistent outcomes (e.g. scores, ratings, ranks, classification) across repeated measurements conducted under similar conditions (e.g. the measurement of a stable personality trait on multiple occasions should produce similar assessments of the trait). Reliable measurement instruments will also produce consistent scores when used by multiple evaluators (e.g. two clinicians using the same measurement instrument to assess the level of depression in the same client should arrive at the same measurement and/or diagnosis). Second, measurement instruments must be valid.[1,2] Valid measurement instruments measure the constructs they are intended to measure (e.g. a measure of motivation truly provides an accurate measure of an individual's current motivational state). But how do psychologists go about determining whether a measurement instrument is reliable and valid? Furthermore, what evidence is required to establish the reliability and validity of a measurement instrument?

Assessing Reliability and Validity

Psychologists rely on a statistic known as a correlation coefficient to assess the reliability and validity of measurement instruments. A correlation coefficient provides a measurement of the strength and direction of the relationship between two variables of interest.[3,4] With respect to the strength of the relationship, correlation coefficients can range in value from .00 to 1.00 with higher values indicating a stronger relationship between the two variables. With respect to the direction of the relationship, correlation coefficients can be either positive (+) or negative (−). A positive (+) correlation coefficient indicates that as one variable increases in value, the second variable also increases in value (e.g. as the number of children in a family increases, the size of the weekly grocery bill also increases). A negative (−) correlation coefficient indicates that as one variable increases in value, the second variable decreases in value (e.g. as the number of children in a family increases, the amount of "quality alone time" available to parents decreases). When strength and direction are combined, correlation coefficients range in value from −1.00 to +1.00. In assessments of reliability and validity, psychologists compute correlation coefficients to measure: (a) the relationship between scores obtained from two measurement instruments (i.e. two different instruments, two versions of the same instrument, two administrations of the same instrument) or (b) the relationship between scores obtained from a measurement instrument and scores from a current/future measure of performance or behavior (e.g. scores on the ACT/SAT and college GPA).[1,2,3,4] The methods commonly used by psychologists to assess the reliability and validity of measurement instruments are described below.

Reliability

There are several methods used by psychologists to evaluate the reliability of a measurement instrument. These methods include the following: **(a)** test-retest reliability, **(b)** parallel-forms reliability, **(c)** split-halves reliability, **(d)** inter-rater reliability, **(e)** inter-method reliability, and **(f)** internal consistency.

Test-Retest Reliability

To assess the test-retest reliability of a measurement instrument, psychologists will use the instrument to take an initial measurement of a group of individuals and record the results (Time 1). Then, at a later point in time, the psychologists will administer the same measurement instrument to the same group of individuals and once again record the results (Time 2). Psychologists will then compute a correlation coefficient to measure the relationship between the measurements collected at Time 1 and Time 2. Since the same instrument is being used at both Time 1 and Time 2, we would expect individual's scores to be consistent across the two measurement times.[1,2] A high positive (+) correlation coefficient would be evidence there is consistency in the measurements over time. Psychologists must be aware, however, of several factors that can influence the consistency of measurements over time and lead psychologists to over- or underestimate the test-retest reliability of a measurement instrument. For example, if individuals remember the content of the measurement instrument from Time 1 to Time 2, it can result in an increase in the consistency of measurements taken over time and an overestimation of the reliability of the measurement instrument.[3,4,5] On the other hand, if the individuals being measured change physically (e.g. maturation), psychologically (e.g. self-esteem), or cognitively (e.g. learning) over time, it can result in a decrease in the consistency of measurements over time and result in an underestimation of the reliability of the measurement instrument.[1,5,6] Measuring constructs that may be unstable over time (e.g. personality, emotions, attitudes) will also result in a decrease in the consistency of measurements over time leading to an underestimation of the reliability of the measurement instrument.[3,4,5]

Parallel-Forms Reliability

To assess the parallel-forms reliability of a measurement instrument, psychologists must first create multiple versions (i.e. forms) of the measurement instrument. While the multiple forms of the measurement instrument will contain different content (e.g. different questions), all forms must measure the same psychological construct and be equivalent (i.e. parallel) in all other respects including the item difficulty, readability, and completion time. Once the multiple forms of the measurement instrument have been created, psychologists will then administer one form of the instrument to a group of individuals and record the results (Form 1). Psychologists will then administer a second form of the instrument to the same group of individuals and once again record the results (Form 2). Psychologists will then compute a correlation coefficient to measure the relationship between scores on the two forms of the measurement instrument.[1,2,3] Since the same construct is being measured by both forms of the measurement instrument, we would expect individual's scores to be consistent across the two forms of the measurement instrument. A high positive (+) correlation coefficient would provide evidence that there is consistency in the measurements across the different forms of the measurement instrument. Psychologists must be aware, however, that the consistency of the measurements across multiple forms of the measurement instrument may be influenced by the order in which the forms of the instrument are administered (e.g. individuals administered Form 1 of the instrument first and Form 2 second may produce a different pattern of consistency than individuals administered Form 2 of the instrument first and Form 1 second). To determine if form order is affecting the consistency of measurements (and therefore affecting the estimation of the reliability of the measurement instrument), psychologists will randomly assign individuals to different administration orders (e.g. ½ assigned to Order A (Form 1–Form 2); ½ assigned to Order B (Form 2–Form 1)) and then compare the two groups with respect to their consistency of measurements across different orders of administration.[1,7]

Split-Halves Reliability

In order to assess the split-halves reliability of a measurement instrument, psychologists will split a measurement instrument into 2 equivalent halves.[3,7] Some psychologists split an instrument into two equal halves by comparing the first ½ of the test with the second ½ of the test. This approach can be problematic if the measurement instrument being split is designed so that easier items are located at the beginning of the instrument and items get progressively more difficult as you proceed through the instrument. If such an instrument is split by comparing the first ½ of the test with the second ½ of the test, you would have one half that contains all of the easier items and one half containing all of the difficult items. Your two halves would therefore not be equivalent. As an alternative approach, psychologists will split such an instrument into two equal halves by comparing the odd # items with the even # items.[1,2,3] Such an approach would create two halves that each contain an equivalent mixture of easy, moderate, and difficult items and would be equivalent. Once psychologists have created 2 equal halves of a measurement instrument, psychologists will administer one half of the instrument to a group of individuals and record the results (Half 1). Psychologists then administer the second half of the instrument to the same group of individuals and again record the results (Half 2). Psychologists will then compute a correlation coefficient to measure the relationship between measurements on the two halves of the test.[1,2,3] Since the two halves of the instrument are equal with respect to content and item difficulty, we would expect individual's scores to be consistent across the two halves of the measurement instrument. A high positive (+) correlation coefficient would be evidence there is consistency in measurements across the two halves of the instrument. Just as in the assessment of parallel-forms reliability, psychologists must assess the influence of order on the consistency of measurements across the two halves of the instrument (e.g. Order A (Half 1–Half 2) vs. Order B (Half 2–Half 1)).

Inter-Rater Reliability

When studying behavior and mental processes, psychologists may have multiple individuals observe and evaluate the variables of interest.[3] After completing their observations, observers may be asked to provide ratings or rankings that summarize their observations or to classify their observations into specified rating categories. Since the observers are all observing the same behavior or mental processes, we would expect the ratings, rankings, or classifications to be consistent across observers. There is no guarantee, however, that two observers who are observing the same behavior or mental processes will provide consistent ratings, rankings, or classifications.[2] In fact, intensive training of observers is often required to establish acceptable levels of inter-rater reliability.[1] A common mistake made by researchers is to have observers make their initial observations, ratings, rankings, or classifications under live experimental conditions and then evaluate the level of inter-rater reliability after the fact. The problem with this approach is that if the level of inter-rater reliability is not acceptable, then the ratings, rankings, or classifications provided by the observers lack reliability and are therefore of little use to the psychologists conducting the research. A better approach would be to train your observers and establish inter-rater reliability prior to allowing them to observe and evaluate the variables of interest under live experimental conditions. By establishing inter-rater reliability prior to collecting experimental data, observers are more likely to produce ratings, rankings, or classifications that are reliable, and therefore of more value to the psychologists conducting the research. To assess inter-rater reliability, psychologists will have two observers observe the same variables of interest and then provide ratings, rankings, or classifications that summarize their observations.[1,2,3] The relationship between ratings, rankings, or classifications of the two observers are then measured through various statistical analyses. If observers provide ratings based on their observations, a correlation coefficient known as a Pearson correlation will be computed.[1,7] If observers provide rankings based on their observations, a correlation known as a Spearman correlation is computed. A high positive (+) correlation once again would indicate consistency in the ratings or rankings of the observers.

If observers classify their observations into specified rating categories, a statistic known as Cohen's Kappa[1] is computed to measure the relationship between the classifications of the observers. The calculation and interpretation of the Cohen's Kappa procedure is described below.

Cohen's Kappa[8,9]

A Social Psychologist interested in studying the nature of relationships has two of her research assistants unobtrusively observe the interactions of 20 couples at a local park. The psychologist instructs her research assistants to observe each couple for 15 minutes and to then independently rate whether they felt each couple was in "like, lust, or love" with one another. The independent ratings of the two research assistants appear below:

	Rater 1	Rater 2
Couple 1	Like	Like
Couple 2	Lust	Love
Couple 3	Lust	Lust
Couple 4	Love	Love
Couple 5	Lust	Lust
Couple 6	Like	Lust
Couple 7	Like	Like
Couple 8	Love	Love
Couple 9	Lust	Like
Couple 10	Love	Love
Couple 11	Like	Like
Couple 12	Like	Like
Couple 13	Love	Lust
Couple 14	Lust	Lust
Couple 15	Love	Lust
Couple 16	Love	Love
Couple 17	Like	Like
Couple 18	Lust	Like
Couple 19	Lust	Lust
Couple 20	Like	Love

Step 1:

Create a new table that summarizes the two research assistants' ratings for the 20 couples. Since the research assistants were given 3 coding category options (i.e. like, lust, love), you will create a 3 × 3 table as shown below (*Note:* If there were only 2 coding category options (i.e. lust, love), you would create a 2 × 2 table). Your completed table will provide a summary of the frequency of agreements and disagreements between the ratings of the two research assistants (Table 1).

Rater #1

Rater #2		Like	Lust	Love	
	Like	5	2	0	**Table 1**
	Lust	1	4	2	
	Love	1	1	4	

To ensure that you are setting up your table correctly, the cell shaded in light gray (frequency = 5) represents the number of times Rater #1 and Rater #2 both rated the same couple as being "in like." The cell shaded in medium gray (frequency = 1), represents the number of times Rater #1 rated a couple as being "in lust" while Rater #2 rated the same couple as being "in love." The cell shaded in dark gray represents the number of times that Rater #1 rated a couple as being "in love" while Rater #2 rated the same couple as being "in lust." You should note the cells along the diagonal of your table represent agreements between the raters while the cells located off the diagonal represent disagreements between raters. When your table is complete, the sum of all cell frequencies should equal 20 (i.e. total number of couples rated by the research assistants).

Step 2:

Using the cell frequency values from Table 1, compute the actual number of agreements between the ratings of the two research assistants (i.e. total number of times there was agreement between the two research assistants' ratings of a couple). To compute the actual number of agreements between the ratings of the two research assistants (**A**), simply sum the frequencies for all of the cells located on the diagonal of Table 1 (cells shaded in gray).

Rater #1

Rater #2		Like	Lust	Love	
	Like	5	2	0	**Table 1**
	Lust	1	4	2	
	Love	1	1	4	

$$A = 5 + 4 + 4 = 13$$

The ratings of the two research assistants were in agreement for 13/20 couples (or 65% of the couples observed).

Step 3:

Using the cell frequency values from Table 1, create a new table containing "row marginal" and "column marginal" frequency values. To compute these values, simply sum the cell frequency values for each row and column in your table as shown below. "Row marginal" values appear in cells shaded in light gray and "column marginal" values appear in cells shaded in dark gray. The sum of your "row marginal" and "column marginal" values should equal 20 (i.e. the total number of couples rated by the two research assistants). We will refer to this new table as Table 2.

Rater #1

		Like	Lust	Love	
	Like	5	2	0	7
Rater #2	**Lust**	1	4	2	7
	Love	1	1	4	6
		7	7	6	20

Table 2

Step 4:

Using the "row marginal" and "column marginal" values you computed in Table 2, create a new table containing "expected frequency values" for each of the cells along the diagonal of the table (cells shaded in gray). The "expected frequency values" indicate the number of times we would expect the two research assistants to agree on a rating of "like, love, and lust" by chance alone. To compute these "expected frequency values," simply select one of the cells along the diagonal and multiply the "row marginal" and "column marginal" values associated with this cell and divide this value by 20 (i.e. the total number of couples rated by the two research assistants). Repeat this process for each cell along the diagonal. We will refer to this new table as Table 3.

Rater #1

		Like	Lust	Love	
	Like	2.45			7
Rater #2	**Lust**		2.45		7
	Love			1.80	6
		7	7	6	20

Table 3

To ensure you are setting up your table correctly, you should compute the following "expected frequency values" for the cells along the diagonal (Like/Like: $7 \times 7 = 49/20 = 2.45$), (Lust/Lust: $7 \times 7 = 49/20 = 2.45$), and (Love/Love: $6 \times 6 = 36/20 = 1.80$), respectively. These "expected frequency values" tell us we would expect the two research assistants to agree on a rating of "like" 2.45 times, a rating of "lust" 2.45 times, and a rating of "love" 1.80 times when rating 20 couples due to chance alone.

Step 5:

Using the "expected frequency values" you computed for the cells along the diagonal in Table 3, compute the "expected number of agreements" (**E**) between the ratings of the two research assistants (i.e. total number of times we would expect the ratings of the two research assistants to agree by chance alone). To compute this value, simply sum the "expected frequency values" for the cells located along the diagonal of Table 3 (cells shaded in gray).

Rater #1

		Like	Lust	Love	
	Like	2.45			7
Rater #2	**Lust**		2.45		7
	Love			1.80	6
		7	7	6	20

Table 3

$$E = 2.45 + 2.45 + 1.80 = 6.7$$

We would expect the ratings of the two research assistants to agree 6.7/20 times by chance alone (or for 33.5% of the couples observed).

Step 6:

Using the values you computed for the "actual number of agreements" (**A**) in Step 2 and the "expected number of agreements" (**E**) you computed in Step 5, compute the value for Cohen's Kappa using the formula below. The calculated Kappa value will be positive (+) if the level of agreement between the ratings of the two research assistants is better than chance and negative (−) if the level of agreement between ratings of the two research assistants is worse than chance.

$$\text{Kappa} = \frac{\text{A (actual number of agreements)} - \text{E (expected number of agreements)}}{\text{N (total couples rated)} - \text{E (expected number of agreements)}}$$

$$\text{Kappa} = \frac{13 - 6.7}{20 - 6.7} = \frac{6.3}{13.3} = \mathbf{.47}$$

Step 7:

To interpret your computed Kappa value ($K = .47$), consult the chart below which provides some generally accepted standards for the interpretation of Kappa values.[10]

Kappa	Level of Agreement	Kappa	Level of Agreement
< 0	Less than Chance Agreement	.41–.60	Moderate Agreement
.01–.20	Slight Agreement	.61–.80	Substantial Agreement
.21–.40	Fair Agreement	.81–.99	Almost Perfect Agreement

Using the values in the table as a standard for comparison, we can conclude there was "moderate agreement" between the ratings of the two research assistants and their assessment of like, lust, and love in the 20 couples observed in the park.

Inter-Method Reliability

Frequently, psychologists will use a variety of measurement instruments to measure their variables of interest. For example, if psychologists are interested in studying attitudes toward the legalization of marijuana, they may assess attitudes through the use of an online survey and a face-to-face interview. If psychologists then want to combine the attitudinal data collected via the two different methods of measurement, they need to verify that the measurements collected via the two methods are consistent (i.e. reliable). To assess the inter-method reliability of two methods of measurement, psychologists will administer the online survey (Method 1) and face-to-face interview (Method 2) to groups of individuals and record the results. Psychologists will then compute a correlation coefficient to measure the relationship between the measurements produced by the two methods of measurement.[1,7,11] A high positive (+) correlation coefficient would indicate consistency in the measurements collected via the two methods. Psychologists must be aware, however, that the consistency of measurements across the two methods may be influenced by differences that exist between the groups of individuals who complete each method of measurement. If there are important differences between groups, it can result in a decrease in the consistency of measurements across the two different methods of measurement and an underestimation of the inter-method reliability. In an effort to create equal groups and to get a more accurate estimation of inter-method reliability, psychologists will often randomly assign individuals to the two methods of measurement being evaluated (e.g. ½ are assigned to Method A (online survey); ½ are assigned to Method B (face-to-face interview)).

Internal Consistency

When psychologists develop a measurement instrument to assess a psychological construct (e.g. honesty), they begin by clearly defining the construct of interest and generating a series of questions designed to measure this construct. Since many constructs are multi-dimensional, psychologists must include questions on the measurement instrument that are designed to measure the full range of a construct's dimensions. With all of the questions on the instrument measuring the same construct, we expect individual's responses to be consistent across questions (i.e. internally consistent). To assess the internal consistency of a measurement instrument, psychologists will administer the instrument to a group of individuals and record the results for each of the questions (or items) on the instrument. Psychologists will then compute correlation coefficients to measure the relationships between responses to each item and every other item on the instrument. An average inter-item correlation value is then computed whose value represents the "internal consistency" of the measurement instrument.[1,2,4,6] Based on these inter-item correlation coefficients, psychologists can remove all questions not highly correlated with the other questions on the instrument. Individuals' responses to these questions were not consistent (i.e. reliable) with their responses to other questions on the instrument.[3] The lack of consistency may be the result of a confusing or poorly worded question, or more importantly, because the question does not provide a good measure of the construct of interest. The final version of the measurement instrument will, therefore, contain a collection of questions that are highly correlated with one another, are measuring the same construct, and are responded to in a consistent manner by individuals who complete the instrument.

Validity

There are several methods used by psychologists to evaluate the validity of a measurement instrument. These methods may include the following: **(a)** face validity, **(b)** content validity, **(c)** criterion-related validity, and **(d)** construct validity.

Face Validity

The assessment of the face validity of a measurement instrument involves nothing more than a subjective judgment as to whether the instrument at first glance appears to measure the construct it is intended to measure.[2,3] For example, a psychologist may develop an instrument to assess quality of sleep. If the instrument has face validity, anyone looking at the instrument would quickly recognize it is designed to measure quality of sleep. However, not all measurement instruments used by psychologists will have face validity. For example, projective personality tests are designed so that individuals completing the instrument are unaware of what construct(s) are being measured. Therefore, anyone looking at these tests would not judge them as having face validity (e.g. anyone looking at the Rorschach Ink Blot[12] test is not likely to look at a series of inkblots and quickly recognize the test as a measure of personality). It is important to remember that face validity provides no evidence that a measurement instrument is valid; only that it "looks" like it would be a valid measure of a construct of interest.[4]

Content Validity

The assessment of the content validity of a measurement instrument involves an analysis of the content (i.e. questions) of the instrument and the extent to which the content of the instrument provides a thorough assessment of the construct of interest.[1,2,3,4] To assess the content validity of a measurement instrument, psychologists will typically compile a panel of experts known as a "content evaluation panel"[1] (or subject-matter experts).[2,4] The panel members have knowledge and/or experience with the construct of interest and can provide expert advice on how best to measure a specific construct. Psychologists will then have the members of the panel examine each question on an instrument and independently rate whether: (a) a question measures the construct and (b) a question is essential to the measurement of that construct. The level of agreement across panel members (i.e. percent agreement) is computed for each question on the instrument.[1,2] Questions that receive a high level of agreement across panel members are considered valid and essential to the measurement of the construct and are included in the final version of the measurement instrument. Questions that fail to receive a high level of agreement across panel members are removed from the measurement instrument. The final version of the measurement instrument, therefore, contains a collection of questions which are measuring the same construct and judged as essential to the measurement of the construct by a panel of experts.

Criterion-Related Validity

For a measurement instrument to demonstrate criterion-related validity, psychologists must be able to use measurements from the instrument to predict current and/or future performance or behavior.[1] There are two approaches used by psychologists to assess the criterion-related validity of a measurement instrument. The two approaches involve the assessment of the: **(a)** predictive validity and **(b)** concurrent validity of an instrument. To assess the predictive validity of an instrument, psychologists will administer the instrument (e.g. a measure of communication skills) to a group of individuals and record the results. At a future point in time, psychologists will then assess the same individuals on a measure of performance or behavior (e.g. job performance as a customer service representative) and once again record the results. Psychologists will then compute a correlation coefficient to measure the relationship between measurements. A high positive (+) or negative (−) correlation coefficient would indicate a strong predictive relationship between the two measurements (e.g. scores from the measure of communication skills are highly predictive of future job performance in customer service).[1,2,3,4]

To assess the concurrent validity of a measurement instrument, psychologists will administer a measurement instrument (e.g. a measure of empathy) to a group of individuals and simultaneously (i.e. concurrently) assess the same individuals on a measure of performance or behavior (e.g. the amount of money donated to charitable organizations in need). Psychologists will then compute a correlation coefficient to measure the relationship between measurements. A high positive (+) or negative (–) correlation coefficient would indicate a strong predictive relationship between the two measurements (e.g. scores on the measure of empathy are highly predictive of the amount of charitable donations).[1,2,3,4] While both predictive and concurrent validity involve an assessment of the relationship that exists between scores from a measurement instrument and a measure of performance or behavior, predictive validity focuses on the ability of psychologists to use scores from a measurement instrument to predict future performance or behavior while concurrent validity focuses on the ability of psychologists to use scores from a measurement instrument to predict current performance or behavior. Quadrant analysis[1,6] is an example of a procedure that is used by psychologists to assess the criterion-related validity of a measurement instrument.

Quadrant Analysis[1,6,13]

A Psychologist is hired by the owner of a car dealership to develop a test that would be used by the dealership to select its new sales personnel. The owner wants the psychologist to develop a test capable of determining which applicants for sales positions would actually be successful salespersons if they were hired by the dealership. After reviewing the salesmanship literature, the psychologist develops a 10-item test designed to measure "salesmanship ability." Scores on the test range from 0–10 with higher scores indicating higher levels of "salesmanship ability." The psychologist decides to use a concurrent validity approach to assess the criterion-related validity of her new test. She administers the test to the 20 salespersons who currently work at the dealership. Concurrently, she examines the dealerships' sales records and measures the number of cars each of the 20 salespersons sold during the last month. The data appear below:

	Score	# Cars		Score	# Cars
Salesman 1	4	3	**Salesman 11**	1	4
Salesman 2	7	7	**Salesman 12**	5	5
Salesman 3	6	6	**Salesman 13**	10	10
Salesman 4	10	3	**Salesman 14**	8	2
Salesman 5	3	9	**Salesman 15**	7	8
Salesman 6	3	2	**Salesman 16**	4	4
Salesman 7	2	1	**Salesman 17**	2	3
Salesman 8	1	1	**Salesman 18**	9	6
Salesman 9	7	10	**Salesman 19**	7	4
Salesman 10	9	9	**Salesman 20**	3	3

Step 1:

Create a graph (as shown below) to illustrate the relationship between the scores on the test of salesmanship ability and number of cars sold by the 20 current salespersons at the dealership. Scores on the measurement instrument (e.g. test of salesmanship ability) should be graphed on the X (i.e. horizontal) axis and the measure of performance (e.g. number of cars sold) should be graphed on the Y (i.e. vertical) axis.

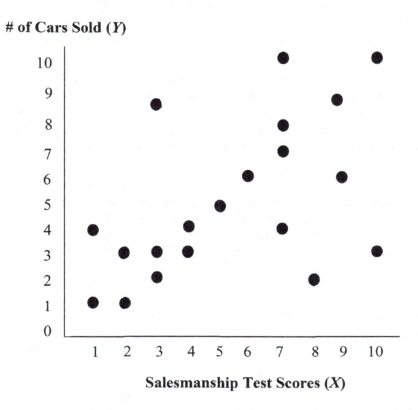

A visual analysis of the graph provides information about the nature of the relationship (i.e. the strength and direction of the correlation) between scores on the test of salesmanship ability and the number of cars sold. If the correlation is weak (a value near .00), there is no clear pattern and the data points will be widely dispersed. If the correlation is strong (a value near 1.00), the data points will line up along a straight-line pattern. The data from the dealership indicates a strong correlation exists between test scores and the number of cars sold (i.e. the pattern of data has the characteristics of a straight-line pattern). If the correlation is positive (i.e. as test scores increase, the number of cars sold increases), the pattern of data will flow from the lower left to the upper right of the graph. If the correlation is negative (i.e. as test scores increase, the number of cars sold decreases), the pattern of data will flow from the upper left to the lower right of the graph. The data from the dealership indicates a positive correlation exists between test scores and the number of cars sold (i.e. the pattern of data flows from the lower left to the upper right of the graph). Combining our visual assessments of the strength and direction of the relationship, the data from the dealership is indicative of a strong positive correlation between scores on the test of salesmanship ability and the number of cars sold.

Step 2:

Identify what level of performance on your measurement instrument will represent "successful" performance (e.g. what level of performance on the test of salesmanship ability will indicate that an individual possesses at least the minimum amount of salesmanship ability to be successful as a salesperson if hired by the dealership). The Psychologist decides based on a review of criteria for "success" used by other tests of salesmanship ability that a score of 5 or higher on the test of salesmanship ability will serve as her criteria for "successful" performance on the test.

Step 3:

Identify what level of performance on your measure of performance or behavior will represent "successful" performance (e.g. what number of cars sold during the last month will indicate that an individual has been a successful salesperson for the dealership). The Psychologist and owner of the dealership meet to discuss this issue and collectively decide based on past sales data from the dealership that in order to be considered "successful" a salesperson at the dealership must sell a minimum of 5 cars per month.

Step 4:

Update the graph you created in Step 1 (as shown below) by adding your criteria for "successful" performance for both your measurement instrument (e.g. test of salesmanship ability) and your measure of performance (e.g. number of cars sold) to the graph. This update will result in your graph being divided up into four separate areas referred to as "quadrants." The four "quadrants" created by your criteria for "success" have been labeled (**A, B, C, D**) in the graph below.

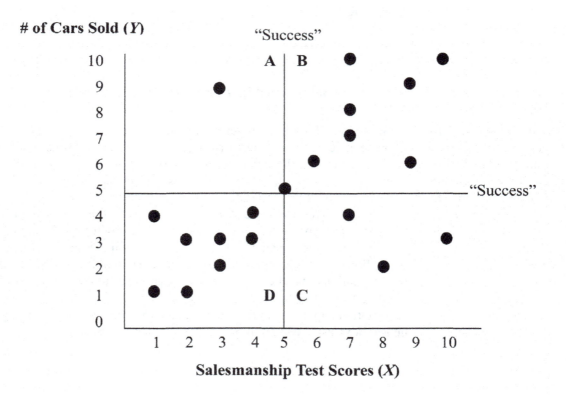

An analysis of your new graph will reveal that two of the quadrants (**B and D**) represent instances in which the test is exhibiting criterion-related validity. Specifically, these quadrants represent instances in which we would make a correct prediction about sales performance based on scores on the test of salesmanship ability. Quadrant B represents those individuals who were successful on the test (scores > 5) and who also exhibited a successful level of sales performance (> 5 cars sold). Individuals in Quadrant B are referred to as "True Positives" (i.e. a successful test score predicts a successful level of performance). Quadrant D represents those individuals who were unsuccessful on the test (scores < 5) and who also exhibited an unsuccessful level of sales performance (< 5 cars sold). Individuals in Quadrant D are referred to as "True Negatives" (i.e. an unsuccessful test score predicts an unsuccessful level of performance).

The other two quadrants (**A and C**) represent instances in which the test is not exhibiting criterion-related validity. Specifically, these quadrants represent instances in which we would make an incorrect prediction about sales performance based on scores on the test of salesmanship ability. Quadrant A represents those individuals who were unsuccessful on the test (scores < 5) but exhibited a successful level of sales performance (> 5 cars sold). Individuals in Quadrant A are referred to as "False Negatives" (i.e. an unsuccessful test score would predict an unsuccessful level of performance, but the individual exhibits a successful level of performance). Quadrant C represents those individuals who were successful on the test (scores > 5), but who exhibited an unsuccessful level of sales performance (< 5 cars sold). Individuals in quadrant C are referred to as "False Positives" (i.e. a successful test score would predict a successful level of performance, but the individual exhibits an unsuccessful level of performance).

Step 5:

Using your updated graph created in Step 4, you should now count the number of individuals located in each of the four quadrants of your graph (**A, B, C, D**). While most of the data points will clearly fall into one of the four quadrants, you will have some individuals whose data falls on one or more of the criteria lines (i.e. criteria for "success" for your measurement instrument and performance measure). When this occurs, you should adhere to the following rules when counting the number of individuals located in each of your four quadrants:

(a) If an individual's data point falls on the criteria line for the measurement instrument (i.e. a score of 5 on the test of salesmanship ability), the individual is considered to have been successful on the test and the individual's data point should be moved to the right into Quadrant **B** or **C**.

(b) If an individual's data point falls on the criteria line for the performance measure (i.e. 5 cars sold in a month), the individual is considered to have exhibited a successful level of performance and the individual's data point should be moved upward into Quadrants **A** or **B**.

(c) If an individual's data point falls on the criteria lines for both the measurement instrument (i.e. a score of 5 on the test of salesmanship ability) and the performance measure (i.e. 5 cars sold in a month), the individual is considered to have been successful on the test and to have exhibited a successful level of performance. The individual's data point should be moved upward and to the right into Quadrant **B**.

Step 6:

Using your updated graph created in Step 4 and your count of the number of individuals in each of your four quadrants, you can now analyze the criterion-related validity of the measurement instrument (e.g. test of salesmanship ability) using the formula below:

$$\frac{\text{\# of Individuals in Quadrant B} + \text{\# of Individuals in Quadrant D}}{\text{Total Number of Individuals Tested}}$$

$$\frac{8+8}{20} = \frac{16}{20} = \textbf{.80}$$

Our calculated value of .80 indicates scores on the test of salesmanship ability accurately predict the level of sales performance for 80% of the individuals who took the test (evidence the test has demonstrated criterion-related validity).

Step 7:

To determine whether the new measurement instrument (e.g. test of salesmanship ability) is an improvement over the current method of selection of sales personnel used by the dealership, we can compute the following formulas:

Formula 1: $\dfrac{\text{\# of Individuals in Quadrant A + \# of Individuals in Quadrant B}}{\text{Total Number of Individuals Tested}}$

$$\frac{1+8}{20} = \frac{9}{20} = \ \mathbf{.45}$$

Our calculated value of .45 indicates that 45% of the sales personnel currently working at the dealership exhibit a successful level of sales performance. This also indicates that the method of selection currently being used at the dealership produces an accurate prediction about sales performance only 45% of the time.

Formula 2: $\dfrac{\text{\# of Individuals in Quadrant B + \# of Individuals in Quadrant D}}{\text{Total Number of Individuals Tested}}$

$$\frac{8+8}{20} = \frac{16}{20} = \ \mathbf{.80}$$

Our calculated value of .80 indicates that scores on the test of salesmanship ability accurately predict level of sales performance for 80% of the individuals who took the test. It also indicates if the test of salesmanship were used by the dealership to select new sales personnel, it would produce an accurate prediction about sales performance 80% of the time.

We can then use our calculations from Formula 1 and Formula 2 to compute the formula below. This formula will be used to determine the percentage of improvement in predictive accuracy the dealership would experience if they stopped using their current method of selection and switched to using the test of salesmanship ability developed by the Psychologist. Your calculated value will be positive (+) if there is an improvement in predictive accuracy and negative (–) if there is a decline in predictive validity.

Formula 2 – Formula 1
$$.80 - .45 = \mathbf{.35}$$

Our calculated value of .35 indicates that the dealership would experience a 35% improvement in predictive accuracy by using the Psychologist's test of salesmanship ability. Over time, this 35% improvement in predictive accuracy would result in the dealership having 35% more of its sales personnel exhibiting a successful level of sales performance.

Construct Validity

A measurement instrument that has construct validity, measures the construct it is intended to measure, and shares predictable relationships with other measurement instruments that measure similar or dissimilar constructs. There are two approaches commonly used by psychologists to assess the construct validity of a measurement instrument. These two approaches involve the assessment of the: **(a)** convergent validity and **(b)** discriminant validity of a measurement instrument.

To assess the convergent validity of a measurement instrument, psychologists administer the measurement instrument (e.g. a measure of optimism) to a group of individuals along with other measurement instruments designed to measure the same construct (i.e. other instruments that measure optimism). Psychologists will then compute correlation coefficients to measure the relationships between scores on the measurement instrument and scores on the other instruments measuring the same construct. Since all of the instruments are measuring the same construct, we would expect scores to be consistent across instruments.[1,2,3,14] A high positive correlation would indicate there is consistency in the scores across instruments and would provide evidence that the measurement instrument demonstrates convergent validity.

To assess the discriminant validity of a measurement instrument, psychologists administer the measurement instrument (e.g. a measure of happiness) to a group of individuals along with other measurement instruments designed to measure dissimilar constructs (i.e. measurement instruments that assess constructs such as hopelessness and depression). Psychologists will then compute correlation coefficients to measure the relationship between scores on the measurement instrument and scores on the other measurement instruments measuring the dissimilar constructs. Since all of the instruments are measuring different constructs, we would expect there would be a lack of consistency in scores across instruments.[1,2,3,14] A weak correlation would indicate a lack of consistency in the scores across instruments and would provide evidence the measurement instrument demonstrates discriminant validity.

EXERCISE 3A

Identifying Types of Reliability and Validity

To produce results that are of value to the scientific community, psychologists must use measurement instruments that are reliable and valid when conducting psychological research. There are numerous approaches psychologists can use to establish the measurement instruments they are using in their research are indeed reliable and valid. Below are 12 scenarios describing different approaches being used by psychologists to examine the reliability and validity of their measurement instruments. For each scenario, please: **(a)** determine which type of reliability (e.g. test-retest, parallel-forms, split-halves, inter-rater, inter-method, internal consistency) or validity (e.g. face, content, predictive, concurrent, convergent, discriminant) is being examined and **(b)** decide whether the evidence collected by the psychologist establishes the reliability or validity of the measurement instrument and provide a rationale for your decision.

PART A

01. An Educational Psychologist creates an instrument designed to measure "teacher readiness" (i.e. higher scores indicating greater "readiness" to have a classroom). To assess her new instrument, she administers the instrument to 20 student teachers preparing to begin their student teaching assignments and records their "readiness" scores. A year later, after the student teachers have completed their teaching assignments, she collects the student teacher evaluation scores (i.e. higher scores indicating better performance in the classroom) for each of the 20 student teachers. She then examines the relationship between "teacher readiness" scores and classroom performance scores and computes a correlation coefficient of +.88.

Type of Reliability/Validity: ☐_____

Supporting Evidence?   Yes ☐   No ☐

Rationale:

02. A Sports Psychologist conducted a study to determine whether Major League umpires call "balls" and "strikes" consistently. He recruited 2 experienced (i.e. 20+ years of experience) Major League umpires and had them observe 10 pitches from a Major League pitcher. After each pitch, the psychologist had the two umpires independently rate whether the pitch was a "ball" or a "strike." The psychologist then examined the relationship between the "ball" and "strike" calls of the two umpires and computed a Kappa value of +.32.

Type of Reliability/Validity: [ ]

Supporting Evidence?   **Yes** [ ]   **No** [ ]

Rationale:

03. A Personality Psychologist develops an instrument designed to measure the personality trait "energetic." She takes copies of her instrument to her local fitness club and asks members of the club to take a look at her instrument and to tell her what they think the instrument is measuring. Her results indicated that 97 of 100 fitness club members (97%) said that they thought her instrument was designed to measure "how energetic a person is."

Type of Reliability/Validity: [ ]

Supporting Evidence?   **Yes** [ ]   **No** [ ]

Rationale:

04. A Cultural Psychologist developed an instrument designed to measure "religiosity" (i.e. higher scores indicating greater importance of religion in one's life). To assess his new instrument, the psychologist administers the instrument to 50 random college students and records their "religiosity" scores. At the same time, the psychologist asks each of the 50 college students to tell him the number of times they had each attended church during the previous 6 months. The psychologist then examines the relationship between church attendance and "religiosity" scores and computes a correlation coefficient of +.03.

Type of Reliability/Validity:

Supporting Evidence?   **Yes** ☐   **No** ☐

Rationale:

05. An Industrial-Organizational Psychologist develops a new instrument designed to measure "motivation" (i.e. higher scores indicating higher motivation). To assess his new instrument, he administers the instrument to 50 job applicants at a local company. He then examines the relationships between the 12 items on the instrument by computing correlation coefficients for all possible pairs of items. He finds the average inter-time correlation is +.81.

Type of Reliability/Validity:

Supporting Evidence?   **Yes** ☐   **No** ☐

Rationale:

06. An Experimental Psychologist develops two versions of a test designed to measure "driving knowledge" (i.e. higher scores indicating higher driving knowledge). The 2 versions contain different questions, but are designed to assess the same content. To assess her instruments, she administers version 1 of her test to a sample of 20 new drivers and records their "driving knowledge" scores. An hour later, she administers version 2 to the same 20 drivers and once again records their "driving knowledge" scores. She examines the relationship between the scores on the 2 versions of the test and computes a correlation coefficient of +.96

Type of Reliability/Validity:

Supporting Evidence?   **Yes** ☐   **No** ☐

Rationale:

07. A Clinical Psychologist develops an instrument designed to measure "anxiety" (i.e. higher scores indicating higher anxiety). To assess his new instrument, he assembles a group of 10 experts in the field of anxiety and asks them to independently rate whether each item on his instrument is a good measure of the construct of "anxiety." The psychologist analyzes the level of agreement between the experts and finds only 5 of the 15 items on his instrument were seen as good measures of the construct of "anxiety" by at least 80% of the experts.

Type of Reliability/Validity:

Supporting Evidence?   **Yes** ☐   **No** ☐

Rationale:

08. After a controversial police shooting, a Community Psychologist develops an instrument designed to measure "attitudes toward law enforcement" (i.e. higher scores indicating more positive attitudes). He administers his instrument to 50 residents and records their "attitude" scores. Before presenting data to the Mayor, he decides to make sure his results accurately represent the attitudes of the community. A week later, he administers his instrument to the same 50 residents and again records their "attitude" scores. He examines the relationship between the two sets of "attitude" scores and computes a correlation coefficient of −.92.

Type of Reliability/Validity:

Supporting Evidence?   **Yes** ☐   **No** ☐

Rationale:

09. A Cognitive Psychologist develops an instrument designed to measure "memory abilities" (i.e. higher scores indicating better memory). To assess her new instrument, she administers the first 20 items (i.e. 1–20) to a sample of 25 college students and records their "memory" scores. She then administers the second 20 items (i.e. 21-40) to the same 25 college students and once again records their "memory" scores. She examines the relationship between the scores on the two sets of items and computes a correlation coefficient of +.09.

Type of Reliability/Validity:

Supporting Evidence?   **Yes** ☐   **No** ☐

Rationale:

10. A Counseling Psychologist develops an instrument designed to measure "self-confidence" (i.e. higher scores indicating greater self-confidence). To assess her new instrument, she administers the instrument to 25 clients and records their "self-confidence" scores. She then administers a popular test of "self-confidence" to the same 25 clients and once again records their "self-confidence" scores. She examines the relationship between scores on the 2 tests and computes a correlation coefficient of +.85. She also discovers her instrument is able to predict the same behaviors (e.g. ambition, risk-taking) as the popular "self-confidence" test.

Type of Reliability/Validity:

Supporting Evidence? **Yes** ☐ **No** ☐

Rationale:

11. A Consumer Psychologist develops an instrument designed to measure "attitudes toward debt" (i.e. higher scores indicating greater acceptance of credit card debt). To assess his new instrument, he administers the instrument to 100 consumers via a telephone survey and records their "attitude toward debt" scores. He administers the instrument to 100 different consumers via in-store customer intercept interviews and records their "attitude toward debt" scores. He then examines the relationship between "attitude toward debt" scores across the two consumer groups and computes a correlation coefficient of −.68.

Type of Reliability/Validity:

Supporting Evidence? **Yes** ☐ **No** ☐

Rationale:

12. A Health Psychologist develops an instrument designed to measure "health consciousness" (i.e. higher scores indicating greater commitment to a healthy lifestyle). To assess her new instrument, she administers her instrument and another instrument measuring the unrelated construct of "spatial ability" (i.e. higher scores indicating greater spatial ability) to people sitting in the waiting rooms at area hospitals. She records their "health consciousness" and "spatial ability" scores. She examines the relationship between scores on her instrument and scores on the instruments measuring "spatial ability" and computes a correlation coefficient of +.18. She also discovers her instrument does not predict the same behaviors (e.g. problem solving, mathematical reasoning) as the measure of "spatial ability."

Type of Reliability/Validity: [   ]

Supporting Evidence?   **Yes** ☐   **No** ☐

Rationale:

PART B

Select **three (3)** of the 12 scenarios and: **(a)** identify a potential flaw in the approach used by the psychologist to establish the reliability or validity of a measurement instrument and **(b)** describe how this identified flaw has the potential to result in the psychologist under- or over-estimating the reliability or validity of his/her measurement instrument.

Scenario 1	Teacher Readiness	☐	**Scenario 7**	Anxiety	☐
Scenario 2	Balls and Strikes	☐	**Scenario 8**	Law Enforcement	☐
Scenario 3	Energetic Personality	☐	**Scenario 9**	Memory Ability	☐
Scenario 4	Religiosity	☐	**Scenario 10**	Self-Confidence	☐
Scenario 5	Motivation	☐	**Scenario 11**	Credit Card Debt	☐
Scenario 6	Driving Knowledge	☐	**Scenario 12**	Health Consciousness	☐

Scenario # and Title:

What potential flaw did you identify in the psychologist's approach and how might this flaw result in an under- or over-estimation of the reliability or validity of the instrument?

_____

_____

_____

_____

_____

_____

_____

_____

Scenario # and Title:

What potential flaw did you identify in the psychologist's approach and how might this flaw result in an under- or over-estimation of the reliability or validity of the instrument?

_____

_____

_____

_____

_____

_____

_____

_____

Scenario # and Title:

What potential flaw did you identify in the psychologist's approach and how might this flaw result in an under- or over-estimation of the reliability or validity of the instrument?

_____

_____

_____

_____

_____

_____

_____

EXERCISE 3B

Analyzing the Criterion-Related Validity of a Measurement Instrument

A Cognitive Psychologist developed a new educational program designed to help people improve their memory skills. People with different types of memory-related issues signed up for the psychologist's program including: (a) people with memory deficits related to brain injuries, (b) people from the world of business unable to get promoted due to an inability to remember important clients' names, (c) people over the age of 60 trying to halt the progressive decline in memory that comes with ageing, and (d) college students wanting to improve their grades by improving their memory skills. A total of 20 people enrolled in the psychologist's program.

The program lasted a total of 10 weeks. At the end of the program, the psychologist administered an instrument designed to measure "memory skills" (i.e. higher scores indicating better memory skills) to each of the 20 people in the program and recorded their "memory skills" scores. Scores on the instrument could range from 0 to 50. After all 20 people in the program completed the "memory skills" instrument, the psychologist took them all to a party attended by 20 other guests. The psychologist told the 20 people in the program to mingle with the other guests for 1 hour. An hour later, the psychologist returned to the party and asked each person in the program to independently recall the names of the 20 guests at the party. Recall scores could range from 0 to 20. The psychologist's data appears below:

	Memory Score	Recall Score		Memory Score	Recall Score
Participant 1	45	20	**Participant 11**	15	18
Participant 2	30	6	**Participant 12**	30	12
Participant 3	20	12	**Participant 13**	10	14
Participant 4	45	10	**Participant 14**	45	8
Participant 5	35	16	**Participant 15**	35	18
Participant 6	25	8	**Participant 16**	20	8
Participant 7	5	10	**Participant 17**	10	4
Participant 8	40	14	**Participant 18**	35	4
Participant 9	20	4	**Participant 19**	45	14
Participant 10	5	20	**Participant 20**	50	16

Step 1:

Create a graph to illustrate the relationship between the scores on the test of memory skills and the number of guest names recalled from the party.

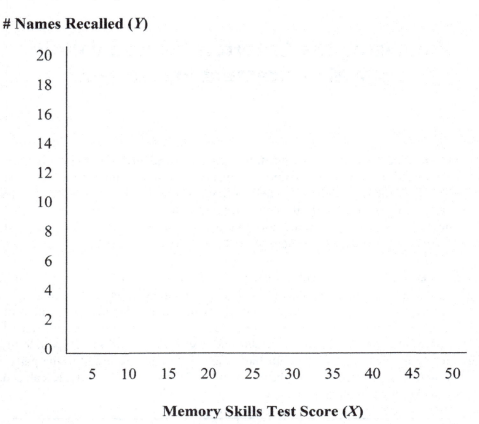

 # Names Recalled (*Y*)

Memory Skills Test Score (*X*)

What does a visual analysis of your graph tell you about the relationship (i.e. the strength and direction of the correlation) between scores on the test of memory skills and the number of guest names recalled from the party?

Strength of the Relationship?	Direction of the Relationship?

Step 2:

The Psychologist selects a score of 30 or higher on the "memory skills" test and recall of 12 or more guest names from the party as the criteria for "successful" performance. Update your graph by adding criteria for "successful" performance & quadrant labels.

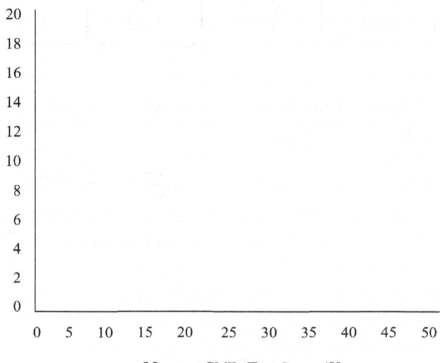

Step 3:

Count the number of individuals located in each of the four quadrants of your graph (A, B, C, D). When a data point falls on one or more of the criteria lines (i.e. criteria for "successful" performance), follow the rules outlined in the module to determine which quadrant (A, B, C, D) the data point should be assigned to during your count.

Step 4:

Now that you have completed your count of the number of individuals located in each of the four quadrants of your graph (A, B, C, D), determine the number of each of the following types of individuals that are present in the psychologist's data set:

True Positives	True Negatives	False Positives	False Negatives
☐	☐	☐	☐

Step 5:

Compute the percentage of individuals whose score on the memory skills test accurately predicts their level of recall of party guest names using the formula below. Show all of your calculations and provide a statement summarizing the results of your calculations.

$$\frac{\text{\# of Individuals in Quadrant B} + \text{\# of Individuals in Quadrant D}}{\text{Total Number of Individuals Tested}}$$

Percentage of Accurate Predictions

Step 6:

Determine whether having knowledge of program participants' scores on the memory skills test will allow the psychologist to predict program participants' level of recall more accurately than merely observing their recall performance at the cocktail party. Show all of your calculations.

Formula 1: $\dfrac{\text{\# of Individuals in Quadrant A} + \text{\# of Individuals in Quadrant B}}{\text{Total Number of Individuals Tested}}$

Formula 2: $\dfrac{\text{\# of Individuals in Quadrant B} + \text{\# of Individuals in Quadrant D}}{\text{Total Number of Individuals Tested}}$

Formula 2 – Formula 1

Percentage of Improvement/Decline in Predictive Accuracy

Based on the results of your quadrant analysis, does the psychologist's memory skills test demonstrate criterion-related validity? Circle your answer and provide a rationale for your decision.

YES VALIDITY   NO VALIDITY

Rationale:

EXERCISE 3C

Analyzing Inter-Rater Reliability

An Industrial-Organizational Psychologist was hired by the CEO of a small company to evaluate the quality of the employees in the company's current workforce. To accomplish this task, the psychologist recruited two senior managers from the company to serve as raters. The psychologist asked the two senior managers to review the performance records for each of the 20 employees who currently worked for the company. After reviewing the performance records, the senior managers were asked to independently classify each of the 20 employees into one of the following three performance ratings categories: (a) "useless," (b) "average," or a (c) "superstar." The independent ratings of the two senior managers appear below:

	Rater 1	Rater 2
Employee 1	Useless	Useless
Employee 2	Superstar	Superstar
Employee 3	Average	Average
Employee 4	Average	Useless
Employee 5	Superstar	Superstar
Employee 6	Average	Average
Employee 7	Superstar	Superstar
Employee 8	Average	Average
Employee 9	Superstar	Superstar
Employee 10	Average	Superstar
Employee 11	Useless	Useless
Employee 12	Useless	Average
Employee 13	Average	Average
Employee 14	Average	Average
Employee 15	Superstar	Superstar
Employee 16	Average	Average
Employee 17	Superstar	Superstar
Employee 18	Superstar	Average
Employee 19	Average	Average
Employee 20	Superstar	Superstar

Step 1:

Create a table that summarizes the two senior managers' ratings for the 20 employees currently working at the company.

Rater #1

	Useless	Average	Superstar
Useless			
Average			
Superstar			

Rater #2 (to the left) **Table 1**

Step 2:

Using the cell frequency values from Table 1, compute the actual number of agreements **(A)** between the ratings of the two senior managers (i.e. the total number of times there was agreement between the two senior managers' ratings of an employee). Show your calculations in the space below:

Actual Number of Agreements (A)

Step 3:

Using the cell frequency values from Table 1, create a table containing "row marginal" and "column marginal" values.

Rater #1

	Useless	Average	Superstar	
Useless				
Average				
Superstar				

Rater #2 (to the left) **Table 2**

Step 4:

Using the "row marginal" and "column marginal" values computed in Table 2, create a table containing "expected frequency values" for each cell along the table diagonal.

Rater #1

	Useless	Average	Superstar	
Useless				
Average				
Superstar				

Rater #2 (label to the left of the Average row)

Table 3

Step 5:

Using the "expected frequency values" you computed for the cells along the diagonal in Table 3, compute the "expected number of agreements" (**E**) between the ratings of the two senior managers (i.e. the total number of times we would expect the ratings of the two senior managers to agree by chance alone).

Actual Number of Agreements (E)

Step 6:

Using the values you computed for the "actual number of agreements" (**A**) in Step 2 and the "expected number of agreements" (**E**) you computed in Step 5, compute the value for Cohen's Kappa using the formula below.

$$\text{Kappa} = \frac{\text{A (actual number of agreements)} - \text{E (expected number of agreements}}{\text{N (total employees rated)} - \text{E (expected number of agreements)}}$$

Kappa (K)

Step 7:

Interpret your computed Kappa value (i.e. consult the chart below which provides some generally accepted standards for the interpretation of Kappa values).[10] What would you: tell the CEO of the company with respect to: **(a)** the quality of the employees within the company's current workforce and **(b)** the inter-rater reliability of the senior managers? Write your responses in the spaces provided below.

Kappa	Level of Agreement	Kappa	Level of Agreement
< 0	Less than Chance Agreement	.41–.60	Moderate Agreement
.01–.20	Slight Agreement	.61–.80	Substantial Agreement
.21–.40	Fair Agreement	.81–.99	Almost Perfect Agreement

Quality of Employees in the Company's Current Workforce?

Inter-Rater Reliability of the Senior Managers?

References

1. Cascio, W. F., & Aguinis, H. (2005). *Applied psychology in human resource management* (6th ed.). Upper Saddle River, NJ: Pearson/Prentice Hall.

2. Muchinsky, P. M. (2011). *Psychology applied to work* (10th ed.). Summerfield, NC: Hypergraphic Press.

3. Cozby, P. C., & Bates, S. C. (2011). *Methods in behavioral research.* (11th ed.). New York, NY: McGraw-Hill Publishers.

4. Rosnow, R. L., & Rosenthal, R. (2012). *Beginning behavioral research: A conceptual primer* (7th ed.). Boston, MA: Pearson Publishers.

5. Bordens, K. S., & Abbot, B. B. (2011). *Research design and methods: A process approach* (8th ed.). Boston, MA: McGraw-Hill Publishers.

6. Levy, P. E. (2012). *Industrial-organizational psychology: Understanding the workplace (*4th ed.). New York, NY: Worth Publishers.

7. Trochim, W. M. (2006). Types of reliability. *The Research Methods Knowledge Base* (2nd ed.). Retrieved from http://www.socialresearchmethods.net/kb/reltypes.php

8. Cohen, J. (1960). A coefficient of agreement for nominal scales. *Educational and Psychological Measurement, 20,* 37–46.

9. Wood, J. M. (2007). Understanding and computing Cohen's Kappa: A tutorial. *WebPsych Empiricist (WPE).* Retrieved from http://www.scribd.com/doc/82858112/Understanding-and-Computing-Cohen-s-Kappa-A-Tutorial

10. Viera, A. J., & Garrett, J. M. (2005). Understanding inter-observer agreement: The Kappa statistic. *Family Medicine, 37*(5), 360–363.

11. Ben-Eliyahu, A. (2013). Methods corner: Let's talk about reliability and validity. *The Chronicle of Evidence-Based Mentoring.* Retrieved from http://chronicle.umbmentoring.org/methods-corner-lets-talk-about-reliability-and-validity/

12. Framingham, J. (2011). Rorschach Inkblot Test. *Psych Central.* Retrieved from http://psychcentral.com/lib/rorschach-inkblot-test/0006018

13. Aamodt, M. G. (1999). *Applied industrial/organizational psychology* (3rd ed.). Belmont, CA: Brooks-Cole/Wadsworth Publishers.

14. Passer, M. W. (2013). *Research methods: Concepts and connections.* New York, NY: Worth Publishers.

MODULE

4

Research Ethics

After psychologists have: (a) established the goals of their research, (b) selected scales of measurement to measure their variables of interest, and (c) identified and/or developed reliable and valid measurement instruments, they must then ensure they design their research studies in such a manner that their procedures, treatment of participants (e.g. recruitment, selection, risks/benefits), and use of the research data conform to the ethical principles and guidelines that have been established for human subjects research. The three major ethical principles that serve as a foundation for all human subjects research are outlined in the Belmont Report (1979).[1]

The Belmont Report

In response to the unethical medical research studies conducted on prisoners at German concentration camps by the Nazis during World War II as well as research conducted in the U.S. involving radiation exposure and observation of an untreated illness in a vulnerable population (e.g. Tuskegee Syphilis Study), the National Commission for the Protection of Human Subjects in Biomedical and Behavioral Research created the Belmont Report. The primary goal of the Belmont Report was to outline for researchers the three basic ethical principles that should form a foundation for all human subjects research. The three basic ethical principles that are outlined in the Belmont Report are: (1) Respect for Persons, (2) Beneficence, and (3) Justice.[1]

Respect for Persons

Individuals who are willing to participate in psychological research are making a valuable contribution to both science and society. Psychologists must show respect for this contribution by ensuring that those individuals who participate in psychological research: (1) are given sufficient information about the research to decide for themselves whether or not to take part in the research and (2) are voluntarily participating in the research.

Before allowing anyone to participate in their research, psychologists must provide all potential participants with information concerning what they will experience if they decide to participate in the research (e.g. purpose, procedures, duration of participation, benefits, risks) as well as their rights as research participants (e.g. confidentiality, request additional information, freedom to withdraw). Psychologists must also ensure that participants fully understand the information they are provided. This is especially important for potential participants whose comprehension abilities may be limited (e.g. children, educationally disadvantaged, mentally disabled). In these special cases, psychologists must ensure that those who represent the best interests of individuals with limited comprehension abilities understand what will occur to those they represent during the research. When potential participants acknowledge they have received sufficient information about the research, fully comprehend this information, and indicate they are willing to take part in the research, they are said to have given their "informed consent." Psychologists typically document participant consent by having potential participants (and/or their representatives) sign an "informed consent" document. This document, in addition to providing information about the research, informs participants who to contact if they were to: (a) have questions about the research or their rights as a research participant, (b) experience a research-related injury, or (c) decide to withdraw from the research.[1,2,3]

Occasionally, psychologists find it necessary to deceive participants. Deception is often used by psychologists when they are concerned that if participants knew the true purpose of the research, or knew what aspects of their behavior and personality were being assessed, it would cause them to change their behavior or to disclose information (i.e. attitudes, values, opinions) in such a way as to appear more socially acceptable (e.g. participants who know they are in a study examining the construct of "empathy" may engage in more helping behavior and express greater concern for others than they would under non-research conditions). The two types of deception used in psychological research are: (a) active deception and (b) passive deception. The "active" forms of deception involve deception by "commission" (i.e. psychologists purposefully mislead participants about the purpose of the study or about elements of the experimental procedures).[4,5] Examples of active deception would include: (1) use of "confederates" (i.e. individuals working for the researcher who play various "roles" and who interact with the participants without them being aware they are part of the research project staff), (2) use of "placebos" (i.e. pills, surgical interventions, or therapy interventions that have no medical value but that are used as a control in the test of actual medical, surgical, or therapeutic interventions), and (3) providing participants with "false feedback" about their behavior, mental processes, personality, or task performance.

The "passive" forms of deception involve deception by "omission" (i.e. psychologists withhold information from participants about the purpose of the study or elements of the experimental procedures). Examples of passive deception would include: (1) partial disclosure of the true purpose of the study to participants, (2) observation of participants without their awareness, and (3) administering measurement instruments to participants that measure constructs they are unaware are being measured.[4,5]

While psychologists might argue that it is necessary to use deception to find meaningful answers to some of their research questions, they are also aware there are negative consequences associated with its use. For example, participants who are placed in distressing situations, learn something negative about themselves, or are observed engaging in embarrassing and/or socially unacceptable behavior as a result of deception may experience varying levels of psychological harm. In addition, deception can diminish trust in the research process making individuals more hesitant to participate in further research. Deception can also diminish societies' respect for the research process and science. Finally, and perhaps most importantly, the use of deception runs counter to the ethical principal of respect for persons that calls for participants to receive a full disclosure of information pertaining to the research before providing informed consent.[1,3,4] As a compromise, the Belmont Report outlined 3 possible conditions under which use of deception may be justifiable. The 3 conditions were as follows: (a) all potential risks that may arise from the use of deception are minimal, (b) use of deception is necessary to conduct a study that will yield reliable and valid results, and (c) all participants exposed to deception will be "debriefed" at the conclusion of the study.[1] During the participant "debriefing" process, psychologists talk with participants to fully inform them about the true purpose of the study, describe why it was necessary for deception to be used during the research, and to ensure they have not been harmed in any way by their participation in the research.

After providing individuals with sufficient information about the research, ensuring they comprehend this information, and documenting their informed consent, psychologists must also ensure they are participating in the research voluntarily. For participation to be considered truly voluntary, psychologists must ensure participants have not been forced or coerced into taking part in the study. This is especially important when participants are drawn from populations vulnerable to coercion (e.g. educationally disadvantaged, mentally disabled). They must also ensure that participants are not taking part in the research due to a sense of obligation or pressure from individuals in positions of authority (e.g. patients, children). Finally, although incentives are frequently provided in exchange for participation in research, psychologists must ensure the incentives offered to potential participants are appropriate for their contribution to the research. This is especially important when participants are drawn from populations vulnerable to offers of excessive financial incentives (e.g. economically disadvantaged, college students).[1,2,3]

Beneficence

Ideally, the research conducted by psychologists would pose no risks to those individuals who serve as participants. In practice, however, psychologists occasionally conduct research that contains a degree of risk for participants. For example, research studies involving the use of deception, the testing of new therapeutic interventions, the disclosure of sensitive personal information, as well as any research studies conducted outside of controlled laboratory settings are inherently risky. Maintaining the health and well-being of participants must be a top priority for all psychologists conducting research. Individuals willing to take part in psychological research must be protected from harm. Therefore, when a degree of risk is involved, psychologists must design their research in such a way as to minimize that risk.

When designing research to minimize the level of risk, psychologists must consider the variety of types of "risk" that participation in research may pose for individuals. There are five types of "risk" psychologists attempt to minimize for participants when designing their research: (a) Physical, (b) Psychological, (c) Social, (d) Legal, and (e) Financial risk.[5,6] Physical risks can include pain, side effects, illness, injury, or death. Psychological risks would include damage to one's self-esteem or self-confidence (e.g. poor task performance or failure), feelings of distress and/or discomfort (e.g. being placed in a stressful situation or asked to relive a traumatic event), and painful insight into one's behavior and personality (e.g. disclosing attitudes that are socially unacceptable or engaging in immoral, illegal, or socially unacceptable behavior). Social, legal, and financial risks would include the loss of current or future employment, loss of membership in social clubs, groups or organizations, damage to one's reputation or community standing, and incarceration. Social, legal, and financial risks typically result from a breach in confidentiality resulting in information being released publicly that leads to a negative societal evaluation of participants. Breaches of confidentiality involving information pertaining to sexual behavior, mental/physical illness, substance use, and past or current criminal activity are especially likely to pose a high degree of social, legal, and/or financial risk for participants. Another factor that potentially places participants at financial risk is the costs associated with being a participant in a psychological research study. For example, individuals participating in long-term studies may be required to travel to the research location on multiple occasions, resulting in expenses (e.g. lost income due to time off from work, money for gas, childcare) that place a financial burden on participants.[3,5,6,7] Because some psychological research involves a degree of risk, psychologists must determine what level of risk is acceptable for the participants in their research studies to assume. To answer this question, psychologists must thoroughly assess the potential benefits and risks associated with their research.

For psychologists to justify exposing their research participants to more than a "minimal risk" of harm (i.e. the risks associated with participation in the research are greater than the risks associated with everyday life), the benefits associated with the research must outweigh the risks to participants.[1,2,3] As a result, when designing their research, psychologists often follow the motto "maximize potential benefits while minimizing potential harms." There are two different types of benefits psychologists must assess when evaluating the potential "benefits" associated with research: (a) Benefits to Participants and (b) Benefits to Others.[1,2,8] Benefits to Participants are those benefits received by individuals as a result of their direct participation in the research. Examples can include: (1) knowledge (e.g. a research study on parenting styles can provide new mothers with knowledge regarding proper parenting practices), (2) insight into one's behavior or mental processes (e.g. a research study on obesity could provide obese individuals with valuable insight into the physical and/or psychological causes of their obesity), and (3) therapy/treatment (e.g. a research study on depression can provide individuals with access to a new medication or an experimental treatment opportunity). Benefits to Others are those benefits received by society as a result of the information learned from research. For example, psychologists may use the results of their research to develop: (1) educational programs (e.g. a research study on sexual harassment can lead to the creation of a training program for employees on sexual harassment in the workplace), (2) therapeutic interventions (e.g. a research study on anxiety can lead to the development of new therapeutic approaches to treating social anxiety), or (3) programs designed to improve the health and well-being of society (e.g. a research study on the eating habits of children can lead to the development of more healthy school lunch programs). Psychologists may also use the results of their research to attempt to shape or change public policy (e.g. a research study on the effects of second-hand smoke can lead to the establishment of smoking bans in public locations like parks, stores, and restaurants).

There are, however, no clear-cut decision rules for psychologists to use when it comes to making the determination as to the benefits/risks ratio that is necessary to consider the level of risk "acceptable" for the participants in their research. As a result, different psychologists might arrive at different "acceptability" decisions when evaluating the same research. Psychologists may also have different thresholds with respect to the level of risk they are personally willing to have participants in their research assume. Psychologists may accept a "balanced" benefits/risks ratio (i.e. benefits = risks), a "more than favorable" benefits/risks ratio (i.e. benefits > risks), or a "substantially more than favorable" benefits/risk ratio (i.e. benefits substantially > risks) based on their personal risk thresholds.[8,9,10]

To get assistance in evaluating the potential benefits and potential risks associated with their research, psychologists can submit their research for review by an IRB (i.e. Institutional Review Board).[9,10] An IRB is an ethics committee composed of individuals with expertise in the design and evaluation of research who evaluate and monitor biomedical and behavioral research. IRBs also contain "community members" whose purpose is to represent the interests of society during IRB evaluations of research. The primary goals of an IRB when evaluating research are to: (1) protect research participants from harm, (2) ensure research is designed in such a way as to minimize risk to participants, and (3) when the research poses more than "minimal risk," to ensure the potential benefits of the research outweigh the potential risks to participants. Based on their evaluations, IRBs can approve a research study, require that a study be modified before it can be granted approval, or disapprove a research study. The strengths of an IRB review are that the evaluation of a research study is based on the collective perspective of individuals who: (a) have appropriate expertise, (b) represent the interests of both science and society, (c) have no vested interests in the outcomes of a research study, and (d) whose primary goal is the protection of human subjects.[1,2,8] IRBs can often be found in both medical (e.g. hospitals, medical schools, VA facilities) and academic settings (e.g. colleges, universities) where biomedical and/or behavioral research is conducted.

Justice

Scientific research has advanced our current understanding of human behavior (e.g. individuals, groups, organizations) and mental processes, and generated knowledge that has been used to improve the health and well-being of individuals and society as a whole. Because the benefits of scientific research are intended to be shared by all members of society, in theory, individuals from all segments of society should share in the responsibility of participating in the research process and contributing to the advancement of science. In practice, however, history has shown us examples of individuals from "vulnerable populations" frequently being targeted by researchers to serve as participants in research involving a high degree of potential risk and the use of deception (e.g. concentration camp prisoners, institutionalized individuals, members of economically and educationally disadvantaged groups). In response, researchers identified specific individuals within society who they considered members of "vulnerable populations" and made it a priority that researchers protect these individuals from being unfairly targeted by researchers conducting high risk research.[1,2,3]

To protect members of these "vulnerable populations," psychologists must be aware of the different vulnerabilities that make these individuals more susceptible than the average society member to the influence of unethical researchers. These vulnerabilities include: (a) diminished physical capacity (e.g. pregnant women, individuals diagnosed with diseases that can diminish physical strength, endurance, immunity, or resistance to stress), (b) diminished mental capacity (e.g. mentally disabled individuals, individuals diagnosed with psychiatric illnesses, individuals diagnosed with diseases that diminish cognitive functioning such as Alzheimer's or dementia), (c) susceptibility to the coercive effects of financial and other incentives (e.g. the economically disadvantaged, prisoners offered reductions in their sentences in exchange for their participation, institutionalized individuals offered extra hospital privileges in exchange for their participation), (d) questionable ability to comprehend the potential risks associated with research and provide informed consent (e.g. educationally disadvantaged, children, non-English speaking individuals) and (e) feelings of obligation toward individuals in positions of authority (e.g. patients who take part in research at the request of a physician or military personnel who participate in research at the request of a superior officer or military authority).[1,2,3] When deciding whether to allow the members of these "vulnerable populations" to enroll in their research studies, psychologists must carefully consider whether their vulnerabilities would place them at more than minimal risk for harm if they were to participate in the research. If so, psychologists have an ethical obligation to exclude these individuals from their research.

In addition to ensuring individuals from all segments of society (and not just the most "vulnerable" members of society) share in the responsibility of participating in psychological research, psychologists must also ensure that individuals from all segments of society share in the benefits derived from the results of psychological research. Specifically, the end products of psychological research (e.g. educational programs, therapeutic interventions, diagnostic tools and measurement instruments, information concerning human behavior and mental processes) must be made available to all members of a society and not just to its more privileged members.[1]

The research process is a partnership between researchers and their participants. Like any successful partnership, their needs to be: (a) full disclosure between parties, (b) freedom to enter into or leave the partnership, (c) clearly defined expectations concerning the partnership, (d) mutual concern for the well-being and interests of both parties, (e) mutual respect between both parties, and (f) the partnership must be mutually beneficial to both parties. These qualities of a successful partnership, and more specifically an ethical relationship between researchers and their participants, are clearly exemplified by three basic ethical principles of respect for persons, beneficence, and justice outlined in the Belmont Report (1979).[1]

EXERCISE 4A

Is the Use of Deception in Research Justifiable?

When conducting research, psychologists strive to collect unbiased measurements of human behavior and mental processes. Psychologists may decide to incorporate deception into their research designs when they are concerned that if participants knew the true purpose of the research it would introduce bias into the study by causing participants to change their behaviors and/or the amount and types of information they are willing to disclose.

Below are 5 research studies that incorporate the use of various types of deception into their designs. For each study, please: **(a)** determine if the researchers are using active deception, passive deception, or both, **(b)** evaluate the deception used by the researchers by examining the level of risk associated with the deception, the necessity of the deception, and whether debriefing is conducted to disclose the use of deception to participants, and **(c)** decide whether the use of deception by the researchers was justified and provide a rationale for your decision.

Research Question #1

Will nurses comply with a request from an authority figure (i.e. physician) to administer a drug to a patient that violates both hospital and professional standards of care?

22 nurses at psychiatric hospitals received a phone call from a researcher who identified himself as a psychiatrist "Dr. Smith." "Dr. Smith" asked each nurse to administer 20 mg of a fictional drug Astroten to a fictional patient "Mr. Jones." "Dr. Smith" told each nurse he would arrive at the hospital shortly to sign the required paperwork. Prior to making the telephone calls, a second researcher placed bottles of the fictional drug Astroten in the hospitals' drug cabinets. The bottles of Astroten actually contained a harmless placebo (i.e. sugar pills). Each bottle of Astroten had a warning label indicating the maximum dose was 10 mg. If a nurse administered the drug, he/she would directly violate both hospital and professional standards of care by giving a patient twice the maximum dose of a non-approved drug based on a physician's order received over the telephone rather than in person. The second researcher observed each of the nurses to see if they would administer the Astroten to "Mr. Jones." If a nurse entered "Mr. Jones" room and moved toward the patient with the Astroten, a second researcher (who was actually a real physician) would intervene and end the study. The results revealed that 21 of the 22 nurses were prepared to administer the Astroten to "Mr. Jones." By comparison, 21 student nurses who were in a comparison control group who were asked on a survey what action they would take in such a circumstance stated they would not have complied with the physician's request. All nurses in the study were debriefed by the researchers as to the purpose of the study, interviewed about their research experiences, and provided with any care they might require as a result of their research experiences.[11,12,13]

Which type(s) of deception was used by the researchers?

Active Deception	Yes ☐	No ☐
Passive Deception	Yes ☐	No ☐
Both	Yes ☐	No ☐

Rationale:

When evaluating the deception used in the research study.........................

Did the use of deception by the researchers pose more than "minimal risk" for the research participants?	Yes ☐	No ☐
Was the use of deception by the researchers a necessity to get reliable and valid results from the research?	Yes ☐	No ☐
Were the research participants debriefed about the use of deception by the researchers?	Yes ☐	No ☐

Based on your overall evaluation of the deception used in the research study, in your opinion, was the use of deception by the researchers justifiable?

Rationale:

Research Question #2

Can sane individuals be reliably distinguished from individuals who are insane
by psychiatrists and/or staff working in psychiatric hospitals?

8 "pseudopatients" (i.e. researchers playing the role of individuals experiencing the symptoms of a psychiatric illness) went to the admissions offices of 12 psychiatric hospitals and reported they had been hearing voices saying the words "empty, hollow, thud." They falsified their names, but answered all other questions about their lives truthfully. The 8 "pseudopatients" were all admitted to the hospitals; 7 with a diagnosis of schizophrenia and 1 with a diagnosis of manic-depressive psychosis. Once admitted, the "pseudopatients" told hospital staff they were no longer hearing voices, exhibited no abnormal behaviors, and followed all instructions from hospital staff. When given medication, they pretended to swallow the pills but later disposed of them. While in their respective hospitals, the "pseudopatients" took notes of their observations of life within psychiatric hospitals in full view of the other patients as well as the hospital staff. The "pseudopatients" were required to stay in the hospital until psychiatrists felt that they had accepted their illness and would comply with a prescribed regiment of psychiatric medication. Results revealed none of the "pseudopatients" were ever detected by hospital staff and all were discharged with diagnoses of schizophrenia in remission. Hospitalizations of "pseudopatients" ranged from 7 to 52 days with an average stay of 19 days. The "pseudopatients" observations revealed little patient-staff interaction, feelings of invisibility and dehumanization, as well as verbal/physical abuse of patients within psychiatric hospitals.[14]

Which type(s) of deception was used by the researchers?

Active Deception	Yes ☐	No ☐
Passive Deception	Yes ☐	No ☐
Both	Yes ☐	No ☐

Rationale:

When evaluating the deception used in the research study.........................

Did the use of deception by the researchers pose more than "minimal risk" for the research participants?	Yes ☐	No ☐
Was the use of deception by the researchers a necessity to get reliable and valid results from the research?	Yes ☐	No ☐
Were the research participants debriefed about the use of deception by the researchers?	Yes ☐	No ☐

Based on your overall evaluation of the deception used in the research study,
in your opinion, was the use of deception by the researcher justifiable?

Rationale:

Research Question #3

Is it possible to "implant" a false childhood memory for an event that never occurred?

24 individuals (ages 18–53) were given a booklet containing 4 stories describing events that had occurred during their childhoods. These stories were provided by an older relative (e.g. sibling, parent, relative) of the participants. Three of the stories in the booklet described events that had occurred during their childhoods while 1 story described a "false event" that had never occurred. The "false event" story described a time when participants had gotten lost in the mall while on a family shopping trip. After being lost, they were found crying and returned to their families by a nice elderly woman. After reading the 4 stories, participants were asked to write down what they could remember about each of the events. If they did not remember an event, they were instructed to write "I do not remember this." The participants were later interviewed at two points in time (i.e. 2 weeks and 4 weeks later) and asked to write down any additional details they had remembered about each of the 4 events. Initially, no one claimed to remember the "false event." Two weeks later, 7 of the 24 participants (29%) now claimed to remember the "false event." After 4 weeks, 6 of the 24 participants (22%) still claimed to have memory of the "false event." Participants were debriefed by the researchers as to the purpose of the study and were told why the use of deception was necessary.[15]

Which type(s) of deception was used by the researchers?

Active Deception	Yes	☐	No	☐
Passive Deception	Yes	☐	No	☐
Both	Yes	☐	No	☐

Rationale:

When evaluating the deception used in the research study.....................

Did the use of deception by the researchers pose more than "minimal risk" for the research participants?	Yes	☐	No	☐
Was the use of deception by the researchers a necessity to get reliable and valid results from the research?	Yes	☐	No	☐
Were the research participants debriefed about the use of deception by the researchers?	Yes	☐	No	☐

Based on your overall evaluation of the deception used in the research study, in your opinion, was the use of deception by the researchers justifiable?

Rationale:

Research Question #4

Is the amount of food people consume influenced by visual cues related to portion size
(e.g. the amount of food remaining on a plate, bowl, or cup)

54 individuals (ages 18-47) were brought into a lab in groups of 4, seated at a restaurant-style table and asked to eat a bowl of tomato soup. The soup was served in either blue or green bowls and participants were led by researchers to believe the study was examining the influence of color on taste perceptions. In reality, color was not the quality of the bowls researchers were interested in studying. Once seated at the table, two of the participants then consumed soup from "normal" bowls while the other two participants consumed soup from "self-filling" bowls (i.e. as participants ate the soup, the bowls were kept continuously full by researchers who pumped soup through a rubber tube hidden under the table connected to the bottom of the bowl). Participants were instructed to eat as much soup as they wanted. After 20 minutes, participants were asked to rate the soup and estimate how many ounces of soup they had consumed. Results revealed that the participants eating from the "self-filling" bowls consumed 73% more soup than those who ate from the "normal" bowls (14.7 ounces to 8.5 ounces). In addition, participants eating from the "self-filling" bowls consumed 140.5 more calories of soup than they estimated, while those who ate from "normal" bowls consumed 32.3 fewer calories of the soup than they had estimated. Participants were debriefed by the researchers as to the purpose of the study, told why the use of deception was necessary, and shown how the deceptive bowls were controlled by the researchers during the experiment.[16]

Which type(s) of deception was used by the researchers?

Active Deception	Yes	☐	No	☐
Passive Deception	Yes	☐	No	☐
Both	Yes	☐	No	☐

Rationale:

When evaluating the deception used in the research study......................

Did the use of deception by the researchers pose more than "minimal risk" for the research participants?	Yes ☐	No ☐
Was the use of deception by the researchers a necessity to get reliable and valid results from the research?	Yes ☐	No ☐
Were the research participants debriefed about the use of deception by the researchers?	Yes ☐	No ☐

Based on your overall evaluation of the deception used in the research study,
in your opinion, was the use of deception by the researchers justifiable?

Rationale:

Research Question #5

Are individuals who are thinking about religion more likely to stop and help
someone in need of assistance? What if they are in a hurry?

67 students enrolled in a seminary college were asked by researchers to give a talk to students in a nearby campus location. Half of the participants were asked to give a talk on job opportunities available to seminary college graduates. The other half were asked to give a talk on the parable of the "Good Samaritan" (i.e. a story that illustrates the value of helping others). Researchers then made one of three statements to participants. Specifically, participants were told that their talks would begin in a few minutes (Low Hurry), were ready to begin (Moderate Hurry), or were supposed to have begun a few minutes ago (High Hurry). Students then went across campus to give their talks. On the way, they encountered a person lying in a doorway in need of assistance. This individual was actually a "confederate" playing the role of a "victim." The "victim" observed each student (without their awareness) to measure the level of assistance they provided. After passing by or providing assistance to the "victim," participants proceeded on to the location of their talks. Results revealed that 40% of the participants offered assistance. With respect to religion, 53% of participants going to give a talk on the parable of the "Good Samaritan" offered assistance, while only 29% of participants going to give a talk on jobs for seminary graduates offered assistance. With respect to being in a hurry, 63% of participants in the "Low Hurry" condition offered assistance, while only 10% in the "High Hurry" condition offered assistance. Even participants giving a talk on the "Good Samaritan" parable offered little assistance when in a hurry. Participants were debriefed as to the purpose of the study, told why the use of deception was necessary and had all their questions answered by the researchers.[17]

Which type(s) of deception was used by the researchers?

Active Deception	Yes ☐	No ☐
Passive Deception	Yes ☐	No ☐
Both	Yes ☐	No ☐

Rationale:

When evaluating the deception used in the research study.....................

Did the use of deception by the researchers pose more than "minimal risk" for the research participants?	Yes ☐	No ☐
Was the use of deception by the researchers a necessity to get reliable and valid results from the research?	Yes ☐	No ☐
Were the research participants debriefed about the use of deception by the researchers?	Yes ☐	No ☐

Based on your overall evaluation of the deception used in the research study, in your opinion, was the use of deception by the researchers justifiable?

Rationale:

EXERCISE 4B

Do the Benefits Outweigh the Risks?

While ideally all psychological research would involve minimal risk to participants (i.e. equivalent to risks associated with everyday life), on occasion, psychologists conduct research that involves deception and/or poses more than minimal risk to participants. To ethically justify this risk, psychologists need to ensure that the potential benefits of the research (e.g. benefits to participants, benefits to society) exceed the potential risks associated with the research.

Below are 5 research studies that involve varying levels of risk for participants. For each study, please: **(a)** evaluate the level of physical, psychological, social, legal, and financial risk for participants and provide a rationale for your evaluation and **(b)** decide what you believe is the ratio of potential benefits/potential risks for the study and provide a rationale for your decision.

Research Question #1

Is the disease known as pellagra caused by an unknown germ or by a poor diet?

In the early 1900s, there was an epidemic-level outbreak primarily in the southern United States of a disease known as pellagra. Pellagra caused severe skin rashes, diarrhea, sores in the mouth, and even dementia if left untreated. The predominant theory at the time was that pellagra was caused by a yet to be identified germ. A researcher studying pellagra noticed that the highest concentrations of the disease were found among the poor as well as in orphanages, asylums, and prisons. The researcher believed the common element among these different populations was a poor diet, and more specifically, a corn-based diet (e.g. cornbread, molasses). The more wealthy segments of society that could afford to eat fresh meats, vegetables, and milk rarely developed pellagra. He hypothesized that a poor diet (i.e. high corn-based diet), and not an unknown germ, was the cause of pellagra. To test his hypothesis, he went to a prison farm in the south and there he recruited 11 healthy prisoners to participate in his study. Prisoners participated in the study in exchange for a pardon from the Governor of the state. The researcher had the 11 prisoners stop eating their normal prison diet and eat a high corn-based diet. Results supported the researcher's hypothesis. Within 5 months of being on the high corn-based diet, 6 of the 11 healthy prisoners were exhibiting severe skin rashes and diagnosed with pellagra. When the results of his research were challenged by some in the medical community, he conducted an additional study to clearly demonstrate pellagra was not caused by a germ. Specifically, the researcher, his assistant, and his wife: **(a)** injected blood from an individual with pellagra into their arms, **(b)** rubbed mucous from the noses and throats of individuals with pellagra into their own noses and throats, and **(c)** swallowed pill capsules containing scabs from skin rashes of individuals with pellagra. None of them became ill, and more importantly, none of them developed pellagra.[18,19]

How would you evaluate the level of physical, psychological, social, legal, and financial risk for the participants?

Risk of Physical Harm	Minimal ☐	Moderate ☐	Significant ☐
Risk of Psychological Harm	Minimal ☐	Moderate ☐	Significant ☐
Risk of Social Harm	Minimal ☐	Moderate ☐	Significant ☐
Risk of Legal Harm	Minimal ☐	Moderate ☐	Significant ☐
Risk of Financial Harm	Minimal ☐	Moderate ☐	Significant ☐

Rationale:

Based on your assessment of the benefits and risks associated with the research, what is your final assessment as to the benefit/risk ratio for the study? (Check One)

Benefits significantly outweigh the risks	☐
Benefits slightly outweigh the risks	☐
Benefits are equivalent to the risks	☐
Risks slightly outweigh the benefits	☐
Risks significantly outweigh the benefits	☐

Rationale:

Research Question #2

Do invasions of our "personal space" produce discomfort (i.e. arousal) that can be
measured through an assessment of physiological responses in the body?

A field experiment was conducted to investigate whether an invasion of personal space produces arousal that can be measured through an assessment of physiological responses occurring within the body. Specifically, the experiment investigated whether an invasion of personal space would increase men's discomfort (i.e. arousal) and negatively affect the speed and the duration of their urination (i.e. physiological response). 60 men using a three-urinal restroom participated in the study. Only those individuals using the leftmost of the three urinals were included in the study. The participants were randomly assigned to one of three personal space invasion conditions (i.e. close distance, moderate distance, control). In the "close distance" condition, a "confederate" (i.e. an individual working with the researcher and playing the role of a person who needed to use the restroom) stood at the middle urinal approximately 16–18 inches away from a participant. The rightmost urinal contained a "Don't use, washing urinal" sign. In the "moderate distance" condition, the confederate stood at the rightmost urinal approximately 52–54 inches away from a participant. The middle urinal contained a "Don't use, washing urinal" sign. Participants were alone in the restroom during the "control condition" and "Don't use, washing urinal" signs were in both the middle and rightmost urinals.

To measure speed and duration of the men's urination, a second "confederate" sat in the toilet stall closest to the three urinals. Using a periscope device hidden in a stack of books on the floor of the toilet stall and two stopwatches, the "confederate" visually monitored the urine flow of each participant and recorded the amount of time it took each of the men to begin urinating (i.e. delay of onset) and the duration of each man's urination (i.e. persistence). It was hypothesized that the closer the "confederate" stood to a participant, the greater discomfort (i.e. arousal) they would experience, which would result in an increase in the delay of onset of urination and also a decrease in duration of the urination (i.e. negative physiological responses). Results supported the hypotheses. Men in the "close distance" condition took longer to begin urinating (close = 8.4 seconds; moderate = 6.2 seconds; control = 4.9 seconds) and also urinated for a shorter duration of time (close = 17.4 seconds; moderate = 23.4 seconds; control = 24.8 seconds) than men in the "moderate distance" and "control" conditions. Results provided evidence that physiological responses in the body can be used by researchers as measures of discomfort (i.e. arousal). Participants were unaware they had taken part in a research study.[20]

How would you evaluate the level of physical, psychological, social, legal,
and financial risk for the participants?

Risk of Physical Harm	Minimal ☐	Moderate ☐	Significant ☐
Risk of Psychological Harm	Minimal ☐	Moderate ☐	Significant ☐
Risk of Social Harm	Minimal ☐	Moderate ☐	Significant ☐
Risk of Legal Harm	Minimal ☐	Moderate ☐	Significant ☐
Risk of Financial Harm	Minimal ☐	Moderate ☐	Significant ☐

Rationale:

Based on your assessment of the benefits and risks associated with the research, what is your final assessment as to the benefit/risk ratio for the study? (Check One)

Benefits significantly outweigh the risks	☐
Benefits slightly outweigh the risks	☐
Benefits are equivalent to the risks	☐
Risks slightly outweigh the benefits	☐
Risks significantly outweigh the benefits	☐

Rationale:

Research Question #3

Who are the men who engage in homosexual acts in public restrooms and what are their motives for engaging in this behavior?

In the 1960s, the majority of arrests for homosexual offenses involved acts of sex between men in public restrooms (i.e. "tea-rooming"). The stereotypic view of these men at the time was that they were all promiscuous homosexuals living deviant lifestyles. To determine if the stereotypic view of these men was accurate, a researcher went to several public parks where men engaged in acts of sex in public restrooms. Over time, he was able to form relationships with several of the men who frequented these restrooms for sex. These men taught him how to be a "watchqueen" (i.e. a man who acts as a lookout while other men engage in acts of sex in the restroom and who signals to the men when the police or strangers approach the restroom) and allowed him to serve in this role. As a "watchqueen," the researcher observed hundreds of acts of sex between men in the restrooms. Having gained the trust of many of the men who frequented the public restrooms, he was able to disclose to them he was actually a researcher studying their behavior. A sample of 50 of these men allowed him to interview them about their sexual orientation, marital status, lifestyle, and motives for engaging in acts of sex at the public restrooms.

After conducting the interviews, the researcher noticed the men willing to be interviewed tended to be more educated and more out-going than the average man who frequented these restrooms. To get a more representative sample of men, the researcher copied down license plate numbers on the cars of men he had observed engaging in acts of sex in the restrooms. Using the license plate numbers, he was able to get the home addresses of the men. One year later, he showed up at the homes of 50 of these men and told them that he was a researcher conducting a community social-health survey. The survey allowed him to collect the same types of lifestyle information he had collected during his interviews with men at the public restrooms. The researcher's final sample therefore contained 100 men who frequented public restrooms to engage in acts of sex with other men. Results failed to support stereotypic views of these men. Only 14% of the men identified themselves as openly homosexual (38% were neither homosexual nor bisexual; 24% were single and covertly homosexual; 24% were bisexual). A majority of the men (54%) were outwardly heterosexual and married to wives unaware of their activities outside of the marriage. Many of the men were productive members of society, lived conventional lifestyles, and went to the public restrooms for a variety of reasons including a decline in the sexual activity within their marriages, a sexual release of the tensions in their lives, and the opportunity to engage in sex without the emotionality required in a committed relationship.[21]

How would you evaluate the level of physical, psychological, social, legal, and financial risk for the participants?

Risk of Physical Harm	Minimal ☐	Moderate ☐	Significant ☐
Risk of Psychological Harm	Minimal ☐	Moderate ☐	Significant ☐
Risk of Social Harm	Minimal ☐	Moderate ☐	Significant ☐
Risk of Legal Harm	Minimal ☐	Moderate ☐	Significant ☐
Risk of Financial Harm	Minimal ☐	Moderate ☐	Significant ☐

Rationale:

Based on your assessment of the benefits and risks associated with the research, what is your final assessment as to the benefit/risk ratio for the study? (Check One)

Benefits significantly outweigh the risks	☐
Benefits slightly outweigh the risks	☐
Benefits are equivalent to the risks	☐
Risks slightly outweigh the benefits	☐
Risks significantly outweigh the benefits	☐

Rationale:

Research Question #4

Is stuttering a learned behavior caused by the labeling of children as stutterers?
If so, can stuttering be induced in healthy, non-stuttering children?

In the 1930s, researchers and speech pathologists believed that the cause of stuttering could be found in the brain (i.e. "misdirected signals in the brain") or had a genetic basis. A researcher who believed that stuttering was not a biological or genetic condition, but rather was a learned behavior caused by the labelling of children as stutters, designed a study to test his hypothesis. If he could successfully induce stuttering in healthy, non-stuttering children, he would have the evidence to support his hypothesis. The researcher hired a research assistant who went to a local orphanage and selected 22 children to participate in the study. The children were not told they were participating in research and the orphanage staff were misled about the true purpose of the research. The children were told they would be receiving speech therapy. 10 of these children were stutterers and 12 of the children were non-stutterers. The 10 children who stuttered were divided into two groups. 5 children in Group 1A were told, "You do not stutter. Your speech is fine" (Stutterers—Positive Therapy). 5 children in Group 1B were told, "Yes, your speech is as bad as people say" (Stutterers—Negative Therapy). The 12 children who did not stutter were also divided into two groups. 6 children in Group 2A were told "Your speech is not normal at all. You are beginning to stutter. It must be corrected immediately" (Non-Stutterers—

Negative Therapy). 6 children in Group 2B all received compliments on their "nice enunciation" of words (Non-Stutterers—Positive Therapy). The research assistant then reinforced these messages over the course of a 5 month period. It was hypothesized children in Group 1A (Stutterers—Positive Therapy) would see a decline in stuttering and improvement in quality of speech while children in Group 2A (Non-Stutterers—Negative Therapy) would see an increase in stuttering and decline in quality of speech. Results failed to support these hypotheses.

In Group 1A (Stutterers—Positive Therapy), 2 children showed a slight improvement, 2 showed a decline, and 1 showed no change in their speech. All of the children in Group 1A continued to stutter. In Group 2A (Non-Stutterers—Negative Therapy), 2 children showed improvement, 2 showed no change, and 2 showed a decline in speech quality. None of the children in Group 2A became stutterers. However, all 6 children in Group 2A began to show the behavioral signs of stutterers. Their school performance declined and they became more withdrawn, less talkative, more self-conscious about their speech, and they exhibited many behavioral "tics" common to stutterers (e.g. snapping their fingers, shuffling their feet, gulping, gasping). They spoke fine, but acted like stutterers. After the study ended, the research assistant returned to the orphanage on 3 occasions to provide follow-up care (i.e. Positive Therapy) and to specifically tell children in Group 2A they did not stutter and that their speech was fine. Due to the failure of the study, learning-based theories of stuttering were abandoned and today the predominant explanation is that there is a genetic predisposition to stuttering.[22]

How would you evaluate the level of physical, psychological, social, legal, and financial risk for the participants?

Risk of Physical Harm	Minimal ☐	Moderate ☐	Significant ☐
Risk of Psychological Harm	Minimal ☐	Moderate ☐	Significant ☐
Risk of Social Harm	Minimal ☐	Moderate ☐	Significant ☐
Risk of Legal Harm	Minimal ☐	Moderate ☐	Significant ☐
Risk of Financial Harm	Minimal ☐	Moderate ☐	Significant ☐

Rationale:

Based on your assessment of the benefits and risks associated with the research, what is your final assessment as to the benefit/risk ratio for the study? (Check One)

Benefits significantly outweigh the risks	☐
Benefits slightly outweigh the risks	☐
Benefits are equivalent to the risks	☐
Risks slightly outweigh the benefits	☐
Risks significantly outweigh the benefits	☐

Rationale:

Research Question #5

If you inject individuals with antibodies from the blood of individuals who have been infected with hepatitis, does it build up immunity to the hepatitis virus?

In 1955, a facility for mentally disabled children experienced a major outbreak of hepatitis (i.e. a disease that affects the liver and causes fatigue, abdominal pain, diarrhea, and fever). Unsanitary conditions at the facility contributed to the spread of the disease. A researcher at the facility was interested in developing a vaccine to provide children at the facility immunity from the hepatitis virus. At that time, more than 50% of the children admitted to the facility became infected with hepatitis within their first year at the facility. When individuals become infected with hepatitis, it causes their immune systems to produce an antibody known as gamma globulin that attempts to fight the virus. The researcher hypothesized that if the children admitted to the facility were vaccinated with these gamma globulin antibodies, they would have immunity built up against the hepatitis virus and would experience only mild symptoms if they were to become infected with the virus. To test his hypothesis, the researcher gave newly admitted children an injection of the gamma globulin antibodies. He then intentionally infected half of the children with the hepatitis virus (taken from blood of children at the facility infected with hepatitis) while the other half of the children were not infected with the hepatitis virus. To protect the children in the study from other diseases they could pick up from the general hospital population, all were housed together in a separate area of the facility known as the "experimental wing." Parents of those children in the study were required to give consent for their children to participate in the study and receive injections of the gamma globulin antibodies and the hepatitis virus. Some parents, before giving their consent, were told by facility officials that due to the overcrowding at the facility and the long waiting list for admission, if they wanted their children admitted to the facility their children would have to be assigned a room on the "experimental wing" which would necessitate they be enrolled in the research study and potentially infected with the hepatitis virus.

Results revealed support for the researcher's hypothesis. The children infected with the hepatitis virus had only mild physical reactions (e.g. swollen liver, slight yellowing of the skin and eyes, some vomiting, and a reduced appetite for a few days). Their physical reactions were much less severe than children at the facility who had not been vaccinated and who were infected with the hepatitis virus via contact with the general hospital population. The researcher also learned that there were two different strains of the hepatitis virus active at the facility known as Hepatitis A and Hepatitis B. After the introduction of the researcher's vaccination program, the overall rate of hepatitis infection at the facility declined.[23]

How would you evaluate the level of physical, psychological, social, legal, and financial risk for the participants?

Risk of Physical Harm	Minimal	☐	Moderate	☐	Significant	☐
Risk of Psychological Harm	Minimal	☐	Moderate	☐	Significant	☐
Risk of Social Harm	Minimal	☐	Moderate	☐	Significant	☐
Risk of Legal Harm	Minimal	☐	Moderate	☐	Significant	☐
Risk of Financial Harm	Minimal	☐	Moderate	☐	Significant	☐

Rationale:

Based on your assessment of the benefits and risks associated with the research, what is your final assessment as to the benefit/risk ratio for the study? (Check One)

Benefits significantly outweigh the risks	☐
Benefits slightly outweigh the risks	☐
Benefits are equivalent to the risks	☐
Risks slightly outweigh the benefits	☐
Risks significantly outweigh the benefits	☐

Rationale:

EXERCISE 4C

Would Reality TV Shows Pass an IRB Ethics Review?

When conducting research, psychologists are interested in studying and observing the way people behave in "real life." They want to understand who people really are, how they really think, and how they really behave under the normal circumstances of their everyday lives. Reality TV shows claim to capture such "real life" behavior. The introduction to the MTV show, *The Real World*,[24] captured the philosophy of reality television (i.e. "what happens when people stop being polite and start getting real"). While reality television has become extremely popular, it has also been criticized for reinforcing stereotypes and exploiting vulnerable people for profit and ratings. So, what would the outcome of an IRB (i.e. Institutional Review Board) review be if a reality television show was proposed as a scientific research study and submitted for review? Would the IRB decide it was an ethical study of human behavior or an unethical experience that would pose more than minimal risk for participants?[25]

Below are descriptions of 4 research studies whose proposed procedures are based on the premises of 4 popular reality television shows. For each study, assume you are a member of an IRB asked to conduct an ethics review and please: **(a)** evaluate the potential benefits and risks associated with the research study and **(b)** determine whether you would grant approval or not grant approval for the proposed research study and provide a rationale for your decision.

Reality TV Show #1: Boiling Points

A researcher will randomly select individuals from the community and create situations designed to intentionally frustrate or annoy them. The individuals will be unaware they are participants in a research study and that their behavior is being videotaped. Examples of situations designed to frustrate or annoy participants will include: (a) having individuals who will not stop talking sit next to them when they are trying to read or watch a movie, (b) having individuals burping and/ or farting sit next to them while they are trying to eat their lunches, (c) having participants order food from employees who keep making mistakes with their orders, (d) having individuals blame participants for breaking items in stores they did not actually break, (e) having the participants sit next to children who are crying or having tantrums when no other seats are available, (f) having individuals continuously make fun of their clothes, hairstyles, and appearances while on a blind date, (g) having participants have their car towed or given a ticket when they have committed no traffic violations, (h) having individuals cut in front of them after they have patiently waited in a long line, and (i) have individuals do unhygienic things to their food (e.g. sneezing or coughing on their food, picking their noses and not washing their hands before handling their food).

Trained actors (i.e. "confederates") working for the researcher will play the roles of frustrating and annoying individuals encountered by participants. The "confederate" actors will attempt to get participants to reach their points of frustration (i.e. "boiling points") within a 10-minute time limit. The "boiling points" of participants will be judged to have been reached if the participants make a verbal and/or physical threat toward a "confederate" actor or they attempt to physically leave a situation. The researcher and a team of research assistants will videotape the behavior of participants from hidden locations and will record the time it takes for participants to reach their "boiling points." When a participant reaches his/her "boiling point" or the 10-minute time limit expires, the study will end. Participants will then be approached by the researcher and told they had taken part in a research study examining frustration. Participants will be told their behavior had been video-taped during the study and will be shown the video footage. Participants will be told the results of the study will help to better our understanding of the individual differences that determine how quickly individuals reach their "boiling points."[26]

1. To what extent will society benefit from the results of this study?

No Societal Benefits	①	②	③	④	⑤	Significant Societal Benefits

2. To what extent will participants personally benefit from participation in the study?

No Personal Benefits	①	②	③	④	⑤	Significant Personal Benefits

3. To what extent does the study place participants "at risk" for harm?

Minimal Risk Level	①	②	③	④	⑤	Significant Risk Level

4. To what extent will the study allow the researcher to observe "real life" behavior?

Poor Study Design	①	②	③	④	⑤	Well-Designed Study

5. To what extent would you personally feel comfortable being a participant in this study?

Very Uncomfortable	①	②	③	④	⑤	Very Comfortable

Would you grant approval to this study?

① YES, I would grant my approval for this study

② NO, I would not grant my approval for this study

Rationale:

Reality TV Show #2: Scare Tactics

A researcher will place individuals into situations designed to frighten them. The individuals will be unaware they are participants in a research study and their behavior is being videotaped. They also will be unaware that their family and friends "volunteered" them to take part in the research study. Participants will be transported by family, friends, and/or "confederate" actors working for the researcher to the locations where participants will be intentionally frightened. Examples of situations designed to frighten participants will include: (a) participants finding a videotape of a murder and then receiving telephone calls from the murderer who wants their videotape back, (b) participants receiving e-mail at home and at work from a coworker who is recently deceased, (c) participants encountering a mysterious cult when they take a wrong turn down a strange road at night, (d) participants encountering the paranormal when the closet in a friend's home turns in to a portal to another universe, (e) participants witnessing an exterminator being attacked by a creature that has eaten through a wall at a friend's home, (f) participants who have stopped at a farm to buy produce being threatened by a shotgun toting farmer after he walks in to the barn and sees them with his daughter who is now topless, (g) participants being attacked by "bigfoot" type creatures while on a camping trip, and (h) participants being asked by a priest to help him kill a member of his congregation who the priest believes is a demon.

Trained actors (i.e. "confederates") working for the researcher will play the role of "frighteners." The researcher and a team of research assistants will videotape the behavior of participants from hidden locations. Medical and psychological professionals will monitor each "frightening" and will intervene in the event a medical or psychological emergency develops. The researcher will monitor the behavior of the participants, watching for signs they are becoming frightened. When participants have clearly reached the point of becoming frightened, the "confederate" actors (i.e. "frighteners") will turn to participants and ask them if they are frightened. When the participants verbally confirm that they are frightened, the research study will end. Each participant will then be approached by the researcher and told they had taken part in a study on human fear and that they had been "volunteered" to participate in the study by their family and friends. Participants will be told their behavior had been videotaped during the study and will be shown the videotape footage of their behavior. Participants will be told that the results of the study will help to better our understanding of: (a) individual differences in responses to frightening situations and (b) the coping mechanisms used by individuals encountering frightening situations.[27]

1. To what extent will society benefit from the results of this study?

No Societal Benefits	①	②	③	④	⑤	Significant Societal Benefits

2. To what extent will participants personally benefit from participation in the study?

No Personal Benefits	①	②	③	④	⑤	Significant Personal Benefits

3. To what extent does the study place participants "at risk" for harm?

Minimal Risk Level	①	②	③	④	⑤	Significant Risk Level

4. To what extent will the study allow the researcher to observe "real life" behavior?

Poor Study Design	①	②	③	④	⑤	Well-Designed Study

5. To what extent would you personally feel comfortable being a participant in this study?

Very Uncomfortable	①	②	③	④	⑤	Very Comfortable

Would you grant approval to this study?

① YES, I would grant my approval for this study

② NO, I would not grant my approval for this study

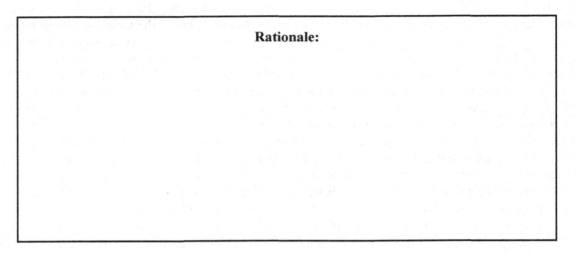

Reality TV Show #3: Survivor

A researcher will recruit 16 individuals to participate in a research study on survival skills under adverse conditions. Participants will be told that the individual who is able to "outwit, outplay, and outlast" the other 15 participants and be the last remaining "survivor" on the island will win $1 million dollars. After signing a consent form and passing a comprehensive physical exam, participants will be transported by the researcher to a remote island and each participant will be assigned to one of two, 8-person teams. Teams will be given no food, clothing, or tools. They must build shelter, find food, build a fire, and set up a base camp using only those materials they can find on the island. Every three days, the researcher will return to the island to serve as the judge for two team challenges. First, a reward challenge will be held. Teams will compete in physical and mental challenges with the winning team receiving items beneficial to survival on the island (e.g. food, clothes, blankets, matches). Second, an immunity challenge will be held in which teams compete in physical and mental challenges with the winning team getting immunity from being voted off the island and out of the research study. Losing teams will have to vote out one member of their team. Prior to team elimination votes, members of the losing team will be given an opportunity to consult with one another, decide whether or not to form voting alliances, and use whatever strategies they personally feel are necessary to allow them to remain on the island and in the research study (e.g. lying to team members, intentionally causing their team to lose an immunity challenge in order to get a specific team member voted off the island, hiding food or supplies from team members in order to gain a competitive advantage). These reward and elimination challenges will continue every three days until 8 participants remain.

The two teams will then be merged and the 8 participants will live together in one of the team camps. All of the reward and immunity challenges will then become competitions among individual participants rather than teams. As the days on the island pass, reward and immunity competitions will become increasingly more difficult for participants as hunger, fatigue, and/or injury may begin to affect their performance. Medical professionals will monitor participants and will intervene in the event of a medical emergency. When only 2 participants remain, they will come before the researcher and a group composed of the last 8 participants who were voted off the island. Each of the 8 eliminated participants will be given a chance to ask the 2 finalists why they believe they deserve to be the last remaining "survivor" on the island and the winner of the $1 million dollars. At this time, some of the 8 eliminated participants may compliment and/or criticize the behaviors, morals, and strategies of the two finalists, and may even vent their own frustrations at being voted off of the island and out of the research study. The two finalists will then get a chance to respond to the questions and comments of the 8 eliminated participants. The 8 eliminated participants will then vote on which of the two finalists they believe should win the $1 million dollars and be declared the "sole survivor." After the final vote, the "sole survivor" will be awarded the $1 million dollar prize and participants will be debriefed by the researcher. Participants will be told that in addition to being a study of team and individual survival skills, the study was also designed to assess whether individuals will: (a) use honesty, physical/mental effort, and teamwork or (b) deception, manipulation, and political strategies to win the $1 million dollars. The study was also designed to assess the extent to which individuals will violate their personal ethics, morals, and principles when faced with a chance to win $1 million dollars.[28]

1. To what extent will society benefit from the results of this study?

No Societal Benefits	①	②	③	④	⑤	Significant Societal Benefits

2. To what extent will participants personally benefit from participation in the study?

No Personal Benefits	①	②	③	④	⑤	Significant Personal Benefits

3. To what extent does the study place participants "at risk" for harm?

Minimal Risk Level	①	②	③	④	⑤	Significant Risk Level

4. To what extent will the study allow the researcher to observe "real life" behavior?

Poor Study Design	①	②	③	④	⑤	Well-Designed Study

5. To what extent would you personally feel comfortable being a participant in this study?

Very Uncomfortable	①	②	③	④	⑤	Very Comfortable

Would you grant approval to this study?

① YES, I would grant my approval for this study

② NO, I would not grant my approval for this study

Rationale:

Reality TV Show #4: Temptation Island

A researcher will recruit heterosexual couples who have been in a committed relationship for a minimum of 1 year to participate in a research study on relationship commitment. The couples will be informed by the researcher that they: (1) will be separated from their partners for 1 week, (2) will be required to go on dates with 4 single individuals of the opposite sex during their week apart, and (3) will re-evaluate their level of commitment to their partners at the end of the week. After signing a consent form and passing a series of medical tests to ensure they do not have any sexually transmitted diseases (STDs), the female members of the couples will be transported to a nearby spa/resort while the male members of the couples will be transported to a nearby casino/resort. When they arrive at their respective locations, the participants will be introduced to the 4 individuals they will be required to go out on a date with during the week. The males' dates will be referred to as "temptresses" while the females' dates will be referred to as "tempters." These "temptresses" and "tempters" will be selected by the researcher based upon their attractiveness, personality, and seductiveness. Participants will be given a dating schedule for the week and the dates may include any of the following: (a) dinner, (b) dancing, (c) swimming, (d) a walk on the beach, (e) breakfast in bed, (f) getting a massage at the spa/resort, (g) gambling, (h) snorkeling, (i) horseback riding, (j) sporting activities, (k) going to a bar, and (l) sitting near a cozy campfire. To ensure the safety of all participants, the researcher will have chaperones accompany couples on their dates and have a team of research assistants videotape all of the dates. Participants will be aware their dates are being videotaped. During the dates, "temptresses" and "tempters" will be instructed by the researcher to dress, behave, and act in such a way as to make the participants interested in having a sexual/intimate relationship with them and test participants' commitment to their partners. Temptresses and tempters will be free to engage in any behaviors they choose, however, chaperones, research assistants, and/or the researcher will intervene if they attempt to engage in any forced or unwelcome physical contact with participants. The chaperones, research assistants, and/or the researcher will not intervene if a date results in consensual sexual activity.

After each of their dates, participants will return to their hotel/spa rooms and videotape their thoughts and feelings about the "temptresses" or "tempters" they have just gone on a date with and any thoughts about implications the date may have for their levels of commitment to their partners. If participants encounter a "temptress" or "tempter" they would like to spend more time with, they will be given the opportunity to cancel dates on their dating schedule and go on additional dates with their "temptresses" or "tempters" of interest. At the end of the week, all participants will be transported home by the researcher to reunite with their partners. Once the couples are reunited, participants will view the videotapes of their partner's dates shot by the research team (the videotapes may or may not document evidence of consensual sexual activity between participants and a "temptress" or "tempter") and the post-date videos recorded by their partners. The "temptresses" and "tempters" will then arrive and give additional feedback about the behaviors of the participants during their dates. Each couple will be given time to examine the video evidence they have been shown as well as the feedback from the "temptresses" and "tempters" and will then be asked to complete a questionnaire concerning the commitment they feel toward their partner and their relationship after the research experience. Participants will then be debriefed by the researcher and told the results of the research study will improve our knowledge of: (a) the factors that tempt individuals into exploring new relationships, (b) how honest individuals are in their statements of commitment to their partners, and (c) how those in committed relationships can better identify the signs of a partner's commitment level changing during the course of a relationship. The researcher will answer all questions from participants and make counselors, therapists, and medical professionals available to couples to provide them any assistance they may need as a result of their experience in the research study.[29]

1. To what extent will society benefit from the results of this study?

No Societal Benefits	①	②	③	④	⑤	Significant Societal Benefits

2. To what extent will participants personally benefit from participation in the study?

No Personal Benefits	①	②	③	④	⑤	Significant Personal Benefits

3. To what extent does the study place participants "at risk" for harm?

Minimal Risk Level	①	②	③	④	⑤	Significant Risk Level

4. To what extent will the study allow the researcher to observe "real life" behavior?

Poor Study Design	①	②	③	④	⑤	Well-Designed Study

5. To what extent would you personally feel comfortable being a participant in this study?

Very Uncomfortable	①	②	③	④	⑤	Very Comfortable

Would you grant approval to this study?

① YES, I would grant my approval for this study

② NO, I would not grant my approval for this study

Rationale:

References

1. U.S. Department of Health, Education, and Welfare, National Commission for the Protection of Human Subjects of Biomedical and Behavioral Research. (1979). *The Belmont Report: Ethical principles and guidelines for the protection of human subjects of research.* Washington, D.C. Retrieved from http://www.hhs.gov/ohrp/policy/belmont.html

2. U.S. Department of Health & Human Services, Office for Human Research Protection. (1974). *Code of federal regulations for the protection of human subjects.* Washington, D.C. (Report No. 45 CFR 46). Retrieved from http://www.hhs.gov/ohrp/humansubjects/guidance/45cfr46.html.

3. Emanual, E., & Abdoler, E., & Stunkel, L. (2010). *Research ethics: How to treat people who participate in research.* Retrieved from http://www.bioethics.nih.gov/education/FNIH_BioethicsBrochure_WEB.PDF.

4. Kimmel, A. J., Smith, N. C., & Klein, J. G. (2010). Ethical decision-making and research design in the behavioral sciences: An application of social contact theory. *INSEAD Faculty & Research Working Paper.* Retrieved from http://www.insead.edu/faculty Research/research/doc.cfm?did=45044.

5. Bordens, K. S., & Abbot, B. B. (2011). *Research design and methods: A process approach* (8th ed.). Boston, MA: McGraw-Hill Publishers.

6. Marshall University, Office of Research Integrity. (2013). Initial IRB full review protocol form. *Marshall University Office of Research Integrity.* Retrieved from http://www.marshall.edu/ori/files/2013/11/Initial-Protocol-Assessment-Form-010313.doc.

7. The Society for Science & Society. (2013). *Human participants: Risk assessment guide* and *online survey procedures.* Retrieved from https://student.societyforscience.org/human-participants#riskass.

8. National Bioethics Advisory Committee. (1998). *Research involving persons with mental disorders that may affect decision-making capacity: The assessment of risk and potential benefit* (Chapter 4). Retrieved https://bioethicsarchive.georgetown.edu/nbac/capacity/TOC.htm.

9. Passer, M. W. (2013). *Research methods: Concepts and connections.* New York, NY: Worth Publishers.

10. Cozby, P. C., & Bates, S. C. (2011). *Methods in behavioral research.* (11th ed.). New York, NY: McGraw-Hill Publishers.

11. Hofling, C., Brotzman, E., Dalrymple, A., Graves, N., & Pierce, C. (1966). An experimental study in nurse-physician relationships. *The Journal of Nervous and Mental Disease, 143*(2), 171–180.

12. Rice, K. E. (n.d.). Key study: Hofling & his nurses. *Integrated SocioPsychology.* Retrieved from http://www.integratedsociopsychology.net/hofling-nurses.html.

13. McLeod, S. A. (2008). Hofling's hospital experiment of obedience. *Simply Psychology.* Retrieved from http://www.simplypsychology.org/hofling-obedience.html.

14. Rosenhan, D. L. (1973). On being sane in insane places. *Science, 179*(4070), 250–258.

15. Loftus, E. F, & Pickrell, J. E. (1995). The formation of false memories. *Psychiatric Annals, 25*(12), 720–725.

16. Wansink, B., Painter, J. E., & North, J. (2005). Bottomless bowls: Why visual cues of portion size may influence intake. *Obesity Research, 13*(1), 93–100.

17. Darley, J. M., & Batson, C. D. (1973). "From Jerusalem to Jericho": A study of situational and dispositional variables in helping behavior. *Journal of Personality and Social Psychology, 27*(1), 100–108.

18. Kraut, A. (2010). Dr. Joseph Goldberger and the war on pellagra. *Office of NIH History.* Retrieved from http://history.nih.gov/exhibits/goldberger/.

19. Elmore, J. G., & Feinstein, A. R. (1994). Joseph Goldberger: An unsung hero of American clinical epidemiology. *Annals of Internal Medicine, 121*(5), 372–375.

20. Middlemist, R. D., Knowles, E. S., & Matter, C. F. (1976). Personal space invasions in the lavatory: Suggestive evidence of arousal. *Journal of Personality and Social Psychology, 33*(5), 541–546.

21. Humphreys, L. (1972). Tearoom trade: Impersonal sex in public places. In W. Feigelman (Ed.), *Sociology Full Circle* (pp. 259–277). Retrieved from http://www.angelfire.com/or3/tss/tearoom.html.

22. Reynolds, G. (2003). The stuttering doctor's "monster study." *New York Times Magazine.* Retrieved from http://www.nytimes.com/2003/03/16/the-stuttering-doctor-s-monster-study.html.

23. Robinson, W. M., & Unruh, B. T. (2008). The hepatitis experiments at the Willowbrook State School. In E.J. Emanuel, C. Grady, & R.F. Lie (Eds.), *The Oxford Textbook of Clinical Research Ethics* (pp. 80–85). Retrieved from http://www.theblackvault.com/m/articles/view/Willowbrook-State-School-Hepatitus-Experiments#.UpNacnQo4cA.

24. Bunim, M. E., & Murray, J. (Executive Producers) (1992–1993). *The Real World: New York.* MTV Music Television (Bunim-Murray Productions). New York City, New York.

25. Spellman, B. A. (2005). Could reality shows become reality experiments? *APS Observer, 18*(3). Retrieved from http://www.psychologicalscience.org/index.php/publications/observer/2005/march-05/could-reality-shows-become-reality-experiments.html.

26. Blitt, J., Berger, I., & Abernathy, A. (Head Writers) (2004–2005). *Boiling Points.* MTV (Fractured Hip Production Company): New York City, New York.

27. Hallock, S., & Healey, K. (Executive Producers) (2003–2013). *Scare Tactics.* SyFy (Hallock-Healey Entertainment): United States Locations.

28. Parsons, C., Burnett, M., & Probst, J. (Executive Producers) (2000–2014). *Survivor.* CBS (Columbian Broadcasting System): Worldwide Locations (Africa; Asia; North America; South America).

29. Silverstein, A., & Wentworth, B. (Head Writers) (2001–2003). *Temptation Island.* Fox (Fox World Productions): Worldwide Locations (Belize, Costa Rica, Honduras).

MODULE 5

Acquiring a Research Sample

Once psychologists have identified the goals of their research, determined which scales of measurement will provide sufficient information to achieve these goals, selected reliable and valid measurement instruments to assess their variables of interest, and established procedures to conduct their research studies in accordance with ethical principles, they can then begin to study their "populations of interest."

A "population of interest" consists of all members of a group of individuals, objects, or events that share a common characteristic that is of interest to researchers (e.g. all women who were diagnosed in 2013 with breast cancer, all personnel records for employees of Fortune 500 companies, all acts of terrorism that have occurred world-wide since 9/11). While studying all members of a population would be an ideal goal for researchers, in most instances, researchers lack the staff, financial resources, time, and access to population members necessary to achieve this ideal goal. As a result, researchers must use available resources to study a smaller portion (or subset) of the population known as a "sample."[1,2,3] When this occurs, the goal for researchers changes to one of identifying a sample of individuals, objects, or events whose characteristics are as similar as possible to those of the population of interest. Such a sample is referred to as a "representative" sample.[2,3,4] When researchers acquire a representative sample of individuals, objects, or events, the information yielded by such a sample is more likely to "generalize," be reliable, and allow the researchers to draw conclusions about the population of interest without having to study all members of the population.

A "representative sample" is also more likely to reduce the amount of "sampling error." Sampling error occurs in research when the statistical characteristics of a sample of individuals, objects, or events are used to estimate the statistical characteristics of the population the sample was drawn from.[1,2,5] For example, assume psychologists are interested in studying the television viewing habits of families in the United States. Ideally, psychologists would measure all of the members of the population of interest (i.e. all U.S. families with a television) and then compute a statistical value to represent that population (e.g. average number of hours of television viewed per week). This statistical value is referred to as a "population parameter."[5] In most instances, however, psychologists would not have the resources to measure all members of the population of interest and would therefore be unable to compute the value of the "population parameter."[2] Psychologists would instead use their available resources to identify a "representative" sample of individuals, objects, or events drawn from the population of interest (i.e. a sample of 1,000 U.S. families with a television). They would then measure all members of the sample and compute a statistical value to represent the sample (e.g. average number of hours of television viewed per week). This statistical value would be referred to as a "sample statistic."[5] Psychologists would then use the value of the "sample statistic" to estimate the value of the unknown "population parameter."

The important question for psychologists is how well the value of the "sample statistic" approximates the value of the unknown "population parameter." Since a "sample statistic" is based on only a subset of the members of the population, its value is unlikely to be identical to that of the "population parameter" that would be based on all members of the population. The discrepancy (i.e. difference) between the values of the "sample statistic" and the "population parameter" is referred to as "sampling error." The amount of "sampling error" is often referred to as the "precision" of the sample and is often presented by researchers as a "margin of error" associated with the "sample statistic."[1,2,5] For example, if psychologists were to study a sample of 1,000 U.S. families, they may compute a "sample statistic" which shows the average number of hours of television viewed per week by these 1,000 U.S. families in 48 hours with a "margin of error" of +/– 4 hours at a 95% confidence level. This would tell us that psychologists are 95% confident that the value of the unknown "population parameter" (i.e. average number of hours of television viewed per week by all families in the U.S.) falls within the range of 44–52 hours of television viewed per week (48 hours +/– 4 hours). Psychologists can increase the precision of their estimate of a "population parameter" by increasing the "representativeness" of the sample they acquire from the population of interest. The more "representative" a sample: (a) the smaller the "sampling error" (i.e. "margin of error"), (b) the more likely a "sample statistic" will provide a precise estimate of a "population parameter," and (c) the more likely information learned from the sample will "generalize" to the population and allow psychologists to draw valid conclusions about the population of interest.[1,2,6]

There are several actions research psychologists can take to increase the likelihood of acquiring a research sample that is "representative" of a population of interest. First, they can ensure that all members of the sample they have acquired are indeed members of the population of interest (also known as the "sampling frame").[1,2,3] When individuals, objects, or events that fall outside of the population of interest are included in a research sample, it is referred to as "over-coverage"[7]; a condition which can reduce the "representativeness" of a research sample. Second, they can ensure all members of the population have an equal opportunity to be selected as a member of the research sample (a process known as "random selection").[4,6] By ensuring all members of the population have an equal opportunity for selection, researchers can reduce the likelihood that they are systematically excluding an important segment of the population from their research sample (a condition referred to as "under-coverage").[8] Third, they can ensure that the size of the sample they have acquired is sufficient to adequately represent the population of interest and to minimize "sampling error" to a level that allows them to make precise estimates of "population parameters" on the basis of "sample statistics" derived from the research sample.[9] Finally, they can ensure they are not allowing personal biases to influence which members of the population are selected for inclusion in the research sample (i.e. "sampling bias").[6,10] This issue is especially important when researchers have an outcome they would like to see supported by the results of their research, and they may be potentially biased toward selecting members of a population who are more likely to provide data in support of this preferred research outcome (e.g. individuals more likely to respond to a treatment intervention; individuals more likely to possess attitudes, values, and/or beliefs preferred by the researchers). Ultimately, the goal for researchers is to acquire an unbiased, randomly selected, "representative" sample of sufficient size from the population of interest and use the statistical characteristics of the sample to make precise estimates of the statistical characteristics of the population.[1,2,9]

There are a variety of techniques researchers can use to acquire a research sample. The sampling technique they ultimately select will be based on a combination of factors including: (a) the amount of time researchers have to acquire a sample and conduct the study, (b) the costs associated with acquiring a sample through various sampling techniques, (c) the number of staff available to assist in the acquisition of a sample, and (d) the sample size and level of "precision" considered sufficient to meet the objectives of the research.[11,12] The sampling techniques which are available to researchers are often classified into two broad categories known as Probability Sampling and Non-Probability Sampling.

Probability Sampling

Probability sampling techniques share a set of common characteristics which include: (a) every member of the population of interest has an opportunity to be selected for inclusion in the research sample, (b) the probability of an individual member of the population being selected for inclusion in the research sample can be determined, (c) the sampling techniques involve the use of the process of "random selection," and (d) the sampling techniques increase the likelihood the research sample will be representative of the population of interest.[1,2,4] A sample of the various probability sampling techniques that are commonly used by researchers are discussed below.

Simple Random Sampling

In simple random sampling, all members of a population of interest have an equal opportunity to be selected as a member of the research sample. To acquire a simple random sample, researchers will first assign a number to each member of the population of interest (e.g. a Health Psychologist interested in conducting research at a 500-member fitness club would assign each fitness club member a number from 1–500). Researchers will then select a desired sample size (e.g. 100 fitness club members). Finally, researchers will randomly select numbers from the list of numbers assigned to members of the population until they have reached their desired sample size (i.e. the Health Psychologist would randomly select 100 numbers from the list of numbers (i.e. 1–500) assigned to the 500 fitness club members).[1,2,3] Techniques that researchers can use to randomly select numbers can range from simply pulling numbers out of a hat to the use of more sophisticated computer-generated tables of random numbers. Members of the population whose numbers are randomly selected will be included in the sample.

A special case of simple random sampling is known as "*random digit dialing*." Random digit dialing is a sampling technique used by researchers conducting a phone survey to acquire a "representative" sample of the population.[2,6] In random digit dialing, researchers will first select area codes for the geographic locations where they want to conduct the phone survey. They will then use either a "*random numbers table*"[4,6,11] or computer-based random numbers generator to randomly generate a desired number of phone numbers within the selected area codes (e.g. 100 randomly generated phone numbers within the 904, 518, and 304 area codes). Members of the population associated with the phone numbers are selected for inclusion in the research sample. Random digit dialing has an important advantage over randomly selecting numbers from a phone book. Randomly selecting numbers from a phone book can be problematic since some members of the population have unlisted landline phone numbers or mobile phone numbers and can't be selected for inclusion in the research sample. By generating all possible phone numbers within selected area codes, random digit dialing ensures all members of selected area code populations who own a phone (i.e. listed and unlisted landline and mobile phones) have an opportunity to be selected for inclusion in the research sample.

Systematic Random Sampling

In a systematic random sample, researchers select every "kth" member of a population of interest.[1,2] To acquire a systematic random sample, researchers will first assign a number to each member of a population of interest (e.g. a School Psychologist interested in conducting research at a 200-student high school would assign each student at the school a number from 1–200). Researchers then select a desired sample size (e.g. 20 students). The researchers will then divide the size of the population by their desired sample size (i.e. 200 students/20 = 10). This value, represented by the letter "k," is referred to as the "skip interval." Researchers will then randomly select a number between 1 and the value of the "skip interval" (i.e. 1–10). The number selected (e.g. 6) represents the number assigned to the first member of the population selected for inclusion in the research sample. Using this number as a starting point, researchers then select every "kth" number based on the "skip interval" (i.e. every 10th number) from the list of numbers assigned to population members until they have reached the desired sample size (e.g. the School Psychologist would first select the student from the school population assigned the number "6" and then select those students assigned every 10th number after this point (i.e. 16, 26, 36, 46, 56, etc.) until acquiring the desired sample of 20 students). Members of the population whose numbers are selected will be included in the sample.[6,11]

Stratified Random Sampling

In addition to studying populations, researchers are also interested in studying subgroups within populations (e.g. Consumer Psychologists are interested in studying the shopping behavior of customers who are part of different income subgroups). In stratified random sampling, researchers divide a population of interest into subgroups (or strata) whose members share a common characteristic and then use simple random sampling to acquire samples from each of these subgroups.[1,3,4] To acquire a "stratified random sample," researchers first decide how they will divide a population of interest into meaningful subgroups. Subgroups must be mutually exclusive and include all population members (e.g. a Consumer Psychologist could divide a population of shoppers into 3 subgroups based on income; < $50,000, $50,001–$100,000, > $100,000 a year). Researchers will then use simple random sampling to acquire a sample from each of these subgroups. Researchers will have to decide at this point whether they want to acquire a *"proportionate"*[1,6] or *"disproportionate"*[1,11] sample. A "proportionate" sample is one in which the proportion of sample members from each subgroup match those found in the population (e.g. if the annual incomes of shoppers are known to be as follows: 40% < $50,000, 25% $50,001–$100,000, and 35% > $100,000, a Consumer Psychologist interested in studying a sample of 100 shoppers will include 40 shoppers with an annual income < $50,000, 25 shoppers with annual incomes of $50,001–$100,000, and 25 shoppers with an annual income > $100,000). By contrast, a "disproportionate" sample is one in which the proportion of sample members from each subgroup do not match those found in the population. "Disproportionate" stratified samples often result from a decision by researchers to sample an equal number of individuals from each subgroup within the population. A "proportionate" sample will be more "representative" of the population of interest in comparison to a "disproportionate" sample.[1,6,11]

Cluster Sampling

In cluster sampling, researchers divide a population of interest into groups (or "clusters") whose members all share a common characteristic.[1,2,13] When "clusters" are based on a geographic location (e.g. states, counties, area codes, zip codes), the process is referred to as "area sampling." The researchers will then randomly select a sample of "clusters" from the population of interest. All members of the selected "clusters" who meet the criteria for inclusion in the research study are then eligible for inclusion in the research sample. To acquire a "cluster" sample, researchers will first decide how they will divide a population of interest into meaningful groups or "clusters" (e.g. an Environmental Psychologist interested in the attitudes of West Virginians toward the future of coal as a source of energy, may divide the population of interest (i.e. residents of West Virginia) into "clusters" (i.e. county of residence)). Researchers will then select the desired number of "clusters" (i.e. 5 counties) they would like to sample (and have the resources to adequately sample). Researchers will then randomly select this number of "clusters" from the population of interest (e.g. an Environmental Psychologist randomly selects 5 of the 55 counties in the state of West Virginia). All population members who reside in these 5 counties can then be selected by researchers for inclusion in the sample. While the processes of stratified random sampling and cluster sampling appear similar, there are important differences between these sampling methods. In stratified random sampling, individual population members are randomly selected and they are randomly selected from all subgroups within the population. By contrast, in cluster sampling, groups or "clusters" of individuals are randomly selected from the population and individuals from only a subset of "clusters" within the population of interest are selected for inclusion in the research sample.[11,13,14]

Panel Sampling

In panel sampling, researchers first use the process of "simple random sampling" to acquire a desired number of members of a population of interest for inclusion in the research sample. Researchers then assess the members of the research sample on the variable of interest on multiple occasions over time.[2,11,15] Researchers then examine the change that occurs in the value of a "sample statistic" over time and use the amount of change in the sample statistic to estimate the amount of change that is occurring in the population of interest over time (e.g. a Political Psychologist interested in studying "likely voting behavior" of registered voters in the two months leading up to a Mayoral election in a small U.S. city, acquires a list of all registered voters in the city and employs simple random sampling to acquire a "representative" sample of 100 registered voters. The psychologist then assesses the "likely voting behavior" of the 100 registered voters in the research sample after each of the three televised Mayoral debates. The psychologist then uses the amount of change in "likely voting behavior" over time for his sample of 100 registered voters to estimate the amount of change in "likely voting behavior" occurring over time within the population of registered voters living in the city where the Mayoral election is occurring).

Multi-Stage Sampling

In multi-stage sampling, researchers employ a combination of sampling methods to acquire a research sample.[1,2,6] For example, let's assume an Experimental Psychologist is interested in studying the career satisfaction of University professors in the U.S. The psychologist could begin the sample acquisition process by using the method of "cluster" sampling to divide the U.S. into 50 meaningful "clusters" (i.e. the 50 U.S. states) and randomly select a desired number of "clusters" (e.g. 5 of the 50 U.S. states). The psychologist could then create a list representing the population of all Universities in these 5 randomly selected states and use the method of "simple random" sampling to select 10 Universities from this population. The psychologist could then use the method of "stratified random" sampling to divide the professors at the 10 Universities into 3 meaningful groups (or "strata") based on faculty rank (i.e. Assistant, Associate, Full professor) and then randomly select a "proportionate" number of professors from each of the three "strata" (e.g. 42 Full, 58 Associate, 50 Assistant). The psychologist's research sample would therefore contain 150 University professors representing 3 faculty ranks randomly selected from the population of faculty at all Universities within the U.S.

Non-Probability Sampling

Non-probability sampling techniques also share a set of common characteristics. These characteristics include: (a) all members of the population of interest do not have an opportunity to be selected for inclusion in the research sample, (b) the probability of an individual member of the population being selected for inclusion in the research sample can't be accurately determined, (c) the sampling techniques do not involve the use of the process of "random selection," (d) the sampling techniques decrease the likelihood that a research sample will be "representative" of a population of interest, and (e) members of the population selected for inclusion in the research sample are selected by researchers on the basis of their availability, convenience, self-selection, and purpose of the research study.[1,2,4] The non-probability sampling techniques commonly used by researchers to acquire a research sample can be classified into the 2 categories of Accidental Sampling and Purposive Sampling.[1]

Non-probability methods of sampling that are categorized as "accidental" sampling are those in which the researchers select members of the population who are: (a) readily available, (b) easily accessible, (c) identified as a result of chance encounters, (d) identified as a result of investigative work associated with a research study, (e) identified as a result of referrals from other members of the population who have participated in the research study, and (f) volunteers for inclusion in the research sample.[1] A sample of the "accidental" non-probability methods of sampling commonly used by researchers to acquire a research sample are described below.

Convenience Sampling

In convenience sampling, researchers select members of the population who are readily available and easily accessible for inclusion in the research sample, rather than taking the time necessary to randomly select members of the population of interest[2,3,4] (e.g. a Military Psychologist selects the first 50 soldiers who enter the mess hall at lunch time to participate in a research study on the psychological effects of exposure to "live combat" rather than taking the time necessary to randomly select 50 soldiers from the population of soldiers serving at the military base).

Quota Sampling

In quota sampling, researchers will divide a population of interest into meaningful subgroups whose members share a common characteristic. Subgroups are mutually exclusive and include all members of the population of interest. Researchers will then make a decision as to the number of population members from each subgroup (i.e. "quotas") they would like to include in the research sample.[1,2,3] The number of individuals selected by the researchers from each subgroup can be "*proportionate*"[1] (i.e. equal to the proportion of the subgroup present within the population of interest) or "*disproportionate*"[1] (i.e. not equal to the proportion of the subgroup present within the population of interest). Rather than randomly selecting the desired number of population members from each subgroup, (as would be done in "stratified random sampling"), researchers select members of the population who are the most readily available and easily accessible for inclusion in the research sample. Quota sampling is essentially the "non-probability" version of stratified sampling.[11] Selection of population members continues until desired "quotas" are met for each of the subgroups (e.g. a Social Psychologist interested in the life satisfaction of single and married women in the U.S., could acquire a "proportionate" quota sample by selecting the first 52 single women and the first 48 married women she meets at a community fundraising event rather than randomly selecting 52 single women and 48 married women from the population of women in the community where the research is being conducted.

Accidental Sampling

In accidental (or haphazard) sampling, researchers have a chance encounter with a member of a population of interest.[1,2,3] As a result of this chance encounter, the researchers select the population member for inclusion in the research sample (e.g. an Industrial-Organizational Psychologist studying the psychological effects of unemployment has a chance encounter at a restaurant while eating dinner with his family with a woman who was recently laid off from her job at an insurance company. As a result of this chance encounter, the psychologist selects the woman for inclusion in his research sample.).

Opportunistic Sampling

In opportunistic sampling, researchers discover information during the course of their investigative work for a research study that leads to the identification of previously unknown members of the population that the researchers would like to select for inclusion in the research sample[10,13,14] (e.g. a Forensic Psychologist studying the psychological profile of children who commit school shootings discovers several school shootings he was previously unaware of while conducting investigative work for his research. Based on this new information, the psychologist selects the children who committed these previously unknown school shootings for inclusion in his research sample.).

Snowball Sampling

In snowball (or chain) sampling, members of the population who have been selected for inclusion in the research sample refer other members of the population who meet the selection criteria for the research study to researchers. Members of the population who have been referred to researchers, will themselves then refer additional population members to researchers. Over time, the referral process gathers momentum and the sample size continues to grow like a snowball rolling down a hill[1,13,14] (e.g. a Developmental Psychologist conducting a study of the parenting behavior of fathers, is given the names of 2 other fathers who are willing to participate in the research study by a father currently in the psychologist's research sample. The two fathers who were referred to the researcher, each provide the researcher with the names of 2 additional fathers who are willing to participate in the research study. As a result of the referral process, the psychologist obtains a large, "representative" sample of the population of interest (i.e. fathers) within a short period of time).

Volunteer Sampling

In volunteer sampling, researchers select population members who volunteer for the research study (i.e. self-select) for inclusion in the research sample.[3,6,13] On the positive side, volunteer sampling reduces the amount of time and resources researchers will need to devote to the recruitment and acquisition of the research sample. However, since volunteers: (a) are selected for inclusion in the research sample through self-selection rather than through the process of "random selection" and (b) may differ in meaningful ways from those individuals who do not volunteer to participate in research (e.g. motivation; personality), the "representativeness" of a sample that contains a large percentage of volunteers may be questionable (e.g. a Cognitive Psychologist conducting research on memory, selects college students who volunteer to take part in the research in exchange for extra course credit for inclusion in the research sample).

Non-probability methods of sampling that are categorized as "purposive" are those in which researchers select members of the population on the basis of: (a) personal judgment as to the individuals, objects, or events that are "representative" of the population, (b) the amount of variability desired in the research sample, (c) the unique qualities associated with members of a population, and (d) the specific purpose of the research study.[1,2,3] A sample of the "purposive" non-probability methods of sampling commonly used by researchers are described below.

Judgment Sampling

In judgment sampling, researchers use their knowledge regarding a population of interest and their personal judgment to select individuals, objects, or events that, in their opinion, are "representative" of the population of interest[9] (e.g. a Counseling Psychologist selects the patients seeking psychological counseling at two community mental health centers for inclusion in her research sample because based on her personal judgment, the patients who seek treatment at these two community mental health centers are "representative" of the population of patients who seek psychological counseling at community mental centers throughout the U.S.).

Heterogeneity Sampling

In heterogeneity (or maximum variation) sampling, researchers select members of the population for inclusion in the research sample with the intent of acquiring a research sample containing as much diversity as possible.[9,13,14] Heterogeneity sampling may be used when researchers want to acquire a research sample that contains a collection of individuals with a wide variety of ideas, attitudes, thoughts, and/or opinions about a specific topic of interest (e.g. a Community Psychologist purposefully selects a diverse sample of residents from the local community to participate in a community forum designed to generate a diverse set of ideas as to how the community should handle its current teen substance use problem).

Homogeneity Sampling

In homogeneity sampling, rather than acquiring a sample that is diverse and "representative" of the entire population of interest, researchers select members of the population of interest for inclusion in the research sample who are as similar as possible and share a common characteristic or experience (i.e. homogeneous).[13,14] Homogeneity sampling is often used when researchers are interested in conducting an in-depth study of a specific subgroup within a population of interest (e.g. a Neuropsychologist interested in studying traumatic brain injuries, decides rather than studying individuals with a wide variety of traumatic brain injuries, that she will instead only select members of the population who have suffered a traumatic brain injury to a highly specific area of the temporal lobe of the brain).

Deviant Case Sampling

In deviant case (or extreme) sampling, researchers will select members of the population who: (a) possess unusual or extreme levels of knowledge, skill, trait, or ability, (b) have had an unusual or extreme (i.e. intense, rare) experience during the course of their lives, or (c) possess an unusual or extreme level of a quality, feature, or characteristic that is of interest to researchers for inclusion in the research sample.[9,13,14] Deviant case sampling may be used by psychologists who desire to learn about a psychological construct or phenomenon by studying the extreme members (i.e. "outliers") of a population of interest (i.e. a Physiological Psychologist interested in studying the role of the brain in human reaction time acquires a sample of population members whose reaction times would place them in the bottom 1% (i.e. extremely slow reaction times) or top 1% (i.e. extremely fast reaction times) of the adult U.S. population).

Modal Instance Sampling

In modal instance (or typical case) sampling, researchers will select those members of the population who best represent a typical, average, or normal member of the population of interest.[1,13,14] Researchers may define "typical, normal, or average" on the basis of existing population statistics and/or on the basis of their personal judgments about the population of interest. The name of the sampling technique is derived from a statistic known as the "mode" which represents the most frequently occurring score or category in a population or sample[5] (e.g. a Quantitative Psychologist interested in studying the mathematical reasoning skills of college students who attend a large, Mid-Atlantic University, selects a sample of 100 college students who are 18–22 years old, first generation college students, from rural hometowns, and are attending college while simultaneously working a full-time job for inclusion in his research sample. The Psychologist specifically selects these 100 college students because, based on the statistics provided to him by the Office of Student Affairs at the University, this is the profile of the "typical student" who attends the University).

Confirming and Disconfirming Case Sampling

In confirming and disconfirming case sampling, researchers first conduct a research study to test a hypothesis of interest. Researchers then divide the members of the research sample who participated in the research study into two categories: (a) those whose results confirmed the research hypothesis and (b) those whose results failed to confirm the research hypothesis. The researchers will then select a desired number of individuals they would like to sample from each category. They then use a non-random process to select the desired number of individuals from each category. Researchers then compare the two groups in an attempt to determine what differences (e.g. individual, behavioral, procedural) exist between the individuals in the two groups that could account for the significant difference in their research outcomes[9,13,14] (e.g. an Industrial-Organizational Psychologist conducts a study testing a research hypothesis that as job satisfaction increases, work productivity also increases. After completing the study, the psychologist selects 5 employees whose results confirmed the research hypothesis and 5 employees whose results failed to confirm the research hypothesis. He then studies the two groups to see whether the difference in their research outcomes can be accounted for by differences in the subjects, experimental procedures, or other variables not accounted for or controlled during the research study.).

Criterion Sampling

In criterion sampling, researchers select only those members of the population of interest who meet the specific eligibility criterion for participation in the research for inclusion in the research sample[14] (e.g. a Clinical Psychologist conducting a research study on depression, selects only the members of the population (i.e. members of the local community diagnosed with depression) who are "male, between the ages of 35–45, have a family history of depression, and who have been taking prescription anti-depressant medication for a minimum of 3 years" for inclusion in the research sample).

Expert Sampling

In expert sampling, researchers identify members of the population who have expertise on a topic of interest to researchers. Researchers then identify a desired number of "experts" they would like to select for inclusion in their research sample. Through a non-random method of selection, researchers then select the desired number of "experts" from the population. Once the members of the research sample are assembled by the researchers, they are often referred to as a "panel of experts."[1,3,9] Researchers then have the "panel of experts" complete a variety of experimental tasks including: (a) providing their expert advice or opinions on important social issues, (b) developing solutions to applied organizational, community, or social-level problems, or (c) evaluating various forms of scientific evidence that are claimed to support or fail to support various research hypotheses or theories (e.g. a Psychiatrist identifies members of the academic community who have expertise in the area of the use of prescription medication for the treatment of psychological illnesses. The psychiatrist then selects 8 of these members of the academic community to serve as a "panel of experts." The psychiatrist then has the "panel of experts" evaluate whether psychologists have the knowledge and/or the training necessary to be granted the same privileges as psychiatrists to prescribe medications for the treatment of psychological illnesses.).

Cohort Sampling

In cohort sampling, researchers select members of a population who have had a specific experience (e.g. a work accident) for inclusion in the research sample.[2,15,16] The researchers then measure the members of the research sample on the variables of interest on several occasions to assess the impact of the experience (e.g. physical, psychological, emotional) with the passage of time. In most instances, researchers also compare the results of the research sample with those of samples drawn from the same population containing individuals who have not had a similar experience (e.g. a Clinical Psychologist conducting a research study on the psychological effects of a workplace accident acquires a sample of employees who were all involved in a workplace accident from a population of employees working at a large construction company. The psychologist administers a battery of psychological tests to the members of his research sample every 6 months for a period of 3 years to examine the impact of the passage of time on the psychological impact of the workplace accident. The psychologist then compares the results from his research sample to those of a sample of employees from the same construction company who were not involved in the workplace accident.).

Trend Sampling

In trend sampling, researchers are interest in studying trends occurring within a population of interest over time. To look for these trends, researchers select members of a population of interest for inclusion in the research sample. Researchers then assess members of the research sample on the variables of interest (e.g. recycling behavior). At a later point in time, researchers collect a second sample from the same population and assess members of this sample on the same variables of interest. The researchers continue this process until they have acquired multiple samples from a population (each containing different members of the population) across a lengthy period of time. Researchers then analyze the results of their collection of samples and use these sample results to estimate whether there are trends occurring in the population on the variables of interest[2,11,16] (e.g. In the year 2000, an Environmental Psychologist selects a sample of individuals living within a large U.S. city and assesses their level of involvement in recycling. Each year from 2000 to 2010, she collects a different sample of individuals from the same U.S. city and assesses their level of involvement in recycling. Each year, she combines the results from her collection of samples to estimate whether there is an upward or downward trend in the recycling behavior occurring within the population of the large U.S. city.).

Sampling for Internet-Based Research

Prior to the emergence of the Internet, researchers who wanted to study a population of interest typically used mail surveys, telephone surveys, in-person paper-and-pencil surveys, and face-to-face interviews to study a "representative" sample of population members. While these traditional methods of studying a population are still widely used today, an expanding number of researchers have begun using online surveys to study a population of interest. Use of an online survey to study a population has several attractive advantages for researchers including: (a) they are inexpensive to create and administer,[12] (b) a large number of population members (many of whom are widely dispersed geographically) can be accessed quickly,[6,12] (c) data can be collected 24 hours a day (which allows population members to complete the survey at a time that best fits their individual lifestyles and schedules),[12] (d) data is immediately available[2,3,12] (unlike a mail survey where researchers face lengthy delays waiting for data to be returned in the mail), (e) they require minimal personnel to administer[3,12] (unlike telephone surveys, in-person paper-and-pencil surveys, and face-to-face interviews that all require significant staff resources to administer), and (f) there are several established online organizations (e.g. SurveyMonkey) which specialize in providing support to researchers conducting online surveys (e.g. technical support, data-bases containing collections of pre-tested survey questions, survey templates for a variety of types of research surveys, data storage, descriptive data analysis, and access to "representative" samples from various population of interest to researchers) at costs that are appropriate for the budgets of researchers in both academic and applied settings.[2,3,17]

Despite all of the advantages online surveys provide, researchers must be aware that the research samples acquired through online surveys may not be "representative" of the population of interest. This lack of "representativeness" may be due to several factors including: (a) despite the rapid expansion of the Internet, there is still a large percentage of people (especially in poorer and rural areas of the population) who don't have access to the Internet and would therefore have no opportunity to be selected for inclusion in the research sample,[3,12] (b) there are individuals in society (e.g. the less educated and elderly) who may not have the technical expertise to complete an online survey,[12] (c) although individuals within the population of interest may have Internet access, they may not have the technology (e.g. software, web browser) necessary to access, view, and/or open survey attachments necessary to complete an online survey,[3,17] and (d) a majority of online surveys are conducted using non-probability methods of sampling.[3,6,17]

A major reason why researchers often use non-probability sampling methods when they conduct an online survey is that they typically do not have access to (or an ability to randomly generate) a list of the e-mail addresses for all the members of a population of interest.[17] Without being able to identify (and therefore access) all members of a population of interest, researchers are unable to use probability methods of sampling or determine the probability that an individual population member will be selected for inclusion in the research sample. As a result, researchers use a variety of non-probability sampling methods to acquire a research sample when conducting an online survey. These methods of non-probability sampling include: (a) site-specific surveys, (b) human subjects site surveys, (c) "pop-up" surveys, and (d) social network site surveys.

To acquire a research sample through a non-probability method of sampling, researchers can post a survey on a specific website and only those individuals who access the website would have the opportunity to participate in the research[2,12,17] (e.g. a Health Psychologist could place a link to an online survey assessing the attitudes of parents toward the nutritional value of school lunches on the websites of the schools located within a local school district. Those parents who access these websites would have the opportunity to complete the online survey.). Researchers can also post surveys on Internet sites devoted to conducting human subjects research which rely on individuals who have access to these sites to volunteer to complete the survey (e.g. College/University researchers can post links to online surveys on research sites that can be accessed by student members of the "human subjects research pool" who can volunteer to complete surveys and to participate in research studies in exchange for extra course credit). Researchers can also post "pop-up" surveys online.[17] These "pop-up" surveys (much like "pop-up" advertisements) will open when individuals open their web browsers to access the Internet. These "pop-up" style surveys typically contain a few items, require limited time to complete, and can provide a quick assessment of the attitudes and opinions of individuals (who respond to the "pop-up" survey) toward a specific topic of interest to researchers (e.g. a Political Psychologist could post a quick 2-item "pop-up" survey online to assess peoples' attitudes toward Obama Care and President Obama's job performance). Finally, researchers can post links to their online surveys on social media sites[2,3,17] (e.g. Facebook, Twitter, LinkedIn, etc.). Individuals who self-select to become members of these social media sites would have the opportunity to participate in the study. The members of the social media sites would also have the opportunity to share the link to the survey with other individuals ("network of friends") who they feel may be interested in participating in the research study (e.g. a Psychologist interested in studying perceptions of the use of animals as subjects in research to test whether new medications, cosmetic products, and food additives are healthy for human consumption, posted a survey on his Facebook page. He shared the survey with his "network of friends" and encouraged those in his network to share the survey with all of the members of their "networks of friends."). As can be seen from these examples, the sampling techniques associated with online surveys are often non-probability methods of sampling.

Although researchers often rely on non-probability methods of sampling, there are ways in which researchers conducting an online survey can use probability methods of sampling to acquire a "representative" research sample. First, researchers can acquire their research samples through organizations and professional associations that provide researchers with access to a list of the e-mail addresses of all of their members (i.e. population).[17] While some organizations and professional associations provide researchers with free access to their membership for research purposes, others will charge researchers a fee to acquire the e-mail address list of their members. Having acquired access to all population members, researchers can use probability methods of sampling to acquire a random sample of e-mail addresses from the population of interest (and a "representative" sample of population members). Population members selected for inclusion in the research sample would then be given access to the online survey. Second, if a population of interest is confined to a specific geographic region, researchers can use methods of sampling that allow them to access all the members of a population (e.g. random digit dialing; address-based sampling) to acquire a sample.[17] Those population members selected for inclusion in the sample would then be given access to the online survey. To increase the survey response rate (and the "representativeness" of the research sample), researchers can provide sample members with the technology necessary to complete the online survey[3] or allow sample members without Internet access or unable to use the Internet to complete the survey through traditional survey methods (e.g. mail, telephone, face-to-face interview). When analyzing the survey results, the researchers must ensure that differences in survey responses are not a result of the differences in the survey method (i.e. online vs. off-line) used to collect sample member responses.[12] Finally, researchers can access "representative" samples of individuals drawn from populations of interest through online companies that specialize in survey development and management (e.g. SurveyMonkey). These companies use sound, scientific methods of sampling to acquire "representative" samples of individuals willing to complete research surveys, and continuously update these samples over time to ensure they remain "representative" of the populations.[2,3,17] For a fee, researchers can then access a "representative" sample from a population of interest and have the members of the sample complete their online survey. In all 3 of the above examples of probability sampling, every member of the population has an opportunity to be selected for inclusion in the research sample and the sampling techniques increase the likelihood that the acquired research sample will be "representative" of the population of interest.

EXERCISE 5A

Probability Methods of Sampling

To acquire a "representative" sample from a population of interest, psychologists rely on methods of sampling known as "probability" sampling. In "probability" sampling, all members of the population of interest have an equal opportunity to be selected for inclusion in the research sample and are selected through a process known as "random selection." Below are 11 scenarios describing research being conducted by psychologists. For each of the scenarios, please identify the method of "probability" sampling being used by the psychologist from the list of probability sampling methods below and write your answer in the space provided.

Cluster Sample	Random Digit Dialing	Simple Random Sample
Multi-Stage Sample	Random Numbers Table	Stratified Random Sample
Panel Sample	Reliable Sample	Systematic Random Sample
Proportionate Sample	Representative Sample	

01. An Industrial-Organizational Psychologist is excited about the quality of the sample he has acquired for his study on employee work motivation after learning that his sample consists of employees whose characteristics match those of employees in his population of interest (i.e. employees of a large manufacturing company).

> **Sampling Method =**

02. To examine the level of fear of violent crime in the major cities of the U.S. (e.g. New York, Los Angeles, Chicago), a team of Social Psychologists randomly select 12 cities from a list of the 1,000 largest cities in the U.S. All residents of the 12 selected cities are then eligible to be surveyed by the team of Social Psychologists about their fear of violent crime.

> **Sampling Method =**

03. An Experimental Psychologist studying the effects of hunger on learning, assigns each of the 100 rats in her lab a number from 1–100. She uses a table of numbers in a statistics book to randomly select 50 numbers between 1–100. The rats assigned to these numbers will be members of her research sample. She will then assign 25 rats to a control group (non-food deprived) and 25 rats to an experimental group (food deprived).

Sampling Method =

04. To assess the impact of economic conditions on prices being paid for groceries, a Consumer Psychologist randomly selects a sample of shoppers from a grocery store. The psychologist contacts the shoppers in her sample each week for 3 consecutive weeks and asks how much money they each spent on groceries and how much they each paid for specific grocery items.

Sampling Method =

05. A Community Psychologist studying attitudes toward a new chemical plant being built in a small town decides to conduct a door-to-door survey at 25 homes in the town. He randomly selects 4 neighborhoods in the town. Then, he randomly selects 10 streets located in these 4 neighborhoods. He then randomly selects 5 blocks located along these 10 streets. Next, he randomly selects 25 homes located on these 5 blocks. Finally, he then conducts a door-to-door survey at these 25 randomly selected homes.

Sampling Method =

06. A Media Psychologist studying attitudes toward the news coverage of a local labor strike selects the local area code (914) and prefix 986 and randomly calls 100 individuals living within the area code and asks them their attitudes toward the news coverage of the strike.

Sampling Method =

07. In an effort to provide his audience with a "representative" view of the types of problems that can occur in relationships, a Counseling Psychologist selects every 10th caller who calls in to the radio station for relationship advice during her afternoon radio program.

Sampling Method =

08. A Cognitive Psychologist places the names of all 30 children enrolled in a preschool class in a bowl. She then randomly selects the names of 15 of the children from the bowl. The 15 children selected will take part in a study of language skills in preschool-age children.

> **Sampling Method =**

09. A Developmental Psychologist is excited about the quality of the sample she acquired for her study on the influence of the temperament of 2-year-old children (i.e. "terrible 2's") on parental stress levels. Her research sample containing 25 mothers of 2-year-old infants has produced results that are consistent over time and multiple measurements and have allowed her to make accurate predictions about parental stress levels for the population of mothers with 2-year-old infants.

> **Sampling Method =**

10. To study the effects of income on quality of life within a community, a Health Psychologist divides the community into 3 socioeconomic status groups (i.e. High SES, Middle SES, and Low SES). He then randomly selects 50 residents of the community from each of the 3 SES groups and has the 150 selected residents complete a survey to assess their quality of life.

> **Sampling Method =**

11. A Quantitative Psychologist studying work-related accidents in manufacturing companies purposefully acquires a research sample containing 35% steel plants, 23% chemical plants, and 42% textile plants to ensure that his research sample accurately reflects the population of manufacturing companies in the U.S.

> **Sampling Method =**

EXERCISE 5B

Non-Probability Methods of Sampling

To acquire a research sample from a population of interest, psychologists frequently rely on methods of sampling known as "non-probability" sampling. In "non-probability" sampling, rather than selecting members of the sample through the process of "random selection," sample members are selected on the basis of availability, convenience, the purpose of the research, or through a process of self-selection. Below are 19 scenarios describing research being conducted by psychologists. For each scenario, please identify the method of "non-probability" sampling being used by the psychologists from the list of non-probability sampling methods below and write your answer in the space provided.

Accidental Sample	Disconfirming Case Sample	Non-Representative Sample
Biased Sample	Disproportionate Sample	Opportunistic Sample
Cohort Sample	Expert Sample	Quota Sample
Confirming Case Sample	Heterogeneity Sample	Snowball Sample
Convenience Sample	Homogeneity Sample	Trend Sample
Criterion Sample	Judgment Sample	Volunteer Sample
Deviant Case Sample	Modal Instance Sample	

01. To study the extremes of human intelligence, a Personality Psychologist acquires a research sample composed of individuals who, based on their IQ scores, fall specifically within either the top 1% or bottom 1% of the adult population with respect to intelligence.

> **Sampling Method =**

02. To determine what types of stores to put in a newly developed shopping mall, a Consumer Psychologist purposefully recruits a diverse sample of individuals from the community to be interviewed about their shopping behavior and store preferences.

> **Sampling Method =**

03. While traveling to a research conference, a Psychologist shares a cab with a woman whose husband recently died. The psychologist recruits the woman to participate in a study she is conducting on the strategies individuals use to cope with the loss of a spouse.

> **Sampling Method =**

04. A School Psychologist conducting a study on the relationship between parental involvement and student's academic performance decides she wants to select 30 parents of students at the school for her research sample. To acquire her 30 parents, she recruits the first 15 men and first 15 women who show up at the first PTA meeting of the school year for her sample.

Sampling Method =

05. To acquire a research sample for her study on the effects of children on marital satisfaction, a Developmental Psychologist places an advertisement in the local newspaper that states, "to be eligible to participate in the research study, you must be married and have a minimum of 2 children currently living with you in your home."

Sampling Method =

06. An Industrial-Organizational Psychologist is interested in conducting a study of employee attitudes toward the company who requires them to work on Thanksgiving. Although 78% of employees at the company work full-time and 22% work part-time, the I/O psychologist decides to recruit an equal number of full- and part-time employees for her research sample.

Sampling Method =

07. A Social Psychologist conducting a study on the level of altruism (i.e. helping behavior) in a community, realizes that he will not be able to draw any meaningful conclusions about the community when he discovers that the characteristics of the individuals in his sample do not closely match those found in the population of community residents.

Sampling Method =

08. A Psychologist who wants to prove women are more intelligent than men recruits female members of her research sample from a local Mensa organization (i.e. members are required to have an IQ > 200) and recruits male members of her sample from the local community.

Sampling Method =

09. A Research Psychologist working at a University has only 1 week left to collect data for a research study he plans on submitting for presentation at an upcoming research conference. To collect the necessary data, he runs frantically around the University campus asking any living, breathing student to participate in his study and complete his research survey.

Sampling Method =

10. After participating in a study on athletic performance in pressure situations, several athletes provide the Sports Psychologist conducting the study with names of other athletes who want to participate in the study. The athletes referred by study participants also provide the Sports Psychologists with referrals of additional athletes after they participate in the research study. The volume of referrals allows the Psychologist to quickly acquire a large research sample.

Sampling Method =

11. In a recent vote, 70% of city residents supported construction of a new international airport, 10% supported construction of a new domestic airport, and 20% did not support construction of a new airport. To study the demographic profile of the "typical" voter, an Experimental Psychologist recruited residents who voted to support construction of a new international airport to complete a survey designed to collect demographic information.

Sampling Method =

12. A Counseling Psychologist is interested in conducting a study on the strategies women use to cope with a diagnosis of breast cancer. Having provided counseling to women diagnosed with breast cancer for 20 years, and having several women in her own family diagnosed with breast cancer, the psychologist uses her knowledge and her personal experiences to select a sample of 100 women who she feels are "representative" of the population of women who have been diagnosed with breast cancer.

Sampling Method =

13. A Military Psychologist examined the physical health, psychological health, and fitness for duty of a sample of soldiers who were wounded during a combat mission. The psychologist conducted the health and fitness for duty assessments each month for an entire year after the soldiers were wounded. The psychologists compared these assessment results to those of a sample of soldiers who had not been wounded in combat to determine how being wounded affects the physical health, psychological health, and fitness for duty of soldiers over time.

Sampling Method =

14. To study the violent crime rate in the U.S., a team of Forensic Psychologists collects violent crime statistics from a sample of 10 U.S. cities. In each subsequent year, the psychologists select 10 different U.S. cities to be in the research sample. The psychologists use the data from the multiple samples of U.S. cities collected over multiple years to estimate whether the violent crime rate in the U.S. is increasing or decreasing over time.

Sampling Method =

15. After conducting a study of the effectiveness of a new anti-depressant medication, a Clinical Psychologist identifies 10 individuals in her research sample for whom the new medication did not work as predicted. She then conducts additional research on these 10 individuals to determine whether factors related to the participants, the medication, research procedures, or experimental error led to the medication not working as predicted for these 10 individuals.

> **Sampling Method =**

16. To study the extent to which an undergraduate degree in Psychology prepares students for a career in the field, an Educational Psychologist recruits a sample of the top minds from the worlds of education, business, and mental health. The psychologist gives them the task of evaluating current Psychology programs and recommending how these programs can be changed to ensure students are adequately prepared for a career in the field of Psychology.

> **Sampling Method =**

17. A Community Psychologist interested in studying homelessness, visits locations in a large city where homeless individuals come in hopes of receiving food and shelter (e.g. missions, churches). The psychologist approaches individuals at these locations and tries to recruit them to participate in his study. His final sample contains only those homeless individuals who volunteer to participate in his research study.

> **Sampling Method =**

18. A Research Psychologist conducting a study on the effectiveness of a new weight loss drug, selects a sample of laboratory rats whose genetics have been controlled by the breeder. The psychologist selected a genetically-controlled sample of rats to ensure the rats in her sample were as identical as possible and allow her to control for the influence of genetic influences on the results of her test of the new weight loss drug.

> **Sampling Method =**

19. While conducting research on paranormal phenomena, a Parapsychologist discovers articles in the local newspaper that describe a man who claims to be able to foresee the future and a woman who claims to communicate with the dead. The Parapsychologist contacts the man and woman and recruits them to take part in a study he is conducting on psychic abilities.

> **Sampling Method =**

EXERCISE 5C

How "Representative" is My Sample?

In order to draw accurate conclusions about a population of interest, psychologists must acquire samples that are "representative" of the population when conducting research. A variety of sampling techniques are used by psychologists to acquire research samples. However, these sampling techniques are not all equally effective in acquiring a "representative" sample. Below are 12 scenarios describing the sampling techniques used by psychologists to acquire a research sample. For each scenario, please identify why the sampling technique used by the psychologist is unlikely to acquire a "representative" sample and write your response in the space provided.

01. A Consumer Psychologist has been hired by a company to study consumer attitudes toward a new barbecue sauce that it has developed. The Consumer Psychologist goes to shopping malls throughout New York and New Jersey and approaches men who appear to be between the ages of 40–55 (i.e. the traditional member of a household who cooks meat on a barbecue grill) and asks them if they would be willing to participate in a research study on a new style of barbecue sauce. Those men who are willing to participate in the study are taken to a room in the mall where they are asked to taste the new barbecue sauce and to give the psychologist a rating as to how likely they would be to buy the new barbecue sauce if it were available in stores and restaurants. Based on his results, the psychologist will make a recommendation to the company as to whether there is enough consumer interest in the product to sell it in stores and restaurants throughout the U.S.

+---+
| **Why is the sample unlikely to be "representative"?** |
| |
| |
| |
| |
| |
| |
| |
| |
| |
| |
+---+

02. To study the attitudes of community residents toward a tax increase proposed by the Mayor and members of the City Council, a Community Psychologist goes to a local Starbucks one morning and interviews randomly selected customers who are standing in line to get coffee about their attitudes toward the Mayor's proposed tax increase.

Why is the sample unlikely to be "representative"?

03. To assess customer opinions of the quality of service being provided by the servers at a local restaurant, an Industrial-Organizational Psychologist has the manager of the restaurant place "Customer Comment" cards at each table and have servers encourage their customers to fill out the "Customer Comment" cards and return them to the cashier when they pay their bill.

Why is the sample unlikely to be "representative"?

04. To curb the growing rate of crime in a community, the Chief of Police proposes a 10:00 p.m. curfew be enforced for all residents. To study the attitudes of community residents toward the proposed curfew, a Research Psychologist conducts a door-to-door survey of homes in the community from 9:00 a.m.–5:00 p.m., Monday thru Friday, for a 1-week period of time.

Why is the sample unlikely to be "representative"?

05. The night before an important statewide political election, a Political Psychologist hired to do political polling for a Republican congressional candidate, stands on the sidewalk outside of campaign headquarters and asks the first 50 people who walk past him whether they are going to vote for his candidate in tomorrow's election. He uses the results from his sample to estimate the likely outcome of the vote in the election.

Why is the sample unlikely to be "representative"?

06. To assess employee attitudes toward the pay, benefits, and promotion opportunities available at a telemarketing call center, a Research Psychologist distributes a paper-and-pencil survey to all employees working the 4:00 p.m.–midnight shift and instructs the employees to return the completed surveys to their immediate supervisors.

Why is the sample unlikely to be "representative"?

---

07. A Forensic Psychologist uses the Internet to find the mailing addresses for all 345 registered sex offenders in the community. He mails each registered offender a survey asking them to rate the extent to which they feel they are likely to reoffend in the future. The psychologist receives 26 surveys back and uses the results to publish an article in which he generalizes the results of his sample to the population of registered sex offenders living in the U.S.

Why is the sample unlikely to be "representative"?

---

08. A Counseling Psychologist conducting a research study on adult survivors of child abuse has only 25 adults in her research sample after the first year of the study. In an attempt to recruit additional participants, she puts an ad in the local paper stating: "Recruiting adult survivors of child abuse to participate in a research study. All participants will receive $500 for taking part in the study. Within a day of the ad running in the paper, the psychologist had acquired the 100 participants she needed to test her research hypotheses and complete the study.

Why is the sample unlikely to be "representative"?

09. To estimate how his class performed on a statistics exam, a Statistician grades the exams of the 15 students who sit in the front row of the classroom and uses the average grade from the sample of 15 students to estimate the average exam score for his entire class of 90 students.

Why is the sample unlikely to be "representative"?

10. A Social Psychologist conducts a study to test a hypothesis that the reason so many women in the city where she lives are single is that there is a lack of quality men in the city. To test her hypothesis, she attends a speed dating event. During the event, she has 6 minute "dates" with 10 different men in 1 hour. At the end of each date, she gives a "quality" rating based on the man's potential as a romantic partner. She uses the "quality" ratings from her sample of "dates" to draw a conclusion about the "quality" of the men available in the city.

Why is the sample unlikely to be "representative"?

11. A Psychologist is hired by an entertainment magazine to identify the sexiest female celebrity alive. The psychologist provides readers with a phone number and for only $3.99 a minute for U.S. callers and $9.99 a minute for International callers, readers can vote for as many as 5 female celebrities. The psychologist uses the results from his sample to identify Jamie Lee Curtis (star of "Halloween") as the world's choice for sexiest female celebrity alive.

Why is the sample unlikely to be "representative"?

12. A Research Psychologist is hired by an attorney defending a client in a death penalty case to determine the likelihood a jury would vote to sentence her client to death if he is convicted of murder. The psychologist begins by calling telephone numbers in the order they are listed in the telephone book for the city where the trial will occur, and continues calling telephone numbers until 50 people have answered his calls. The psychologist asks the 50 people who answer his calls whether they each could vote for the death penalty if they were a member of a jury that had found a defendant guilty of murder. The psychologist uses the results of her telephone survey to estimate the likelihood that a jury selected from the city where the trial will occur would vote for the death penalty if the attorney's client is found guilty of murder.

Why is the sample unlikely to be "representative"?

References

1. Trochim, W. M. (2006). Sampling terminology. *The Research Methods Knowledge Base* (2nd ed.). Retrieved from http://www.socialresearchmethods.net/kb/sampterm.php.

2. Cozby, P. C., & Bates, S. C. (2011). *Methods in behavioral research.* (11th ed.). New York, NY: McGraw-Hill Publishers.

3. Passer, M. W. (2013). *Research methods: Concepts and connections.* New York, NY: Worth Publishers.

4. Jackson, S. L. (2014). *Research methods: A modular approach* (3rd ed.). Stamford, CT: Cengage Learning.

5. Gravetter, F. J., & Wallnau, L. B. (2012). *Statistics for the behavioral sciences* (9th ed.). Belmont, CA: Wadsworth-Cengage Learning.

6. Bordens, K. S., & Abbot, B. B. (2011). *Research design and methods: A process approach* (8th ed.). Boston, MA: McGraw-Hill Publishers.

7. OECD. (2004). Over-coverage. *Glossary of Statistical Terms*. Retrieved from http://stats.oecd.org/glossary/detail.asp?ID=4545.

8. OECD. (2005). Under-coverage. *Glossary of Statistical Terms*. Retrieved from http://stats.Oecd.org/glossary/detail.asp?ID=5069.

9. Marshall, M. N. (1996). Sampling for qualitative research. *Family Practice, 13*(6), 522–525.

10. Rosnow, R. L., & Rosenthal, R. (2012). *Beginning behavioral research: A conceptual primer* (7th ed.). Boston, MA: Pearson Publishers.

11. Daniel, J. N. (2011). *Sampling essentials: Practical guidelines for making sampling choices.* Thousand Oaks, CA: Sage Publishers.

12. Beins, B. C. (2012). *Research methods: A tool for life* (3rd ed.). Boston, MA: Pearson Publishers.

13. Teddlie, C., & Yu, F. (2007). Mixed methods sampling: A typology with examples. *Journal of Mixed Methods Research, 1*(1), 77–100.

14. Onwuegbuzie, A. J., & Collins, K. M. T. (2007). A typology of mixed methods sampling Designs in social science research. *The Qualitative Report, 12*(2), 281–316.

15. Ruspini, E. (1999). Longitudinal research and the analysis of social change. *Quality and Quantity, 33*, 219–227.

16. Palmquist, R. (1999). Survey methods. *Research Methods*. Retrieved from http://www.ischool.utexas.edu/~palmquis/courses/survey.html.

17. Schonlau, M., Fricker, R. D., & Elliott, M. N. (2002). *Conducting research via e-mail and the web.* Santa Monica, CA: RAND Corporation.

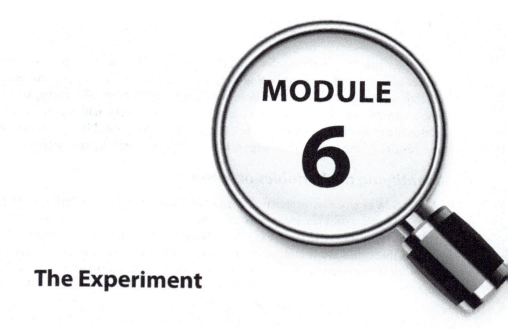

MODULE

6

The Experiment

Psychologists who conduct psychological research are often motivated by a desire to get answers to the questions of "why?" Specifically, psychologists want answers to questions such as: (a) Why do people act the way they do? (b) Why do people think the way they do? (c) Why are some people more influenced by the people and the events in their environment than others? (d) Why do some people respond more favorably to planned or self-initiated efforts to change behavior or mental processes than others? and (e) Why do some people respond more favorably to therapeutic and educational interventions designed to improve physical, psychological, and emotional well-being than others. To answer these questions of "why," psychologists must be able to identify the causes of human behavior and mental processes. In order to identify causes of behavior and mental processes, psychologists conducting psychological research must utilize the one type of research design that allows for a causal conclusion to be drawn. This type of research design is known as "the experiment."[1,2,3]

Preliminary Activities Prior to Conducting an Experiment

Before psychologists can conduct an experiment, they must complete several preliminary activities. They must first come up with an idea for an experiment. Ideas for research can come from both personal and professional sources. Personal sources of research ideas include personal experiences, our observations of the world, and problems in one's life that need to be solved.[4,5,6] Professional sources of research ideas include the research literature, scientific theories, research agenda of professional associations and societies, calls for research from grant-funding agencies, recommendations from colleagues, and one's own prior research.[2,4,6] After selecting an idea for an experiment, the next activity for psychologists is to conduct a review of the research literature to determine if prior research exists which specifically examined their idea for an experiment.[1,4,6] If prior research does exist, psychologists should examine the methods used by prior researchers and the knowledge learned from the research. Based on their review of the research literature, psychologists must then design a research study that will: (a) attempt to replicate the results of prior research, (b) use a new methodology to study the idea of interest, or (c) "fill in gaps" in the research by examining a dimension or element of the idea of interest not previously studied by researchers.[2,4,7] Regardless of the specific focus of the research, the primary goal is to add new knowledge to the existing research literature.[8]

After selecting a research idea and reviewing the research literature, psychologists must then decide upon a specific 'research question'[5] that they would like to design an experiment to answer. To answer their research questions experimentally, psychologists must: (a) identify the variables of interest, (b) define precisely how each variable of interest will be measured in the experiment, (c) develop a research hypothesis that clearly states the predicted outcome of the experiment, and (d) establish criteria that will be used to determine whether the results of the experiment support (or fail to support) the research hypothesis.

Identifying the Variables of Interest

A variable is any characteristic of a person, object, or event that can change (vary) or assume multiple values.[1,2,4] Some variables are quantitative in nature (i.e. can assume multiple numerical values) while other variables are qualitative in nature (i.e. can assume multiple non-numerical categorical values).[4,6,7] Some examples of variables that are quantitative in nature would include height, IQ, annual income, number of hospitalizations for depression, and number of errors made by a rat running a maze. Quantitative variables can be either discrete or continuous.[6,9] A discrete variable is one that can assume multiple numerical values which are whole numbers (e.g. number of children, number of therapy sessions attended, number of sexual partners). A continuous variable can assume multiple numerical values which may contain fractional or decimal values (e.g. time required to run a marathon, amount of weight lost after bariatric surgery, temperature inside a steel manufacturing plant). Some examples of variables that would be qualitative in nature include political affiliation (Republican, Democrat, Independent), gender (Male, Female), marital status (Single, Married, Separated), and underwear preference (Boxers, Briefs, Thongs, None).

As examples of the types of research questions and variables of interest to psychologists, a Developmental Psychologist conducting an experiment to answer the research question, "Does consuming sugar cause the activity level of children to increase?" would want to know if there is a "causal relationship" between the consumption of sugar and level of activity, while a professor of Psychology conducting an experiment to answer the research question, "Will adding humor to my class lectures cause student exam scores to increase?" would want to know whether a causal relationship exists between lecture content and exam performance. Since the variables of interest can assume multiple quantitative or qualitative values, psychologists must decide how they will measure each variable of interest during the experiment.

Defining the Variables of Interest

Once psychologists have selected a research question to examine and identified their variables of interest, they must then decide how each variable will be defined and measured in the experiment. The definitions used to describe how variables will be measured during an experiment are referred to as "operational definitions."[1,2,4] Operational definitions serve several functions which include: (a) providing all members of the research staff with a common understanding of the research variables,[1,4,5] (b) removing all uncertainty from the processes used to measure the research variables,[1,4] (c) increasing the consistency (or reliability) of the measurements of the research variables,[6,8] (d) providing researchers who want to replicate or build upon the results of the experiment precise instructions as to how to measure the research variables,[1,4,8] and (e) determining the precise dimensions (or "boundaries") of the population to which results of the experiment would be applicable (i.e. "generalize").[5,7,8] Below are examples of two research questions as they might be "operationalized" by psychologists.

Research Question

Does consuming sugar cause the activity level of children to increase?

Does consuming sugar (i.e. consuming 1 king-size Snickers candy bar and a 20-ounce bottle of Mountain Dew soda pop) cause the activity level (i.e. a rating on a 7-point scale: 1 = Extremely Inactive; 7 = Extremely Hyperactive provided by a child's pre-school teacher) of children (i.e. children ages 4–5 enrolled in pre-school) to increase (i.e. be higher than a comparison group of children ages 4–5 enrolled in pre-school who do not consume sugar).

Research Question

Will adding humor to my class lectures cause student exam scores to increase?

Will adding humor (i.e. jokes, funny stories, amusing personal anecdotes) to my class lectures (i.e. lectures in a college-level Research Methods course) cause student (i.e. Psychology majors enrolled in a college-level Research Methods course) exam scores (i.e. scores on the mid-term exam for the course) to increase (i.e. be higher than a comparison group of Psychology majors enrolled in a college-level Research Methods course whose class lectures contain no humor).

Stating the Research Hypotheses

Once psychologists have selected a research question, reviewed the research literature, identified their research variables, and operationally defined the research variables, they are now ready to formally state their research hypothesis. A hypothesis is a formal statement of the predicted relationship between the research variables. Specifically, it is a statement of the predicted outcome of an experiment.[4,5,6] A hypothesis is often referred to as an "educated guess" because the outcome predicted by psychologists is often based on a review of the results of prior research related to their research question. A quality research hypothesis should be: (a) clearly stated, (b) testable, and (c) falsifiable (i.e. there must be an opportunity for the results of an experiment to support, or fail to support, the research hypothesis).[2,3,6] In many cases, psychologists will use an "if...then" format when writing research hypothesis[1,6,10] (i.e. if certain conditions are present, then a specific outcome will occur). Below are examples of two research hypotheses as they might be stated by psychologists using an "if...then" format.

Research Question

Does consuming sugar cause the activity level of children to increase?

If pre-school age children consume sugar, then they will exhibit a significantly higher level of activity at school than pre-school age children who do not consume sugar.

Research Question

Will adding humor to my class lectures cause student exam scores to increase?

If college students listen to lectures containing humor, then they will score significantly higher on a class exam than college students who listen to lectures containing no humor.

Establishing Criteria to Test the Research Hypothesis

In order to determine whether the results of an experiment support (or fail to support) a research hypothesis, psychologists must establish the test criteria they will use to evaluate the results of their experiment. This criteria is established through a process known as "hypothesis testing."[3,7,9] The first step in the "hypothesis testing" process is to develop competing hypothesis statements known as the null and alternative hypotheses.[3,7,9] The null hypothesis is a statement predicting no causal relationship between the research variables. By contrast, the alternative hypothesis is a statement predicting that a causal relationship exists between the research variables. Since, the null hypothesis serves as the focus of the "hypothesis testing" process, the task for psychologists is to determine whether the results of their experiment support (or fail to support) the null hypothesis. Below are two examples of null and alternative hypotheses as they may be stated by psychologists conducting experiments.

Research Question

Does consuming sugar cause the activity level of children to increase?

Null Hypothesis

Pre-school age children who consume sugar will exhibit a level of activity at school that is not significantly different from pre-school age children who do not consume sugar.

Alternative Hypothesis

Pre-school age children who consumer sugar will exhibit a significantly higher level of activity at school than pre-school age children who do not consume sugar.

Research Question

Will adding humor to my class lectures cause student exam scores to increase?

Null Hypothesis

College students who listen to lectures containing humor will have exam scores that are not significantly different from college students who listen to lectures containing no humor.

Alternative Hypothesis

College students who listen to lectures containing humor will score significantly higher on a class exam than college students who listen to lectures containing no humor.

The second step in the "hypothesis testing" process is to establish the criteria that will be used to determine if the experimental results support (or fail to support) the null hypothesis. To establish this criteria, psychologists will need to make three important decisions. First, they will have to decide what statistical analysis they will use to analyze the results of the experiment. The statistical analysis chosen by the psychologists will be based on the goals of the research and the scales of measurement used to measure the research variables.[9] Second, they must decide on a level of confidence they would like to have when evaluating the results of their experiment.[3,7,9] Since all experiments are subject to potential sources of error (e.g. measurement error, biased or non-representative sample, uncontrolled factors in the experimental environment), psychologists can never be 100% confident in the accuracy of their evaluation of the results of the experiment. Instead, psychologists establish criteria that allow them to be 95% or 99% confident. At a 95% "confidence level," psychologists would be 95% confident in their evaluation of the relationship between the research variables and have a 5% chance of making a Type 1 error (i.e. concluding there is a causal relationship between the research variables when no causal relationship actually exists). By comparison, at a 99% "confidence level," psychologists would be 99% confident in their evaluation of the relationship between the research variables and have only a 1% chance of making a Type 1 error.[3,4,7,9] While there is less chance of a Type 1 error at the 99% "confidence level," the trade-off is that a higher criteria must be met in order to conclude that the results of the experiment support the existence of a causal relationship between the research variables. Third, psychologists must decide how many individuals they will select for inclusion in their research sample to ensure that: (a) their sample is "representative" of the population of interest and (b) will provide a valid assessment of the relationship between the research variables.[4,6,9]

After selecting the statistical analysis they will use to analyze their experimental data, a level of confidence, and a sample size, psychologists can then consult statistical tables created by statisticians to determine the exact value of the test criteria (i.e. the "critical value") they will use to determine if the results of the experiment support (or fail to support) the null hypothesis.[9] To ensure they conduct an objective and ethical evaluation of the relationship that exists between the research variables, psychologists must complete steps 1 and 2 of the "hypothesis testing" process prior to conducting their experiment and collecting their experimental data. Psychologists will then complete the final 2 steps of the "hypothesis testing" process after they have collected their experimental data.

Developing a Strategy to Acquire the Research Sample

The final preliminary activity psychologists need to complete before conducting an experiment is to decide what method of sampling will be used to acquire a research sample that is "representative"[4,6,11] of the population and sufficient in size to provide a valid assessment of the relationship that exists between the research variables.[9,12] When conducting an experiment, the research sample should be acquired through a "probability" method of sampling[4,11,13] to ensure that all members of the population of interest have an equal chance of being selected for inclusion in the research sample and that they are selected through a process of "random selection." All members of the research sample must also meet the eligibility criteria established by the psychologists (i.e. they must fall within the target "sampling frame")[4,6,13] and have the ability to provide informed consent to participate in the experiment. Psychologists must also decide at this time what methods they are going to use to advertise the study and what (if any) incentives and/or compensation members of the research sample will receive in exchange for participating in the experiment. The preliminary activities psychologists must complete prior to conducting an experiment are summarized below.

Develop an Idea for an Experiment	Review the Research Literature	Select a Research Question to Answer
Identify the Research Variables	Operationally Define Research Variables	Develop and State Research Hypotheses
Establish Criteria to Test Research Hypotheses	Select a Desired Research Sample Size	Select a Method of Sampling to Acquire Research Sample

Conducting an Experiment

After completing all necessary preliminary activities, psychologists are ready to conduct their experiment. An experiment should be a well-planned and highly controlled investigation.[6,7] Members of the research staff should be trained to: (a) maintain objectivity, (b) exhibit precision and accuracy in measurement of research variables, (c) strictly adhere to the procedural protocol, (d) monitor and document potential sources of error throughout the experiment, and (e) behave in a highly professional and ethical manner.[2,3,4] For psychologists to conduct an experiment that allows them to determine with a high degree of confidence whether a causal relationship exists between the variables of interest, the experiment must possess 7 essential characteristics. These 7 essential characteristics are described below.

(1) Random Selection of Subjects

A valid assessment of the relationship between the variables of interest should begin with psychologists using a probability method of sampling to select members of the population for inclusion in the research sample.[4,11,13] Use of a probability method of sampling (e.g. simple random, systematic random, stratified random, cluster, panel, multi-stage), will ensure: (a) all members of the population of interest have an equal opportunity to be selected for inclusion in the research sample, (b) members of the research sample will be selected through a process of "random selection,"[5,11] and (c) the research sample is more likely to be representative and more likely to produce results that are generalizable to the population of interest. Below are two examples of how the "random selection" process might be used to acquire a research sample by psychologists conducting experiments.

Research Question

Does consuming sugar cause the activity level of children to increase?

The Developmental Psychologist will use a multi-stage method of sampling to acquire a research sample. First, the psychologist will use "cluster sampling" to select 10 pre-school classes from a list provided by the WV Department of Education of all pre-school classes within West Virginia. Psychologists will then assign each of the 10 selected pre-school classes a number between 1–10, place the numbers in a hat, and randomly select 3 classes. The psychologist will then create a list of the 60 children enrolled in these 3 classes and assign each child on the list a number between 1–60. Finally, the psychologist will use a random numbers table to randomly select 20 of these children for inclusion in the research sample.

Research Question

Will adding humor to my class lectures cause student exam scores to increase?

The Psychology professor will assign a number from 1–4 to the 4 sections of a Research Methods course she teaches. She will then place the numbers in a hat and randomly select 2 classes. The students enrolled in these two classes will be selected for inclusion in the research sample.

(2) Random Assignment to Groups

After using a process of random selection to acquire a sample that is representative of the population, psychologists should use a process of "random assignment" to assign members of the research sample to groups (i.e. "conditions"). In "random assignment," all members of the research sample have an equal opportunity to be assigned to any of the conditions in an experiment. The primary goals of "random assignment" are: (a) to assign participants to conditions in an unbiased manner and (b) to create groups of participants who are as equivalent as possible (preferably identical!).[1,2,4]

With respect to unbiased assignment to conditions, psychologists must ensure they are not intentionally or unintentionally assigning participants to conditions in a manner that unfairly increases the likelihood of achieving a desired experimental outcome.[14,15] For example, assume that an Industrial-Organizational Psychologist has developed a new program to teach individuals how to perform more professionally during a job interview. To test the effectiveness of his new program, he plans on having 10 individuals complete his program (i.e. "program group") and 10 individuals who do not complete his program (i.e. "control group") serve as a comparison group. He will then have all 20 individuals take part in a "mock job interview" and have an experienced interviewer rate their professionalism during the interview. If successful, his new program has the potential to be extremely profitable. Clearly, he has a vested interest in the outcome of his experiment! As an I-O Psychologist, he is aware of research indicating that individuals who are articulate (i.e. speak well) typically receive high ratings for professionalism in a job interview. If he were to use this knowledge and assign the 10 most articulate participants to his "program group" and the 10 least articulate participants to his "control group," he would have assigned his participants to conditions in a biased manner and unfairly increased the likelihood of achieving his desired outcome (i.e. supporting the effectiveness of his new program). Random assignment ensures that participants are assigned to conditions in an unbiased manner.

There are two main problems associated with the biased assignment of participants to the conditions in an experiment. First, if it is done intentionally by psychologists, it's unethical! An experiment should provide an unbiased assessment of the effectiveness of a treatment, program, or variable of interest. Second, whether intentional or not, psychologists who assign participants to conditions in a biased manner are introducing a source of error into the experiment which can lead to conclusions being drawn that are not valid.[4,5] This can result in members of society being exposed to treatments and/or programs that are ineffective (or harmful) or to information that is inaccurate and/or misleading.

With respect to the creation of equivalent groups of participants across the conditions in an experiment, creating equivalent groups can be a difficult task for psychologists given the wide range of variability (e.g. demographic, experiences, knowledge) found among members of most research samples. The process of "random assignment" theoretically creates equal groups by distributing this variability evenly across groups.[4,5,11] It is critical that all groups are equivalent at the outset of an experiment so that any differences between groups at the end of the study can be attributed to the effects of the research variables and are not simply a result of differences in the characteristics and/or composition of the groups.

(3) Manipulation of an Independent Variable

Once the psychologists have randomly assigned members of the research sample to groups, they will then introduce a variable into the experiment known as the "independent variable." The independent variable is a variable that is controlled or "manipulated" by psychologists to create different "experiences" for groups in an experiment.[2,4,5] The independent variable is also the main variable of interest in the experiment.[1] In a well-designed and controlled experiment, the independent variable should be the only thing allowed to vary across groups. If differences are then observed between groups, psychologists can conclude the independent variable is the cause of that difference.[2,3,4] When psychologists conduct an experiment in which their independent variable can be isolated as the cause of any significant differences between groups, the experiment is said to have "internal validity."[2,5,11] Experiments that have "internal validity" will produce results more likely to generalize to the larger population of interest.

An independent variable must have a minimum of two values (i.e. "levels").[4,5,7] As a result, experiments will involve a comparison of a minimum of 2 groups. Since independent variables can have more than two "levels," psychologists may also conduct experiments that compare the performance of more than two groups. While some independent variables used by psychologists are quantitative in nature[2,7] (i.e. the different levels of the independent variable represent different quantitative values of size, amount, or time), other independent variables are qualitative in nature[2,7] (i.e. different levels of the independent variable represent different non-quantitative, categorical values). Examples of quantitative independent variables could include the dosage level of a psychiatric drug (e.g. 0 mg, 5 mg, 10 mg), the amount of time allotted to memorize a list of 50 words (e.g. 0 minutes, 15 minutes, 30 minutes), and number of required therapy sessions in a program for the treatment of social anxiety (e.g. 0 sessions, 3 sessions, 5 sessions). Some examples of qualitative independent variables could include the type of therapy received for the treatment of major depression (e.g. no therapy, behavioral, cognitive), the type of reinforcement used to teach rats to complete a maze error-free (e.g. no reinforcement, positive, negative), and the style of presentation used to teach employees a new safety procedure (e.g. no presentation, video, lecture).

The process of "random assignment" used to assign members of the research sample to groups will also determine the "level" of the independent variable that members of the research sample will be exposed to during the experiment. The classic experimental design involves the comparison of 2 groups known as the "experimental" and "control" groups. The "experimental" group consists of members of the research sample who experience the treatment, intervention, or variable of interest to the psychologists conducting the experiment.[5,7,8] The experimental group in an experiment is often referred to as the "treatment" group. The "control" group consists of members of the research sample who do not experience the treatment, intervention, or variable of interest to the psychologists conducting the experiment.[5,7,8] Therefore, the classic experimental design involves the comparison of a "treated" and an "untreated" group of participants. If the experiment were well-designed and significant differences were observed between the groups, psychologists could conclude that the cause of these differences was the treatment, intervention, or variable of interest to the psychologists conducting the experiment. Below are two examples of independent variables (as well as the "levels" of the independent variables) as they might be defined by psychologists conducting experiments.

Research Question

Does consuming sugar cause the activity level of children to increase?

Independent Variable = Sugar Consumption

Level 1 (Experimental Group) = Sugar (i.e. 1 king-size Snickers candy bar and a 20-ounce Mountain Dew soda) will be consumed by pre-school age children

Level 2 (Control Group) = No sugar will be consumed by a comparison group of pre-school age children

Research Question

Will adding humor to my class lectures cause student exam scores to increase?

Independent Variable = Exposure to Humor

Level 1 (Experimental Group) = College students will listen to a professor's lectures that contain humor (i.e. jokes, funny stories, and amusing personal anecdotes)

Level 2 (Control Group) = A comparison group of college students will listen to a professor's lectures that contain no humor

(4) Measurement of One or More Dependent Variables

Once the psychologists have manipulated the independent variable to create different experiences for groups in an experiment, they will then introduce a variable into the experiment known as the "dependent variable." The dependent variable is a variable that is "measured" by psychologists to assess the influence of the independent variable in an experiment.[2,4,6] The dependent variable is measured by psychologists in order to determine whether there is a significant difference between the "experimental group" that is exposed to the treatment, intervention, or variable of interest to the psychologists and the "control group" who is not exposed to the treatment, intervention, or variable of interest. The name of the variable derives from the fact that its measured value "depends" on the influence of the independent variable.[1,2,3] The dependent variable in an experiment is often referred to as the "outcome" variable. When conducting an experiment, psychologists are not limited to assessing one dependent variable. The influence of the independent variable can be assessed through the measurement of multiple dependent variables.[1,4,7] To increase the likelihood the results of their experiment will generalize to the larger population of interest, psychologists must ensure they use reliable and valid methods of assessment (e.g. tests, scores, observations, ratings) to measure the dependent variable(s) in their experiment.[1,7] Below are two examples of dependent variables that psychologists conducting experiments could use to assess the influence of their independent variables.

Research Question

Does consuming sugar cause the activity level of children to increase?

Dependent Variable

A rating of a child's activity level at school on a 7-point scale (1 = Extremely Inactive; 7 = Extremely Hyperactive) provided by a child's pre-school teacher

Research Question

Will adding humor to my class lectures cause student exam scores to increase?

Dependent Variable

The score (0–100 points) earned by a college student on the mid-term examination of a college-level Research Methods course

(5) Control of Extraneous Variables

In a well-designed and controlled experiment, the independent variable manipulated by the psychologists should be the one thing that varies across groups. Any factor present during an experiment with the potential to influence the outcome of the study that has not been purposefully manipulated is known as an "extraneous variable."[1,2,8] Extraneous variables can be problematic for psychologists conducting experiments because they: (a) add a source of error into an experiment,[5] (b) can influence the outcome of an experiment,[2,5] and (c) can make it difficult for psychologists to accurately assess the true relationship between the independent and dependent variables.[5,6] In some cases, extraneous variables can influence the outcome of an experiment in such a way that psychologists conclude that there is a causal relationship between an independent and dependent variable when no causal relationship actually exists. Alternatively, extraneous variables can influence the outcome of an experiment in such a way that psychologists will conclude that there is no causal relationship between an independent and dependent variable when a causal relationship actually does exist.[2,5] These errors result from psychologists being unable to see the true relationship between the independent and dependent variables through the error (i.e. "noise")[16] created by the presence of an extraneous variable.

There are several types of "extraneous variables" that have the potential to influence the outcome of an experiment. Subject variables[6,8] are individual differences among participants that can influence the outcome of an experiment (e.g. motivations, health, emotions, demographics). Task variables[5,8] are characteristics associated with the task completed by the participants during an experiment that can influence the outcome of an experiment (e.g. clarity of the instructions, time allotted, difficulty level, individual vs. group). Experimental variables are characteristics associated with the psychologists and members of the research staff conducting the experiment[6] that can influence the outcome of an experiment (e.g. personal biases, demographics, personality, attention to detail). Situational variables are the characteristics associated with the experimental environment that can influence the outcome of an experiment[6] (e.g. noise, temperature, comfort, distractions). In the event any of these different types of extraneous variables are present during an experiment, psychologists must attempt to minimize the potential influence of these variables on the outcome of the experiment. Psychologists can attempt to minimize the influence of these extraneous variables through: (a) elimination,[1,6,7] (b) control, and (c) randomization.

The most effective method available to psychologists to minimize the potential effects of extraneous variables is to eliminate them.[1,6,7] One potential way for psychologists to identify and eliminate potential extraneous variables is to conduct a "pilot study" prior to running their actual experiment.[4,8] During a "pilot study," psychologists can observe all aspects of their experiment in action and identify and eliminate any factors in the experimental environment that could have an influence on the outcome of the experiment (e.g. rewrite unclear instructions, change the time allotted to complete an experimental task, repair experimental apparatus that are malfunctioning, control the lighting, temperature, and noise in the laboratory, write a detailed script for members of the research staff to follow when interacting with participants). Psychologists can also try to minimize the potential effects of extraneous variables through control and standardization.[1,4,5,7] The more psychologists standardize what groups "experience" during the experiment and control all aspects of the environment in which the experiment occurs, the less likely the outcome of the study will be influenced by factors other than the independent variable. This explains why most psychologists conduct their experiments in highly controlled laboratory settings and follow strict protocols to ensure the research "experience" for participants is as identical as possible. Finally, if psychologists are unable to eliminate or control potential effects of extraneous variables, they can rely on the process of "randomization" (i.e. random assignment) to distribute the effects of extraneous variables evenly across the groups in an experiment.[1,2,4,5]

No matter which method is used to minimize the potential effects of extraneous variables, psychologists and members of their research staff should continuously observe and monitor all aspects of the experiment for any unanticipated occurrences (e.g. participants, procedures, staff-participant interactions, experimental task, environmental factors) and make note of any factors they observe that have the potential to influence the outcome of the experiment. Psychologists can then use these observations to determine whether there is data from individual participants or entire experimental sessions that need to be excluded from the experiment due to the presence of extraneous variables. Below are examples of potential extraneous variables that could influence the outcomes of experiments conducted by psychologists.

Research Question

Does consuming sugar cause the activity level of children to increase?

Potential Extraneous Variables

Subject Variables = appetite size, ability to follow instructions, temperament

Task Variables = amount and types of sugar consumed, time allotted to consume sugar

Experimental Variables = teacher observation skills, attitudes toward individual children

Situational Variables = behavior of other children in the classroom, classroom management style, size and layout of the classroom environment

Research Question

Will adding humor to my class lectures cause student exam scores to increase?

Potential Extraneous Variables

Subject Variables = sense of humor, attentiveness in class, attitudes toward professor

Task Variables = type of exam (multiple choice, essay), time allotted to complete exam

Experimental Variables = relationship with individual students, varied lecture content/quality

Situational Variables = distractions in classroom environment (noise, temperature, lighting), level of stress in the classroom during the exam

(6) Elimination of Confounding Variables

A type of extraneous variable referred to as a "confounding" variable is the most problematic for psychologists conducting experiments. A confounding variable is a factor that has the potential to influence the outcome of an experiment that systematically varies across groups at the same time as the independent variable. In a well-designed and controlled experiment, psychologists will allow only 1 factor (i.e. the independent variable) associated with the "experiences" of the experimental and control groups to vary. If a confounding variable is present in an experiment, there are actually two differences between the "experiences" of the participants in the experimental and control groups; 1 intended difference (i.e. the independent variable) and 1 unintended difference (i.e. the confounding variable).[2,4,5,6] The problem the presence of a confounding variable in an experiment creates for psychologists is that when the results of an experiment indicate that there is a significant difference between the experimental and control groups on a dependent variable, psychologists are unable to determine whether the cause of the difference is the independent variable, the "confounding variable," or a combination of the variables.[4,8,11] As a result, the experiment will lack internal validity[5] and the psychologists will be: (a) unable to determine the true relationship between the independent and dependent variables and (b) more likely to draw erroneous conclusions about the true nature of the relationship that exists between the independent and dependent variables.

To prevent the outcome of an experiment from being influenced by the presence of a "confounding variable," psychologists can: (a) eliminate any confounding variables that may be observed during a "pilot study"[4,8] or identified by psychologists and research staff during a pre-experiment review of the procedures that would be used during the experiment or (b) through using a controlled environment, standardized procedures, and random assignment to minimize participant differences between groups as well as differences between the research "experiences" of participants during the experiment.[2,4,5] Even after their experiment has been completed, the psychologists should conduct a post-experiment review of their research design and procedures to consider whether the results of their experiment could be due to the presence of a confounding variable that had not been identified prior to, or during the experiment. Below are examples of confounding variables that have the potential to influence the outcomes of experiments being conducted by psychologists.

Research Question

Does consuming sugar cause the activity level of children to increase?

Possible Confounding Variables

Teacher vs. Substitute Teacher, Day of Assessment

A substitute teacher is in the classroom on the day the pre-school age children assigned to the experimental group consume sugar and have their activity levels assessed. The regular teacher is in the classroom on the day the pre-school age children assigned to the control group do not consume sugar and have their activity levels assessed.

Problem

If children in the experimental group exhibit a significantly higher level of activity than children in the control group, this difference could have been caused by the consumption of sugar (i.e. the independent variable), the presence of a substitute teacher who may have a different classroom management style (i.e. confounding variable), or the assessment of the activity level of the children occurring on different school days (i.e. confounding variable).

Solution

The confounding variables present in the experiment could have been eliminated by having the activity levels of children in both the experimental and control groups assessed on the same school day when the regular classroom teacher was present in the classroom.

Research Question

Will adding humor to my class lectures cause student exam scores to increase?

Potential Confounding Variables

Quiet Class vs. Noisy Class, Day of Assessment

Noisy construction is occurring in the next classroom on the day college students assigned to the control group who had heard lectures that contained no humor took a mid-term exam for a Research Methods course. No construction was occurring in the next classroom on the day college students assigned to the control group who had heard lectures containing humor took a mid-term exam for a Research Methods course.

Problem

If college students in the experimental group scored significantly higher on the mid-term exam than college students in the control group, this difference could have been caused by the exposure to humor in class lectures (i.e. the independent variable), the absence of noise on the day of the mid-term exam (i.e. the confounding variable), or the assessment of student learning occurring on different school days (i.e. confounding variable).

Solution

The confounding variables present in the experiment could have been eliminated by having the college students take the mid-term exam for the Research Methods course on the same school day and under the same level of noise coming from the next classroom.

(7) Appropriate Statistical Analysis of Experimental Data

After the psychologists have collected their experimental data, they are ready to complete the final 2 steps in their "hypothesis testing" process. Recall there are 4 steps in the "hypothesis testing" process. Step 1 (i.e. stating the null and alternative hypotheses) and Step 2 (i.e. establishing a test criteria or "critical value") were completed prior to the collection of any experimental data.[3,7,9] In Step 3, the experimental data will undergo a statistical analysis conducted by the psychologists. The psychologists will select an appropriate statistical analysis based on the goal of the research, the specific research question being examined, and the scales of measurement being used to measure the variables of interest.[2,9] The statistical analysis will yield a numerical value representing the strength of the relationship between the independent and dependent variables in the experiment (i.e. the higher the value, the stronger the relationship). This numerical value is referred to as the "calculated value." After verifying the accuracy of their statistical analysis, psychologists will proceed to the fourth and final step in the "hypothesis testing" process.

In Step 4 of the hypothesis testing process, psychologists will compare the "calculated value" computed in Step 3 with the test criteria (or "critical value") established in Step 2 of the hypothesis test to draw their conclusion about the results of the experiment.[9] Recall that the null hypothesis serves as the focus of the hypothesis testing process. Therefore, conclusions drawn by the psychologists about the results of the experiment will be in relation to the null hypothesis. Based on a comparison of the "calculated" and "critical" values, psychologists will make one of two decisions: (a) if the "calculated value" is significantly different than the "critical value," the psychologists will make a decision to Reject the Null Hypothesis and will conclude that there is a causal relationship between the independent and dependent variables, or (b) if the "calculated value" and the "critical value" are not significantly different, psychologists will make a decision to Fail to Reject the Null Hypothesis and will conclude there is not a causal relationship between the independent and dependent variables.[3,6,7,9] The confidence level chosen for the statistical analysis will determine whether the psychologists are 95% or 99% confident in their conclusion about the relationship between the independent and dependent variables. Below are examples of potential results for statistical analyses performed by psychologists conducting experiments.

Research Question

Does consuming sugar cause the activity level of children to increase?

If a t-test is conducted at a 95% confidence level and the "calculated t value" is significantly different than the "critical t value," the psychologist would Reject the Null Hypothesis and be 95% confident there is a significant difference in the activity level at school of pre-school age children who consumed sugar and pre-school age children who did not consume sugar.

Research Question

Will adding humor to my class lectures cause student exam scores to increase?

If an analysis of variance (ANOVA) is conducted at a 99% confidence level and the "calculated F value" and "critical F value" are not significantly different, the Psychology professor would be 99% confident there is no significant difference between mid-term exam scores of students who listened to lectures containing humor and students who listened to lectures containing no humor.

After completing an experiment, it would be tempting for psychologists to immediately inform society about the results of their research. However, before disclosing the results of their research to society, psychologists must complete two additional activities in order to ensure the results of their research are valid and that their research does not pose a risk to society. The first activity is to replicate the results of their experiment.[2,6] If the results of the experiment are valid, psychologists should be able to replicate their results across multiple research samples tested on different occasions. Replication of the results by fellow psychologists working at other research facilities would provide further support for the validity of the experimental results. The second activity for psychologists is to make their research available for critical review by the scientific community. This critical review should be conducted by members of the scientific community who have the expertise to evaluate all aspects of the research (e.g. design, procedures, analyses) and to evaluate the extent to which the research adds new knowledge to the area of study. This critical review is known as "peer review."[4,5] The credibility of researchers who bypass the "peer review" process and present the results of their research directly to the media and/or society is considered highly questionable in the eyes of the scientific community. If research undergoes "peer review" and gets a positive review, it has finally reached the stage at which it is deemed to have sufficient merit to be shared with members of the scientific community and/or society. Research conferences and scholarly research journals are two common avenues psychologists can use to share the results of their research.[1,4,8]

Sharing Experimental Results with the Scientific Community and Society

To share the results of their research with the members of the scientific community and society, psychologists can submit their research for presentation at the annual meeting of a state, regional, or national professional society or research association (e.g. the Society for Industrial-Organizational Psychology).[1,4,8] In order to present their research at a conference, psychologists are required to submit an abstract or a completed paper describing the research for "peer review." If their research is accepted by conference reviewers, psychologists can present their research in one of several presentation formats including a poster, oral presentation, a symposium, a roundtable discussion, or a panel presentation. In each of these presentation formats, psychologists have an opportunity to engage in scholarly discussions with individuals who have expertise or an interest in the same area of study. Members of the conference committees who are in charge of public relations often alert the media to research that will be presented at the conference that is likely to be of interest to the general public in an effort to share the results of research with those outside the academic community. Psychologists can also share the results of their research by submitting the research for publication in a scholarly research journal.[4,6,8] When psychologists submit an article to a scholarly research journal, it is typically reviewed by a minimum of two reviewers (assigned by the Editor of the journal) who have appropriate expertise. Each reviewer evaluates the research and makes a decision as to whether the article should be: (a) rejected, (b) revised and resubmitted, or (c) accepted for publication (with recommended revisions). If there is disagreement among reviewers, the editor of the journal casts the tie-breaking vote which will determine whether or not the article will be published.[4,6] Once it's published, the research can be accessed by the scientific community, the media, and the general public through use of online databases and Internet search engines that are designed to locate scholarly research articles.

EXERCISE 6A

Identifying Independent, Dependent, and Control Variables

The goal of an experiment is to determine whether there is a cause-and-effect relationship between an independent variable that is "manipulated" and one or more dependent variables that are "measured" by psychologists. To isolate the independent variable as the sole "cause" of any differences in the dependent variable, all other factors in the experimental environment need to be controlled (i.e. kept constant) by psychologists throughout the experiment. The factors that are held constant are known as "control variables."

Below are 6 experiments conducted by psychologists across a variety of laboratory and/or applied settings. For each of these experiments, please: **(a)** identify the independent variable, its levels, and its nature (i.e. quantitative or qualitative), **(b)** identify the dependent variable(s) in the experiment, and **(c)** identify three variables that must be controlled by psychologists throughout the experiment and provide a rationale for the variables you feel must be controlled.

01. A Consumer Psychologist conducts an experiment to study the effect of music on shopping behavior. First, she randomly selects 50 shoppers at a large retail store. She then randomly assigns the shoppers to one of two groups. Shoppers in the first group do their Christmas shopping while Christmas carols are playing throughout the store. Shoppers in the second group do their Christmas shopping while no music is playing in the store. Shoppers are all given two hours to complete their shopping. After two hours of shopping, she measures the number of items purchased and amount of money spent by each shopper. She predicts that shoppers who do their Christmas shopping while Christmas carols are playing in the store will buy significantly more items and spend significantly more money than shoppers who do their Christmas shopping when no music is playing.

Independent Variable =

    Level 1 =

    Level 2 =

    What type of independent variable is being manipulated by the psychologist?

        Quantitative   Qualitative

Dependent Variable 1 =

Dependent Variable 2 =

What are 3 variables the psychologist must control during the experiment?

1. _____

2. _____

3. _____

Rationale:

02. An Industrial-Organizational Psychologist conducts an experiment to test the effect of taking naps at work on employee productivity. The psychologist randomly selects 100 employees at an insurance company and randomly assigns them to one of two groups. For one month, the first group of employees is allowed to take a nap at work whenever they feel tired. The second group of employees is not allowed to take a nap at work during the same one-month period. At the end of the month, the psychologist measures the number of new customers and the number of insurance policies sold for each employee. He predicts that there will be no significant difference in the average number of new customers or insurance policies sold for employees who are allowed to nap and employees who are not allowed to nap.

Independent Variable =

    Level 1 =

    Level 2 =

What type of independent variable is being manipulated by the psychologist?

Quantitative   Qualitative

Dependent Variable 1 =

Dependent Variable 2 =

What are 3 variables the psychologist must control during the experiment?

1. _____

2. _____

3. _____

Rationale:

03. A Health Psychologist who supervises a weight loss program at a fitness club requires all program members to walk 1 mile per day to maximize weight loss. One day, a member of the program says to him, "If I walk more than 1 mile per day, will I lose more weight?" In response, he conducts an experiment on the effect of walking more than 1 mile per day on weight loss. He randomly selects 30 members of the program and randomly assigns them to one of three groups. The first group is required to follow his normal recommendation and walk 1 mile per day for one month. The second group is required to walk 5 miles per day for the same one-month period. The third group is required to walk 10 miles per day for the same period of one month. At the end of the month, he measures the number of pounds lost by each participant. He predicts that there will be no significant difference in the average amount of weight lost by participants who walk 1 mile, 5 miles, or 10 miles per day.

Independent Variable =

    Level 1 =

    Level 2 =

    Level 3 =

What type of independent variable is being manipulated by the psychologist?

Quantitative   Qualitative

Dependent Variable 1 =

What are 3 variables the psychologist must control during the experiment?

1. _____

2. _____

3. _____

Rationale:

04. A Cognitive Psychologist conducts an experiment to test the effect of time on the accuracy of recall. She randomly selects 60 students from a University and randomly assigns them to one of three groups. All groups watch a video of a robbery at a liquor store. The first group is asked to recall details of the robbery immediately after the video (0-minute delay). The second group is asked to recall details of the robbery 30 minutes after the video (30-minute delay). The third group is asked to recall details of the robbery 60 minutes after the video (60-minute delay). He then measures the number of accurate details about the robbery each student recalled. He predicts that students who recall details of the robbery after the passage of time (30 and 60-minute delay) will recall significantly fewer accurate details than students who recall details of the robbery immediately after the crime (0-minute delay).

Independent Variable =

   Level 1 =

   Level 2 =

   Level 3 =

What type of independent variable is being manipulated by the psychologist?

Quantitative   Qualitative

Dependent Variable 1 =

What are 3 variables the psychologist must control during the experiment?

1. _____

2. _____

3. _____

Rationale:

05. After reading a magazine article that offered dating advice to men that claimed women are more likely to flirt with men who wear a wedding ring, a Social Psychologist decides that she will conduct an experiment in order to test the accuracy of this dating advice for men. She randomly selects 30 men from the local community and randomly assigns them to one of two groups. She has the men in both groups attend a two-hour "mixer" attended by 30 single women from the local community. The men in the first group are required to wear a wedding ring during the "mixer." The men in the second group are required to wear no wedding ring during the "mixer." At the end of the two-hour "mixer," she asks each of the men how many women flirted with them, how many women kissed them, and how many women asked them for their phone number during the two-hour "mixer." She predicts that there will be no significant difference in the average number of women who flirt, kiss, or ask for the phone numbers of men wearing wedding rings and men not wearing wedding rings.

Independent Variable =

    Level 1 =

    Level 2 =

What type of independent variable is being manipulated by the psychologist?

Quantitative   Qualitative

Dependent Variable 1 =

Dependent Variable 2 =

Dependent Variable 3 =

What are 3 variables the psychologist must control during the experiment?

1. _____

2. _____

3. _____

Rationale:

06. A Psychiatrist conducts an experiment to test the effectiveness of a new medication designed to treat depression. He randomly selects 20 of his patients who have been diagnosed with depression and randomly assigns them to one of two groups. He requires the first group to swallow a pill containing a 10 mg dose of the new medication twice a day for 6 months. He requires the second group to swallow a "placebo" (i.e. a pill which does not contain any of the new medication—0 mg dose) twice a day for the same 6 month period. After 6 months, he measures the depression level of each patient. He predicts that patients who took the 10 mg dose of the new medication will be significantly less depressed than patients who took the "placebo" (0 mg dose of the new medication).

Independent Variable =

  Level 1 =

  Level 2 =

What type of independent variable is being manipulated by the psychologist?

Quantitative   Qualitative

Dependent Variable 1 =

What are 3 variables the psychologist must control during the experiment?

1. _____

2. _____

3. _____

Rationale:

EXERCISE 6B

Identifying Confounding Variables in Experiments

In a well-designed and carefully controlled experiment, the only factor allowed to vary across the experimental and control groups is the independent variable. In some experiments, however, a confounding variable is mistakenly allowed to vary across groups at the same time as the independent variable. When a confounding variable is present, psychologists are unable to conclude that the independent variable is the sole cause of any significant differences observed between the experimental and control groups. Below are the descriptions of 8 experiments. For each experiment, please identify the: **(a)** independent variable, **(b)** confounding variable(s), and **(c)** actions the psychologist should have taken to eliminate the confounding variable(s) from the experiment and write your responses in the spaces provided.

01. A Health Psychologist conducts an experiment to determine if running or walking results in greater weight loss for women. She randomly selects 30 female students from a University and randomly assigns students to one of two groups. She has the students in the first group run 1 mile per day on the outdoor track at the University for 7 days. She has the students in the second group walk 1 mile per day on a treadmill inside the University fitness center for the same 7 day period. She measures the amount of weight lost by each student. The results revealed that the female students who ran 1 mile per day lost significantly more weight than the female students who walked 1 mile per day.

Independent Variable =

Confounding Variable(s) =

What actions should the psychologist have taken to eliminate the influence of the confounding variable from her experiment?

02. A Clinical Psychologist conducts an experiment to determine if male clients respond more favorably to a male or female therapist. He randomly selects 40 male clients from his case load diagnosed with an anxiety disorder and he randomly assigns them to one of two groups. He sends men in the first group to a male therapist who specializes in behavioral therapy for 3 therapy sessions. He sends men in the second group to a female clinician who specializes in cognitive therapy for 3 therapy sessions. After all the men completed 3 therapy sessions, he measures the anxiety level of each of the men. The results revealed that the male clients who received therapy from a male therapist had a significantly lower anxiety level than the male clients who received therapy from a female therapist.

Independent Variable =

Confounding Variable(s) =

What actions should the psychologist have taken to eliminate the influence of the confounding variable from his experiment?

03. A Behavioral Psychologist conducts an experiment to determine if the use of punishment or positive reinforcement results in quicker learning in lab rats. He randomly selects 40 lab rats and randomly assigns them to one of two groups. He has rats in the first group learn to turn left to find food in a "T maze" (i.e. a maze shaped like the letter T). Rats are given positive reinforcement (food) each time they make the correct turn. He has rats in the second group learn to turn right to find food in a "Y maze" (i.e. a maze shaped like the letter Y). Rats are given punishment (shock) each time they make an incorrect turn. He measures the number of trials it takes each rat to learn to make the correct turn. The results revealed that the rats who received positive reinforcement while in the maze learned to make the correct turn in significantly fewer trials than rats who received punishment while in the maze.

Independent Variable =

Confounding Variable(s) =

What actions should the psychologist have taken to eliminate the influence of the confounding variable from his experiment?

04. A Psychology professor conducted an experiment to determine if college students perform better in a Research Methods course if they read an e-textbook or a traditional textbook. He has 25 students enrolled in a MWF section of the course read an e-textbook while taking the course. He has 25 students enrolled in a TR section of the course read a traditional textbook while taking the course. He measures the course performance of each student by recording the grade each student earns on the final exam for the course. The results revealed college students who read an e-textbook scored significantly higher on the final exam than college students who read a traditional textbook in a college Research Methods course.

Independent Variable =

Confounding Variable(s) =

What actions should the psychologist have taken to eliminate the influence of the confounding variable from his experiment?

05. A Forensic Psychologist conducted an experiment to determine if jurors are more likely to convict an individual if they are sequestered or not sequestered during a trial. She randomly selects 20 individuals from the community and randomly assigns them to one of two groups. She has the first group serve as a jury for a mock trial involving a man accused of murder. Jurors are sequestered in a local hotel during the 7 day trial. She has the second group serve as a jury for a mock trial involving a woman accused of shoplifting. During the 7 day trial, jurors are not sequestered. At the end of the trials, she has each juror rate how likely he/she is to vote to convict the accused (1 = Definitely Not Convict; 10 = Definitely Convict). The results revealed that the jurors who were sequestered during the trial were significantly more likely to vote to convict the accused than jurors who were not sequestered during the trial.

Independent Variable =

Confounding Variable(s) =

What actions should the psychologist have taken to eliminate the influence of the confounding variable from her experiment?

06. A Consumer Psychologist conducted an experiment to determine if shoppers are more likely to purchase a product if it's endorsed by a celebrity endorser or a non-celebrity endorser. She randomly selects 40 shoppers at a local pharmacy and randomly assigns them to one of two groups. She has shoppers in the first group watch a commercial for a new cold medicine in which the product is endorsed by a popular celebrity. She has shoppers in the second group watch a commercial for a new hemorrhoid cream in which the product is endorsed by a non-celebrity endorser. She asks each shopper to rate how likely he/she is to buy the product advertised in the commercial (1 = Definitely Not Purchase; 10 = Definitely Purchase). The results revealed that the shoppers who watched the commercial with the celebrity endorser were significantly more likely to purchase the product than the shoppers who watched the commercial containing a non-celebrity endorser.

Independent Variable =

Confounding Variable(s) =

What actions should the psychologist have taken to eliminate the influence of the confounding variable from her experiment?

07. A Military Psychologist conducted an experiment to determine if there is a difference in the performance of soldiers who face live ammunition and non-live ammunition. She has a group of 25 soldiers complete a drill where they attempt to rescue a captured soldier being held in an underground cave complex. No live ammunition is fired at soldiers during the drill. She has a second group of 25 soldiers complete a drill where they attempt to capture a small squad of enemy soldiers driving a truckload of explosives through a small village. Live ammunition is fired at soldiers during the drill. She assigns each soldier a performance score (0–50 points). The results revealed that soldiers who faced the live ammunition had significantly higher performance scores than soldiers who faced no live ammunition.

Independent Variable =

Confounding Variable(s) =

What actions should the psychologist have taken to eliminate the influence of the confounding variable from her experiment?

08. An Experimental Psychologist conducted an experiment to determine if older individuals are able to learn to use technology just as fast as younger individuals. She randomly selects 15 individuals over the age of 65 from a local retirement home and 15 college students who are under the age of 22 from the local University. She has all 30 participants listen to a 3-hour lecture in which she explains how to e-mail, text, tweet, Instagram, and set up a Facebook page. After her lecture, she has all 30 participants attempt to send 3 e-mails, 3 texts, 3 tweets, 3 Instagram photos, and set up a new Facebook page and profile. Retirement home residents are asked to complete these tasks using the laptop computers the psychologist has supplied. College students are asked to attempt to complete the tasks using their personal cell phones. She records the amount of time it takes each participant to complete the required tasks. The results revealed that the younger college students completed the assigned tasks significantly faster than the older retirement home residents.

Independent Variable =

Confounding Variable(s) =

What actions should the psychologist have taken to eliminate the influence of the confounding variable from her experiment?

EXERCISE 6C

Designing an Experiment to Test the Wisdom of Proverbs

According to the Merriam-Webster online dictionary,[17] a "proverb" is, "a brief popular saying that gives advice about how people should live or that expresses a belief that is generally thought to be true" (e.g. Too many cooks spoil the broth). Although the wisdom and the advice offered by proverbs is "generally thought to be true," it is important that we determine whether this wisdom and advice is supported by scientific research before using it to make the important decisions in our lives. Below are 12 popular proverbs and their associated meanings.[18] Please select one proverb from the list below and design an experiment to determine if the wisdom and advice offered by the proverb is supported by scientific research. Use the question prompts on the following pages to describe how you will: **(a)** acquire your research sample, **(b)** assign the participants to groups, **(c)** define, control, manipulate, and measure your research variables, and **(d)** determine if there is a causal relationship between your independent and dependent variables.

1. Absence makes the heart grow fonder
   "When you are away from someone you love, you love them even more"

2. Actions speak louder than words
   "What a person actually does is more important than what they say they will do"

3. Blood is thicker than water
   "Family relationships are stronger than relationships with other people"

4. Don't judge a book by its cover
   "Don't judge by appearances"

5. Honesty is the best policy
   "It's always better to be honest"

6. Laughter is the best medicine
   "Laughter makes people feel good"

7. Love is blind
   "A person in love does not see the faults of the person he/she loves"

8. The squeaky wheel gets the grease
   "The person who complains the loudest gets the most attention"

9. The way to a man's heart is through his stomach
   "Feed a man well and he will love you"

10. When the cats away, the mice will play
    "People sometimes misbehave when the person in authority is absent"

11. You are what you eat
    "What you eat has an effect on your well-being"

12. You can't teach an old dog new tricks
    "A person who is used to doing things a certain way cannot change"

Proverb Selected:

_____

What research question will you attempt to answer with your experiment?

Research Question	
	_____
	_____
	_____
	_____

What is the population of interest for your experiment?

Population of Interest =

What method of sampling will you use to acquire your research sample?

Sampling Method =

Describe specifically how you will use this method of sampling to acquire your research sample from your population of interest.

_____

_____

_____

_____

_____

_____

How many groups will you have in your experiment?   **# of Groups =**

Describe specifically how you will randomly assign members of your research sample to the groups in your experiment.

_____

_____

_____

_____

_____

_____

What independent variable will you "manipulate" and how will you operationally define each level of your independent variable?

```
┌─────────────────────────────────────────────────────────────────────┐
│                                                                       │
│   Independent Variable =                                              │
│                                                                       │
│   Level 1:  _____         │
│                                                                       │
│             _____         │
│   Level 2:  _____         │
│                                                                       │
│             _____         │
│   Level 3:  _____         │
│                                                                       │
│             _____ (if necessary)      │
│                                                                       │
└─────────────────────────────────────────────────────────────────────┘
```

What dependent variable(s) will you "measure" to assess the influence of the independent variable and how will you operationally define your dependent variable(s)?

```
┌─────────────────────────────────────────────────────────────────────┐
│                                                                       │
│   Dependent Variable 1 =                                              │
│                                                                       │
│   Definition:  _____         │
│                                                                       │
│                _____         │
│                                                                       │
│                _____         │
│                                                                       │
│   Dependent Variable 2 =                                              │
│                                                                       │
│   Definition:  _____         │
│                                                                       │
│                _____         │
│                                                                       │
│                _____ (if necessary)   │
│                                                                       │
└─────────────────────────────────────────────────────────────────────┘
```

Based on the operational definitions you will use to define your independent and dependent variable(s), describe specifically what participants in the control group and experimental group(s) will "experience" during your experiment.

Control Group	
Experimental Group 1	
Experimental Group 2 (if necessary)	

What are **three (3)** specific variables you will need to control to ensure that your independent variable is the true "cause" of any significant differences you observe between the control and experimental group(s)? Provide a rationale for the variables you select.

Variable 1: _____

Variable 2: _____

Variable 3: _____

Rationale:

What are the null and alternative hypotheses that you will test in your experiment?

Null Hypothesis	
Alternative Hypothesis	

Which of your hypotheses (i.e. null or alternative) would you predict the results of your experiment will support? Provide a rationale for your prediction.

☐ Null Hypothesis

☐ Alternative Hypothesis

Rationale:

If your results were to support your prediction, will your decision be to Reject the Null Hypothesis or Fail to Reject the Null Hypothesis? Provide a rationale for your decision.

☐ Reject the Null Hypothesis

☐ Fail to Reject the Null Hypothesis

Rationale:

Based on your decision, will you conclude that there is (or is not) a causal relationship between your independent and dependent variable(s)? Provide a rationale for your conclusion.

☐ No, there is no causal relationship between the independent and the dependent variable
☐ Yes, there is a causal relationship between the independent and the dependent variable
Rationale:

After you complete your experiment, what will your next step be if: **(a)** the results support your prediction or **(b)** the results fail to support your prediction?

If the results support my prediction, I would then	If the results fail to support my prediction, I would then .....

References

1. Smith, R. A., & Davis, S. F. (2012). *The psychologist as detective: An introduction to conducting research in psychology* (6th ed.). Boston, MA: Pearson Publishers.

2. Beins, B. C. (2012). *Research methods: A tool for life* (3rd ed.). Boston, MA: Pearson Publishers.

3. Rosnow, R. L., & Rosenthal, R. (2012). *Beginning behavioral research: A conceptual primer* (7th ed.). Boston, MA: Pearson Publishers.

4. Cozby, P. C., & Bates, S. C. (2011). *Methods in behavioral research.* (11th ed.). New York, NY: McGraw-Hill Publishers.

5. Bordens, K. S., & Abbot, B. B. (2011). *Research design and methods: A process approach* (8th ed.). Boston, MA: McGraw-Hill Publishers.

6. Passer, M. W. (2013). *Research methods: Concepts and connections.* New York, NY: Worth Publishers.

7. Kantowitz, B. H., Roediger, H. L., & Elmes, D. G. (2014). *Experimental psychology* (10th ed.). Stamford, CT: Cengage Learning.

8. Maclin, M. K., & Solso, R. L. (2007). *Experimental psychology: A case approach* (8th ed.). Boston, MA: Pearson/Allyn & Bacon.

9. Gravetter, F. J., & Wallnau, L. B. (2012). *Statistics for the behavioral sciences* (9th ed.). Belmont, CA: Wadsworth-Cengage Learning.

10. Trochim, W. M. (2006). Experimental design. *The Research Methods Knowledge Base* (2nd ed.). Retrieved from http://www.socialresearchmethods.net/kb/desexper.php.

11. Jackson, S. L. (2014). *Research methods: A modular approach* (3rd ed.). Stamford, CT: Cengage Learning.

12. Marshall, M. N. (1996). Sampling for qualitative research. *Family Practice, 13*(6), 522–525.

13. Trochim, W. M. (2006). Sampling terminology. *The Research Methods Knowledge Base* (2nd ed.). Retrieved from http://www.socialresearchmethods.net/kb/sampterm.php.

14. Myers, A., & Hansen, C. H. (2011). *Experimental psychology* (7th ed.). Belmont, CA: Wadsworth/ Cengage Learning.

15. Schultz, K. F., & Grimes, D. A. (2002). Generation of allocation sequences in randomized trials: Chance not choice. *The Lancet, 359,* 515–519.

16. Trochim, W. M. (2006). Classifying experimental designs. *The Research Methods Knowledge Base* (2nd ed.). Retrieved from http://www.socialresearchmethods.net/kb/expclass.php.

17. Definition of "proverb" reprinted by permission from Merriam-Webster's Collegiate® Dictionary © 2014 by Merriam-Webster, Inc. (www.Merriam-Webster.com).

18. English proverbs and sayings. (n.d.). *Learn English Today.* Retrieved from http://www.learn-english-today.com/proverbs/proverbs.html.

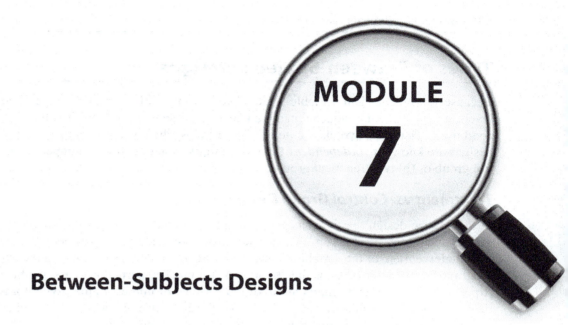

MODULE
7

Between-Subjects Designs

During an experiment, psychologists manipulate an independent variable and observe its effect by measuring one or more dependent variables.[1,2,3] The independent variable manipulated by psychologists will have two or more levels.[1,3,4] During an experiment, participants assigned to the various levels of the independent variable will be exposed to different "experiences." These different "experiences" are referred to as "conditions" in an experiment. To determine if there is a significant difference on the dependent variable for participants exposed to various conditions, psychologists can elect to use one of two types of research designs. These two research designs are known as "between-subjects" and "within-subjects" designs.

Between-subjects research designs are also referred to as "independent-group" designs or "randomized group" designs.[2,3,5] In between-subjects designs, the participants are randomly assigned to the different conditions in an experiment. Each participant is assigned to only one condition and is exposed to only one level of the independent variable.[1,2,3] Participants are then measured on the dependent variable and average scores are computed for participants assigned to each of the conditions. The average scores on the dependent variable are then analyzed to determine if there is a significant difference across conditions.

Within-subjects research designs are also referred to as "repeated measures" designs.[3,6,7] In within-subjects designs, participants are not randomly assigned to different conditions. The participants take part in all of the conditions in an experiment and are exposed to all levels of the independent variable.[1,3,6] After completing each of the conditions, participants are measured on the dependent variable and average scores are then computed for each condition. The average scores on the dependent variable are then analyzed to determine whether there is a significant difference across conditions.

Therefore, to determine if there is a significant difference on the dependent variable for participants exposed to the different conditions in an experiment, psychologists have to decide whether to examine: (a) multiple groups of participants who take part in only one condition in an experiment (i.e. "between-subjects" design) or (b) a single group of participants who take part in all of the conditions in an experiment (i.e. "within-subjects" design). There are challenges posed by each of these research designs. The choice of design will influence the time, resources, and participants needed to conduct the experiment, as well as the sources of error that psychologists will need to eliminate/control to conduct a valid test of the relationship between the independent and dependent variables. The types of between-subjects designs that are used by psychologists to conduct experiments, as well as the advantages, disadvantages, and challenges associated with these designs will be the focus of the current module. Types of within-subjects designs used by psychologists to conduct experiments, as well as the advantages, disadvantages, and challenges associated with these designs will be the focus of Module 8.

Types of Between-Subjects Designs

Because the independent variable manipulated by psychologists in an experiment will have two or more levels, an experiment conducted using a between-subjects design will involve a comparison of two or more conditions. There are two classic designs used by psychologists to compare two different conditions. These designs are known as *Independent Groups Designs*[2,3,5] and involve a comparison of: (a) a treatment and control group or (b) two treatment groups.

Treatment vs. Control Group Design

In this classic design, participants are randomly assigned to one of two groups known as the "experimental group" and the "control group." The participants assigned to the experimental group are exposed to the treatment, intervention, or the variable of interest to the psychologists conducting the experiment. The experimental group is also referred to as the "treatment" group. The participants assigned to the control group are not exposed to the treatment, intervention, or the variable of interest to the psychologists conducting the experiment.[1,2,8] The participants are then measured on the dependent variable(s) and average scores are computed for both the treatment and control groups. Average scores on the dependent variable(s) are then analyzed to determine if there is a significant difference between the control and treatment groups. This research design is often used by psychologists who want to test the effectiveness of a new treatment or intervention. This design allows psychologists to establish that the health and well-being of individuals who are exposed to the treatment or intervention is significantly better than that of individuals who are not exposed to the treatment or intervention.

Treatment vs. Treatment Group Design

In this classic design, participants are randomly assigned to one of two "treatment groups." Participants who are assigned to different "treatment groups" are exposed to different amounts or types of a treatment or intervention.[1,2,8] Participants are then measured on the dependent variable(s) and average scores are computed for each of the treatment groups. Average scores on the dependent variable(s) are then analyzed to determine if there is a significant difference between the two treatment groups (i.e. the two different amounts or types of treatment or intervention received). This classic between-subjects design is typically used by psychologists after they have established the effectiveness of a treatment or intervention through the use of the treatment-control group design. For example, psychologists may use the treatment-control group design to first establish the effectiveness of psychotherapy in reducing level of anxiety (e.g. the anxiety level of individuals who attend a session of psychotherapy (i.e. treatment group) is significantly lower than the anxiety level of individuals who do not attend (i.e. control group) a therapy session). Having established the effectiveness of psychotherapy in reducing anxiety, psychologists can then use the treatment-treatment group design to compare the effectiveness of: (a) different amounts of psychotherapy (e.g. 1 session vs. 5 sessions) or (b) different types of psychotherapy (e.g. psychoanalysis vs. cognitive therapy) in reducing anxiety.

When using one of these classic between-subjects designs to conduct an experiment, it is essential psychologists accomplish three key goals when assigning participants to conditions in the experiment. First, they must ensure that they assign participants to conditions in an unbiased manner so that participants have an equal opportunity to be assigned to any of the conditions in the experiment.[2,3,6] Second, they must ensure that the size of the groups of participants assigned to each of the conditions in the experiment is comparable and that the number of participants is sufficient to conduct a meaningful comparison across conditions. Finally, they must ensure the groups of participants assigned to the conditions in the experiment are as equivalent as possible (preferably identical!).[2,3,5] It is critical that the groups of participants assigned to each of the conditions are equivalent at the start of an experiment so that any differences between groups at the end of the experiment can be attributed to the effects of the independent variable rather than to differences between the groups that were present at the beginning of the experiment. In many experiments, psychologists will rely on "random assignment"[3,5,7] of participants to conditions to accomplish these three key goals.

Creation of Comparable Sized Groups

While random assignment does ensure psychologists assign participants to the conditions in an experiment in an unbiased manner, it does not guarantee the groups of participants assigned to each condition will be comparable in size.[8,9,10] To illustrate, let's assume a psychologist wants to enroll 12 participants in her experiment and would like to randomly assign the 12 participants to two conditions (i.e. a "treatment group" and a "control group"). She decides to use a coin flip to randomly assign participants to groups as they enroll in the experiment over time. She decides a flip of "tails" (T) will assign a participant to the "treatment group" (TG) while a flip of "heads" (H) will assign a participant to the "control group" (CG). She begins by flipping a "tails" (T) for her first participant and assigns the participant to the "treatment group" (TG). Over time, as each new participant enrolls in her experiment, she once again flips a coin and assigns the participant to a condition based on the outcome of the coin flip. She continues until she has enrolled her 12 participants in the experiment and has assigned all participants to a condition. Below are three potential outcomes of the psychologist's random assignment process.

Participant #	1	2	3	4	5	6	7	8	9	10	11	12
Coin Toss Result	T	T	T	H	T	T	H	H	T	T	T	T
Group Assignment	TG	TG	TG	CG	TG	TG	CG	CG	TG	TG	TG	TG

Outcome 1: 9 "treatment group" and 3 "control group"

Participant #	1	2	3	4	5	6	7	8	9	10	11	12
Coin Toss Result	T	H	T	H	T	T	H	H	T	H	H	T
Group Assignment	TG	CG	TG	CG	TG	TG	CG	CG	TG	CG	CG	TG

Outcome 2: 6 "treatment group" and 6 "control group"

Participant #	1	2	3	4	5	6	7	8	9	10	11	12
Coin Toss Result	T	H	H	H	T	H	H	H	T	T	H	H
Group Assignment	TG	CG	CG	CG	TG	CG	CG	CG	TG	TG	CG	CG

Outcome 3: 4 "treatment group" and 8 "control group"

In looking at the results, we can see that two groups of equivalent size were created in only one of the three outcomes (i.e. Outcome 2: 6 "treatment group" and 6 "control group"). In the other two outcomes, there were sizeable differences in the size of the groups created through random assignment. This type of outcome is more likely when the size of the research sample is small.[8,9,10] If the size discrepancy between groups is too large, psychologists will be unable to conduct a meaningful comparison across conditions. This can be especially problematic when the target population is small in size. Fortunately for psychologists, as the size of their research sample increases, random assignment becomes increasingly more likely to produce groups that are equivalent in size across conditions. So, while random assignment has the potential to create groups that are comparable in size across conditions (especially as the research sample increases in size), psychologists need to be aware that it does not guarantee that groups will be comparable in size across conditions (especially when studying target populations that are small in size).

A second way to randomly assign participants to conditions in an experiment is through the use of a computerized randomization program (e.g. http://www.randomization.com/).[11] Let's assume that the same psychologist elects to use a computerized randomization program to assign her 12 participants to her two conditions (i.e. a "treatment group" and a "control group"). When she opens the computerized randomization program, it will prompt her to enter her number of participants (i.e. 12) and the number of conditions in her experiment (i.e. 2). The program then uses the information to generate a "randomization plan." The "randomization plan" emerges in the form of a randomly ordered list of 6 treatment group" and 6 "control group" assignments. The psychologist could then use this "randomization plan" to assign her 12 participants to her two conditions over time as they enroll in her experiment. A potential "randomization plan" the computerized randomization program might generate for the psychologist appears below:

"Randomization Plan"

Participant 1	Treatment	
Participant 2	Treatment	
Participant 3	Treatment	
Participant 4	Control	MONTH 1
Participant 5	Treatment	
Participant 6	Treatment	
Participant 7	Treatment	
Participant 8	Control	
Participant 9	Control	
Participant 10	Control	MONTH 2
Participant 11	Control	
Participant 12	Control	

In looking at the "randomization plan," the first thing to notice is that unlike the coin flip method of random assignment, the computerized randomization program is designed to create groups of participants that are equal in size across conditions. If the psychologist were to run the randomization program multiple times for her experiment, the randomization program would continue to create randomly ordered lists that contain 6 "treatment group" and 6 "control group" assignments (a new random order will be generated each time she runs the program). However, the second thing you should notice is that the two groups become equivalent in size only after all of the participants in the experiment have been assigned to conditions (i.e. the "treatment group" and "control group" both contain 6 participants only after the 12th and final participant has been randomly assigned to a condition).[11] But why is this an important consideration?

Let's assume that it takes the psychologist two months to enroll the 12 participants in her experiment. She enrolls 6 participants during the first month of the experiment and following the "randomization plan," she assigns 5 participants to the "treatment group" (Participants 1, 2, 3, 5, and 6) and assigns 1 participant to the "control group" (Participant 4). If she were to analyze the results of her experiment at the end of the first month, there would be a sizeable difference in the size of her groups and she would be unable to conduct a meaningful comparison across the two conditions. She enrolls her final 6 participants during the second month of the experiment and following the "randomization plan," assigns 1 participant to the "treatment group" (Participant 7) and 5 of the participants to the "control group" (Participants 8, 9, 10, 11, and 12). If she were to analyze the results of her experiment at the end of the second month, she would have an equal number of participants in each of her groups which would allow her to conduct a meaningful comparison across the two conditions. Her groups have only now become equivalent in size after all of the participants had been assigned to a condition in the experiment.

Now let's assume during the first month of the experiment, an event occurs in the local community (e.g. community tragedy, economic crisis, weather event) that is likely to influence the performance of participants who are enrolled in the experiment during this time. During the second month of the experiment, no similar event occurs. If we look at the "randomization plan" created for the psychologist, we notice that during the first month of the experiment, 5 of the 6 participants enrolled were assigned to the "treatment group." Therefore, the event occurring in the local community is likely to have a greater influence on participants in the "treatment group" compared to participants in the "control group" who were enrolled primarily during the second month of the experiment (5 of the 6 "control group" members were enrolled during the second month of the experiment). As a result, if the psychologist were to find a significant difference between the "treatment group" and the "control group" at the end of the experiment, she would be unable to determine whether that difference was due to the effectiveness of the treatment or to the differential effects of the community event across the two conditions.

So, although the computerized randomization program is designed to create groups that are equivalent in size across conditions: (a) the groups are only equivalent after all participants have been assigned to conditions, and (b) the groups are not equivalent in size at all times during the course of the experiment.[10,11] This can be problematic when the enrollment of participants occurs over an extended period of time and events which can influence the performance of the participants are not constant throughout the experiment. There is a method of randomization that allows psychologists to randomly assign participants to conditions and create groups which are equal in size throughout an experiment. This method is known as "block randomization."[2,8,9]

In "block randomization," psychologists create a "randomization plan" that they can use to randomly assign participants to conditions and which creates groups that are equivalent in size at any point throughout an experiment. To develop a "randomization plan" through the process of "block randomization," psychologists will follow the process outlined below.[2,8,9]

Step 1:   Select a desired sample size for the experiment (e.g. 40)

Step 2:   Select a desired number of conditions (e.g. 2; "treatment group"/"control group")

Step 3:   Select a "block size" that divides evenly into the desired sample size and which is evenly divisible by the desired number of conditions (e.g. "block size" of 4)

  (a)   Dividing the desired sample size by the block size will determine the total number of blocks needed to assign all the participants to the conditions in the experiment (e.g. 40/4 = 10 blocks needed)

  (b)   The "block size" value will determine the number of participants in each block (e.g. there will be 4 participants in each block)

  (c)   Dividing the block size by the number of conditions will determine the number of participants assigned to each condition in each block (e.g. 4/2 = 2 participants will be assigned to the "treatment group" and 2 participants will be assigned to the "control group" in each block

Based on the calculations in Step 3, the "randomization plan" that the psychologist will create to randomly assign participants to conditions will contain ten blocks of four participants and in each of the blocks, two participants will be assigned to the treatment group (T) and two participants will be assigned to the control group (C).

Step 4: Generate a random sequence of conditions for each block. The "treatment group" and "control group" must appear twice in each random sequence of conditions (e.g. since the psychologist will need 10 blocks to assign all of the participants to conditions, 10 random sequences of conditions will need to be generated. Examples of some of the random sequences that might be generated would be TTCC; TCTC; CTTC).

Step 5: Randomly assign the random sequence of conditions generated in Step 4 to blocks (e.g. the 10 random sequences of conditions generated in Step 4 will be randomly assigned to the 10 blocks that are needed to assign all the participants to conditions).

Step 6: Create the final "randomization plan" (e.g. the psychologist will create a master list containing the random sequence of conditions assigned to each block; *See Table 1*).

Step 7: Assign participants to conditions according to the "randomization plan" (e.g. as each participant enrolls in the study, the psychologist will consult the "randomization plan" and assign the participant to the condition dictated by the plan. The process continues until all blocks have been filled and all participants have been assigned to conditions.).

TABLE 1	Final "Randomization Plan"	
Block #	**Participants**	**Condition Assignments**
1	1–4	TTCC
2	5–8	TCCT
3	9–12	CTTC
4	13–16	TCTC
5	17–20	CTCT
6	21–24	TTCC
7	25–28	TCTC
8	29–32	CCTT
9	33–36	CTCT
10	37–40	CTTC

Although it can take some time to develop a "block randomization plan," when the plan has been developed it ensures psychologists that: (a) the participants will be randomly assigned to conditions in an unbiased manner, (b) groups will be equivalent in size across conditions after all participants have been assigned to conditions, (c) groups will be equivalent in size after each block in the "randomization plan" has been filled and therefore, they will be equivalent in size throughout the duration of the experiment, and (d) since the groups will be equivalent in size throughout the experiment, if there are environmental events that occur during the course of the experiment, the influence of these events will have an equal influence on the treatment and the control group.[2,8,9,10] All of these conditions increase the likelihood that psychologists will be able to conduct a meaningful comparison across conditions.

Creation of Equivalent Groups across Conditions

In "random assignment," all members of the research sample have an equal opportunity to be assigned to any of the conditions in an experiment. The process of "random assignment" theoretically creates equal groups by distributing the variability found among members of the research sample (e.g. demographics, life experiences, personality) evenly across conditions.[2,3,12] To illustrate how "random assignment" can create equal groups by distributing variability among members of a research sample evenly across conditions, let's examine a potential outcome of a "random assignment" process for an experiment being conducted by an Industrial-Organizational Psychologist to answer the question: "Do 'casual Fridays' increase employee job satisfaction?" In this experiment, 10 employees at a law firm will be allowed to dress in casual clothes at work on Fridays for a month (i.e. "treatment group"). A second group of 10 employees who work at the same law firm will not be allowed to dress casually at work on Fridays during the same time period (i.e. "control group"). At the end of the month, all 20 of the employees will have their job satisfaction measured by the I/O psychologist. A variable which could influence the outcome of the experiment is the current level of job satisfaction for the 20 employees in the experiment. In order to conclude "causal Fridays" is the cause of any increase in job satisfaction observed at the end of the experiment, the psychologist must be sure that the job satisfaction of her two groups of employees are equivalent at the start of the experiment. Otherwise, if an increased level of job satisfaction is observed in employees who are allowed to dress casually, the psychologist would be unable to determine if this increased level of job satisfaction is due to "casual Fridays" or to the fact that the group of employees who were allowed to dress casually had a higher level of job satisfaction at the start of the experiment than employees who were not allowed to dress casually.

Below is a table displaying some hypothetical data for this experiment. In the table, each employee in the experiment has been assigned a number from 1–20 and a pre-experiment rating of job satisfaction (1 = Extremely Dissatisfied; 7 = Extremely Satisfied) has been supplied to the I/O psychologist by each of the 20 employees. Let's assume that the psychologist uses a random numbers table to randomly assign 10 employees to the "treatment group" (i.e. 10 employees who get to dress casually on Fridays) and 10 employees to the "control group" (i.e. 10 employees who do not get to dress casually on Fridays). Results of the "random assignment" appear below.

Current Job Satisfaction for the 20 Employees in the Experiment

Employee #	1	2	3	4	5	6	7	8	9	10	11	12	13	14	15	16	17	18	19	20
Satisfaction	4	1	6	4	6	7	3	1	6	5	2	4	6	4	6	5	4	7	2	6

Employee #'s 1, 4, 6, 7, 11, 13, 14, 16, 17, and 20 are randomly assigned to "treatment group"

Employee #	1	4	6	7	11	13	14	16	17	20
Satisfaction	4	4	7	3	2	6	4	5	4	6

Average Job Satisfaction = 45/10 = **4.5**

Employee #'s 2, 3, 5, 8, 9, 10, 12, 15, 18, and 19 are randomly assigned to "control group"

Employee #	2	3	5	8	9	10	12	15	18	19
Satisfaction	1	6	6	1	6	5	4	6	7	2

Average Job Satisfaction = 44/10 = **4.4**

As can be seen from the data, the random assignment process was successful in distributing the variability in the current job satisfaction of employees in the experiment evenly across the two conditions. The random assignment process produced two equivalent groups of employees with respect to their average level of current job satisfaction (Treatment Group = 4.5; Control Group = 4.4). Since the two groups are equivalent, the psychologist can be more confident (although not 100% confident!) that any difference in the job satisfaction of the two groups at the end of the experiment can be attributed to "casual Fridays" rather than a difference in job satisfaction across groups that existed at the start of the experiment.

There is no guarantee, however, that random assignment will produce equivalent groups in an experiment.[2,4] It only guarantees that if there is a difference between the groups after the participants have been randomly assigned to conditions, the difference is due to chance. Let's examine another possible outcome of "random assignment" for the experiment conducted to answer the research question: "Do 'casual Fridays' increase employee job satisfaction?"

Current Job Satisfaction for the 20 Employees in the Experiment

Employee #	1	2	3	4	5	6	7	8	9	10	11	12	13	14	15	16	17	18	19	20
Satisfaction	4	1	6	4	6	7	3	1	6	5	2	4	6	4	6	5	4	7	2	6

Employee #'s 3, 5, 6, 9, 10, 13, 15, 16, 18, and 20 are randomly assigned to "treatment group"

Employee #	3	5	6	9	10	13	15	16	18	20
Satisfaction	6	6	7	6	5	6	6	5	7	6

Average Job Satisfaction = 60/10 = **6.0**

Employee #'s 1, 2, 4, 7, 8, 11, 12, 14, 17, and 19 are randomly assigned to "control group"

Employee #	1	2	4	7	8	11	12	14	17	19
Satisfaction	4	1	4	3	1	2	4	4	4	2

Average Job Satisfaction = 29/10 = **2.9**

In this outcome, the random assignment process was unsuccessful in distributing the variability in the current level of job satisfaction of employees in the experiment evenly across the groups. The random assignment process produced two groups of employees who are not equivalent with respect to the average level of current job satisfaction (Treatment Group = 6.0; Control Group = 2.9). Since the two groups are not equivalent, the psychologist would have a difficult time determining whether a difference in job satisfaction across groups at the end of the experiment was due to "casual Fridays" or to the fact that the group of employees who dressed casually had a higher level of job satisfaction at the start of the experiment than the group of employees who did not dress casually. Since random assignment provides no guarantee it will produce equivalent groups, psychologists frequently turn to a technique known as "matching" to produce equivalent groups.[1,2,3] When psychologists use the process of "matching" to create equivalent groups, the research design is referred to as a "matched groups" design.

Matched Groups Design

In the process known as "matching," prior to the start of the experiment, members of the research sample are measured on a variable that is likely to affect their performance during the experiment[1,2,3] (but which is not the main variable of interest for the psychologists conducting the experiment). For example, if a Psychology professor is interested in conducting an experiment to answer the question, "Does providing students with a study guide increase exam performance?," the academic ability of the students in the research sample (i.e. as measured by college GPA) would likely influence exam performance during the experiment. So, prior to the start of the experiment, members of the research sample would be asked to provide their current college GPA. Members of the research sample would then be "matched" based on their current college GPA's (e.g. two members of the research sample who have identical GPA's would be considered a "matched pair"). After all the members of the research sample have been placed into "matched pairs," the members of each "matched pair" are then randomly assigned to the different conditions in the experiment[2,3,5] (e.g. 1 member of the "matched pair" is assigned to the "treatment group" that will receive a study guide for the exam and 1 member of the "matched pair" is assigned to the "control group" that would not receive a study guide for the exam). The "matching" process will create two groups of college students whose average college GPA's are identical. While the process of "random assignment" provides an opportunity for equal groups to be created, the process of "matching" forces the groups in an experiment to be equivalent.[1,3,7] The one disadvantage to the "matching" process is that members of the research sample who do not have a "match" (i.e. another member of the research sample who has an identical GPA) are removed from the experiment, thus reducing the size of the research sample.[1,13]

To illustrate how the "matching" process can be used to create equivalent groups in an experiment, let's look at some hypothetical data for the Psychology professor's experiment. In the table below, each college student in the research sample has been assigned a number from 1–20 and each student has provided the Psychology professor with his/her current college GPA.

Student #	GPA	Student #	GPA	Student #	GPA	Student #	GPA
1	3.7	6	2.9	11	3.1	16	4.0
2	3.2	7	3.3	12	2.8	17	3.7
3	4.0	8	3.4	13	2.4	18	2.9
4	2.6	9	3.2	14	3.3	19	3.8
5	3.1	10	3.4	15	2.8	20	2.4

Using the GPA's, the professor would first form "matched pairs" of sample members.

Student #	GPA	GPA	Student #
1	3.7	3.7	17
2	3.2	3.2	9
3	4.0	4.0	16
5	3.1	3.1	11
6	2.9	2.9	18
7	3.3	3.3	14
8	3.4	3.4	10
12	2.8	2.8	15
13	2.4	2.4	20

Student # 4 (GPA = 2.6) and Student # 19 (GPA = 3.8) will be removed from the experiment since they do not have a "match" for their GPA among members of the research sample. The size of the research sample has been reduced to 18 college students. Nine students will be randomly assigned to each group in the experiment.

The professor will then randomly assign members of each "matched" pair to groups.

Student #'s 1, 9, 16, 5, 18, 7, 8, 12, and 20 are randomly assigned to "treatment group"

Student #	1	9	16	5	18	7	8	12	20
GPA	3.7	3.2	4.0	3.1	2.9	3.3	3.4	2.8	2.4

Average GPA = 28.8/9 = **3.2**

Student #'s 17, 2, 3, 11, 6, 14, 10, 15, and 13 are randomly assigned to "control group"

Student #	17	2	3	11	6	14	10	15	13
GPA	3.7	3.2	4.0	3.1	2.9	3.3	3.4	2.8	2.4

Average GPA = 28.8/9 = **3.2**

As can be seen from the data, the "matching" process successfully created two groups of college students with identical average college GPA's (Treatment Group = 3.2; Control Group = 3.2). Since the two groups are equivalent, the professor can be more confident (although not 100% sure) that any difference in the exam performance of the two groups can be attributed to whether or not the students received a study guide for the exam rather than to a difference in academic ability (i.e. as measured by college GPA) across groups (i.e. conditions).

While "matching" produces groups that appear equivalent, psychologists must be aware that while the groups are equivalent with respect to the "matching variable," there may be other variables which might influence the performance of members of the research sample during the experiment for which the groups have not been "matched" (e.g. In the professor's experiment designed to answer the research question, "Does providing students with a study guide increase exam performance?," the groups were not "matched" with respect to "study skills"; a variable that could definitely influence the performance of participants during the experiment). If there are significant differences between the groups with respect to a potentially influential variable, psychologists will be unable to rule out the effect of this variable as a potential cause of any significant differences between groups observed during the experiment. As a remedy to this potential problem, psychologists can "match" members of the research sample across multiple variables before randomly assigning them to the conditions in the experiment.[1,7,13] While this remedy will increase the equivalence of the groups in an experiment, the trade-off is that it is likely to decrease the size of the research sample by increasing the number of sample members for whom there is no "match" and who must therefore be excluded from the experiment.[1,7,13]

There are also instances when psychologists may be unable to use "matching" to create equivalent groups in their experiments. The most common instance is when psychologists face time or staff resource constraints that prohibit the measurement of all members of the research sample on the "matching" variable prior to the start of an experiment.[1,7] Psychologists may also be unable to use "matching" when they are concerned that measuring members of the research sample on a "matching" variable will make them aware of the true purpose of the experiment[2] (e.g. In the professor's experiment designed to answer the question, "Does providing students with a study guide increase exam performance?," measuring the "study skills" or "study time" of all members of the research sample as a "matching" variable prior to the experiment could make participants aware that the main focus of the experiment involves exam performance. If the participants are aware of the purpose of the experiment, it might influence their performance during the experiment and ultimately influence the conclusions that can be drawn about the relationship between whether or not one is provided a study guide and exam performance). In both of these instances, psychologists would have to instead rely on "random assignment" to create equivalent groups for their experiments.

Psychologists also conduct experiments in which they manipulate independent variables that have more than two levels. As a result, the experiments will involve a comparison of more than two conditions. These experiments are typically conducted using between-subjects designs (i.e. independent groups, matched groups) which are modified by psychologists to accommodate more than two conditions. Experiments which compare more than two conditions will typically include: (a) a control group and two or more treatment groups or (b) three or more treatment groups. While there are several design options available, psychologists typically conduct these experiments using an independent groups design.

Control Group vs. Multiple Treatment Groups Design

In this design, participants are randomly assigned to either a "control group" or one of multiple "treatment groups."[1,2,8] Those participants assigned to the different "treatment groups" are then exposed to different treatments, interventions, or levels of the variable of interest to the psychologists conducting the experiment. The participants assigned to the "control group" are not exposed to the treatment, intervention, or variable of interest to the psychologists conducting the experiment. Each participant is assigned to only one condition and is exposed to only one level of the independent variable. Participants are then measured on the dependent variable(s) and average scores are computed for participants in each of the conditions. The average scores on the dependent variable(s) are then analyzed to determine if there is a significant difference between the control group and treatment groups.

As an example, let's assume an Experimental Psychologist is interested in conducting an experiment to determine whether exposure to humor can reduce patients' pain following a joint replacement surgery. She also wants to determine if exposure to visual humor (e.g. episodes of a TV sitcom) is more effective in reducing patients' pain following joint replacement surgery than exposure to printed humor (e.g. comic books). To conduct the experiment, she would randomly assign participants to either a "control group" (i.e. patients who receive no exposure to humor following their joint replacement surgery), treatment group A (i.e. patients who watch episodes of a TV sitcom following joint replacement surgery), or treatment group B (i.e. patients who read comic books following joint replacement surgery). After the humor exposure manipulation has been completed, the psychologist will then collect a "pain rating" from each of the patients in the experiment (e.g. 1 = I feel no pain; 7 = The pain is unbearable!). The psychologist will compute an average pain rating for the participants in each condition in the experiment. The average pain ratings will then be analyzed to determine: (a) if there is a significant difference in ratings of pain between the control group (who received no exposure to humor) and the two treatment groups (who both received exposure to humor) and (b) if there is a significant difference in ratings of pain between treatment group A (who received exposure to visual humor) and treatment group B (who received exposure to printed humor).

Multiple Treatment Groups Design

In this design, participants are randomly assigned to one of multiple "treatment groups" in an experiment. Participants assigned to the different "treatment groups" are exposed to different amounts or types of the treatment, intervention, or variable of interest to the psychologists conducting the experiment.[1,2,8,14] All of the participants are then measured on the dependent variable(s) and average scores are computed for participants in each of the treatment groups. Average scores on the dependent variable(s) are then analyzed to determine if there are significant differences between the treatment groups (different amounts or types of treatment, intervention, or variable received).

As an example, let's assume the results of the Experimental Psychologist's experiment on exposure to humor and patients' pain following joint replacement surgery revealed that patients exposed to visual humor reported significantly lower pain than patients exposed to printed humor or no humor following joint replacement surgery. Because there are a variety of types of visual humor, she could conduct a follow-up experiment in which she compared the effectiveness of 4 different types of visual humor (e.g. TV sitcom, comedy film, animated TV comedy, TV sketch comedy) in reducing patients' pain following joint replacement surgery. In order to conduct her experiment, she would randomly assign her participants to treatment group A (i.e. patients who watch episodes of a TV sitcom show following joint replacement surgery), treatment group B (i.e. patients who watch a comedy film following joint replacement surgery), treatment group C (i.e. patients who watch an animated TV comedy show following joint replacement surgery), or to treatment group D (i.e. patients who watch a TV sketch comedy show after joint replacement surgery). After the humor exposure manipulation is complete, the psychologist will collect a "pain rating" from each of the patients in the experiment (e.g. 1 = I feel no pain; 7 = The pain is unbearable!). She will then compute average pain ratings for each condition in the experiment. The average pain ratings will then be analyzed to determine if there are significant differences between participants in the 4 "treatment groups" (i.e. differences in pain ratings due to exposure to the 4 different types of visual humor).

Advantages and Disadvantages of Between-Subjects Designs

There are several advantages for psychologists who use a between-subjects design to conduct an experiment in which they compare two or more conditions. These advantages are a direct result of participants taking part in only one condition during the experiment. First, the performance of participants during the experiment will not be adversely affected by factors such as stress, fatigue, and boredom, or artificially inflated by a practice/learning effect that can result when participants are required to complete multiple conditions.[2,10,12] Second, participants will be less able to discern the true purpose of the experiment due to being "blind" to what is occurring in the other conditions in the experiment.[2,12] Participants will, therefore, be less likely to alter their behavior during an experiment in response to perceptions of how they believe they are expected to behave or to the outcome desired by the psychologists conducting the experiment. Third, the potential for carry-over effects are eliminated.[2,4,7] A "carry over" effect can occur when the effects of one condition during an experiment carry-over or contaminate participant performance during a subsequent condition (e.g. if participants take part in a condition with a lasting effect on their physical, psychological, emotional, or cognitive state, it can influence their performance in subsequent condition(s) during the experiment). Fourth, the potential for "order effects" are also eliminated.[12] An "order effect" can occur when the order in which conditions are administered in an experiment can have a significant effect on participant performance (e.g. if participants are administered two drugs during an experiment (i.e. Drug A and Drug B), those participants who are administered Drug A followed by Drug B may show a different outcome than participants who are administered Drug B followed by Drug A). Finally, since participants take part in only one condition and the amount of time participants are involved in the research is kept to a minimum, participants are less likely to drop out of the experiment. Therefore, subject attrition (i.e. "drop out") is minimized.[10]

Although there are several advantages associated with a between-subjects design, there are also several important disadvantages that psychologists must take into consideration. First, since different groups of participants are assigned to each condition in the experiment, a larger number of participants will be required than if psychologists had a single group of participants take part in all conditions in the experiment.[2,5,7] The larger number of participants required by the between-subjects design can be problematic for psychologists who have limited financial or staff resources or who are studying populations with limited members (e.g. individuals who have been diagnosed with rare medical or psychological conditions, individuals who have had unique life experiences). Second, psychologists have to expend time and resources to create the equivalent groups across conditions in an experiment (e.g. "matching") which are essential for a between-subjects design to provide a valid test of the relationship between an independent and dependent variable.[1,6] This is not a concern for a within-subjects design in which a single group of participants completes all the conditions in an experiment. Finally, error introduced into an experiment through the creation of groups that are "similar but not identical" across conditions, makes a between-subjects design less sensitive to the effect of an independent variable (i.e. less able to detect the true relationship that exists between an independent variable and one or more dependent variables) than a within-subjects design.[2,4,5,13]

EXERCISE 7A

Analysis of Random Assignment Strategies

When conducting an experiment using a between-subjects design, psychologists must: (a) assign participants to conditions in an unbiased manner so participants have an equal opportunity to be assigned to any of the conditions in the experiment, (b) create groups that are comparable in size and that contain a sufficient number of participants to allow for a meaningful comparison across conditions, and (c) create groups that are as equivalent as possible (preferably identical!) across conditions so that any differences between the groups at the end of the experiment can be attributed to the effect of the independent variable rather than to differences between groups that existed at the start of the experiment. Psychologists rely on the process of "random assignment" to achieve these three objectives.

Below are 10 scenarios describing different methods used by psychologists to randomly assign participants to the conditions in their experiments. For each scenario, please determine if: **(a)** the assignment of participants is truly "random", **(b)** the assignment process will create two groups of equal size, **(c)** the psychologists allowed their personal biases to effect the assignment process, and **(d)** the assignment process will create groups that are equivalent across conditions. Please provide a rationale for your decisions in the spaces provided.

01. A Cognitive Psychologist studying the effect of sleep deprivation on memory, assigns the first 10 individuals who enroll in her study to a treatment group (i.e. deprived of sleep) and the last 10 individuals who enroll in her study to a control group (i.e. not deprived of sleep).

Is the assignment of participants truly random?	YES	NO
Will the process result in groups of equal size?	YES	NO
Did personal bias enter the assignment process?	YES	NO
Will the process produce equivalent groups?	YES	NO

Rationale:

02. A Psychiatrist studying a new depression medication, assigns the 10 participants who appear most suicidal to a treatment group (i.e. receive medication) and the remaining 10 participants to a control group (i.e. do not receive medication).

Is the assignment of participants truly random?	YES	NO
Will the process result in groups of equal size?	YES	NO
Did personal bias enter the assignment process?	YES	NO
Will the process produce equivalent groups?	YES	NO

Rationale:

03. An Experimental Psychologist studying the effect of time pressure on performance, assigns participants to conditions based on their last names. Individuals whose last names start with the letters A–L are assigned to a treatment group (i.e. time pressure) while those whose last names start with the letters M–Z are assigned to a control group (i.e. no time pressure).

Is the assignment of participants truly random?	YES	NO
Will the process result in groups of equal size?	YES	NO
Did personal bias enter the assignment process?	YES	NO
Will the process produce equivalent groups?	YES	NO

Rationale:

04. A Health Psychologist studying the effect of exercise on self-esteem, places 20 ping-pong balls numbered 1–20 in a bowl. She has her 20 participants each take 1 ball from the bowl. Participants selecting an odd numbered ball are assigned to a treatment group (i.e. exercise). Those selecting an even numbered ball are assigned to a control group (i.e. no exercise).

Is the assignment of participants truly random?	YES	NO
Will the process result in groups of equal size?	YES	NO
Did personal bias enter the assignment process?	YES	NO
Will the process produce equivalent groups?	YES	NO

Rationale:

05. A Clinical Psychologist studying the effects of behavioral and cognitive therapy on anxiety, assigns individuals who can attend a morning therapy session (8:00–9:00 a.m.) to treatment group A (i.e. receive behavioral therapy) and individuals who can attend an evening therapy session (6:00–7:00 p.m.) to treatment group B (i.e. receive cognitive therapy).

Is the assignment of participants truly random?	YES	NO
Will the process result in groups of equal size?	YES	NO
Did personal bias enter the assignment process?	YES	NO
Will the process produce equivalent groups?	YES	NO

Rationale:

06. A Military Psychologist studying the effect of dehydration on alertness, has 20 soldiers each draw a card from a deck of playing cards. Those soldiers who draw a red card are assigned to a treatment group (i.e. deprived of water) while those who draw a black card are assigned to a control group (i.e. not deprived of water).

Is the assignment of participants truly random?	YES	NO
Will the process result in groups of equal size?	YES	NO
Did personal bias enter the assignment process?	YES	NO
Will the process produce equivalent groups?	YES	NO

Rationale:

07. An Educational Psychologist studying the effectiveness of a new reading program for high school students, rotates the assignment to his conditions (i.e. treatment, control, treatment, control, etc...) until all 20 of his participants have been assigned to a treatment group (i.e. complete reading program) or a control group (i.e. do not complete reading program).

Is the assignment of participants truly random?	YES	NO
Will the process result in groups of equal size?	YES	NO
Did personal bias enter the assignment process?	YES	NO
Will the process produce equivalent groups?	YES	NO

Rationale:

08. A School Psychologist studying the effectiveness of a new anti-bullying program, assigns 10 high school students who, according to the school principal, will take the program seriously to a treatment group (i.e. complete anti-bullying program) and 10 other high school students to a control group (i.e. do not complete anti-bullying program).

Is the assignment of participants truly random?	YES	NO
Will the process result in groups of equal size?	YES	NO
Did personal bias enter the assignment process?	YES	NO
Will the process produce equivalent groups?	YES	NO

Rationale:

09. A Psychology Professor studying student perceptions of two new Experimental Psychology textbooks, assigns students who want to complete the textbook evaluation survey online to treatment group A (i.e. evaluate textbook 1) and students who want to complete the textbook evaluation survey in his office to treatment group B (i.e. evaluate textbook 2).

Is the assignment of participants truly random?	YES	NO
Will the process result in groups of equal size?	YES	NO
Did personal bias enter the assignment process?	YES	NO
Will the process produce equivalent groups?	YES	NO

Rationale:

10. A Physiological Psychologist studying the effect of a stressful event on chemical reactions in the brains of lab rats, assigns 10 lab rats with prior experience participating in experiments to a treatment group (i.e. experience stressful event) and 10 lab rats with no prior experience participating in experiments to a control group (i.e. do not experience stressful event).

Is the assignment of participants truly random?	YES	NO
Will the process result in groups of equal size?	YES	NO
Did personal bias enter the assignment process?	YES	NO
Will the process produce equivalent groups?	YES	NO

Rationale:

EXERCISE 7B

Evaluating Between-Subjects Design Options

A team of Forensic Psychologists are interested in conducting an experiment to study the effectiveness of a "victim-offender dialogue" program for men incarcerated in prison. The goals of the program are to teach offenders to: (a) show remorse for their crimes, (b) show empathy for their victims, and (c) take personal responsibility for their crimes. During the program, trained mediators will facilitate one-hour meetings between victims (or family members of the victims) and their offenders. During the meetings, the victims can ask their offenders questions about the crimes, ask why the offenders committed their crimes, and talk with the offenders about what it is like to be the victim of a crime, and how being a victim has negatively affected their lives and the lives of their families. A week after these meetings, after the inmates have had some time to reflect on the words of their victims, the psychologists will have each of the inmates complete a questionnaire. The questionnaire will assess inmates' levels of remorse, empathy, and personal responsibility in relation to their crimes and the victims of their crimes.

There is currently disagreement among the team of Forensic Psychologists with respect to the type of between-subjects research design that would provide the most meaningful assessment of the "victim-offender dialogue" program. Their disagreement centers on the method that will be used to assign participants to conditions and create groups of participants that are equivalent across conditions. A description of the research design ideas of each member of the team appear below. Please read each team member's research ideas and then: **(a)** identify the strengths of the proposed research design, **(b)** the weaknesses of the proposed research design, and **(c)** rate the likelihood the proposed design will allow the team of Forensic Psychologists to conduct a valid and meaningful assessment of the "victim-offender dialogue" program.

After you have evaluated each of the team member's research design ideas, you will be asked to provide your recommendation as to the research design that the Forensic Psychologists should use to assess the effectiveness of the "victim-offender dialogue" program and provide a rationale for your recommendation in the space provided.

Forensic Psychologist A

Forensic Psychologist A wants to conduct a classic between-subjects design. She wants to ask the warden of the prison for a list containing the names of all 500 inmates incarcerated at the prison. She will then assign each inmate on the list a number from 1–500 and use a random numbers table to randomly select 50 inmates from the list. She will then assign each of these 50 inmates a number from 1–50 and once again use a random numbers table to assign 25 inmates to a treatment group (i.e. inmates who will participate in the "victim-offender dialogue" program) and 25 inmates to a control group (i.e. inmates who will not participate in the "victim-offender dialogue" program). Finally, after the 25 inmates assigned to the treatment group complete their meetings with their victims, she will have all 50 inmates complete a questionnaire designed to assess their feelings of remorse, empathy, and personal responsibility in relation to their crimes.

Strengths of the Research Design	Weaknesses of the Research Design

What is the likelihood this research design would allow the Forensic Psychologists to conduct a meaningful assessment of the "victim-offender dialogue" program?

Extremely   1   2   3   4   5   6   7   Extremely
Unlikely   Likely

Rating =

Rationale:

Forensic Psychologist B

Forensic Psychologist B wants to conduct a "matched groups" between-subjects design. He hypothesizes that the amount of time an inmate has been incarcerated in prison for his crime would influence the extent to which the "victim-offender dialogue" program would teach him to express remorse, empathy, and/or personal responsibility in relation to his crime. Therefore, he proposes that "years of incarceration" be used as a "matching" variable. He would like to ask the warden of the prison for a list containing the names of all 500 inmates incarcerated at the prison and the number of years each of the inmates on the list has been incarcerated at the prison. Once he acquires the list from the warden, he plans to go through the list and create "matched pairs" of inmates who have been incarcerated at the prison for the same number of years (e.g. two inmates who have been incarcerated at the prison for 5 years would be considered a "matched pair"). He will continue this "matching" process until he has found 25 "matched pairs" of inmates. He will then take each "matched pair" of inmates and randomly assign the letters A and B to the inmates. He will then flip a coin. If he flips "heads," inmate A will be assigned to the treatment condition (i.e. inmates who will participate in the "victim-offender dialogue" program) and inmate B will be assigned to the control condition (i.e. inmates who will not participate in the "victim-offender dialogue" program). If he flips "tails," inmate B will be assigned to the treatment condition and inmate A will be assigned to the control condition. He will continue this process for each of the 25 "matched pairs" of inmates until all 50 of the inmates have been assigned to the treatment and control conditions. Finally, after the 25 inmates assigned to the treatment group complete their meetings with their victims, he will have all 50 inmates complete a questionnaire designed to assess their feelings of remorse, empathy, and personal responsibility in relation to their crimes.

Strengths of the Research Design	Weaknesses of the Research Design

What is the likelihood this research design would allow the Forensic Psychologists to conduct a meaningful assessment of the "victim-offender dialogue" program?

Extremely   1   2   3   4   5   6   7   Extremely
Unlikely   Likely

Rating =

Rationale:

Forensic Psychologist C

Forensic Psychologist C wants to conduct an "alternative" between-subjects design. He hypothesizes inmates who live together in a prison cell and experience the highly structured and routine lifestyle of prison together will come to think and behave in a highly similar manner over time. He proposes that inmates who are currently "cellmates" can be considered similar enough to one another to be treated as a "matched pair." He will ask the warden of the prison for a list containing the names of all 500 inmates incarcerated at the prison along with the names of their "cellmates." He will then assign the 250 pairs of cellmates a number from 1–250 and then use a random numbers table to randomly select 25 pairs of cellmates. He will then take each pair of cellmates and assign the numbers 1 and 2 to the inmates. He will place slips of paper containing the numbers 1 and 2 into a bowl and draw out one slip of paper. If he draws a "1," inmate 1 will be assigned to the treatment condition (i.e. inmates who will participate in the "victim-offender dialogue" program) and inmate 2 will be assigned to the control condition (i.e. inmates who will not participate in the "victim-offender dialogue" program). If he draws a "2," inmate 2 will be assigned to the treatment condition and inmate 1 to the control condition. He will continue this process for each of the 25 "matched pairs" of inmates until all 50 inmates have been assigned to conditions. Finally, after all 25 of the inmates assigned to the treatment condition complete their meetings with their victims, he will have all 50 inmates complete a questionnaire to assess their feelings of remorse, empathy, and personal responsibility in relation to their crimes.

Strengths of the Research Design	Weaknesses of the Research Design

What is the likelihood this research design would allow the Forensic Psychologists to conduct a meaningful assessment of the "victim-offender dialogue" program?

Extremely   1   2   3   4   5   6   7   Extremely
Unlikely   Likely

Rating = [   ]

Rationale:

Having evaluated the design ideas of each Forensic Psychologist, which of the proposed research designs would you recommend that the psychologists use to have the best chance of conducting a meaningful assessment of the "victim-offender dialogue" program? Provide a rationale for your recommendation in the space provided below.

Forensic Psychologist 1: Classic Between-Subjects Design ☐

Forensic Psychologist 2: Matched-Groups Design ☐

Forensic Psychologist 3: Alternative Design ☐

Rationale:

What *modifications* to this design would you recommend to improve its ability to provide a meaningful assessment of the "victim-offender dialogue" program?

EXERCISE 7C

Analysis of a Block Randomization Plan

An Industrial-Organizational Psychologist wants to conduct an experiment to investigate the effectiveness of 3 incentive programs for increasing employee productivity. The 3 incentive programs she wants to investigate are as follows: (**A**) a "Time-Off Incentive" (i.e. employees can earn one week of paid leave (valued at $500) by achieving the target level of productivity set by the company), (**B**) a "Stock-Options Incentive" (i.e. employees can earn $500 of company stock by achieving the target level of productivity set by the company), and (**C**) a "Financial Incentive" (i.e. employees can earn a one-time $500 bonus for achieving the target level of productivity set by the company). She plans on using a between-subjects design to conduct her experiment. She has recruited 30 employees from a local company to participate in her experiment and she would like to use a "block randomization plan" to randomly assign the 30 employees to her 3 incentive conditions. Having slept through her Research Methods course in college, she is having trouble remembering how to create a "block randomization plan"! She finds her "drool covered" notes from her college Research Methods course and after reading through her limited notes, attempts to create a "block randomization plan." Her "block randomization plan" appears below.

Block Randomization Plan

Block #	Participants	Condition Assignment
1	1–4	CBBA
2	5–8	CACB
3	9–12	BBBA
4	13–16	CABB
5	17–20	BABC
6	21–24	CBCB
7	25–28	ACBC
8	29–30	CB

Please review the "block randomization plan" created by the Industrial-Organizational Psychologist and identify **four (4)** specific errors the psychologist has made in setting up her "block randomization plan."

Identify **four (4)** specific errors made by the Industrial-Organizational Psychologist in setting up her "block randomization plan."

Error 1: _____

_____

_____

_____

Error 2: _____

_____

_____

_____

Error 3: _____

_____

_____

_____

Error 4: _____

_____

_____

_____

Additional Errors?

Being an expert on "block randomization plans," you volunteer to create a "plan" that the Industrial-Organizational Psychologist can use to assign her participants to the three conditions in her experiment. Based on the number of participants who will take part in the experiment (i.e. 30) and the number of incentive conditions the psychologist would like to investigate (i.e. 3), you decide to create a "block randomization plan" that uses a "block size" of 3. Using a "block size" of 3, please create a correctly designed "block randomization plan" and place your final "block randomization plan" in the space provided below.

Block Randomization Plan

Block #	Participants	Condition Assignment

Identify **three (3)** specific ways in which your "block randomization plan" is an improvement over the "plan" created by the I/O Psychologist.

References

1. Bordens, K. S., & Abbot, B. B. (2011). *Research design and methods: A process approach* (8th ed.). Boston, MA: McGraw-Hill Publishers.

2. Passer, M. W. (2013). *Research methods: Concepts and connections.* New York, NY: Worth Publishers.

3. Cozby, P. C., & Bates, S. C. (2011). *Methods in behavioral research.* (11th ed.). New York, NY: McGraw-Hill Publishers.

4. Kantowitz, B. H., Roediger, H. L., & Elmes, D. G. (2014). *Experimental psychology* (10th ed.). Stamford, CT: Cengage Learning.

5. Smith, R. A., & Davis, S. F. (2012). *The psychologist as detective: An introduction to conducting research in psychology* (6th ed.). Boston, MA: Pearson Publishers.

6. Beins, B. C. (2012). *Research methods: A tool for life* (3rd ed.). Boston, MA: Pearson Publishers.

7. Jackson, S. L. (2014). *Research methods: A modular approach* (3rd ed.). Stamford, CT: Cengage Learning.

8. Myers, A., & Hansen, C. H. (2011). *Experimental psychology* (7th ed.). Belmont, CA: Wadsworth/Cengage Learning.

9. Schultz, K. F., & Grimes, D. A. (2002). Generation of allocation sequences in randomized trials: Chance not choice. *The Lancet, 359,* 515–519.

10. Maclin, M. K., & Solso, R. L. (2007). *Experimental psychology: A case approach* (8th ed.). Boston, MA: Pearson/Allyn & Bacon.

11. Dallal, G. E. (2013). Welcome to randomization.com: Where it's never the same thing twice. *Randomization.com.* Retrieved from http://www.randomization.com

12. Leary, M. R. (2007). *Introduction to behavioral research methods* (5th ed.). Boston, MA: Pearson/Allyn & Bacon.

13. Gravetter, F. J., & Wallnau, L. B. (2012). *Statistics for the behavioral sciences* (9th ed.). Belmont, CA: Wadsworth-Cengage Learning.

14. Evans, A. N., & Rooney, B. F. (2007). *Methods in psychological research.* Thousand Oaks, CA: Sage Publications.

MODULE
8

Within-Subjects Designs

When psychologists want to conduct an experiment in which two or more levels of an independent variable (i.e. two or more conditions) are compared, there are two primary research design options for them to consider. As discussed in Module 7, the first design option is known as the "between-subjects" design.[1,2,3] Recall that in a between-subjects design, a different group of participants is assigned to each condition in the experiment. Each group of participants is then exposed to a different level of the independent variable. All the participants are then measured on the dependent variable. Average scores on the dependent variable are then computed for each group of participants (i.e. for each condition). Finally, these average scores undergo a statistical analysis to determine if there is a significant difference across conditions.

There are, however, some characteristics associated with the "between-subjects" research design that may prevent psychologists from making it their design of choice. First, the between-subjects design often requires a large number of participants.[1,2,3] The need for a large number of participants can be problematic for psychologists who lack the time and/or resources necessary to recruit and test a large number of participants or who want to study populations that contain a small number of members.[2,3] Second, when using a between-subjects design, psychologists have to devote time and resources toward the creation of equivalent groups of participants across the conditions in an experiment[2,4] (e.g. matching, block randomization). Third, the between-subjects design does not allow psychologists to study the behavior and/or mental processes of individual participants under different conditions or study changes in individual participants that can occur over time.[3] As a result of these characteristics of the "between-subjects" design, psychologists may decide to select the second design option as their research design of choice. This second design option is known as the "within-subjects" design.

In the "within-subjects" research design, a different group of participants is not assigned to the different conditions in the experiment with each group exposed to a different level of the independent variable. Instead, a single group of participants completes all of the conditions in the experiment and are exposed to all levels of the independent variable.[2,3,5] After completing each of the conditions in the experiment and being exposed to each level of the independent variable, participants are measured on the dependent variable. The process continues until the participants have completed all conditions in the experiment. Average scores on the dependent variable are then computed for each condition. The average scores then undergo a statistical analysis to determine whether there is a significant difference in the behavior and/or mental processes of the group across conditions or whether the behavior and/or mental processes of the group have changed significantly over time. Because participants are repeatedly measured on the dependent variable after completing each of the conditions in the experiment, the within-subjects design is also referred to as a "repeated measures" design.[2,5,6]

Types of Within-Subjects Designs

Because the independent variable manipulated by psychologists in an experiment will have two or more levels,[1,2,4] an experiment conducted using a within-subjects design will involve a single group of participants who complete two or more conditions (i.e. exposed to two or more levels of the independent variable). There are two "within-subjects" designs commonly used by psychologists to compare two different conditions (i.e. two different levels of the independent variable). These within-subjects designs involve a comparison of: (a) a treatment and control group or (b) two treatment groups.

Treatment vs. Control Group Design

In this type of research design, a single group of participants completes both a treatment condition and a control condition.[1,2,5,6] In the treatment condition, the participants are exposed to the treatment, intervention, or variable of interest. In the control condition, the participants are not exposed to the treatment, intervention, or variable of interest. After completing each of the conditions, participants are measured on the dependent variable and average scores on the dependent variable are then computed for both the treatment and the control conditions. The average scores on the dependent variable are then statistically analyzed to determine if there is a significant difference in the behavior or mental processes of the group of participants across conditions. This research design is often used by psychologists who want to test the effectiveness of a new treatment or intervention.

As an example, assume a Neuropsychologist is interested in conducting an experiment to test the effectiveness of a new drug designed to reduce the frequency of nightmares experienced by individuals diagnosed with post-traumatic stress disorder (PTSD). If the Neuropsychologist were to use a "within-subjects" design, he could have a single group of participants take the new drug every day for 1 month. At the end of the month, he would have each participant report the number of nightmares he/she experienced during the 1-month period. He would then have the same group of participants take a "placebo" (i.e. a pill that does not contain the new medication) every day for 1 month. At the end of the month, the Neuropsychologist would again ask each of the participants to report the total number of nightmares he/she experienced during the 1-month period. He would then compute the average number of nightmares experienced by participants during the treatment condition (i.e. when taking the new medication) and the average number of nightmares experienced by participants during the control condition (i.e. when taking a placebo). If the average number of nightmares experienced by participants is significantly lower during the treatment condition, the Neuropsychologist would have evidence the new medication is effective in reducing the frequency of nightmares in individuals diagnosed with PTSD.

Treatment vs. Treatment Group Design

In this type of research design, a single group of participants complete two different treatment conditions. While completing the two treatment conditions, participants are exposed to two different amounts of a treatment or intervention or to two different types of treatment or intervention.[2,3,5] After completing each treatment condition, participants are measured on the dependent variable. Average scores on the dependent variable are computed for each treatment condition and statistically analyzed to determine whether there is a significant difference in the behavior and/or mental processes of participants across the two treatment conditions. The results of the experiment would provide psychologists with evidence as to the relative effectiveness of: (a) two different amounts of a treatment or intervention or (b) two different types of treatment or intervention.

As an example, assume a Sports Psychologist is interested in conducting an experiment to compare the effectiveness of two different interventions designed to increase the self-confidence of professional athletes returning to competition following a significant injury. Specifically, the Sports Psychologist wants to compare the effectiveness of a motivational speaker and self-help motivational audiotapes in increasing the self-confidence of athletes. If the Sports Psychologist were to use a within-subjects design, she could have a single group of professional athletes who are preparing to return to competition following a significant injury listen to a 3-hour lecture by a motivational speaker (i.e. Intervention A). After the 3-hour presentation, she would have each of the athletes rate his/her level of self-confidence. She would then have the same group of athletes listen to a 3-hour self-help motivational audiotape (i.e. Intervention B). At the conclusion of the 3-hour motivational audiotape, she would ask each of the athletes to once again rate his/her level of self-confidence. She would then compute the average self-confidence ratings for Intervention A (i.e. motivational speaker) and Intervention B (i.e. self-help motivational audiotape). If there is a significant difference between the average ratings of self-confidence, the Sports Psychologist would have evidence as to which treatment is more effective in increasing the self-confidence of professional athletes returning to competition following a significant injury.

Psychologists also use "within-subjects" designs to conduct experiments in which they manipulate an independent variable that has more than two levels. These experiments involve a single group of participants who complete three or more conditions (i.e. are exposed to three or more levels of the independent variable). Psychologists have used the "within-subjects" design to conduct a variety of experiments in which they have manipulated independent variables with more than two levels. These experiments have involved: (a) studying changes in a single group of participants over time (e.g. over repeated trials, sessions, administrations of a test, treatments, doses, performances), (b) comparing the relative effectiveness of multiple methods of treatment, (c) comparing the effectiveness of multiple intervention programs, or (d) comparing perceptions of people, places, or things whose characteristics have been manipulated.[2,3]

Studying Change Over Time

In this type of research design, psychologists will make three or more measurements of a single group of participants over time. Specifically, they will measure the group of participants on the dependent variable after the group completes each of the three or more conditions in the experiment. Depending upon the nature of the experiment being conducted, psychologists may measure the group of participants on the dependent variable after the group has completed multiple: (a) trials (e.g. the time it takes rats to complete a maze is measured after each of 6 maze trials), (b) sessions (e.g. the likelihood of divorce is measured for married couples after each of 4 marital therapy sessions), (c) test administrations (e.g. Graduate Record Exam (GRE) scores for Psychology majors applying to Graduate psychology programs are measured after each of 3 administrations of the GRE), (d) doses (e.g. the intensity of pain for individuals experiencing migraine headaches is measured after each of 5 doses of a new migraine medication, (e) performances (e.g. the number of defective products produced is measured at the end of each month during employees' 3 month probation period), or (f) treatments (e.g. mobility of elderly patients is measured after each of 4 sessions of physical therapy).[2,3] Average scores on the dependent variable are then computed for each conditions (i.e. each trial, session, treatment, administration, dose, performance). Average scores on the dependent variable are then analyzed to determine whether there is a significant difference in the behavior and/or mental processes of the group of participants across conditions (i.e. over time).

As an example, assume a Human Factors Psychologist has been hired to train employees on how to safely use a new piece of manufacturing equipment. Specifically, she has been hired by the company to conduct a 5-day safety training program for employees who will be required to use the new piece of machinery. In addition to conducting the 5-day training, she is interested in conducting an experiment to determine if 5 days of training are necessary to teach employees how to use the new equipment safely. To conduct her experiment, she has the employees attend the first day of the training program. At the end of the day, she administers a test that is designed to assess their knowledge as to how to operate the new piece of machinery safely. She then has the employees attend days 2–5 of the training program and administers the same safety test at the end of each day of training. She then computes an average test score for each day of the training program and conducts a statistical analysis to determine if there is a significant difference in the average tests scores across days of the program. In analyzing her results, she might discover that scores on the test increase significantly from day 1 to day 3, but then remain stable on days 4 and 5 of the program. From these results, she would have evidence that employees are able to learn how to use the new piece of equipment safely in only 3 days of training and that days 4 and 5 of the training program do not provide any additional significant increase in safety knowledge.

Comparing Treatment Effectiveness

In this type of design, psychologists will measure a single group of participants on the dependent variable after the group experiences each of 3 or more: (a) different amounts of a treatment method or (b) different methods of treatment.[1,2,3] The average scores on the dependent variable are then computed for each amount of a treatment or each method of treatment. The average scores then undergo a statistical analysis to determine if there is a significant difference in the behavior and/or mental processes of participants across the different amounts of a treatment method or across the different methods of treatment.

As an example, assume that an Experimental Psychologist is interested in conducting an experiment to identify the dosage level of a new insomnia medication that is the most effective in helping insomniacs fall asleep at night. To conduct the experiment, the psychologist has a group of individuals diagnosed with insomnia take a 5 mg dose of the insomnia medication every day for 1 month. At the end of the month, he has each individual report the total number of sleepless nights he or she had during the month. He then has the same group take a 50 mg dose of the new insomnia medication every day for 1 month. At the end of the month, he once again has each individual report the number of sleepless nights he or she had during the month. Finally, he has the same group take a 500 mg dose of the new insomnia medication each day for 1 month. Once again, each individual is asked to report the number of sleepless nights he or she had during the month. He then computes an average number of sleepless nights for each of the conditions (i.e. for each dosage level of the insomnia medication) and conducts a statistical analysis to determine whether there is a significant difference in the average number of sleepless nights across dosage levels. If a significant difference emerges, he would then have evidence as to the dosage level of the medication that is most likely to be effective in helping insomniacs fall asleep at night.

Comparing Intervention Effectiveness

In this type of research design, psychologists will measure a single group of participants on the dependent variable after the group experiences each of 3 or more intervention programs.[2,3] Average scores on the dependent variable are then computed for each of the intervention programs. The average scores then undergo a statistical analysis to determine if there is a significant difference in the behavior and/or mental processes of the participants across intervention programs.

As an example, assume that a Community Psychologist is interested in conducting an experiment to determine what type of intervention program is the most effective in helping teens who are currently a member of a gang make the decision to no longer live the gang lifestyle. To conduct the experiment, she has a group of teenage gang members who have been court-ordered to attend an intervention program attend a 2-day "boot camp" program. During the "boot camp" program, military-style discipline and exhausting physical labor are used to break the teens down and rebuild them by teaching them to have self-respect, personal responsibility for their actions, respect for authority, and to strive to make a positive contribution to society. At the end of the 2-day boot camp program, each of the teens is asked to provide a rating of the likelihood he or she will leave the gang lifestyle (e.g. 1 = Not At All Likely; 7 = Highly Likely). The same group of teens then attends a 2-day "prison visitation" program. During the "prison visitation" program, the teens experience what it's like to be sent to prison. The teens are booked, finger printed, strip searched, have mug shots taken, and are issued a prison uniform and prisoner number. The teens then meet with real inmates who are current or former gang members. The inmates talk with the teens about life in prison and how the gang lifestyle led to a life behind bars. Inmates use verbal and physical intimidation tactics to further encourage the teens to leave the gang lifestyle. At the end of the 2-day prison visitation program, each teen is once again asked to provide a rating of his or her likelihood of leaving the gang lifestyle. Finally, the same group of teens attends a 2-day "morgue visitation" program. During the "morgue visitation" program, the teens get to see the deadly consequences of gang-related activity. The teens visit several morgues and view the bodies of gang members killed during gang-related violence and observe an autopsy performed on the body of a deceased gang member.

Coroners who work at the morgues talk with the teens about the gruesome ways people have died as a direct result of gang-related activity. At the end of the 2-day morgue visitation program, each teen is once again asked to provide a rating of his or her likelihood of leaving the gang lifestyle. After the teens have completed the intervention programs, she computes an average likelihood of leaving the gang lifestyle rating for each of the intervention programs. Average scores are then statistically analyzed to determine if there is a significant difference in likelihood of leaving the gang ratings across conditions. If a significant difference emerges, she would then have evidence as to the intervention program that is the most likely to be effective in helping teens make the decision to no longer live the gang lifestyle.

Comparing Perceptions of People, Places, or Things

In this type of research design, psychologists will measure the perceptions of a single group of participants after the group has been exposed to people, places, or things whose characteristics have been manipulated.[2,3] These manipulations result in the creation of three or more versions of the people, places, or things that are being evaluated. Each "version" is then considered a separate condition in the experiment. Appearance is a characteristic of people that could be manipulated (e.g. a Research Psychologist studying the effect of appearance on perceptions of attractiveness could take photographs of an individual wearing 4 different styles of clothing (e.g. jeans and t-shirt, suit and tie, casual wear, athletic wear) and have a group of participants provide their perceptions of the attractiveness of the individual in the 4 photographs). The attractiveness rating for each version of the photograph would serve as the dependent variable. Temperature is a characteristic of a place that could be manipulated (e.g. a Psychology Professor could manipulate the temperature in a classroom and have a group of students solve statistics problems for 15 minutes while the temperature in the classroom is 25 degrees, 50 degrees, 75 degrees, and 100 degrees). The number of problems solved correctly in each of the temperature conditions would serve as the dependent variable.

Advertising slogans used by companies to market and sell a product are an example of a thing that can be manipulated. Assume a Consumer Psychologist has been hired by a company that sells the most unhealthy donuts in the world. During laboratory testing, rats who consumed the donuts became obese, developed heart disease, developed extremely high cholesterol levels, and died significantly earlier than rats who did not consume the donuts! In an effort to sell their donuts to health-conscious consumers, the company decided to use humor in its advertisements for the donuts. The advertising department at the company created 4 humorous slogans they are considering using in an upcoming advertising campaign. The company wants the psychologist to conduct an experiment to determine which of the 4 humorous slogans is the most likely to lead to higher sales if used in the company's upcoming advertising campaign. The 4 humorous slogans the company would like to have evaluated are as follows:

(a)   Guns don't kill people, our donuts do!

(b)   If you're going to clog your arteries, it might as well be with our donuts!

(c)   Every one of our donuts you eat is one step closer to Heaven!

(d)   Our donuts are to die for!

To conduct his experiment, the Consumer Psychologist presents each of the 4 slogans to a group of consumers. After presenting each slogan, he has each of the consumers rate the extent to which the slogan makes them more likely to buy the company's donuts (e.g. 1 = I am no more likely to buy these donuts; 5 = I am extremely more likely to buy these donuts). He computes an average likelihood of purchase rating for each of the 4 slogans. He then statistically analyzes the average likelihood of purchase ratings to determine if there is a significant difference in ratings across slogans. If a significant difference emerges, he would then have evidence as to which of the 4 humorous slogans is most likely to lead to higher sales if used in the company's upcoming advertising campaign for its donuts.

Advantages of Within-Subjects Designs

There are two main advantages for psychologists who decide to use a within-subjects research design. First, the within-subjects design requires fewer participants than the between-subjects design.[3,7,8] For example, assume a Health Psychologist wants to conduct an experiment to study the effectiveness of 4 diet programs in helping individuals lose weight. Specifically, she wants to evaluate the effectiveness of a No Fat Diet, a Low Fat Diet, a Low Carbohydrate Diet, and a Vegetarian Diet. If she decided to use a between-subjects design with a different group of 25 participants assigned to each diet conditions, she would need 100 participants to conduct the experiment (i.e. 4 diet conditions × 25 participants per condition = 100 total participants). If she decided to use a within-subjects design with a single group of 25 participants completing all 4 of the diet conditions, she would only need a total of 25 participants (i.e. 1 group of 25 participants that completes all 4 diet conditions = 25 total participants). The reduced number of participants required to conduct a within-subjects design is especially beneficial for psychologists who don't have the time, resources, staff, or access to acquire a large research sample,[1,2,5] or psychologists who are studying a population whose membership is small in size (e.g. rare psychological or medical conditions, atypical personal experiences, unique cognitive abilities).[1,7]

The second advantage of a within-subjects design is that it reduces the amount of error that is introduced into an experiment by the individual differences that exist among the members of the research sample. Recall that in a between-subjects design, a different group of participants is assigned to each of the conditions in the experiment. Creating groups of participants that are equivalent across conditions poses a major challenge for psychologists. Even after having used techniques such as "random assignment" or "matching," the groups of participants assigned to each condition of the experiment, although similar, are not likely to be identical to one another. Any differences that exist between the groups of participants across the conditions represents a source of error.[1,2,3] The larger the difference between groups (i.e. the larger the error), the less likely psychologists will be able to assess the true relationship between the independent and dependent variable, and the more likely they will be to draw conclusions that are not valid. By contrast, in the within-subjects design, since the same group of participants completes all of the conditions in the experiment, there are no differences between the group of participants across conditions. In a sense, the single group of participants in the within-subjects design serves as a "match" for itself across conditions, thus creating equivalent "groups" across conditions.[4,9,10] With this potential source of error eliminated, psychologists who use a within-subjects research design are more likely to be able to assess the true relationship between the independent and the dependent variable and draw valid conclusions based on the results of the experiment than if they used a between-subjects design. As a result, researchers often refer to within-subjects designs as having more "power"[5,6,7] and being more "sensitive" to the effect of the independent variable (i.e. able to detect the effect of the independent variable, even when the effect size is small).[1,2,10]

Disadvantages of Within-Subjects Designs

There are also some disadvantages associated with using a within-subjects design. Some of these disadvantages are a result of participants being required to complete all of the conditions in an experiment. First, since participants are required to complete multiple conditions, there is a greater potential for participants to drop out of the experiment over time. This "dropping out" of participants during an experiment is often referred to as "attrition or mortality."[1,2,7] A significant loss of participants can prevent psychologists from accurately assessing the relationship between the independent and dependent variables. Second, since the participants may be involved in the experiment over an extended period of time, there is a greater potential for events (e.g. personal, community, societal) outside the experiment to influence the performance of participants during the experiment. The performance of participants may be affected differently across conditions in the experiment depending on the timing of these outside events.[7,8] Third, since the participants may be involved in the experiment over an extended period of time, there is a greater likelihood that participants may change in a meaningful way over time. As an example, psychologists who conduct experiments with younger children, elderly individuals, or individuals diagnosed with a progressive illness are likely to see meaningful changes in participants (decline or development) if their experiments are conducted over extended periods of time. When participants change in a meaningful way during an experiment it is referred to as "maturation."[7,8] If participants change over time: (a) the group of participants can no longer be considered equivalent across conditions, and (b) in the event there is a significant difference on the dependent variable across conditions, psychologists may be unable to determine if this difference is due to the effect of the different conditions (i.e. different levels of the independent variable) or to the change in the participants occurring over time (and conditions).

There are also some disadvantages associated with using a within-subjects design that are a result of the inclusion of multiple conditions (i.e. multiple levels of the independent variable) in the experiment. First, if there is equipment being used to manipulate the independent variable or measurement instruments being used to measure participants on the dependent variable that need to be reset, restarted, or recalibrated after each condition, it increases the likelihood error will be introduced into the experiment. Measurement instruments would also include any raters, judges, or observers used to measure the participants on the dependent variable who may grow tired over time or have difficulty remaining consistent in their evaluation of participants across conditions.[6] Second, the more conditions included in an experiment, the more opportunities participants have to discover the true purpose of the study or the hypothesized outcome of the experiment and alter their behavior in such a way as to support (or fail to support) the hypothesized outcome.[3,11,12]

There are also some disadvantages associated with using a within-subjects design that are a result of the order in which the conditions in an experiment are administered to the participants. First, in within-subjects designs, there is a potential for "order effects." Order effects occur in an experiment when the performance of participants is effected by the order in which the conditions are completed.[1,3,5] For example, if a Cognitive Psychologist has participants complete 3 different problem-solving tasks (e.g. an easy, moderate, and difficult task), the performance of participants on the difficult problem-solving task may be significantly worse if the difficult task is the first task that they complete as opposed to the third task they complete. Second, in within-subjects research designs, there is a potential for "carry-over effects."[3,8,13] Carry-over effects occur when participants complete a condition during an experiment and the effect of that condition has an influence on their performance in subsequent conditions in the experiment (i.e. the effects of a condition "carry over" into subsequent conditions). Examples of "carry-over" that can occur in experiments are presented in the table below.

Effect	Description of Effect
Fatigue	Participants who complete a strenuous task in a condition may perform poorly in subsequent conditions as a result of fatigue[1,2,5]
Boredom	Participants who complete a tedious or boring task in a condition may perform poorly in subsequent conditions as a result of boredom[2]
Practice	Participants who complete a task in a condition may perform better if they are asked to complete the task again in subsequent conditions[4,5,8]
Contrast	Participants exposed to an extreme condition (e.g. emotional, arousing, surprising, challenging), may be less responsive to subsequent conditions that by contrast are less extreme[1,2,11]
Habituation	Participants exposed to a shocking or surprising stimulus (e.g. graphic photographs) in a condition, may become less responsive when exposed to the stimulus again in subsequent conditions[2]

Effect	Description of Effect
Sensitization	Participants exposed to a shocking or surprising stimulus (e.g. graphic photographs) in a condition, may become more responsive when exposed to the stimulus again in subsequent conditions[2,8]
Learning	Participants who acquire new knowledge or information in a condition may perform better in subsequent conditions as a result of the new knowledge or information they have learned[1,2]
Familiarity	Participants who complete a condition in an experiment may perform better in subsequent conditions as a result of becoming more familiar with the experimental setting and the experience of being a participant[2]

Counterbalancing

To control for the effects of order and carry-over in an experiment, psychologists can use a technique known as "counterbalancing." In "counterbalancing," psychologists create different orders of the conditions in the experiment (e.g. Order 1 = ABC; Order 2 = BCA) and then assign an equal number of participants to each of the condition orders. By having participants complete the conditions in different orders, counterbalancing is designed to distribute the effects of order and carry-over equally across the conditions in the experiment.[2,3,5] By controlling for the effects of order and carry-over, if a significant difference in average ratings on the dependent variable emerges across conditions, psychologists would be more confident that the significant difference could be attributed to the effect of the independent variable.

As an example of how counterbalancing is designed to distribute the effects of order and carry-over equally across the conditions in an experiment, let's examine the carry-over effect of boredom. In an experiment, if participants complete several conditions (e.g. Conditions A,B,C), they may become increasingly bored over time. If all participants completed the conditions in the same order (e.g. ABC), the participants would all be most bored during the same condition (i.e. Condition C; the last condition in the experiment). If an analysis of the average ratings on the dependent variable across conditions revealed that the average rating for Condition C was significantly lower than the average ratings for Condition A and Condition B, psychologists may erroneously attribute this difference to the effect of the independent variable, when in fact it was the result of the carry-over effect of boredom. If instead, psychologists were to create different orders of the conditions (e.g. CBA; ACB; BAC) and assign an equivalent number of participants to each order, participants would not all be most bored during the same condition. In fact, 1/3 of the participants would be most bored during Condition A (i.e. CBA), 1/3 would be most bored during Condition B (i.e. ACB), and 1/3 would be the most bored during Condition C (i.e. BAC). Counterbalancing would have successfully distributed the carry-over effect of boredom equally across conditions. If an analysis of average ratings on the dependent variable across conditions revealed that the average rating for Condition C was significantly lower than the average ratings for Condition A and Condition B, psychologists would now be more confident the significant difference was due to the effect of the independent variable.

There are multiple counterbalancing strategies available to psychologists who want to control for the effects of order and carry-over during an experiment. The strategies chosen by psychologists will depend on their available resources, staff, access to participants, and time in which to complete the experiment. Counterbalancing strategies are typically organized into the two categories of: (a) Complete Counterbalancing and (b) Partial Counterbalancing.

Complete Counterbalancing

In "complete counterbalancing," psychologists create all possible orders of the conditions in the experiment and assign an equal number of participants to each of the condition orders.[13,14] But how do psychologists know how many possible orders can be created from the conditions in their experiment? The answer is they can use the formula k! (where k equals the number of conditions in an experiment) to calculate the number of possible orders that can be created from the conditions in an experiment.[1,3] For example, if psychologists are conducting an experiment in which they are comparing two conditions, there would be two possible orders of conditions they could create (k! = 2 × 1 = 2 possible orders). If psychologists want 10 participants assigned to each order, a total of 20 participants would be needed to conduct the experiment (i.e. 10 participants would be assigned to each of the 2 orders). The two orders that could be created are presented below:

	1st Condition	**2nd Condition**
Order 1	A	B
Order 2	B	A

By comparison, if psychologists want to conduct an experiment in which they compare three conditions, there would now be six possible orders of conditions that they could create (k! = 3 x 2 x 1 = 6 possible orders). If psychologists want 10 participants assigned to each order, a total of 60 participants would be needed to conduct the experiment (i.e. 10 participants would be assigned to each of the 6 orders). The six orders that could be created are presented below:

	1st Condition	**2nd Condition**	**3rd Condition**
Order 1	A	B	C
Order 2	A	C	B
Order 3	B	A	C
Order 4	B	C	A
Order 5	C	A	B
Order 6	C	B	A

As the number of conditions in an experiment increases, the number of possible orders of conditions that can be created increases dramatically, as does the number of participants needed to conduct the experiment.[3,6,7] To illustrate this point, assume psychologists want to conduct an experiment in which they want to compare four conditions. There would be twenty-four possible orders of conditions they could create! (k! = 4 × 3 × 2 × 1 = 24 possible orders). If psychologists want 10 participants assigned to each order, a total of 240 participants would now be needed to conduct the experiment (i.e. 10 participants assigned to each of the 24 orders). The twenty-four orders that could be created are presented below:

	Condition					Condition			
	1st	**2nd**	**3rd**	**4th**		**1st**	**2nd**	**3rd**	**4th**
Order 1	A	B	C	D	**Order 13**	C	A	B	D
Order 2	A	C	D	B	**Order 14**	C	B	D	A
Order 3	A	D	B	C	**Order 15**	C	D	A	B
Order 4	A	B	D	C	**Order 16**	C	A	D	B
Order 5	A	C	B	D	**Order 17**	C	B	A	D
Order 6	A	D	C	B	**Order 18**	C	D	B	A
Order 7	B	A	C	D	**Order 19**	D	A	B	C
Order 8	B	C	D	A	**Order 20**	D	B	C	A
Order 9	B	D	A	C	**Order 21**	D	C	A	B
Order 10	B	A	D	C	**Order 22**	D	A	C	B
Order 11	B	C	A	D	**Order 23**	D	B	A	C
Order 12	B	D	C	A	**Order 24**	D	C	B	A

Complete counterbalancing is the most effective strategy for controlling for the effects of order and carry-over during an experiment. Complete counterbalancing distributes the effects of order and carry-over equally across all conditions in an experiment by ensuring:[2,3]

(a) Each condition appears an equal number of times in each ordered position (e.g. each condition appears in the 1st, 2nd, 3rd, etc. ordered position an equal number of times).

(b) Each condition appears before and after every other condition an equal number of times (e.g. Condition A will precede and follow Condition B an equal number of times).

(c) Each condition appears before and after every other condition an equal number of times in each pair of ordered positions in the experiment (e.g. Condition A will precede and follow Condition B an equal number of times when comparing the 1st vs. 2nd ordered positions, the 2nd vs. 3rd ordered position, the 3rd vs. 4th ordered position, etc.).

Although complete counterbalancing is the most effective strategy for controlling for the effects of order and carry-over during an experiment, psychologists with limited resources, staff, access to participants, and time to complete experiments, will face a difficult challenge in trying to recruit a sufficient number of participants to assign to all possible orders of conditions as the number of conditions in an experiment increases.[2,3,5] While complete counterbalancing may be the optimal strategy to use, in these instances, psychologists may instead have to use a strategy from the second category of counterbalancing strategies known as "partial counterbalancing."

Partial Counterbalancing

In "partial counterbalancing," psychologists select a subset of all possible orders of the conditions in an experiment and assign an equal number of participants to each of the selected condition orders.[2,7,14] There are three "partial counterbalancing" strategies that are commonly used by psychologists. These strategies are: (a) Random selection of a subset of orders, (b) the Latin Square, and (c) the Balanced Latin Square.

In the *"random selection of a subset of orders"* strategy, psychologists select a subset of all of the possible orders of the conditions in an experiment and then assign an equal number of participants to each of the selected orders.[3,5,6] When selecting a subset of orders, psychologists must select a subset of orders in which each condition appears an equal number of times in each of the ordered positions (e.g. Condition A must appear in the 1st, 2nd, 3rd, etc. ordered position an equal number of times). For example, if complete counterbalancing is used in an experiment with three conditions, there would be a total of 6 possible orders that could be created (k! = 3 × 2 × 1 = 6 possible orders). Rather than assign participants to all 6 possible orders, psychologists could instead select a subset of three orders in which each condition in the experiment appeared once in each ordered position and assign participants to each of the selected orders (see below).

Condition

	1st	2nd	3rd
Order 1	A	B	C
Order 2	A	C	B
Order 3	B	A	C
Order 4	B	C	A
Order 5	C	A	B
Order 6	C	B	A

Condition

	1st	2nd	3rd
Order 1	A	B	C
Order 2	C	A	B
Order 3	B	C	A

While the "random selection of a subset of orders" strategy does ensure that each of the conditions appears an equal number of times in each ordered position (i.e. it controls for effects of order), it is still a less effective strategy than complete counterbalancing because each of the conditions does not precede and follow every other condition an equal number of times (i.e. it does not control for effects of carry-over). Note that in the 3 randomly selected orders above, Condition A precedes Condition B twice (Order 1; Order 2), but Condition A never follows Condition B in any of the selected orders.

In the *"Latin Square"* strategy of "partial counterbalancing," psychologists will create a table with dimensions of k rows × k columns (where k is the number of conditions compared in the experiment).[1,2,10] When the "Latin Square" table is completed, it will: (a) contain a subset of all possible orders of the conditions in an experiment and (b) each condition in the experiment will appear in each ordered position an equal number of times (e.g. Condition A will appear in the 1st, 2nd, 3rd, etc. ordered position an equal number of times). Psychologists can then assign an equal number of participants to each order of conditions created in the table.

For example, if psychologists are interested in conducting an experiment in which they compare three conditions, they would need to create a 3 × 3 "Latin Square." To create the "Latin Square," they would first create a blank 3 × 3 table. Next, they would select a random order of their three conditions and write this sequence of conditions across Row 1 of the table.

C	B	A

Then, they would fill in the second row of the table by rotating each condition in Row 1 of the table one position to the right. When this rotation is complete, Condition C would rotate to position 2, Condition B would rotate to position 3, and Condition A would rotate to position 1.

C	B	A
A	**C**	**B**

Finally, they would fill in the third row of the table by rotating each condition in Row 2 of the table one position to the right. When this rotation is complete, Condition A would rotate to position 2, Condition C would rotate to position 3, and Condition B would rotate to position 1.

C	B	A
A	C	B
B	**A**	**C**

When the table is completed, the three rows in the table represent a subset of all of the possible orders of the conditions in the experiment. The psychologists can now assign an equal number of participants (e.g. 10) to each order of conditions (i.e. each row of the table). The final "Latin Square" the psychologists would use to conduct their experiment appears below.

		1st	2nd	3rd
Order 1	10 participants	C	B	A
Order 2	10 participants	A	C	B
Order 3	10 participants	B	A	C

The same sequence of steps can be followed to create a "Latin Square" for experiments in which 4, 5, 6, etc. conditions are compared. For example, assume a Health Psychologist wants to conduct an experiment to study perceptions of four types of fitness equipment. Specifically, the Health Psychologist wants to study perceptions of treadmills, stationary bikes, stair climbers, and elliptical machines. Since there are four conditions in his experiment, he will need to create a 4 × 4 "Latin Square" as shown below.

Step 1: Create a 4 × 4 table

Step 2: Assign a random sequence of the 4 conditions to Row 1 of the table

Bike	Climber	Elliptical	Treadmill

Step 3: To create Row 2, rotate each condition in Row 1 one position to the right

Bike	Climber	Elliptical	Treadmill
Treadmill	**Bike**	**Climber**	**Elliptical**

Step 4: To create Row 3, rotate each condition in Row 2 one position to the right

Bike	Climber	Elliptical	Treadmill
Treadmill	Bike	Climber	Elliptical
Elliptical	**Treadmill**	**Bike**	**Climber**

Step 5: To create Row 4, rotate each condition in Row 3 one position to the right

Bike	Climber	Elliptical	Treadmill
Treadmill	Bike	Climber	Elliptical
Elliptical	Treadmill	Bike	Climber
Climber	**Elliptical**	**Treadmill**	**Bike**

When the table is completed, the four rows in the table represent a subset of all of the possible orders of the conditions in the experiment. He can now assign an equal number of participants (e.g. 20) to each order of conditions (i.e. each row of the table). The final "Latin Square" he would use to conduct his experiment appears below.

		1st	**2nd**	**3rd**	**4th**
Order 1	20 participants	Bike	Climber	Elliptical	Treadmill
Order 2	20 participants	Treadmill	Bike	Climber	Elliptical
Order 3	20 participants	Elliptical	Treadmill	Bike	Climber
Order 4	20 participants	Climber	Elliptical	Treadmill	Bike

Like the "random selection of a subset of orders" strategy, the "Latin Square" strategy of counterbalancing ensures that each of the conditions appears an equal number of times in each ordered position (i.e. it controls for effects of order). However, like the "random selection of a subset of order" strategy, the "Latin Square" strategy is a less effective strategy than complete counterbalancing because each condition does not precede and follow every other condition an equal number of times[1,2,3] (i.e. does not control for effects of carry-over). Note in the 4 randomly selected orders above, the Treadmill condition precedes the Bike condition three times (Order 2; Order 3; Order 4), but the Treadmill condition never follows the Bike condition in any of these orders). To create a "Latin Square" in which each condition precedes and follows every other condition an equal number of times, psychologists will create a "balanced Latin Square."

In the "***Balanced Latin Square***" strategy of partial counterbalancing, psychologists will create a table with the dimensions of k rows × k columns (where k is the number of conditions in the experiment). When the table is complete, it will: (a) contain a subset of all possible orders of the conditions, (b) each condition will appear in each ordered position an equal number of times (i.e. it controls for effects of order), and (c) each of the conditions in the experiment precedes and follows every other condition an equal number of times.[3,4,5,10] (i.e. it controls for effects of carry-over). Psychologists can then assign an equal number of participants to each order of conditions created in the table. Unlike a traditional "Latin Square," a "balanced Latin Square," can only be created when there is an even number of conditions in an experiment.[3,4]

For example, if psychologists are interested in conducting an experiment in which they will compare four conditions (e.g. ABCD), they would need to create a 4 × 4 "balanced Latin Square." To create a "balanced Latin Square," they would first create a 4 × 4 table. Next, they would use the formula (A, B, n, C; where n equals the number of conditions in the experiment) to create the sequence of conditions that will appear in Row 1 (see below).

A	B	D	C

Then, they would fill in the second row of the table by replacing each condition in Row 1 of the table with the condition that would follow it in an ordered sequence (i.e. Condition A will be replaced by Condition B, Condition B will be replaced by Condition C; Condition C will be replaced by Condition D, and Condition D will be replaced by Condition A as you return to the beginning of the ordered sequence).

A	B	D	C
B	**C**	**A**	**D**

Next, they would fill in the third row of the table by replacing each condition in Row 2 of the table with the condition that would follow it in an ordered sequence.

A	B	D	C
B	C	A	D
C	**D**	**B**	**A**

Finally, they would fill in the fourth row of the table by replacing each condition in Row 3 of the table with the condition that would follow it in an ordered sequence.

A	B	D	C
B	C	A	D
C	D	B	A
D	**A**	**C**	**B**

When the table is completed, the four rows in the table represent a subset of all of the possible orders of the conditions in the experiment. The psychologists can now assign an equal number of participants (e.g. 25) to each order of conditions (i.e. each row of the table). The final "balanced Latin Square" the psychologists would use to conduct their experiment appears below.

		1st	2nd	3rd	4th
Order 1	25 participants	A	B	D	C
Order 2	25 participants	B	C	A	D
Order 3	25 participants	C	D	B	A
Order 4	25 participants	D	A	C	B

The same sequence of steps can be followed to create a "balanced Latin Square" for an experiment in which 6 conditions will be compared. Assume a Consumer Psychologist wants to conduct an experiment to study consumer perceptions of six different brands of spaghetti sauce. Since there are six conditions in his experiment, she will need to create a 6×6 "balanced Latin Square" as shown below.

Step 1: Create a 6×6 table

Step 2: Use the formula (A, B, n, C, n – 1, D, n – 2; where n equals the number of conditions) to create the sequence of conditions that will appear in Row 1

Brand A	**Brand B**	**Brand F**	**Brand C**	**Brand E**	**Brand D**

Step 3: To create Row 2 of the table, replace each condition in Row 1 of the table with the condition that would follow it in an ordered sequence

Brand A	Brand B	Brand F	Brand C	Brand E	Brand D
Brand B	**Brand C**	**Brand A**	**Brand D**	**Brand F**	**Brand E**

Step 4: To create Row 3 of the table, replace each condition in Row 2 of the table with the condition that would follow it in an ordered sequence

Brand A	Brand B	Brand F	Brand C	Brand E	Brand D
Brand B	Brand C	Brand A	Brand D	Brand F	Brand E
Brand C	**Brand D**	**Brand B**	**Brand E**	**Brand A**	**Brand F**

Step 5–7: Fill in Rows 4–6 of the table using the same replace process used in Steps 2–4

Brand A	Brand B	Brand F	Brand C	Brand E	Brand D
Brand B	Brand C	Brand A	Brand D	Brand F	Brand E
Brand C	Brand D	Brand B	Brand E	Brand A	Brand F
Brand D	**Brand E**	**Brand C**	**Brand F**	**Brand B**	**Brand A**
Brand E	**Brand F**	**Brand D**	**Brand A**	**Brand C**	**Brand B**
Brand F	**Brand A**	**Brand E**	**Brand B**	**Brand D**	**Brand C**

When the table is completed, the six rows in the table represent a subset of all of the possible orders of the conditions in the experiment. She can now assign an equal number of participants (e.g. 10) to each order of conditions (i.e. each row of the table). The "balanced Latin Square" she would use to conduct her experiment appears below.

		1st	2nd	3rd	4th	5th	6th
Order 1	10 participants	A	B	F	C	E	D
Order 2	10 participants	B	C	A	D	F	E
Order 3	10 participants	C	D	B	E	A	F
Order 4	10 participants	D	E	C	F	B	A
Order 5	10 participants	E	F	D	A	C	B
Order 6	10 participants	F	A	E	B	D	C

Since a "balanced Latin Square" can only be created when there is an even number of conditions in an experiment, psychologists who want to conduct an experiment in which they compare an odd number of conditions must use a different "partial counterbalancing" strategy to ensure that: (a) each condition in the experiment appears an equal number of times in each of the ordered positions, and (b) each condition in the experiment precedes and follows every other condition in the experiment an equal number of times. This strategy involves the creation of two "mirror image" traditional "Latin Squares."[3,4]

As an example, assume that a Military Psychologist wants to conduct an experiment to determine which of 3 activities is the most effective in improving the physical fitness of soldiers. Specifically, he wants to study the effectiveness of running, hiking, and swimming in improving the fitness of soldiers. Since he has three conditions in his experiment, he is unable to create a "balanced Latin Square." Instead, he will begin by creating a traditional 3 × 3 "Latin Square" using the procedure outlined earlier in the module. His "Latin Square" appears below.

3 × 3 "Latin Square"

Hiking	Running	Swimming
Swimming	Hiking	Running
Running	Swimming	Hiking

He will then create a second "Latin Square" that is a "mirror image."

Hiking	Running	Swimming
Swimming	Hiking	Running
Running	Swimming	Hiking

Swimming	Running	Hiking
Running	Hiking	Swimming
Hiking	Swimming	Running

Original "Latin Square"   **"Mirror Image" Latin Square**

He will then combine his two "mirror image" Latin Squares into a single table.

Hiking	Running	Swimming
Swimming	Hiking	Running
Running	Swimming	Hiking
Swimming	Running	Hiking
Running	Hiking	Swimming
Hiking	Swimming	Running

When the table is completed, the six rows in the table represent a subset of all possible orders of the conditions in the experiment. The table also provides the psychologist with all of the benefits of a "balanced Latin Square" in that each condition will appear an equal number of times (i.e. 2 times) in each ordered position, (i.e. it controls for effects of order) and each of the conditions in the experiment will precede and follow every other condition in the experiment (i.e. it controls for effects of carry-over) an equal number of times (i.e. 2 times). He can now assign an equal number of soldiers (i.e. 5) to each order of conditions (i.e. each row of the table).

		1st	2nd	3rd
Order 1	5 participants	Hiking	Running	Swimming
Order 2	5 participants	Swimming	Hiking	Running
Order 3	5 participants	Running	Swimming	Hiking
Order 4	5 participants	Swimming	Running	Hiking
Order 5	5 participants	Running	Hiking	Swimming
Order 6	5 participants	Hiking	Swimming	Running

The same sequence of steps can be followed for an experiment in which 5 conditions will be compared. Assume that a Media Psychologist wants to conduct an experiment in which she will study TV viewer's perceptions of 5 new TV shows (i.e. ABCDE) debuting on a television network during the new Fall TV schedule.

Step 1: Create a traditional 5 × 5 "Latin Square"

A	C	B	E	D
D	A	C	B	E
E	D	A	C	B
B	E	D	A	C
C	B	E	D	A

Step 2: Create a "mirror image" 5 × 5 Latin Square

A	C	B	E	D
D	A	C	B	E
E	D	A	C	B
B	E	D	A	C
C	B	E	D	A

D	E	B	C	A
E	B	C	A	D
B	C	A	D	E
C	A	D	E	B
A	D	E	B	C

Step 3: Combine the two "mirror image" Latin Squares into a single table.

A	C	B	E	D
D	A	C	B	E
E	D	A	C	B
B	E	D	A	C
C	B	E	D	A
D	E	B	C	A
E	B	C	A	D
B	C	A	D	E
C	A	D	E	B
A	D	E	B	C

When the table is completed, the 10 rows in the table represent a subset of all possible orders of the conditions in the experiment. The table also provides the Media Psychologist with all the benefits of a "balanced Latin Square" in that each condition appears an equal number of times in each ordered position (i.e. 2 times) and each condition will precede and follow every other condition in the experiment an equal number of times (i.e. 4 times). She can now assign an equal number of TV viewers (i.e. 10) to each order of conditions (i.e. each row of the table).

		1st	**2nd**	**3rd**	**4th**	**5th**
Order 1	10 Participants	Show A	Show C	Show B	Show E	Show D
Order 2	10 Participants	Show D	Show A	Show C	Show B	Show E
Order 3	10 Participants	Show E	Show D	Show A	Show C	Show B
Order 4	10 Participants	Show B	Show E	Show D	Show A	Show C
Order 5	10 Participants	Show C	Show B	Show E	Show D	Show A
Order 6	10 Participants	Show D	Show E	Show B	Show C	Show A
Order 7	10 Participants	Show E	Show B	Show C	Show A	Show D
Order 8	10 Participants	Show B	Show C	Show A	Show D	Show E
Order 9	10 Participants	Show C	Show A	Show D	Show E	Show B
Order 10	10 Participants	Show A	Show D	Show E	Show B	Show C

While the "balanced Latin Square" and "mirror image" Latin Square techniques ensure that each condition in an experiment: (a) appears an equal number of times in each of the ordered positions, and (b) precedes and follows every other condition in the experiment an equal number of times, they may still be less effective than "complete counterbalancing" for controlling for the effects of order and carry-over during an experiment. Why? Because when psychologists use the strategy of "complete counterbalancing," all possible orders of conditions are tested during the experiment as opposed to only a subset of all possible condition orders that is tested when a "partial counterbalancing" strategy is used.

But how do psychologists ultimately know the counterbalancing strategy they have used has been successful in distributing the effects of order and carry-over equally across conditions? To determine whether counterbalancing has been effective, psychologists will assess the effect of "condition order" during their statistical analysis of their experimental data.[2,10] If the results of the statistical analysis reveals that the effect of "condition order" is non-significant, it would indicate counterbalancing has been successful in distributing the effects of order and carry-over equally across conditions. This is the preferred result. If, however, the results of the statistical analysis reveals the effect of "condition order" is significant, it would indicate counterbalancing has been unsuccessful. If counterbalancing has been unsuccessful, psychologists would be aware that there are order or carry-over effects that have not been controlled for during the experiment.

The Choice of a Between-Subjects vs. Within-Subjects Design

When psychologists want to conduct an experiment in which they will compare two or more conditions (i.e. two or more levels of an independent variable), they must decide whether they will use a between-subjects design or a within-subjects design. But how do psychologists decide which design they will use? In some instances, due to the nature of the research study, psychologists may not have a choice as to which design they will use.[3,5,7] For example, if the goal of an experiment is to study the behavior or mental process of participants over time or to study the performance of participants over successive trials, sessions, test administrations, doses, or treatments, psychologists would have no choice but to use the within-subjects design. In other instances, the choice of design may be made on the basis of: (a) available resources, (b) ethical considerations, (c) the risk of participants discovering the true purpose of the research, or (d) the types of activities psychologists want to devote time and resources to during an experiment (i.e. creating equivalent groups vs. counterbalancing to control for order and carry-over effects).

With respect to available resources, if psychologists have limited resources, staff, access to participants, or time to conduct their experiment, they are likely to choose a within-subjects design which requires fewer participants to conduct.[1,2] By contrast, if psychologists have access to participants and sufficient resources to collect a large research sample, they will likely choose a between-subjects design. With respect to ethical considerations, psychologists must determine whether having participants complete multiple conditions places them at more than minimal risk. If participating in multiple conditions during the experiment creates more than minimal risk for participants (e.g. excessive fatigue, stress, emotional discomfort, arousal),[1,2,5] psychologists have an ethical obligation to use a between-subjects design in which participants would only have to complete one condition. With respect to the risk of participants discovering the true purpose of the study, psychologists may elect to minimize this risk by using a between-subjects design in which participants complete only one condition and are unaware of what is occurring in other conditions.[3,4,5] Keeping participants "blind" to what is occurring in other conditions makes it less likely they will discover the true purpose of the study and alter their behavior in response.

Finally, with respect to the types of activities psychologists want to devote their time and resources to during an experiment, psychologists must determine whether they want to devote their time and resources to the creation of equivalent groups of participants across conditions or to the implementation of a counterbalancing strategy to control for the effects of order and carry-over during the experiment. If psychologists would rather devote their time and resources to the creation of equivalent groups of participants via random assignment or matching, they are likely to use a between-subjects design.[1,2,3] By contrast, if psychologists would rather use a single group of participants and devote their time and resources to implementing a counterbalancing strategy to control for the effects or order and carry-over as the participants complete all of the conditions in the experiment, they are likely to use a within-subjects design.[1,2,3]

Clearly, there are advantages and disadvantages associated with both a between-subjects design and a within-subjects design. Psychologists must carefully evaluate the advantages and disadvantages associated with each design before making their final design decision. Ultimately, the goal for psychologists is to select the design which provides the best opportunity to assess the true relationship between the independent and dependent variables examined in the experiment.

EXERCISE 8A

Comparing Between-Subjects vs. Within-Subjects Designs

When psychologists want to conduct an experiment in which two or more levels of an independent variable (i.e. two or more conditions) are compared, they must decide whether they will use a between-subjects or a within-subjects research design. In order to decide which type of design provides them with the best opportunity to assess the relationship that exists between the independent and dependent variable being examined in the experiment, psychologists must be knowledgeable of the defining characteristics of between- and within-subjects designs.

Below is a list of characteristics that may or may not be associated with between-subjects and within-subjects research designs. For each characteristic, use the scale below to indicate whether the characteristic: **(a)** applies only to a between-subjects design, **(b)** applies only to a within-subjects design, **(c)** applies to both between-subjects and within-subjects designs, or **(d)** does not apply to either a between-subjects or within-subjects design and write your answer in the space provided.

BS	Characteristic applies only to a between-subjects design
WS	Characteristic applies only to a within-subjects design
BOTH	Characteristic applies to both a between-subjects and within-subjects design
X	Characteristic does not apply to a between-subjects or within-subjects design

_____ The design allows psychologists to examine changes in the behavior and/or mental processes of individual participants over time

_____ An independent variable with more than two levels is manipulated by psychologists

_____ Psychologists create "matched" groups of participants

_____ Participants complete only one of the conditions in the experiment

_____ Psychologists can draw causal conclusions about the relationship between the independent and dependent variable

_____ There is an increased risk that participants will drop out of the experiment over time

_____ Multiple groups of participants take part in the experiment

_____ Psychologists can compare the effectiveness of different intervention programs

_____ The design can be used for an experiment that involves a comparison of two or more conditions (i.e. a comparison of two or more levels of an independent variable)

BS	Characteristic applies only to a between-subjects design
WS	Characteristic applies only to a within-subjects design
BOTH	Characteristic applies to both a between-subjects and within-subjects design
X	Characteristic does not apply to a between-subjects or within-subjects design

_____ Participants are randomly assigned to the different conditions in the experiment

_____ Two or more independent variables are manipulated by psychologists

_____ Participants are exposed to only one level of the independent variable

_____ Design choice for psychologists with resources to acquire a large research sample

_____ Design contains a control group of participants who are not exposed to the treatment, intervention, or variable of interest to psychologists conducting the experiment

_____ The design is appropriate for use with only healthy, adult populations

_____ Participants may consume a "placebo" (i.e. a pill that does not contain the medication being studied by psychologists) during the experiment

_____ There is an increased risk participants will grow fatigued or bored over time

_____ If psychologists want to have 25 participants complete each of the 4 conditions in their experiment, they will need 100 participants to conduct the study

_____ One or more dependent variables are measured by psychologists

_____ The design is also referred to as an "independent groups design"

_____ Average scores on the dependent variable are computed for each condition and are statistically analyzed to see if there is a significant difference across conditions

_____ There is an increased risk that over time participants will learn the true purpose of the experiment and potentially alter their behavior during the experiment

_____ There is an increased risk that the results of the experiment may be contaminated by the effects of the individual differences among members of the research sample

_____ Design choice for psychologists with limited resources or access to participants

_____ Participants complete all of the conditions in the experiment

_____ Design contains a treatment group of participants who are exposed to the treatment, intervention, or variable of interest to psychologists conducting the experiment

BS	Characteristic applies only to a between-subjects design
WS	Characteristic applies only to a within-subjects design
BOTH	Characteristic applies to both a between-subjects and within-subjects design
X	Characteristic does not apply to a between-subjects or within-subjects design

_____ There is an increased risk that the results of the experiment may be influenced by factors or events occurring outside of the experiment

_____ The design is also referred to as a "repeated measures" design

_____ Psychologists must ensure that participants are not placed at more than minimal risk as a result of their participation in the experiment

_____ A single group of participants takes part in the experiment

_____ The design is also referred to as a "factorial" design

_____ Participants are exposed to all of the levels of the independent variable

_____ Participants are measured on the dependent variable once during the experiment

_____ The design requires psychologists to implement a counterbalancing strategy

_____ Psychologists can compare the effectiveness of different amounts of a treatment or the effectiveness of different types of treatments

_____ If psychologists want to have 25 participants complete each of the 4 conditions in their experiment, they will need 25 participants to conduct the study

_____ Participants are measured on the dependent variable multiple times in the experiment

_____ The design is immune to both order effects and carry-over effects

_____ The design guarantees that there will be an equal number of participants in each condition throughout the course of the experiment

EXERCISE 8B

Choosing a Between-Subjects vs. Within-Subjects Design

When psychologists want to conduct an experiment in which two or more conditions (i.e. two or more levels of an independent variable) are compared, they must decide whether they will use a between-subjects or a within-subjects research design. Psychologists must carefully weigh the advantages and the disadvantages of both designs before making a final design decision. The research design they ultimately choose should provide them with the best opportunity to evaluate the relationship that exists between the independent and dependent variables in their experiment.

Below are descriptions of 8 experiments psychologists are interested in conducting. For each of these 8 experiments, please: **(a)** provide your recommendation to the psychologist as to which research design you would recommend that he or she use to conduct the experiment, and **(b)** provide a rationale for your recommendation in the space provided. Your rationale should be based on the specific advantages and disadvantages associated with the between-subjects and within-subjects research designs.

01. An Industrial-Organizational Psychologist wants to conduct an experiment on the effect of sleep deprivation on work performance. She wants to determine whether there is a significant difference in the average number of errors made by employees who have been deprived of sleep for 12, 24, 36, and/or 48 hours.

☐ Between-Subjects Design

☐ Within-Subjects Design

Rationale:

02. A Consumer Psychologist wants to conduct an experiment on consumer perceptions of four different perfumes. He wants to know if there is a significant difference in the average smell ratings provided by consumers for perfumes A, B, C, and/or D.

☐ Between-Subjects Design

☐ Within-Subjects Design

Rationale:

03. A Physiological Psychologist wants to conduct an experiment on the effect of consumption of caffeine on heart rate. She wants to determine whether there is a significant difference in the average heart rate of individuals who have consumed a 20-ounce energy drink, a 20-ounce bottle of soda, a 20-ounce cup of coffee, and/or a 20-ounce glass of tea.

☐ Between-Subjects Design

☐ Within-Subjects Design

Rationale:

04. An Experimental Psychologist wants to conduct an experiment on the effect of distraction on pain tolerance. He wants to know if there is a significant difference in the average amount of time people can keep their hand submerged in a bucket of ice water normally and/or when they attempt to distract themselves from the pain by counting from 1–100 in their heads.

☐ Between-Subjects Design

☐ Within-Subjects Design

Rationale:

05. A Statistics Professor wants to conduct an experiment on the effect of taking practice tests on student exam performance. He wants to know if there is a significant difference in the average statistics exam scores for students who complete 1, 2, and/or 3 practice tests.

☐ Between-Subjects Design

☐ Within-Subjects Design

Rationale:

06. An Environmental Psychologist wants to conduct an experiment on the effect of temperature on problem-solving abilities. He wants to determine whether there is a significant difference in the average problem-solving scores of individuals placed in an extremely cold (10 degrees) and/or extremely warm (100 degrees) environment.

☐ Between-Subjects Design

☐ Within-Subjects Design

Rationale:

07. A Neuropsychologist wants to conduct an experiment on the effect of odor on male arousal. She wants to determine whether there is a significant difference in the average arousal levels of men exposed to the odors of cinnamon, bacon, steak, and/or beer.

☐ Between-Subjects Design

☐ Within-Subjects Design

Rationale:

08. A Social Psychologist wants to conduct an experiment on self-improvement techniques and self-confidence in males. He wants to determine whether there is a significant difference in the average self-confidence ratings of men who buy a new wardrobe, dye and style their hair, and/or get their teeth whitened.

☐ Between-Subjects Design

☐ Within-Subjects Design

Rationale:

EXERCISE 8C

Evaluation of Counterbalancing Strategies

There are a variety of counterbalancing strategies psychologists can use to control for the effects of order and carry-over during an experiment in which they use a within-subjects design to compare two or more levels of an independent variable (i.e. compare two or more conditions). This exercise will test your knowledge of complete and partial counterbalancing strategies.

The Experiment

A Clinical Psychologist who specializes in the treatment of anxiety disorders is interested in conducting an experiment to compare the effectiveness of 2 different treatment methods. She wants to know whether there is a significant difference in the effectiveness of: (a) an anti-anxiety drug and (b) psychotherapy in treating the symptoms of an anxiety disorder. In order to compare the effectiveness of the 2 treatments, she will use a within-subjects design and expose individuals who have been diagnosed with an anxiety disorder to a method of treatment for a month. At the end of the month, she will assess their levels of anxiety. She will then expose the same group of individuals to a second method of treatment for a month. At the end of the month, she will once again assess their levels of anxiety. She will then compute average anxiety scores for each of the two treatment methods and analyze the average scores to determine whether there is a significant difference in anxiety across treatment methods.

01. If the Clinical Psychologist wants to use "complete counterbalancing" to control for the effects of order and carry-over during the experiment and assign 20 participants to all of the possible orders of conditions that can be created; **(a)** how many orders of conditions could the Clinical Psychologist create, and **(b)** how many participants will she need to conduct her experiment?

$\square$ = possible orders of conditions

$\square$ = number of participants required

> **List all the possible orders of conditions the Clinical Psychologist could create from the conditions in her experiment:**

02. The Clinical Psychologist decides she would like to add a 3rd method of treatment to her experiment (i.e. hypnosis). If she wants to use "complete counterbalancing" to control for the effects of order and carry-over during the experiment and assign 15 participants to all of the possible orders of conditions that can be created: **(a)** how many orders of conditions could she create, and **(b)** how many participants will she need to conduct her experiment?

☐ = possible orders of conditions
☐ = number of participants required

List all the possible orders of conditions the Clinical Psychologist could create from the conditions in her experiment:

03. If she adds a 4th treatment (i.e. meditation) to her experiment and assigns 10 participants to all possible orders of conditions that can be created: **(a)** how many orders of conditions could she create, and **(b)** how many participants will she need to conduct her experiment?

☐ = possible orders of conditions
☐ = number of participants required

What if she decides to get really ambitious and add a 5th condition (i.e. aroma therapy) to her experiment and assign 5 participants to all possible orders of conditions?

☐ = possible orders of conditions
☐ = number of participants required

04. A colleague recommends she compare 3 methods of treatment in her experiment (i.e. anti-anxiety drug, psychotherapy, hypnosis) and to use a "partial counterbalancing" strategy to control for order and carry-over effects. He recommends she use the "random selection of a subset of orders" strategy of partial counterbalancing. He shows her how to create all of the possible orders of conditions and randomly select a subset of 3 of the orders. He tells her she can now assign an equal number of participants to each of these 3 selected orders.

Please: **(a)** identify the flaws in his counterbalancing strategy, **(b)** decide if his strategy will control for the effects of order and/or carry-over, and **(c)** describe the changes you would make to strengthen his counterbalancing strategy.

	1st	2nd	3rd
Order 1	Drug	Therapy	Hypnosis
Order 2	Drug	Hypnosis	Therapy
Order 3	Therapy	Drug	Hypnosis
Order 4	Therapy	Hypnosis	Drug
Order 5	Hypnosis	Drug	Therapy
Order 6	Hypnosis	Therapy	Drug

All Possible orders

	1st	2nd	3rd
Order 1	Drug	Therapy	Hypnosis
Order 2	Hypnosis	Therapy	Drug
Order 3	Hypnosis	Drug	Therapy

Randomly selected subset of orders

What are the flaws in his counterblancing strategy?

Will his counterbalancing strategy control for.................? (**Explain**).

Order	Carry-Over

What changes would you make to strengthen his partial counterbalancing strategy so that it provides greater control for the effects of order and carry-over during the experiment?

Recommended Changes:

05. Ultimately, she decides to compare 4 treatments in her experiment (i.e. anti-anxiety drug, psychotherapy, hypnosis, meditation) and to use a "partial counterbalancing" strategy to control for the effects of order and carry-over. She decides she will use a "balanced Latin Square" strategy of partial-counterbalancing. She creates a 4 × 4 "balanced Latin Square" containing 4 orders of the conditions in her experiment and plans to assign an equivalent number of participants to each order of conditions (i.e. each row of the table). Below is the 4 × 4 "balanced Latin Square" she created.

4 × 4 "balanced Latin Square"

	1st	2nd	3rd	4th
Order 1	Meditation	Hypnosis	Therapy	Drugs
Order 2	Hypnosis	Therapy	Drugs	Meditation
Order 3	Therapy	Drugs	Hypnosis	Meditation
Order 4	Therapy	Meditation	Drugs	Hypnosis

Has she really created a "balanced Latin Square"? (Explain)

Using the procedures outlined in the module, please create a "balanced Latin Square" that the Clinical Psychologist could use to counterbalance the 4 conditions in her experiment and that will control for the effects of both order and carry-over during her experiment. Use the 4 × 4 square below for your final "balanced Latin Square."

"balanced Latin Square"

	1st	2nd	3rd	4th
Order 1				
Order 2				
Order 3				
Order 4				

Which strategy of counterbalancing listed below will provide the Clinical Psychologist with the greatest amount of control for the effects of order and carry-over during her experiment? Provide your rationale in the space provided.

☐ = Complete Counterbalancing

☐ = Balanced "Latin Square"

Rationale:

References

1. Cozby, P. C., & Bates, S. C. (2011). *Methods in behavioral research.* (11th ed.). New York, NY: McGraw-Hill Publishers.

2. Bordens, K. S., & Abbot, B. B. (2011). *Research design and methods: A process approach* (8th ed.). Boston, MA: McGraw-Hill Publishers.

3. Passer, M. W. (2013). *Research methods: Concepts and connections.* New York, NY: Worth Publishers.

4. Kantowitz, B. H., Roediger, H. L., & Elmes, D. G. (2014). *Experimental psychology* (10th ed.). Stamford, CT: Cengage Learning.

5. Jackson, S. L. (2014). *Research methods: A modular approach* (3rd ed.). Stamford, CT: Cengage Learning.

6. Smith, R. A., & Davis, S. F. (2012). *The psychologist as detective: An introduction to conducting research in psychology* (6th ed.). Boston, MA: Pearson Publishers.

7. Beins, B. C. (2012). *Research methods: A tool for life* (3rd ed.). Boston, MA: Pearson Publishers.

8. Leary, M. R. (2007). *Introduction to behavioral research methods* (5th ed.). Boston, MA: Pearson/Allyn & Bacon.

9. Maclin, M. K., & Solso, R. L. (2007). *Experimental psychology: A case approach* (8th ed.). Boston, MA: Pearson/Allyn & Bacon.

10. Mackenzie, I. S. (2013). *Within-subjects vs. between-subjects designs: Which to use?* Retrieved from http://www.yorku.ca/mack/RN-Counterbalancing.html.

11. Price, P., & Oswald, K. (2008). Carryover effects and counterbalancing. *Research Methods for Dummies.* Retrieved from http://psych.csufresno.edu/psy144/Content/Design/Experimental/carryover.html.

12. Lambdin, C. & Shaffer, V. A. (2009). Are within-subject designs transparent? *Judgment and Decision Making, 4*(7), 554–566.

13. Evans, A. N., & Rooney, B. F. (2007). *Methods in psychological research.* Thousand Oaks, CA: Sage Publications.

14. Brown, C. (n.d.). *Counterbalancing.* Retrieved from http://www.csub.edu/~lvega/counterbalancing.htm.

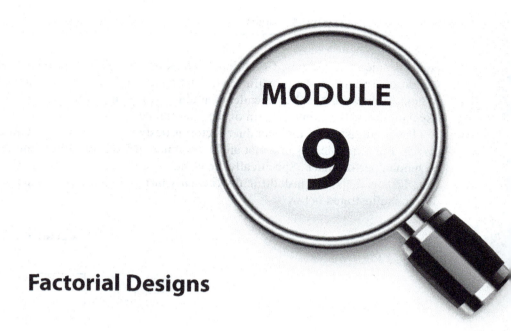

MODULE 9

Factorial Designs

For psychologists, one of the most important goals of psychological research is to explain the behavior and mental processes of both human and non-human subjects.[1,2] In order to be able to explain behavior and mental processes, psychologists have to conduct experiments to uncover the underlying causes.[3,4] In some instances, behaviors and/or mental processes may be caused by a single variable that psychologists can study by using the between-subjects and within-subjects designs discussed in Modules 7 and 8 which involved the manipulation of a single independent variable. In other instances, behaviors and/or mental processes may be caused by the combined effects of two or more variables. Rather than conduct a separate experiment for each variable, it would be preferable for psychologists to use a research design which allowed them to study both the individual and combined effects of two or more variables in one experiment.[1,2,5] Fortunately for psychologists, such a research design exists. It is known as a "factorial design."[1,2,6]

A "factorial design" is a design that contains two or more independent variables.[2,6,7] In a factorial design, the independent variables are known as "factors."[1,2,6] Each of the "factors" (i.e. independent variables) in a factorial design will have two or more levels.[8] Psychologists use the number of factors and the number of levels associated with each factor to describe a factorial design. For example, assume that a Media Psychologist is interested in studying the factors that influence enjoyment of a motion picture. Specifically, she wants to study how the color of a film (i.e. black and white version of a film vs. full color version of a film) and the viewing conditions (i.e. watch film alone vs. watch film with an audience) influence movie patrons' enjoyment of a film. The Media Psychologist's design is illustrated below.

	Factor B (Film Color)	
	Black/White	Full Color
Watch Alone	1	2
With Audience	3	4

Factor A (Viewing Condition)

Since her design contains 2 factors (i.e. independent variables) and each of her factors has 2 levels, she would describe her design as a "2 × 2 factorial design."[1,2,7] If we multiply 2 × 2, we get a value of "4." This value tells her how many unique conditions there are in her experiment. By combining all the levels of her 1st factor (Factor A: Viewing Condition) with all the levels of her 2nd factor (Factor B: Film Color), she can create 4 unique conditions: Condition 1 (black and white film—alone), Condition 2 (full color film—alone), Condition 3 (black and white film - with audience), and Condition 4 (full color film - with audience). Ratings of enjoyment would be the dependent variable in the experiment. The 2×2 factorial design used by the Media Psychologist is the simplest form of the factorial design.[1,9]

Psychologists will also conduct factorial designs in which one or more factors has more than two levels.[1,3,10] For example, assume that an Environmental Psychologist is interested in studying the effect of noise on human performance. Specifically, he wants to study how noise level (i.e. 30 decibels, 60 decibels, 90 decibels, 120 decibels) and task difficulty (i.e. easy task, difficult task) influence human performance. His research design is illustrated below.

Factor B (Task Difficulty)

		Easy	Difficult
	30 decibels	1	2
	60 decibels	3	4
Factor A (Noise Level)	90 decibels	3	3
	120 decibels	3	3

Since his design contains 2 factors (i.e. independent variables) and his 1st factor (Factor A: Noise Level) has 4 levels and his 2nd factor (Factor B: Task Difficulty) has 2 levels, he would describe his research design as a "4 × 2 factorial design." If we multiply 4 × 2, we get a value of "8." By combining all the levels of his two factors, he can create 8 unique conditions: Condition 1 (easy task—30 dB), Condition 2 (easy task—60 dB), Condition 3 (easy task—90 dB), Condition 4 (easy task—120 dB), Condition 5 (difficult task—30 dB), Condition 6 (difficult task—60 dB), Condition 7 (difficult task—90 dB), and Condition 8 (difficult task—120 dB). Task performance would be the dependent variable in the experiment.

Psychologists also conduct factorial designs in which they study more than two factors.[1,2] For example, assume that a Cognitive Psychologist is interested in studying the factors that may affect our ability to recall a list of words. Specifically, she wants to study the effects of method of presentation (i.e. auditory: individuals listen to an audio recording of the word list vs. visual: individuals watch a slide show presentation of the word list), frequency of presentation (i.e. the list of words is presented once vs. the list of words is presented multiple times), and method of rehearsal (i.e. individuals rehearse the list of words alone vs. individuals rehearse the list of words in a group). The Cognitive Psychologist's design is illustrated below.

Factor C (Rehearsal)

Alone				Group		
Factor B (Frequency)				**Factor B (Frequency)**		
	Once	Multiple			Once	Multiple
Auditory	1	2		Auditory	5	6
Visual	3	4		Visual	7	8

Factor A (Method)

Since her design contains 3 factors (i.e. independent variables) and her three factors (i.e. Factor A: Method of Presentation; Factor B: Frequency of Presentation; Factor C: Method of Rehearsal) each have 2 levels, she would describe her design as a "2 × 2 × 2 factorial design." If we multiply 2 × 2 × 2, we get a value of "8." By combining all the levels of her three factors, she can create 8 unique conditions: Condition 1 (auditory—one presentation of list - rehearsed alone), Condition 2 (auditory—multiple presentations of list—rehearsed alone), Condition 3 (visual—one presentation of the list—rehearsed alone), Condition 4 (visual—multiple presentations of the list—rehearsed alone), Condition 5 (auditory—one presentation of list—group rehearsal), Condition 6 (auditory—multiple presentations of list—group rehearsal), Condition 7 (visual—one presentation of list—group rehearsal), and finally Condition 8 (visual—multiple presentations of list—group rehearsal). The number of words recalled from the list would be the dependent variable in the Cognitive Psychologist's experiment.

The factorial design allows psychologists to study a variety of factor types. Specifically, when psychologists conduct factorial designs, they study: (a) quantitative and qualitative factors, (b) between-subjects and within-subjects factors, and (c) manipulated and non-manipulated (i.e. subject) factors. When studying a quantitative factor, the different levels of the factor represent different quantitative amounts of the factor.[1,2,11] For example, a Developmental Psychologist could study the effect of reading time on cognitive development in young children. Her reading time factor could have four levels representing different quantitative amounts of time parents read to their children each day (e.g. 15 minutes, 30 minutes, 45 minutes, 60 minutes). When studying a qualitative factor, different levels of the factor represent different, non-quantitative, categorical values associated with the factor.[1,2,11] For example, a Forensic Psychologist could study the effect of prison cell color on the level of aggression displayed by prisoners. His prison cell color factor could have 5 levels representing different, non-quantitative, categorical values (e.g. pink prison cells; green prison cells; blue prison cells; white prison cells; grey prison cells).

When psychologists include a between-subjects factor in their factorial design, different groups of participants are randomly assigned to each level of the factor.[1,2,6] As a result, each of the groups will have a different experience during the experiment. For example, a Community Psychologist could study the effectiveness of different community-based programs in reducing substance use in at-risk teens. His community program factor could have 3 levels representing different types of programs for at-risk teens (e.g. athletics program, music program, job training program). If the community program factor is studied as a between-subjects factor, different groups of at-risk teens would be randomly assigned to the different programs. After all of the groups have completed their assigned program, the Community Psychologist could then compare the rate of substance-use among teens across programs. By comparison, if psychologists include a within-subjects factor in their factorial design, a single group of participants experiences all of the levels of the factor.[1,2,4] For example, a psychology professor teaching a course in Research Methods could study college students' perceptions of different textbook formats that could be used in the course. Her textbook format factor may have 4 levels representing different textbook formats that could be adopted for the course (i.e. e-book, audio book, standard print textbook, large print textbook). Students would evaluate each of the 4 textbook formats and the professor would then compare student perceptions across formats.

While the independent variables in a factorial design are typically "manipulated" by the psychologists conducting the experiment[1,2,4] (i.e. psychologists determine the levels of the factors participants will be exposed to and what the participants will experience during the experiment), psychologists may also incorporate "non-manipulated" factors into factorial designs. A "subject variable" is an example of a "non-manipulated" factor that psychologists will incorporate into a factorial design.[2,6,7] Subject variables (i.e. "participant variables") are personal characteristics (i.e. sex, age, race, marital status, sexual orientation) and/or personal experiences (i.e. divorce, fired from a job, victim of a crime, diagnosed with a medical/psychological illness) individuals possess prior to participating in an experiment. Because individuals already possess a specific level of these factors (i.e. personal characteristics or personal experiences) prior to participating in an experiment, individuals are not randomly assigned to the different levels of the factor as is done with a "manipulated" independent variable.[2,3,6] Rather, individuals are placed into groups based on the level of the factor that they each bring with them to the experiment. For example, if the subject variable of marital status is incorporated into a factorial design, individuals will already possess a level of marital status prior to participating in the experiment. It would make no sense for psychologists to then randomly assign these individuals to the different levels of the marital status factor (e.g. single, married, separated, divorced). Instead, the psychologists place individuals into groups based on the marital status that they bring with them to the experiment.

There are two styles of the factorial design that are commonly used by psychologists to study the individual and combined effects of a "manipulated" independent variable and a non-manipulated "subject variable." These factorial designs allow psychologists to study the effect of a "manipulated" independent variable on a behavior and/or mental process and to determine whether the effect generalizes to different groups of individuals who share a common personal characteristic and/or personal experience.[7] Specifically, these designs focus on whether different types of individuals respond in a similar manner when exposed to different situations or different types of treatments. These two styles of factorial designs are known as: (a) a Person × Situation factorial design and (b) a Person × Treatment factorial design.

Person × Situation Factorial Design

In a simple "person × situation" factorial design, psychologists examine the individual and combined effects of a single non-manipulated subject variable (i.e. person) and a single manipulated situational variable (i.e. situation).[1,2,3] Assume that a Social Psychologist is interested in determining whether there is a difference in the level of discomfort experienced by men and women across a variety of stressful situations. Specifically, he wants to determine if there is a difference in the level of discomfort experienced by men and women who have to give a public speech, go on a blind date, or complete a job interview. His research design is illustrated below.

Factor B (Stressful Situation)

		Speech	Date	Interview
	Males	1	2	3
Factor A (Gender)				
	Females	3	4	6

The non-manipulated "subject variable" in his design is gender. Each of the participants possessed a gender prior to participating in the experiment, so he can simply assign participants to groups based on the gender they "brought with them" to the experiment. The "manipulated" situation variable in his design is a stressful situation. He can manipulate the stressful situation participants experience during the experiment and randomly assign different groups of men and different groups of women to the different stressful situations if he treats situation as a between-subjects factor, or have a single group of men and a single group of women experience all of the different stressful situations if he treats situation as a within-subjects factor. For his experiment, he is treating situation as a between-subjects factor.

Since his design contains 2 factors (i.e. independent variables) and his 1st factor (Factor A: Gender) has 2 levels and his 2nd factor (Factor B: Stressful Situation) has 3 levels, he would describe his research design as a "2 × 3 factorial design." If we multiply 2 × 3, we get a value of "6." By combining all the levels of his two factors, he can create 6 unique conditions: Condition 1 (males—public speech), Condition 2 (males—blind date), Condition 3 (males—job interview), Condition 4 (females—public speech), Condition 5 (females—blind date), and finally Condition 6 (females—job interview). Level of discomfort would be the dependent variable.

Person × Treatment Factorial Design

In a simple "person × treatment" factorial design, psychologists examine the individual and combined effects of a single non-manipulated subject variable (i.e. person) and a single manipulated treatment variable (i.e. treatment).[2,6,12] Assume that a Clinical Psychologist is interested in studying the effectiveness of different methods of treatment for women diagnosed with post-traumatic stress disorder (PTSD) after experiencing a traumatic event during their lives. Specifically, she wants to compare the effectiveness of three methods of treatment (i.e. Cognitive Behavioral Therapy (CBT), Eye Movement Desensitization Reprocessing (EMDR), Selective Serotonin Uptake Inhibitor (SSRI)) in the treatment of women diagnosed with PTSD after experiencing child abuse, domestic violence, or a sexual assault. Her research design is illustrated below.

	Factor B (Treatment Method)		
	CBT	EMDR	SSRI
Child Abuse	1	2	3
Domestic Violence	4	5	6
Sexual Assault	7	8	9

Factor A (Trauma) labels the rows: Child Abuse, Domestic Violence, Sexual Assault.

The non-manipulated "subject variable" in her design is the type of trauma experienced. Each participant experienced a specific type of trauma prior to participating in the experiment, so she can simply assign participants to groups based on the trauma history they brought with them to the experiment. The "manipulated" treatment variable in her design is treatment method. For her experiment, treatment method is a between-subjects factor.

Since her design contains 2 factors (i.e. independent variables) and her 1st factor (Factor A: Trauma) has 3 levels and her 2nd factor (Factor B: Treatment Method) has 3 levels, she would describe her design as a "3 × 3 factorial design." If we multiply 3 × 3, we get a value of "9." By combining all the levels of her 2 factors, she can create 9 unique conditions: Condition 1 (child abuse—CBT), Condition 2 (child abuse—EMDR), Condition 3 (child abuse—SSRI), Condition 4 (domestic violence—CBT), Condition 5 (domestic violence—EMDR), Condition 6 (domestic violence—SSRI), Condition 7 (sexual assault—CBT), Condition 8 (sexual assault—EMDR), and Condition 9 (sexual assault—SSRI). Level of improvement of PTSD symptoms would be the dependent variable in the experiment.

While the inclusion of non-manipulated "subject variables" in factorial designs allows psychologists to study whether different types of individuals respond in a similar manner when exposed to different situations or different types of treatments[7], psychologists have to use caution when interpreting the results of these experiments. Why? Because when psychologists include a subject variable in a factorial design, participants are not randomly assigned to groups. Instead, they are placed into groups based on the level of the subject variable they possess prior to taking part in the experiment. While psychologists might assume this is the only difference that exists across groups, since participants were not randomly assigned to groups, psychologists cannot be sure that individual differences among participants have been equally distributed across groups. Therefore, there may be additional personal characteristics and/or personal experiences that are different across groups in the experiment.[2,3] For example, if a psychologist places participants into groups based on the variable of "gender," there may be additional personal characteristics and/or personal experiences (e.g. knowledge, skills, abilities, personality, attitudes, beliefs, etc.) that are different across the groups of males and females in the experiment. As a result, when the psychologists interpret the results of their experiment, they might conclude that the significant differences that exist between men and women on the dependent variables are due to the effect of participant gender, when in fact, the significant differences are due to the effects of the additional personal characteristics and/or personal experiences which differ across the groups of males and females in the experiment. The potential error introduced by the inclusion of a "subject variable" in a factorial design forces psychologists to be cautious in the conclusions they can draw.[2,3,6,7]

Types of Factorial Designs

When psychologists are interested in studying the individual and combined effects of two or more factors of independent variables (i.e. factors), there are 3 types of factorial designs they can use. The type of factorial design psychologists use will depend on whether the factors they are studying in their experiments are all between-subjects factors, all within-subjects factors, or a combination of both between-subjects and within-subjects factors. These three factorial designs are known as: (a) the between-subjects factorial design, (b) the within-subjects factorial design, and (c) the mixed factorial design.

Between-Subjects Factorial Design

The between-subjects factorial design is used by psychologists to study the individual and combined effects of two or more independent variables, all of which are between-subjects factors.[1,2,5,7] Different conditions are created by combining all of the levels of the factors in the experiment. Psychologists will then randomly assign different groups of participants to the different conditions in the experiment. Since different groups are assigned to the different conditions in the experiment, a between-subjects factorial design is also known as an "independent-groups factorial design."[1,2] Some psychologists use between-subjects factorial designs to study the effects of two or more manipulated between-subjects factors. As an example, assume a Parapsychologist is interested in studying the factors which influence whether individuals report experiencing paranormal phenomena in a reportedly "haunted" location. She wants to know whether the amount of knowledge individuals have about the haunted history of a location and the time of day when they investigate the location effects the number of paranormal experiences individuals report. Her research design is illustrated below.

	Factor B (Historical Information)	
	No Information	Information
Daytime	**1** Participant Group 1 n = 10	**2** Participant Group 2 n = 10
Nighttime	**3** Participant Group 3 n = 10	**4** Participant Group 4 n = 10

Factor A (Investigation Time)

Since her research design contains 2 factors (i.e. independent variables) and her 1st factor (Factor A: Investigation Time) has 2 levels and her 2nd factor (Factor B: Historical Information) has 2 levels, she would describe her design as a "2 × 2 between-subjects factorial design." When she combines all of the levels of her 2 factors, she can create 4 conditions: Condition 1 (daytime—no knowledge), Condition 2 (daytime —knowledge), Condition 3 (night time—no knowledge), and Condition 4 (night time—knowledge). Since her factors are all between-subjects factors, she will randomly assign a different group of participants to each of her 4 conditions. If she wants to have 10 participants in each of her conditions, she would need a total of 40 participants in order to conduct her experiment. The number of paranormal phenomena observed by each participant during the investigation would be the dependent variable in the experiment.

Other psychologists use the between-subjects factorial design to study the effects of both manipulated and non-manipulated (i.e. subject variables) between-subjects factors. For example, assume an Industrial-Organizational Psychologist is interested in studying the influence of work breaks on the performance of employees with different levels of work experience. He wants to know whether the manner in which work breaks are scheduled throughout the work day affects the work performance of new hires and experienced employees. His design is below.

		Factor B (Employee Work Experience)	
		New Hires	Employees
	1—60 Minute Break	**1** New Hire Group 1 n = 20	**4** Employee Group 1 n = 20
Factor A (Breaks)	2—30 Minute Breaks	**2** New Hire Group 2 n = 20	**5** Employee Group 2 n = 20
	4—15 Minute Breaks	**3** New Hire Group 3 n = 20	**6** Employee Group 3 n = 20

Since his research design contains 2 factors (i.e. independent variables) and his 1st factor (Factor A: Break Schedule) has 3 levels and his 2nd factor (Factor B: Worker Experience) has 2 levels, he would describe his design as a "3 × 2 between-subjects factorial design." Factor A is his manipulated, between-subjects factor and Factor B is his non-manipulated, between-subjects factor (i.e. subject variable). By combining all levels of his 2 factors, he can create 6 conditions: Condition 1 (1—60–minute break—new hires), Condition 2 (2—30-minute breaks—new hires), Condition 3 (4—15-minute breaks—new hires), Condition 4 (1—60–minute break—employees), Condition 5 (2—30-minute breaks—employees), and finally Condition 6 (4—15-minute breaks—employees). Since his two factors are both between-subjects factors, he would randomly assign a different group of new hires to three of his conditions (i.e. Conditions 1–3) and randomly assign a different group of experienced employees to his other three conditions (i.e. Conditions 4–6). If he wants 20 participants in each condition, he would need a total of 120 participants to conduct his experiment. The work performance of each participant during the experiment would be the dependent variable in the experiment.

Psychologists who use the between-subjects factorial design to study the individual and combined effects of two or more between-subjects factors, face the very same challenges faced by psychologists who use a between-subjects design to study a single independent variable. If a different group of participants is assigned to each condition in the experiment, psychologists will need a greater number of participants to conduct the experiment than if they had a single group of participants complete all of the conditions in the experiment.[2,3,8] In addition, psychologists have to expend time and resources to create equivalent groups across conditions in order to: (a) reduce the error associated with the individual differences among the members of the research sample and (b) conduct a valid assessment of the individual and combined effects of their two or more factors on the dependent variable(s).[4,6,12]

Within-Subjects Factorial Design

Psychologists use the within-subjects factorial design to study the individual and combined effects of two or more independent variables, all of which are within-subjects factors.[1,2,6] Different conditions are created by combining all of the levels of the factors in the experiment. A single group of participants then completes all the conditions in the experiment. Since a single group of participants is measured on the dependent variable after they complete each condition in the experiment, the within-subjects factorial design is referred to as a "repeated-measures factorial design."[1,4,7] Assume a psychologist who conducts research in the area of sensation and perception is interested in studying the factors that influence the ability of individuals to recognize distant objects. Specifically, he wants to know the extent to which the distance at which objects are viewed and the movement of objects influences recognition accuracy. His research design is illustrated below.

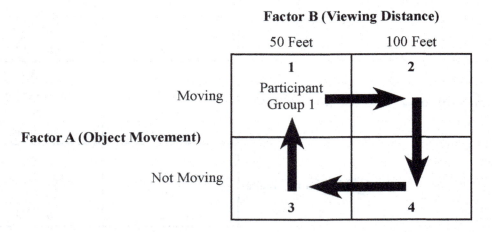

Since his research design contains 2 factors (i.e. independent variables) and his 1st factor (Factor A: Object Movement) has 2 levels and his 2nd factor (Factor B: Viewing Distance) has 2 levels, he would describe his design as a "2 × 2 within-subjects factorial design." By combining all the levels of his factors, he can create 4 conditions: Condition 1 (moving—50 feet), Condition 2 (moving—100 feet), Condition 3 (not moving—50 feet), and finally Condition 4 (not moving—100 feet). Since his two factors are both within-subjects factors, he would have a single group of participants complete all the conditions. If he wants 20 participants to complete each condition, he would need a total of 20 participants to conduct his experiment. The recognition accuracy of each participant during the experiment would be the dependent variable in the experiment.

Psychologists who use the within-subjects factorial design to study both the individual and combined effects of two or more within-subjects factors, face the very same challenges faced by psychologists who use a within-subjects design to study a single independent variable. Since a single group of participants will complete all of the conditions in the experiment, psychologists will have to implement a full or partial counterbalancing strategy in order to control for potential order effects and carry-over effects during the experiment.[1,2,6] Also, since participants will spend a longer amount of time in the experiment in order to complete all the conditions, psychologists must attempt to minimize the influence of outside events on participants' performance during the experiment. Finally, psychologists must be aware of the increased potential for subject attrition (i.e. drop-out)[1,4,6] and for participants to learn the purpose of the experiment and potentially alter their behavior as they complete each condition in the experiment.[2,8,11]

Mixed Factorial Design

The mixed factorial design is used by psychologists to study the individual and combined effects of a combination of between-subjects and within-subjects factors.[1,2,3] The mixed factorial design is also known as a "split plot design."[6] Mixed factorial designs are used by some psychologists to study both the individual and combined effects of a manipulated between-subjects factor and a manipulated within-subjects factor. As an example, assume a Cognitive Psychologist is interested in studying the factors which influence the ability of individuals to remember a list of words. Specifically, she is interested in studying the effects of memory strategy (i.e. mnemonics) and memory task (i.e. recall vs. recognition) on the ability to remember a list of words. Her research design is illustrated below.

Factor B (Memory Task)

	Recall	Recognition
Mnemonic A	**1** Participant Group 1 n = 15	**2**
Mnemonic B	**3** Participant Group 2 n = 15	**4**

Factor A (Memory Strategy)

Since her research design contains 2 factors (i.e. independent variables) and her 1st factor (Factor A: Memory Strategy) is a between-subjects factor with 2 levels and her 2nd factor (Factor B: Memory Task) is a within-subjects factor with 2 levels, she would describe her design as a "2 × 2 mixed factorial design." By combining all of the levels of her two factors, she can create 4 unique conditions: Condition 1 (mnemonic A—recall), Condition 2 (mnemonic A—recognition), Condition 3 (mnemonic B—recall), and Condition 4 (mnemonic B—recognition). Since Factor A (Memory Strategy) is a between-subjects factor, she will randomly assign a different group of participants to the different memory strategies (i.e. mnemonic A and mnemonic B). Since Factor B is a within-subjects factor, all participants will complete both memory tasks (i.e. recall and recognition). If she wants to have 15 participants complete each condition, she would need a total of 30 participants to conduct her experiment. The number of words correctly identified from the word list would be the dependent variable in the experiment.

Psychologists also use the mixed factorial design to study the individual and combined effects of a non-manipulated, between-subjects factor (i.e. subject variable) and a manipulated within-subjects factor. For example, assume that a Sports Psychologist is interested in studying the effect of adverse weather conditions on the performance of amateur and professional athletes. Specifically, he wants to study the performance of amateur and professional golfers in different adverse weather conditions (e.g. extreme cold, extreme wind, extreme rain). His research design is illustrated below.

Factor B (Type of Golfer)

	Amateur	Professional
Cold	**1** Amateur Group 1 n = 30	**4** Professional Group 1 n = 30
Wind	**2**	**5**
Rain	**3**	**6**

Factor A (Weather)

Since his research design contains 2 factors (i.e. independent variables) and his 1st factor (Factor A: Weather) is a within-subjects factor with 3 levels and his 2nd factor (Factor B: Type of Golfer) is a between-subjects factor with 2 levels, he would describe his design as a "3 × 2 mixed factorial design." By combining all levels of his 2 factors, he can create 6 conditions: Condition 1 (cold—amateur), Condition 2 (wind—amateur), Condition 3 (rain—amateur), Condition 4 (cold—professional), Condition 5 (wind—professional), and Condition 6 (rain—professional). Since Factor B (Type of Golfer) is a non-manipulated, between-subjects factor (i.e. subject variable), he will simply place golfers who participate in his experiment into groups based on each golfer's current amateur or professional status. Since Factor A is a within-subjects factor, all golfers will play 3 rounds of golf (i.e. 1 round when it is extremely cold, 1 round when it is extremely windy, and 1 round when it is extremely rainy). If he wants 30 amateur and 30 professional golfers to play a round of golf under each of the 3 adverse weather conditions, he would need a total of 60 golfers to conduct his experiment. For each round of golf played, the score shot by each golfer would be the dependent variable for the experiment.

Analyzing a Factorial Design

A factorial design allows psychologists to study both the individual and combined effects of two or more independent variables on one or more dependent variables. The individual effect of each independent variable in a factorial design is known as a "main effect."[1,2,4] To illustrate how psychologists analyze the "main effect" for each independent variable in a factorial design, we can take a look at the following example.

A fast-food restaurant chain is considering adding "bison burgers" (i.e. healthier burgers made out of bison meat rather than hamburger) to its menu. A Consumer Psychologist has been hired by the company to study consumer perceptions of its "bison burgers." The company wants the Consumer Psychologist to study both the individual and combined effects of cooking method (i.e. fried vs. grilled) and burger size (i.e. ¼ pound vs. ½ pound) on consumer perceptions of the "bison burgers." The psychologist decides to conduct a 2 × 2 between-subjects factorial design. Combining all the levels of his two factors, he creates 4 unique conditions: Condition 1 (fried—¼ pound), Condition 2 (fried—½ pound), Condition 3 (grilled—¼ pound), and Condition 4 (grilled—½ pound). He then randomly assigns a different group of 8 consumers to each of the different conditions in his experiment. Participants then consume their assigned "bison burger" and give the "bison burger" a taste rating using a 10-point rating scale (1 = Wow! This burger is awful!; 10 = Wow! This burger is awesome!). The taste rating data is presented below.

	Factor B (Burger Size)	
	¼ Pound	½ Pound
Fried	**1** 6 8 8 9 7 9 8 9	**2** 4 6 6 6 5 4 4 5
Grilled	**3** 7 6 5 6 5 4 6 9	**4** 8 7 8 9 9 8 7 8

Factor A (Cooking Method)

To analyze the "main effect" for Factor A (Cooking Method) on the dependent variable (i.e. taste rating), we start by computing the means for each level of Factor A (i.e. each row in the table).[5,6,8] These row means are referred to as "marginal means."[2] To compute the row mean for the "fried" level of Factor A, we simply add the taste ratings for all participants who ate a "fried bison burger" (regardless of the size of the bison burger they ate) and divide by the total number of participants who ate a "fried bison burger." To compute the row mean for the "grilled" level of Factor A, we simply add the taste ratings for all participants who ate a "grilled bison burger" (regardless of the size of the bison burger they ate) and divide by the number of participants who ate a "grilled bison burger." The computed "marginal means" for Factor A are presented below.

Factor B (Burger Size)

	¼ Pound		½ Pound		
	1		**2**		
Fried	6	8	4	6	104/16 = **6.5**
	8	9	6	6	
	7	9	5	4	
	8	9	4	5	
	3		**4**		
Grilled	7	6	8	7	112/16 = **7.0**
	5	6	8	9	
	5	4	9	8	
	6	9	7	8	

Factor A (Cooking Method)

If this were a real experiment, the Consumer Psychologist would conduct a statistical analysis to determine if there was a significant difference between the means. For our purposes, however, we will simply consider a difference of 2 points or more between the means to be a significant difference. Our analysis revealed that the average taste rating for the "fried" bison burger was 6.5 while the average rating for the "grilled" bison burger was 7.0. Since there is only a ½ point difference between the row means, we would conclude that there is no significant difference in the average taste rating given by consumers to "fried" and "grilled" bison burgers. Therefore, there is no "main effect" for Factor A. The method used to cook the bison burgers is not having a significant effect on consumers' taste ratings.

To analyze the "main effect" for Factor B (Burger Size) on the dependent variable (i.e. taste rating), we start by computing the means for each level of Factor B (i.e. each column in the table). These column means are referred to as "marginal means." To compute the column mean for the "¼ pound" level of Factor B, we simply add up the taste ratings for all participants who ate a "¼ pound bison burger" (regardless of the method used to cook the bison burger) and then divide by the total number of participants who ate a "¼ pound bison burger." To compute the column mean for the "½ pound" level of Factor B, we add up the taste ratings for all participants who ate a "½ pound bison burger" (regardless of the method used to cook the bison burger) and divide by the total number of participants who ate a "½ pound bison burger." The computed "marginal means" for Factor B are presented following.

Factor B (Burger Size)

		¼ Pound		½ Pound	
		1		**2**	
	Fried	6	8	4	6
		8	9	6	6
		7	9	5	4
		8	9	4	5
Factor A (Cooking Method)		**3**		**4**	
	Grilled	7	6	8	7
		5	6	8	9
		5	4	9	8
		6	9	7	8

12/16 = **7.0** 104/16 = **6.5**

Our analysis revealed that the average taste rating for the "¼ pound" bison burger was 7.0 while the average rating for the "½ pound" bison burger was 6.5. Since there is only a ½ point difference between the column means, we would conclude there is no significant difference in the average taste rating given by consumers to the "¼ pound" and "½ pound" bison burgers. Therefore, there is no significant "main effect" for Factor B. The size of these bison burgers is not having a significant effect on consumers' taste ratings.

In addition to analyzing the "main effects" for each individual independent variable in a factorial design, psychologists can also analyze the combined effect of the independent variables on one or more dependent variables. The combined effect of two or more independent variables on a dependent variable is known as an "interaction."[1,2,4,5] To analyze the "interaction" between Factor A (Cooking Method) and Factor B (Burger Size), the Consumer Psychologist would begin his analysis by computing average taste ratings for each condition (i.e. "cell") in his experiment. These average ratings are referred to as "cell means."[13] To compute a "cell mean," we simply add up the taste ratings in a condition and then divide by the number of participants assigned to that condition. The "cell" means for each condition are presented below.

Factor B (Burger Size)

		¼ Pound	½ Pound
		1	**1**
	Fried	64/8 = **8.0**	40/8 = **5.0**
Factor A (Cooking Method)		**3**	**4**
	Grilled	48/8 = **6.0**	64/8 = **8.0**

After computing the "cell means" for each condition in his experiment, the Consumer Psychologist would then prepare a graph displaying the "cell means." In preparing the graph, Factor A is placed on the horizontal axis and the dependent variable (i.e. average taste ratings) is placed on the vertical axis.[13] The cell means for each of the levels of Factor B are then displayed in the main body of the graph. A graph displaying the "cell means" in the "bison burger" study are presented below.

Average Taste Rating

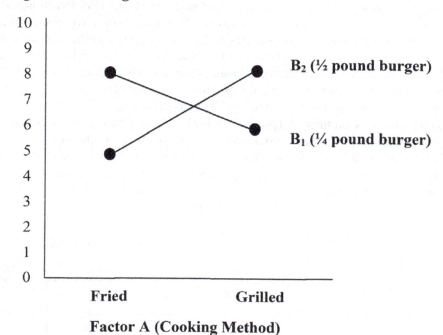

Factor A (Cooking Method)

So how do we determine whether there is an "interaction" between Factor A (Cooking Method) and Factor B (Burger Size)? If this were a real experiment, the Consumer Psychologist would conduct a statistical analysis to determine if there was a significant interaction between the two factors. For our purposes, we will use 2 general rules of thumb to identify the presence of an "interaction." First, when an "interaction" is present between factors, the lines on a graph that represent each level of Factor B will cross one another (or run non-parallel to one another). When there is no "interaction" present, the lines on a graph that represent each level of Factor B will run parallel to one another (much like railroad tracks) and will not cross.[3,6,7] If we take a look at the Consumer Psychologist's graph, the lines on the graph which represent each level of Factor B cross one another. This indicates the presence of an "interaction" between the factors. Second, when interpreting the "interaction," it is necessary to: (a) use both Factor A and Factor B when stating the conclusion or (b) use the phrase "it depends" when stating the conclusion.[1,2,3,13] If we look at the Consumer Psychologist's graph, we can conclude that if a bison burger is fried, consumers prefer the taste of a ¼ pound burger, but if a bison burger is grilled, consumers prefer the taste of the ½ pound burger. Notice how we need to include information about both factors when stating our conclusion. So, if the restaurant were to ask the Consumer Psychologist, "How do consumers want us to cook their bison burgers?," the Consumer Psychologist would have to say that "it depends on the size of the bison burger they order" and if the restaurant were to ask, "What size of bison burger do consumers prefer?," the Consumer Psychologist would have to say that "it depends on how they want it cooked." This once again indicates the presence of an "interaction" between factors. So, in looking at the overall results for the "bison burger" study, there was no significant "main effect" for Factor A (Cooking Method), there was no significant "main effect" for Factor B (Burger Size); however, there was a significant "interaction" between Factors A × B (Cooking Method × Burger Size). Each factor by itself had no significant effect on consumer taste ratings, but when the two factors were combined, they did have a significant effect on consumer taste ratings.

The same type of analysis can be applied to a factorial design that includes factors that have more than two levels. As an example, assume the fast-food restaurant wants the Consumer Psychologist to conduct a second study on consumer perceptions of their "bison burgers." The second study will focus on consumer perceptions of the "toppings" that can be added to a bison burger. The company wants the Consumer Psychologist to study the individual and combined effects of the type of cheese (i.e. swiss vs. provolone vs. cheddar) and type of sauce (i.e. ranch vs. barbecue vs. buffalo) on consumer perceptions of taste. The psychologist decides to conduct a 3 × 3 between-subjects factorial design. Combining all the levels of his two factors, he creates 9 unique conditions: Condition 1 (Swiss–ranch), Condition 2 (Swiss-barbecue), Condition 3 (Swiss–buffalo), Condition 4 (provolone–ranch), Condition 5 (provolone–barbecue), Condition 6 (provolone–buffalo), Condition 7 (cheddar–ranch), Condition 8 (cheddar–barbecue), and Condition 9 (cheddar–buffalo). He then randomly assigns a different group of 8 consumers to each of the different conditions in his experiment. Participants then consume the assigned "bison burger" and give the "bison burger" a taste rating using a 10-point rating scale (1 = Wow! This burger is awful!; 10 = Wow! This burger is awesome!). The taste rating data is presented below.

Factor B (Burger Size)

		Ranch		Barbecue		Buffalo	
		1		**2**		**3**	
		3	4	8	6	9	10
	Swiss	2	5	6	6	9	10
		2	2	5	5	8	9
		3	3	6	6	8	9
		4		**5**		**6**	
Factor A		4	6	5	7	9	9
(Cheese Type)	Provolone	1	2	8	9	8	10
		2	2	5	5	9	10
		3	4	5	4	8	9
		7		**8**		**9**	
		3	2	3	6	9	9
	Cheddar	4	3	4	7	9	10
		5	4	7	6	7	10
		2	1	7	8	9	9

To analyze the "main effect" for Factor A (Cheese Type) on the dependent variable (i.e. taste rating), we start by computing the "marginal means" for each level of Factor A (i.e. each row in the table). To compute the row mean for the "Swiss" cheese level of Factor A, we simply add up the taste ratings for all participants who ate a bison burger with Swiss cheese (regardless of the type of sauce put on the bison burger) and divide by the number of participants who ate a bison burger with Swiss cheese. We can then use the same process to compute the row means for both the "provolone" and "cheddar" cheese levels of Factor A. The computed "marginal means" for Factor A are presented below.

Factor B (Burger Size)

		Ranch		Barbecue		Buffalo		
		1		**2**		**3**		
	Swiss	3	4	8	6	9	10	144/24 = **6.0**
		2	5	6	6	9	10	
		2	2	5	5	8	9	
		3	3	6	6	8	9	
		4		**5**		**6**		
Factor A	Provolone	4	6	5	7	9	9	144/24 = **6.0**
(Cheese Type)		1	2	8	9	8	10	
		2	2	5	5	9	10	
		3	4	5	4	8	9	
		7		**8**		**9**		
	Cheddar	3	2	3	6	9	9	144/24 = **6.0**
		4	3	4	7	9	10	
		5	4	7	6	7	10	
		2	1	7	8	9	9	

If this were a real experiment, the Consumer Psychologist would conduct a statistical analysis to determine if there was a significant difference between the means. For our purposes, however, we will once again consider a difference of 2 points or more between the means to be a significant difference. Our analysis revealed that the average taste rating was the same for bison burgers with Swiss, provolone, or cheddar cheese. The average taste rating was 6.0 for each type of cheese. Since there was no difference between the row means, we would conclude that there is no significant difference in the average taste rating given by consumers to bison burgers with Swiss, provolone, or cheddar cheese. Therefore, there is no "main effect" for Factor A. The type of cheese on a bison burger is not having a significant effect on consumers' taste ratings.

To analyze the "main effect" for Factor B (Sauce Type) on the dependent variable (i.e. taste rating), we start by computing the "marginal means" for each level of Factor B (i.e. each column in the table). To compute the column mean for the "ranch" sauce level of Factor B, we add up the taste ratings for all participants who ate a bison burger with ranch sauce (regardless of the type of cheese on the bison burger) and divide by the number of participants who ate a bison burger with ranch sauce. We can then use the same process to compute the column means for the "barbecue" and "buffalo" sauce levels of Factor B. The computed "marginal means" for Factor B are presented below.

Factor B (Sauce Type)

		Ranch		Barbecue		Buffalo	
		1		**2**		**3**	
		3	4	8	6	9	10
	Swiss	2	5	6	6	9	10
		2	2	5	5	8	9
		3	3	6	6	8	9
		4		**5**		**6**	
Factor A		4	6	5	7	9	9
(Cheese Type)	Provolone	1	2	8	9	8	10
		2	2	5	5	9	10
		3	4	5	4	8	9
		7		**8**		**9**	
		3	2	3	6	9	9
	Cheddar	4	3	4	7	9	10
		5	4	7	6	7	10
		2	1	7	8	9	9
		72/24 = **3**		144/24 = **6**		216/24 = **9**	

Our analysis revealed the average taste ratings for a bison burger with ranch, barbecue, or buffalo sauce were 3.0, 6.0, and 9.0 respectively. Since there is more than a 2 point difference between at least two column means, we would conclude that there is a significant difference in the average taste ratings given by consumers to bison burgers with ranch, barbecue, and buffalo sauce. Therefore, there is a significant "main effect" for Factor B. The type of sauce is having a significant effect on consumers' taste ratings. A further analysis of the "column means" reveals that consumers: (a) rated bison burgers with barbecue sauce as being tastier than bison burgers with ranch sauce (barbecue sauce 6.0 > ranch sauce 3.0) and (b) rated bison burgers with buffalo sauce as being tastier than bison burgers with either barbecue or ranch sauce (buffalo sauce 9.0 > barbecue sauce 6.0 and ranch sauce 3.0).

To analyze the interaction between Factor A (Cheese Type) and Factor B (Sauce Type), the Consumer Psychologist would begin his analysis by computing the average taste rating for each condition (i.e. "cell") in his experiment. These average ratings are known as "cell means." To compute a "cell mean," we simply add up the taste ratings in a condition and then divide by the number of participants who are assigned to that condition. We continue this process until a "cell mean" has been computed for every condition in the experiment.13 The "cell" means for each condition are presented below.

Factor B (Sauce Type)

		Ranch	Barbecue	Buffalo
Factor A (Cheese Type)	Swiss	1 24/8 = **3.0**	2 48/8 = **6.0**	3 72/8 = **9.0**
	Provolone	4 24/8 = **3.0**	5 48/8 = **6.0**	6 72/8 = **9.0**
	Cheddar	7 24/8 = **3.0**	8 48/8 = **6.0**	9 72/8 = **9.0**

After computing the "cell means" for each condition in his experiment, the Consumer Psychologist would then prepare a graph displaying the "cell means." In preparing the graph, Factor A is placed on the horizontal axis and the dependent variable (i.e. average taste ratings) is placed on the vertical axis.[13] The cell means for each of the levels of Factor B are then displayed in the main body of the graph. A graph displaying the "cell means" in the "bison burger" study are presented below.

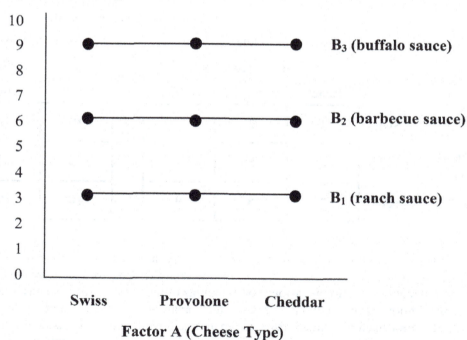

If we take a look at the Consumer Psychologist's graph, the lines that represent each level of Factor B run parallel to one another and do not cross one another. This indicates that there is no "interaction" between factors. Looking at the graph, we can conclude that consumers prefer the taste of bison burgers with buffalo sauce regardless of the type of cheese on the bison burger. Notice how we do not need to include information about both factors in stating our conclusion. So, if the restaurant were to ask the Consumer Psychologist, "What kind of sauce do consumers want on their bison burgers?," the Consumer Psychologist would simply say "buffalo" sauce. If the restaurant were to ask the Consumer Psychologist, "What kind of cheese do consumers want on their bison burgers?," the Consumer Psychologist would simply say "there is no preference for one type of cheese over the others." Notice how an "it depends" statement is not necessary when stating the conclusions about the results of the study. So, in looking at the overall results of the second "bison burger" study, there was no significant "main effect" for Factor A (Cheese Type), there was a significant "main effect" for Factor B (Sauce Type), and there was not a significant Factor A × B "interaction." While the type of sauce by itself had a significant effect on consumer taste ratings, the type of cheese by itself and the combination of cheese type × sauce type did not have a significant effect on consumer taste ratings.

The analysis of a factorial design becomes more complex when psychologists include more than two factors (i.e. independent variables) in their factorial design.[1,2,6] For example, assume the fast-food restaurant wants the Consumer Psychologist to conduct a third study to determine whether there is a difference in male and female consumers' ratings of bison burgers containing different sauce type × cheese type combinations. If consumer gender is added to his factorial design, the Consumer Psychologist would now have to conduct a 3 (Factor A: Cheese Type) × 3 (Factor B: Sauce Type) × 2 (Factor C: Gender) between-subjects factorial design. The combination of all the levels of the 3 factors would create a total of 18 unique conditions. His design is illustrated below.

Factor C (Consumer Gender)

		Male				Female		
		Factor B (Sauce Type)				**Factor B (Sauce Type)**		
		Ranch	Barbecue	Buffalo		Ranch	Barbecue	Buffalo
	Swiss	1	2	3		10	11	12
Factor A (Cheese Type)	Provolone	4	5	6		13	14	15
	Cheddar	7	8	9		16	17	18

To analyze the results of his experiment, the Consumer Psychologist would once again have to determine whether there is a significant "main effect" for each individual factor as well as determine whether there are any significant "interactions" between various combinations of his factors. Since he has 3 factors in his factorial design, he would now have to conduct 3 main effect" analyses (i.e. the main effect for Factor A: Cheese Type, the main effect for Factor B: Sauce Type, the main effect for Factor C: Consumer Gender).

When he analyzes his data to determine whether there are any significant "interactions" present, he will find the process to be much more complex than when there were only 2 factors in his factorial design. Remember that in a factorial design that contains 2 factors, there is only one possible "interaction" (Factor A × Factor B). Since this represents an interaction between 2 factors, it is referred to as a "2-way interaction."[2,5,6] Because he now has 3 factors in his design, he will have 3 different "2-way interactions" to analyze (Factor A × Factor B, Factor A × Factor C, Factor B × Factor C). In addition to these 2-way interactions, he will also have an additional "interaction" to analyze. This additional "interaction" would be the "3-way interaction" between all his factors (Factor A × Factor B × Factor C).[2,3,5] If there was a significant "3-way interaction" in his experiment, the Consumer Psychologist would conclude that male and female consumers preferred the taste of different cheese type × sauce type combinations on their bison burgers. As is evident from the example, increasing the number of factors in a factorial design increases the complexity of the design as well as the complexity of the analysis and interpretation of results. It is for these reasons that most psychologists who use a factorial design will limit their designs to 2–3 factors (i.e. independent variables).[3,4,6] Psychologists must carefully weigh the benefits of the knowledge gained by adding additional factors to a factorial design, against the increased complexity and interpretation challenges associated with the inclusion of the additional factors. The analysis of a factorial design containing 3 factors is beyond the scope of this discussion.

Advantages of the Factorial Design

There are 3 main advantages associated with using a factorial design. First, the factorial design allows psychologists to study more than one independent variable (i.e. factor) in a single experiment rather than having to conduct multiple experiments that each examine the effect of a single independent variable.[3,4,11] By studying more than one independent variable (i.e. factor) in a single experiment, psychologists can study the individual and combined effects of their factors more efficiently (i.e. less time, fewer staff/resources)[2,5,7] when compared to conducting multiple experiments which examine a single independent variable. Second, the factorial design allows psychologists to study how different factors (and different levels of factors) interact to produce unique and significant effects on behavior and/or mental processes.[2,3,9,11] The opportunity to examine the combined effect of multiple independent variables is not available to psychologists who conduct experiments in which they study the effect of only a single independent variable. Third, given that human behavior is complex and often caused by the effects of multiple factors in our environment, the "factorial design" allows psychologists to conduct experiments which provide a more realistic assessment of the causes of "real world" behavior.[1,2,9,11] By allowing psychologists to study the combined effects of two or more independent variables, a "factorial design" helps psychologists understand how even subtle differences in combinations of factors can produce dramatically different outcomes.

Disadvantages of the Factorial Design

While there are several advantages associated with the use of a factorial design, there are also some important disadvantages psychologists need to consider when deciding if the factorial design is the best design to use to answer their research question(s). First, as psychologists add additional independent variables (i.e. factors) to their research designs, it increases the number of unique conditions that can be created when all of the levels of the different factors are combined. As the number of unique conditions increases, a greater amount of time, resources, research staff, and participants may be required to conduct the experiment.[1,2,5] Second, since factorial designs are used to study different combinations of both between-subjects and within-subjects factors, they are vulnerable to the same sources of error as the between- and within-subjects designs that are used to study a single independent variable. As an example, when a manipulated, between-subjects variable is included in a factorial design, psychologists must take the appropriate actions (e.g. random assignment, matching) to ensure there are equivalent groups of participants across conditions.[1,2,3,7] When a within-subjects factor is included in a factorial design, psychologists must take the appropriate actions (e.g. full and partial counterbalancing strategies) to control for both order effects and carry-over effects that may occur during the experiment.[1,2,6] Available resources and access to members of a target populations will also play a role in decisions as to whether to treat an independent variable (i.e. factor) in a factorial design as a between-subjects or within-subjects variable. Third, as the number of independent variables in a "factorial design" increases: (a) the complexity of the design increases, (b) conducting the experiment free of error becomes more difficult, (c) the data analysis becomes more complex, and (d) interpretation of the results of the experiment becomes more challenging.[5,6,7] Before making a decision to use a "factorial design," psychologists should take the necessary time to carefully consider both the advantages and the disadvantages associated with such a design.

EXERCISE 9A

Factorial Design Analysis 1

A Social Psychologist is interested in studying how middle-aged men can increase their self-confidence. She wants to determine whether making changes to one's physical appearance (Factor A) and/or acquiring a new skill (Factor B) can increase the self-confidence of middle-aged men. Specifically, she wants to examine the individual and combined effects of 3 different methods of changing one's physical appearance (i.e. professional haircut, new wardrobe, teeth whitening) and the acquisition of 2 new skills (i.e. learning to dance, learning to cook) on the self-confidence of middle-aged men. She has decided to conduct a between-subjects factorial design and wants to have 8 middle-aged men in each of the conditions in her experiment. After acquiring their assigned skill and making the assigned change in their physical appearance, each middle-aged man will provide a rating of his level of self-confidence on a 10-point rating scale (1 = I have absolutely no self-confidence; 10 = I have the self-confidence to take on the world!).

01. Numerically, how would the Social Psychologist describe her factorial design?

$\boxed{}$ × $\boxed{}$ factorial design

02. How many independent variables (i.e. factors) are in the Social Psychologist's design?

$\boxed{}$ Independent Variables (i.e. factors)

03. How many unique conditions can the Social Psychologist create by combining all the levels of her independent variables (i.e. factors)?

$\boxed{}$ Conditions

04. How many middle-aged men will the psychologist need to conduct her experiment?

$\boxed{}$ Middle-Aged Men

05. How many "main effects" and "interactions" will the Social Psychologist have to analyze to interpret the results of her experiment?

$\boxed{}$ Main Effects

$\boxed{}$ Interactions

Below is the *raw data* from the Social Psychologist's experiment.

	Factor B (Skill Acquired)			
	Dance		Cook	
Haircut	6	8	4	6
	4	3	6	6
	7	3	5	4
	4	5	4	5
Wardrobe	6	4	7	7
	5	6	7	9
	5	4	9	5
	4	6	7	5
Teeth	7	4	9	10
	5	6	9	9
	5	4	8	9
	6	3	9	9

Factor A (Appearance Change) labels the rows.

06. Compute the "*marginal means*" for Factor A

	Factor B (Skill Acquired)				
	Dance		Cook		
Haircut	6	8	4	6	= ☐
	4	3	6	6	
	7	3	5	4	
	4	5	4	5	
Wardrobe	6	4	7	7	= ☐
	5	6	7	9	
	5	4	9	5	
	4	6	7	5	
Teeth	7	4	9	10	= ☐
	5	6	9	9	
	5	4	8	9	
	6	3	9	9	

Factor A (Appearance Change) labels the rows.

Assuming a 2 point difference between means represents a "significant difference," is there a "main effect" for Factor A (Appearance Change)?

[ ] Yes   [ ] No

What can the Social Psychologist conclude about the effect of a change in one's physical appearance on the self-confidence of middle-aged men?

---

07. Compute the "*marginal means*" for Factor B

Factor B (Skill Acquired)

		Dance		Cook	
	Haircut	6	8	4	6
		4	3	6	6
		7	3	5	4
		4	5	4	5
Factor A (Appearance Change)	Wardrobe	6	4	7	7
		5	6	7	9
		5	4	9	5
		4	6	7	5
	Teeth	7	4	9	10
		5	6	9	9
		5	4	8	9
		6	3	9	9

[ ]   [ ]

Assuming a 2 point difference between means represents a "significant difference," is there a "main effect" for Factor B (Skill Acquired)?

☐ Yes   ☐ No

What can the Social Psychologist conclude about the effect of acquiring a new skill on the self-confidence of middle-aged men?

08. Compute the "*cell means*" for each condition in the experiment

Factor B (Skill Acquired)

	Dance	Cook
Haircut	☐	☐
Factor A (**Appearance Change**) Wardrobe	☐	☐
Teeth	☐	☐

09. Create a *graph* illustrating the results of the psychologist's experiment

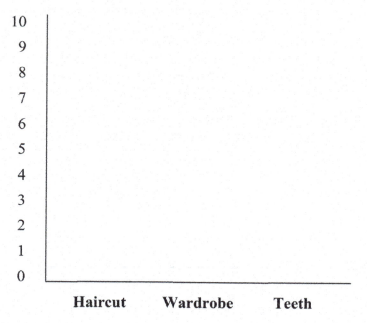

Self-Confidence Rating

Factor A (Appearance Change)

Haircut   Wardrobe   Teeth

Is there a "significant interaction" between Factor A × Factor B?

☐ Yes   ☐ No

What can the Social Psychologist conclude about the "interaction" between Factor A: (Appearance Change) × Factor B (Skill Acquired) in middle-age men?

If a middle-aged man asked you how he could increase his self-confidence, what would you recommend he do based on the results of the experiment conducted by the Social Psychologist?

EXERCISE 9B

Factorial Design Analysis 2

Every morning for the past 20 years, a Psychology professor has had an apple fritter and a 16 ounce cup of coffee for breakfast. The apple fritter and cup of coffee provided him with the energy to get through his long days of teaching. Recently, as he reached the age of 49, he found he no longer had the energy at the end of the day to teach at a high level. He wants to determine whether increasing his apple fritter and/or coffee intake will provide him with the extra energy he needs. He decides to conduct a between-subjects factorial design with the amount of coffee (i.e. 1 cup, 2 cups, 3 cups) as Factor A and the number of apple fritters (i.e. 1 fritter, 2 fritters, 3 fritters) as Factor B. He recruits a sample of professors who are 49 years of age or older to take part in the experiment. He randomly assigns 8 professors to each condition. After consuming their assigned amount of coffee and number of apple fritters, each professor will provide a rating of his energy level at the end of the day using a 10-point rating scale (1 = I have absolutely no energy. I need to take a nap! 10 = I have so much energy I feel like I am going to explode!).

01. Numerically, how would the Psychology professor describe his factorial design?

□ × □ factorial design

02. How many independent variables (i.e. factors) are in the Psychology professor's design?

□ Independent Variables (i.e. factors)

03. How many unique conditions can the Psychology professor create by combining all the levels of his independent variables (i.e. factors)?

□ Conditions

04. How many professors 49 years of age or older will be needed to conduct the experiment?

□ Professors

05. How many "main effects" and "interactions" will the Psychology professor have to analyze to interpret the results of his experiment?

□ Main Effects

□ Interactions

Below is the *raw data* from the Psychology professor's experiment.

Factor B (Fritters)

		1 Fritter		2 Fritters		3 Fritters	
		3	1	8	6	9	10
	1 Cup	2	3	6	6	9	9
		4	4	7	6	8	9
		3	4	4	5	9	9
Factor A		6	7	7	6	7	7
(Coffee)	2 Cups	5	6	5	7	7	5
		5	8	6	5	5	5
		5	6	7	5	7	5
		8	10	5	8	2	4
	3 Cups	9	10	8	8	2	3
		9	9	5	6	4	1
		8	9	5	5	5	3

06. Compute the "*marginal means*" for Factor A

Factor B (Fritters)

		1 Fritter		2 Fritters		3 Fritters			
		3	1	8	6	9	10		
	1 Cup	2	3	6	6	9	9	=	☐
		4	4	7	6	8	9		
		3	4	4	5	9	9		
Factor A		6	7	7	6	7	7		
(Coffee)	2 Cups	5	6	5	7	7	5	=	☐
		5	8	6	5	5	5		
		5	6	7	5	7	5		
		8	10	5	8	2	4		
	3 Cups	9	10	8	8	2	3	=	☐
		9	9	5	6	4	1		
		8	9	5	5	5	3		

Assuming a 2 point difference between means represents a "significant difference," is there a "main effect" for Factor A (Amount of Coffee)?

☐ Yes   ☐ No

What can the Psychology professor conclude about the effect of the amount of coffee consumed on the energy level of professors 49 years of age or older?

07. Compute the "*marginal means*" for Factor B

Factor B (Fritters)

		1 Fritter		2 Fritters		3 Fritters	
	1 Cup	3	1	8	6	9	10
		2	3	6	6	9	9
		4	4	7	6	8	9
		3	4	4	5	9	9
Factor A	2 Cups	6	7	7	6	7	7
(Coffee)		5	6	5	7	7	5
		5	8	6	5	5	5
		5	6	7	5	7	5
	3 Cups	8	10	5	6	2	4
		9	10	8	8	2	3
		9	9	5	6	4	1
		8	9	5	5	5	3

☐   ☐   ☐

Assuming a 2-point difference between means represents a "significant difference," is there a "main effect" for Factor B (Number of Fritters)?

☐ Yes   ☐ No

What can the Psychology professor conclude about the effect of the number of apple fritters consumed on the energy level of professors 49 years of age or older?

08. Compute the "*cell means*" for each condition in the experiment

Factor B (Fritters)

	1 Fritter	2 Fritters	3 Fritters
1 Cup	☐	☐	☐
2 Cups	☐	☐	☐
3 Cups	☐	☐	☐

Factor A (Coffee)

09. Create a *graph* illustrating the results of the professor's experiment

Energy Level Rating

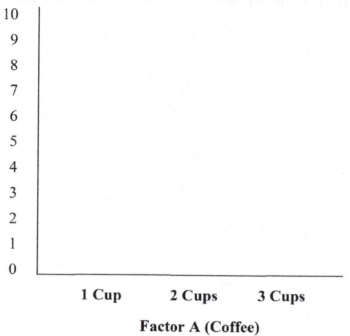

Factor A (Coffee)

Is there a "significant interaction" between Factor A × Factor B?

☐ Yes   ☐ No

What can the professor conclude about the "interaction" between Factor A: (Amount of Coffee) × Factor B (Number of Fritters) in professors 49 years of age or older?

If a professor 49 years of age or older asked you how many cups of coffee and the number of apple fritters he should eat for breakfast to maximize his level of energy, what would you recommend based on the results of the experiment conducted by the Psychology professor?

EXERCISE 9C

How Many Participants Will I Need?

An Industrial-Organizational Psychologist is interested in studying the effectiveness of five different work-place wellness programs in improving the health and wellness of employees currently working for a nation-wide chain of retail stores. The five workplace wellness programs she is interested in evaluating are as follows: (a) a smoking cessation program, (b) a weight loss program, (c) a depression screening program, (d) a blood pressure screening program, and (e) an employee assistance program for employees who are experiencing problems with stress, personal problems, or substance use. To conduct a meaningful assessment of the five different wellness programs, the Industrial-Organizational Psychologist wants to have 25 employees in each of the conditions in her experiment.

How many employees will she need if she conducts a ....

01. Between-Subjects Design?

Smoking	Weight	Depression	Blood	EAP		
					=	

02. Within-Subjects Design?

Smoking	Weight	Depression	Blood	EAP		
					=	

03. 2 (Male, Female) × 5 (Smoking, Weight, Depression, Blood, EAP) Design with wellness program as a Between-Subjects factor?

	Smoking	Weight	Depression	Blood	EAP		
Male							
Female						=	

04. 2 (Male, Female) × 5 (Smoking, Weight, Depression, Blood, EAP) Design with wellness program as a Within-Subjects factor?

	Smoking	Weight	Depression	Blood	EAP	
Male						
Female						=

05. 2 (Male, Female) × 3 (Employee, Store Manager, Regional Manager) × 5 (Smoking, EAP, Weight, Depression, Blood) Design with employee gender, position, and wellness program all as Between-Subjects factors?

	Males			**Females**		
	Employee	Store Manager	Regional Manager	Employee	Store Manager	Regional Manager
Smoking						
Weight						
Depression						
Blood						
EAP						

=

06. 2 (Male, Female) × 3 (Employee, Store Manager, Regional Manager) × 5 (Smoking, EAP, Weight, Depression, Blood) Design with gender and position as Between-Subjects factors and wellness program as a Within-Subjects factor?

	Males				**Females**		
	Employee	Store Manager	Regional Manager		Employee	Store Manager	Regional Manager
Smoking							
Weight							
Depression							
Blood							
EAP							

= ☐

07. 2 (Male, Female) × 3 (Employee, Store Manager, Regional Manager) × 5 (Smoking, EAP, Weight, Depression, Blood) Design with employee gender and position as Within-Subjects factors and wellness program as a Between-Subjects factor?

	Males				**Females**		
	Employee	Store Manager	Regional Manager		Employee	Store Manager	Regional Manager
Smoking							
Weight							
Depression							
Blood							
EAP							

= ☐

Look closely at the Industrial-Organizational Psychologist's design #7 on the previous page. As an expert in factorial design, please explain to the Industrial-Organizational Psychologist why it is impossible for her to conduct this design.

References

1. Cozby, P. C., & Bates, S. C. (2011). *Methods in behavioral research.* (11th ed.). New York, NY: McGraw-Hill Publishers.

2. Passer, M. W. (2013). *Research methods: Concepts and connections.* New York, NY: Worth Publishers.

3. Smith, R. A., & Davis, S. F. (2012). *The psychologist as detective: An introduction to conducting research in psychology* (6th ed.). Boston, MA: Pearson Publishers.

4. Beins, B. C. (2012). *Research methods: A tool for life* (3rd ed.). Boston, MA: Pearson Publishers.

5. Evans, A. N., & Rooney, B. F. (2007). *Methods in psychological research.* Thousand Oaks, CA: Sage Publications.

6. Bordens, K. S., & Abbot, B. B. (2011). *Research design and methods: A process approach* (8th ed.). Boston, MA: McGraw-Hill Publishers.

7. Leary, M. R. (2007). *Introduction to behavioral research methods* (5th ed.). Boston, MA: Pearson/Allyn & Bacon.

8. Jackson, S. L. (2014). *Research methods: A modular approach* (3rd ed.). Stamford, CT: Cengage Learning.

9. Maclin, M. K., & Solso, R. L. (2007). *Experimental psychology: A case approach* (8th ed.). Boston, MA: Pearson/Allyn & Bacon.

10. Rosnow, R. L., & Rosenthal, R. (2012). *Beginning behavioral research: A conceptual primer* (7th ed.). Boston, MA: Pearson Publishers.

11. Kantowitz, B. H., Roediger, H. L., & Elmes, D. G. (2014). *Experimental psychology* (10th ed.). Stamford, CT: Cengage Learning.

12. Ray, W. J. (2011). *Methods: Towards a science of behavior and experience* (10th ed.). Belmont, CA: Wadsworth/Cengage Learning.

13. Gravetter, F. J., & Wallnau, L. B. (2012). *Statistics for the behavioral sciences* (9th ed.). Belmont, CA: Wadsworth-Cengage Learning.

MODULE 10

Quasi-Experimental Research

When psychologists want to draw a causal conclusion about the effect of an independent variable (i.e. treatment or intervention) on a dependent variable (i.e. outcome measure), they use an experimental research design. In a "true experiment," psychologists will: (a) randomly assign participants to groups (i.e. conditions), (b) systematically manipulate an independent variable so the "experimental group" receives the treatment or intervention and the "control group" does not receive the treatment or intervention, (c) measure one or more dependent variables to assess the effect of the independent variable (i.e. treatment or intervention) on the experimental and control groups, and (d) control all extraneous and confounding variables so that any differences observed between the experimental and control groups on the dependent variables can be attributed to the effect of the independent variable (i.e. treatment or intervention).[1,2] Through creating equivalent groups, systematically manipulating an independent variable, reliably measuring one (or more) dependent variables, and maintaining a high degree of control over the factors in an experimental environment, psychologists can draw causal conclusions regarding the effect of their independent variable (i.e. treatment or intervention) on one or more dependent variables (outcome measures).

It is not always possible, however, for psychologists to conduct a "true experiment" when conducting research. Psychologists may face situational, methodological, and ethical constraints that prevent them from using an experimental design to answer their research questions.[2,3,4] In response to these constraints, psychologists use an alternative type of research design known as a "quasi-experimental" design to conduct their research. A "quasi-experimental" research design is a research design that resembles a "true experiment" but that lacks one or more of the essential elements of a "true experiment"[2,5,6] (e.g. random assignment of participants,[1,3,7] manipulation of a "true" independent variable,[3,5,8] a control group,[1,5] a high degree of control over factors within the experimental environment[2,3,4]). Although "quasi-experimental" research designs, like "true experiments," allow psychologists to study the relationship between an independent variable (i.e. treatment or intervention) and one or more dependent variables (i.e. outcome measures), they are vulnerable to a variety of "threats" that can diminish the ability of psychologists to make a causal statement about the effect of their treatment or intervention.[6,9,10]

Types of Quasi-Experimental Research Designs

There are a variety of different types of "quasi-experimental" research designs available to psychologists to study the effects of an independent variable (i.e. treatment or intervention) on one or more dependent variables (i.e. outcome measures). Some of these "quasi-experimental" research designs contain only a single group of participants (i.e. an "experimental group" that is exposed to a treatment or intervention). Therefore, these designs lack a comparison group (i.e. a "control group") that is not exposed to a treatment or intervention; an essential element of a "true experiment." These designs are often referred to as "pre-experimental" designs.[1,6,11] There are three "pre-experimental" research designs commonly used by psychologists to conduct a "quasi-experimental" research study. These three "pre-experimental" designs are known as the: (a) One Group Post-Test Only design, (b) One Group Pre-Test/Post-Test design, and (c) Interrupted Time Series Design.

One Group Post-Test Only Design

In the "One Group Post-Test Only" design, a group of participants is exposed to a treatment or intervention (X), and then members of the group are assessed on an outcome measure (O).[1,2,5] The "One Group Post-Test Only" design is also known as a "One Shot Case Study."[1,11,12] The "One Group Post-Test Only" design is shown below.

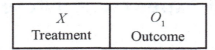

X	O_1
Treatment	Outcome

In some cases, psychologists have control over the design, content, and administration of the treatment or intervention (X). For example, a Health Psychologist interested in the study of "happiness" develops an educational program designed to teach people how to live a happier life. She places an ad in the local newspaper to recruit participants for her study. The first 30 people who respond to her ad are enrolled in the study and take part in her 4 week educational program. At the end of the 4 week program, the Health Psychologist has each of the participants complete an instrument designed to measure his/her current level of "happiness." Scores on the instrument range from 0–50 with higher scores indicating greater happiness. The Health Psychologist then analyzes the data and finds that the average "happiness" rating for the 30 people who completed her 4 week educational program was $M = 48.5$. Clearly, participants in the study reported being extremely happy with their lives after completing the Health Psychologist's educational program.

Based on the results of her study, can the Health Psychologist conclude her educational program was successful in teaching people how to live a happier life? Unfortunately, the answer to that question is no. Why? First, without measuring the "happiness" of her participants before they completed her educational program, the Health Psychologist would be unable to determine whether completing her educational program had produced any change in their "happiness." For example, it's possible that the average "happiness" of her participants was $M = 38.5$ before they completed her educational program. This would have told the Health Psychologist that there had been a 10-point increase in the average level of "happiness" after the participants had completed her program. It's also possible, the average "happiness" of her participants was $M = 48.5$ before they completed her program. This would have told the Health Psychologist that there had been no change in the average level of "happiness" after the participants had completed her program. Without a pre-intervention (i.e. pre-test) measure of the participant's "happiness," the amount of change in their level of "happiness" after completing the Health Psychologist's program would be unknown.[2,5,7] Secondly, the Health Psychologist has no comparison group in her study (i.e. a group of participants who do not complete her educational program).[1,4,11] Without a comparison group, the Health Psychologist is unable to determine whether her participants would have been extremely happy with their lives, even without participating in her educational program.

In other cases, rather than evaluating the effectiveness of a treatment or intervention that they have developed, psychologists may evaluate the effectiveness of a treatment or intervention that has been developed and administered by an organization (e.g. business, school, community agency). For example, an Educational Psychologist may be interested in studying the effect of an after-school reading program on the scores of elementary school students on a test of reading comprehension. Rather than developing and administering an after-school reading program, he decides to evaluate the effectiveness of an after-school reading program that was developed and administered by teachers at a local elementary school. To evaluate the effectiveness of the after-school reading program, he examines the scores of those students who completed the program on a test of reading comprehension they are required to take at the end of the school year. Based on his/her score on the test, a student is classified as having demonstrated a Novice, Partial Mastery, Mastery, Above Mastery, or Distinguished level of performance. The Educational Psychologist analyzes the data and finds that 92% of the elementary school students who completed the after-school reading program scored at the Above Mastery or Distinguished level of performance on the test. Clearly, those students who completed the after-school reading program demonstrated a high level of performance on the test of reading comprehension.

Based on the results of his evaluation, can the Educational Psychologist conclude that the after-school reading program was successful in improving reading comprehension in elementary school students? As was the case in the Health Psychologist's study of "happiness," the answer is no. Why? First, without having a measure of the reading comprehension of students before they completed the after-school reading program, the Educational Psychologist would be unable to determine whether completing the after-school reading program produced any change in their level of reading comprehension. Second, without a comparison group (i.e. a group of students at the elementary school who did not complete the after-school reading program), the Educational Psychologist is unable to determine whether the students would have performed well on the test of reading comprehension, even without completing the after-school reading program. Because of these limitations, psychologists who use a "One Group Post-Test Only" design are unable to make a causal statement about the effect of a treatment or intervention.

One Group Pre-Test/Post-Test Design

In the "One Group Pre-Test/Post-Test" design, a group of participants is assessed on an outcome measure both before (O_1) and after (O_2) being exposed to a treatment or intervention (X).[2,5,13] The "One Group Pre-Test/Post-Test" design is an improvement over the "One Group Post-Test Only" research design due to the inclusion of a pre-intervention (i.e. pre-test) assessment of the outcome measure.[1,2,5] This allows psychologists to assess the amount of change that occurs in an outcome measure following exposure of the group to the treatment or intervention. The "One Group Pre-Test/Post-Test" design is shown below.

O_1	X	O_2
Pre-Test	Treatment	Post-Test

In some cases, psychologists have control over the design, content, and administration of the treatment or intervention (X). For example, a Psychology professor who teaches a Research Methods course wants to know whether changing the format of his course from a lecture format to a discussion format will increase his class attendance. There are 75 students currently enrolled in his Research Methods course. To evaluate the effect of a course format change, the professor counts the number of students who attend his class each day for a period of three weeks. He then uses this data to compute an average daily attendance for his class. The average daily attendance was $M = 52$ students. The Psychology professor then introduces the treatment or intervention by changing the format of his course from a lecture format to a discussion format. After changing the format of his course, the Psychology professor then counts the number of students who attend his class each day for a period of three weeks. He then uses the data to compute an average daily attendance for his class. The average daily attendance was $M = 64$ students. Clearly, attendance in the Psychology professor's Research Methods course increased following the change made to the format of the course.

Based on the results of his study, can the Psychology professor conclude that the change in the format of his course was responsible for the increase in class attendance? Unfortunately, the answer to that question is no. Why? First, without having a comparison group (i.e. a group of students in a Research Methods course who did not experience a change in the format of their course), the Psychology professor would be unable to determine whether class attendance would have increased over time, even without the change in the format of the course.[1,5,6] Second, while the increase in the professor's class attendance may have been due to the change in the format of his course, there are a variety of "threats" to the internal validity of a "One Group Pre-Test/

Post-Test" design that could also account for the increase in the professor's class attendance. These "threats" to the internal validity of the "One Group Pre-Test/Post-Test" research design would include: (a) maturation, (b) history, (c) instrumentation, and (d) attrition.[14]

Maturation refers to meaningful changes in the participants that occur during the course of a research study[1,2,8] (e.g. as students adjust to the demands of college they learn how important it is to attend class on a regular basis). History refers to events that occur during a research study that can influence the behavior of participants[1,2,5] (e.g. release of mid-term grades may motivate students to attend class more frequently). Instrumentation refers to a change in the consistency of the measurements taken during a research study[2,7,8] (e.g. the professor's count of daily class attendance may not be accurate throughout the study). Attrition refers to the loss of participants as individual participants drop out of the research study over time[2,7,13] (e.g. students who drop out of the professor's class during the semester). As a result, participants who are measured during the pre-test phase are different from the participants measured during the post-test phase. To the extent that they can't be ruled out as "threats" to the internal validity of the study, the potential effects of factors such as maturation, history, instrumentation, and attrition prevent psychologists who use the "One Group Pre-Test/ Post-Test" research design from being able to conclude their treatment or intervention is the sole cause of an observed change in the outcome measure.

In other cases, rather than evaluating the effect of a treatment or intervention they have developed, psychologists may evaluate the effect of a treatment or intervention implemented by an organization (e.g. business, government agency, organization). As an example, a Consumer Psychologist may be interested in studying the effect of a uniform change on the tips received by female servers at a sports bar. In an effort to increase business at the bar, the bar owner recently started requiring his female servers to wear a more "revealing" uniform at work. To determine whether this change in uniform resulted in an increase in the tips received by the female servers at the bar, the Consumer Psychologist had the bar owner compute the average tip received by his female servers during the week prior to making the change to the more revealing uniforms. The bar owner informs the Consumer Psychologist the average tip received by his female servers was 8%. The Consumer Psychologist then has the bar owner compute the average tip received by his female servers during the week after making the change to the more revealing uniforms. The bar owner informs the Consumer Psychologist the average tip received by his female servers was 26%. Clearly, customers at the sports bar gave the female servers much higher tips following the change to the more revealing uniforms.

Based on the results of her study, can the Consumer Psychologist conclude the change to the more revealing uniforms was the cause of the increase in tips received by the female servers at the sports bar? As was the case in the Psychology professor's study of "class attendance," the answer is no. Why? First, without having a comparison group (i.e. a group of female servers at the sports bar who do not change to the more "revealing" uniform), the Consumer Psychologist would be unable to determine whether the average tip received by the female servers would have increased over time, even without the change to the more revealing uniform. Second, while the increase in the average tip received by the female servers may have been due to the change to the more revealing uniform, it is also possible the increase in the average tip received was due to the effects of: (a) maturation (e.g. female servers may have gotten better at their job over time which lead to larger tips from customers), (b) history (e.g. the customers may have received paychecks from their employers during the post-test phase of the study which lead to larger tips being given to female servers after the change to the more revealing uniform), (c) instrumentation (e.g. the bar owner may not have been consistent in monitoring all the tips received by the female servers throughout the study), and (d) attrition (e.g. some of the female servers who worked at the sports bar may have quit during the course of the study. As a result, the female servers whose tips were measured during the pre-test phase of the study may have been different from the female servers whose tips were measured during the post-test phase of the study). To the extent that she could not rule out these potential "threats" to the internal validity of her study, the potential effects of these factors would prevent the Consumer Psychologist from being able to conclude the change to the more revealing uniform was the sole cause of the increase in the average tip received by the female servers at the sports bar.

Interrupted Time Series Design

In the "Interrupted Time Series" design, a group of participants is assessed on an outcome measure multiple times both before (O_1, O_2, O_3) and after (O_4, O_5, O_6) being exposed to a treatment or intervention (X).[1,2,3] The "Interrupted Time Series" design is an improvement over the "One Group Pre-Test/Post-Test" design due to the inclusion of multiple pre-intervention (i.e. pre-test) and post-intervention (i.e. post-test) assessments of the outcome measure.[2,6,7] This allows psychologists to gain a better understanding of: (a) the trend in the outcome measure for the group prior to the introduction of the treatment or intervention,[2,3] (b) the amount of change that occurs in the outcome measure after the group has been exposed to the treatment or intervention,[3,5] and (c) both the short-term and long-term effects of the treatment or intervention (X) on the outcome measure over time.[5,11] The "Interrupted Time Series" design is shown below.

O_1 Pre-Test	O_2 Pre-Test	O_3 Pre-Test	X Treatment	O_4 Post-Test	O_5 Post-Test	O_6 Post-Test

In some cases, psychologists have control over the design, content, and administration of the treatment or intervention (X). For example, an Industrial-Organizational Psychologist who is interested in customer service develops a training program to improve the customer service skills of retail employees. The CEO of a national retail chain store agrees to allow the psychologist to test the effectiveness of her training program on employees at 5 of the company's 50 nationwide store locations. To assess the level of customer satisfaction with the customer service provided by store employees, the company prints an address for a website on all store receipts. Customers can visit the website and complete an on-line survey in which they evaluate the customer service they received from store employees as being Unacceptable, Poor, Average, Above Average, or Exceptional. Every month, each store manager uses the feedback from customers to compute the percentage of customers who have received Exceptional customer service. To assess her training program, she begins by computing the average percentage of customers across the 5 stores who received Exceptional customer service for each of the previous 6 months. Then, she has all the employees at each of the 5 stores complete her training program. After all the employees have completed her training program, she then computes the average percentage of customers across the 5 stores who received Exceptional customer service for each of the next 6 months following the employee training program. A graph of the results of her evaluation of the effectiveness of her training program appears below.

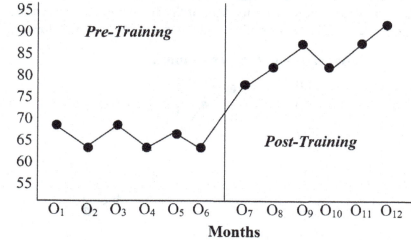

Based on the results of her study, can the Industrial-Organizational Psychologist conclude that her customer service training program was responsible for the increase in the percentage of customers who received Exceptional customer service from store employees? Unfortunately, the answer to that question is no. Why? First, without a comparison group (i.e. a group of stores in which store employees did not complete the training program), she would be unable to determine whether the average percentage of customers who received Exceptional customer service would have increased over time, even without employees having completed the training program.[1,13,16] Second, while the increase in the percentage of customers who received Exceptional service may have been due to the psychologist's training program, it is also possible the increase was due to the effects of: (a) uncontrolled events that occurred during the course of the study (i.e. history) or (b) differences in the demographic characteristics of customers (e.g. sex, age) who completed the on-line survey each month during the study. To the extent each of these "threats" to the internal validity of the study can't be ruled out, the potential effects of these factors would prevent the Industrial-Organizational Psychologist from being able to state her training program was the sole cause of the increase in the average percentage of customers who received Exceptional service.

A strength of the "Interrupted Time Series" research design is that due to the inclusion of multiple assessments of the outcome measure during the pre-intervention (i.e. pre-test) phase of the research study, psychologists can rule out several potential "threats" to the internal validity of the study.[2,5] These "threats" would include "maturation" (i.e. meaningful change in participants that occurs over the course of a research study) and "testing" (i.e. a change in scores (increase or decrease) on the outcome measure resulting from repeated testing).[1,2,8] Psychologists are able to rule out these potential "threats" if the assessments of the outcome measure for a group remain stable across multiple measurements during the pre-intervention (i.e. pre-test) phase of the study. If the assessments of the outcome measure remain stable over time, it would indicate participants in the group are not changing in a meaningful way over time (i.e. "maturation") and the group's score on the outcome measure is not changing in a meaningful way over time as the group is repeatedly assessed on the outcome measure (i.e. "testing").

In other cases, rather than evaluating the effect of a treatment or intervention they have developed, psychologists may evaluate the effect of a treatment or intervention implemented by a community, organization, or business. For example, a Community Psychologist interested in the effectiveness of crime prevention programs in reducing crime, decides to study the effectiveness of a 10:00 p.m. curfew initiated by the Mayor and members of City Council in reducing crime in his local community. To study the effectiveness of the 10:00 p.m. curfew, he asks the Chief of police to provide him with the number of crimes that were committed in the 3 neighborhoods in the community with the highest crime rates for each of the 3 weeks prior to the start of the 10:00 p.m. curfew as well as for each of the 3 weeks after the start of the 10:00 p.m. curfew. He uses this data to compute the average number of crimes that occurred across the 3 neighborhoods for each of the 3 weeks prior to the start of the 10:00 p.m. curfew and for each of the 3 weeks after the start of the 10:00 p.m. curfew. The data for the Community Psychologist's evaluation of the effectiveness of the 10:00 p.m. curfew appears below.

Average # of Crimes Committed

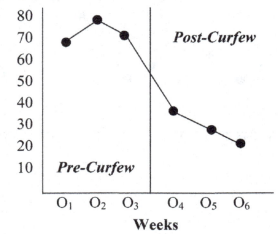

Weeks

Based on the results of his study, can the Community Psychologist conclude the 10:00 p.m. curfew initiated by the Mayor and City Council was effective in reducing crime within the community? Unfortunately, the answer is no. Why? First, without having a comparison group (i.e. a group of neighborhoods with similar high rates of crime in which a 10:00 p.m. curfew was not implemented), he would be unable to determine whether the average number of crimes that were committed in these 3 neighborhoods would have declined over time, even without a 10:00 p.m. curfew being implemented. Second, while the decrease in crime may have been due to the 10:00 p.m. curfew, it is also possible the decrease in crime was due to the effects of uncontrolled events (i.e. history) that occurred in the community or in the 3 neighborhoods during the course of the study (e.g. the people who committed a large number of the crimes in the 3 neighborhoods may have moved or been incarcerated for their criminal activity). Third, the decrease in crime may have been due to a "threat to internal validity" known as "statistical regression." Statistical regression can occur when a group displays an extreme score on an outcome measure during the pre-test phase of a research study. As repeated measurements of the group are taken over time, the group's score on the outcome measure may naturally become less extreme and move (i.e. or "regress") toward a more average score.[8,12,15] If this occurs during the time when the group is exposed to the treatment or intervention, it can give the appearance the treatment or intervention is responsible for the observed increase or decrease in the group's score on the outcome measure. In the Community Psychologist's research study, the neighborhoods selected for study were the 3 neighborhoods in the community with the highest (i.e. most extreme) crime rates. Over time, the crime rates in these neighborhoods may have naturally become less extreme and "regressed" (i.e. decreased) towards a more average level of crime. If this "statistical regression" occurred while the 10:00 p.m. curfew was in effect, it could have given the appearance that the 10:00 p.m. curfew was responsible for the decrease in crime. To the extent these potential "threats" can't be ruled out, the potential effects of these factors would prevent the Community Psychologist from concluding the curfew was the sole cause of the decrease in crime within the community.

There are some "quasi-experimental" research designs that attempt to improve upon the "pre-experimental" designs by including a comparison group (i.e. a "control group"). Although these "quasi-experimental" research designs include a "control group," they do lack an essential element of a "true experiment." This essential element is the random assignment of participants to groups (i.e. conditions). There are three research designs which include a "control group" that are commonly used by psychologists to conduct "quasi-experimental" research. These research designs are known as the: (a) Non-Equivalent Control Group Post-Test Only design, (b) Non-Equivalent Control Group Pre-Test/Post-Test Design, and (c) Non-Equivalent Control Group Interrupted Time Series Design.

Non-Equivalent Control Group Post-Test Only Design

The "Non-Equivalent Control Group Post-Test Only" research design is created by adding a "control group" to the "One Group Post-Test Only" pre-experimental research design. In the "Non-Equivalent Control Group Post-Test Only" research design, one group of participants is exposed to the treatment or intervention (X), and then members of the group are assessed on an outcome measure (O). A second group of participants acts as a comparison group (i.e. "control group"). This second group is not exposed to the treatment or intervention. The members of this group are simply assessed on the outcome measure.[1,2,5] In the "Non-equivalent Control Group Post-Test Only" design, the participants are not randomly assigned to groups. Instead, participants are assigned to groups on the basis of a preexisting characteristic or membership in pre-existing groups.[5,9,17] Since random assignment is not used to assign participants to groups, there is no assurance that the "experimental" and "control" groups are equivalent; hence the name "Non-Equivalent Control Group" design.[1,2,5] The "Non-Equivalent Control Group Post-Test Only" design is shown below.

X Treatment	O_1 Outcome
	O_1 Outcome

In some cases, psychologists have control over the design, content, and administration of the treatment or intervention (X). For example, a Psychology professor who teaches Statistics wants to know whether giving students practice problems to work on before an exam improves exam performance. To examine the effect of practice problems on exam performance, he gives students in one of his Statistics classes practice problems to work on before an exam. He does not give the students in his other Statistics class practice problems to work on before the same exam. After students in both of his Statistics classes have taken the exam, he computes average exam scores for each of his classes. He finds the average exam score for the class of students who received practice problems to work on before the exam was $M = 92$, and the average exam score for the class of students who did not receive practice problems to work on before the exam was $M = 83$.

Based on the results of his study, can the Psychology professor conclude that providing his students with practice problems to work on before an exam improves exam performance? Unfortunately, the answer is no. Why? First, there is no pre-intervention (i.e. pre-test) measure of exam performance.[2,11] A pre-intervention (i.e. pre-test) measure of exam performance would allow the professor to determine if there was a difference in exam performance across his two groups before the introduction of his "practice problem" intervention. Perhaps, students in the "experimental group" (i.e. students enrolled in his first class who were given practice problems) had a higher average score on the previous course exam than students in the "control group" (i.e. students enrolled in his second class who were not given practice problems). In such a case, the students in the "experimental group" may have outperformed the "control group" on the exam during the study even without having been given practice problems to work on before the exam. Second, the students in the Psychology professor's study were not randomly assigned to groups (i.e. conditions). Instead, the students were assigned to groups (i.e. conditions) based on which of the Psychology professor's Statistics classes they were enrolled in. Students in his first class were assigned to the "experimental group" (i.e. received practice problems) and students in his second class were assigned to the "control group" (i.e. received no practice problems). By not randomly assigning students to groups, the professor has introduced a potential "threat to internal validity" known as "selection" into his study. Selection refers to when participants are assigned to groups in a way that creates significant differences between the groups at the beginning of the study.[2,8,12] The problem created by "selection" is that if there is a difference between the groups on the outcome measure after the "experimental group" has been exposed to the treatment or intervention (i.e. during the post-test phase of the research study), psychologists will be unable to determine whether this difference was due to the effect of the treatment or intervention, or a difference between the groups that existed before the introduction of the treatment/ intervention. To rule out the "threat" of "selection," the professor would have to measure his two groups on additional variables likely to have an influence on the outcome measure (i.e. exam performance) to assess the extent to which his two groups were equivalent at the start of the study.[4,6,13] If the groups were not equivalent at the start of the study, the Psychology professor would be unable to determine whether the difference in exam performance between the groups was due to the effect of the practice problems or to a difference that existed between the two groups at the start of the study (e.g. difference in math skills, work ethic, study skills, etc.).

In other cases, rather than evaluating the effect of a treatment or intervention they have developed, psychologists may evaluate the effect of a treatment or intervention implemented by a community, organization, or business. For example, a Psychologist interested in the prevention of workplace injuries decides to study the effectiveness of a "workplace yoga" program in the prevention of back pain in construction workers. The Psychologist goes to a construction site where the site supervisor requires all of his employees to participate in a 30 minute yoga session each morning before beginning their shifts. The site supervisor believes that yoga can increase employees' strength and flexibility and reduce the amount of back pain they experience on the job. She decides to use another construction site where the employees do not participate in a 30 minute yoga session each morning before beginning their shifts as her "control group." She has all the employees at both construction sites rate their current level of back pain using a 10-point rating scale (1 = I am currently experiencing no back pain; 10 = I am currently experiencing an intolerable level of back pain). She then computes an average "back pain rating" for each of the two construction sites. She finds that the average "back pain rating" for the construction workers who participate in a yoga session each morning before work was $M = 3.5$, and the average "back pain rating" for the construction workers who do not participate in a yoga session each morning before work was $M = 7.8$.

Based on the results of her study, can the Psychologists conclude the "workplace yoga" program was effective in reducing back pain in construction workers? Unfortunately, the answer is no. Why? As was the case with the students in the Psychology professor's study of "practice problems," the Psychologist had no pre-intervention (i.e. pre-test) measure of "back pain" for her two groups of construction workers. In addition, the construction workers in the Psychologist's study were not randomly assigned to groups (i.e. conditions). Instead, construction workers were assigned to groups (i.e. conditions) based on the construction site they worked at. Construction workers at the first construction site were all assigned to the "experimental group" (i.e. workers participated in a workplace yoga program) and construction workers at the second construction site were all assigned to the "control group" (i.e. workers did not participate in a workplace yoga program). By not having a pre-intervention (i.e. pre-test) measure of "back pain," nor randomly assigning the construction workers to groups, the Psychologist will be unable to determine if the difference in the level of back pain reported by the two groups during the post-intervention phase of the study was due to the beneficial effect of the "yoga sessions" or to a difference that existed between the two groups at the start of the study (e.g. construction workers who worked at the site assigned to the "experimental group" may have had healthier backs or fewer prior back injuries than construction workers who worked at the site assigned to the "control group").

Non-Equivalent Control Group Pre-Test/Post-Test Design

The "Non-Equivalent Control Group Pre-Test/Post-Test" design is created by adding a "control group" to the "One Group Pre-Test/Post-Test" pre-experimental research design. In the "Non-Equivalent Control Group Pre-Test/Post-Test" research design, two groups of participants are first assessed on an outcome measure (O_1). One group of participants is then exposed to a treatment or intervention (X). The second group of participants is not exposed to the treatment or intervention. Finally, the two groups are once again assessed on the outcome measure (O_2).[1,2] In the "Non-Equivalent Control Group Pre-Test/Post-Test" design, the participants are not randomly assigned to groups. Instead, participants are assigned to groups based on a preexisting characteristic or membership in pre-existing groups.[2,3,5] The "Non-Equivalent Control Group Pre-Test/Post-Test" design is an improvement over the "Non-Equivalent Post-Test Only" design as a result of the addition of a pre-intervention (i.e. pre-test) assessment of the outcome measure for both groups.[2,5] This allows psychologists to: (a) determine whether the groups are different on the outcome measure prior to the introduction of the treatment or intervention,[3,5,8] (b) determine if the groups are different on the outcome measure after the introduction of the treatment or intervention, and (c) determine the amount of change each group experienced on the outcome measure from the pre-test to post-test phases of the study.[1,2,5] If the treatment or intervention has a significant effect on the outcome measure, the experimental group should experience a greater amount of change on the outcome measure than the control group from the pre-test to post-test phases of the research study. The "Non-Equivalent Control Group Pre-Test/Post-Test" design is shown below.

O_1 Outcome	X Treatment	O_2 Outcome
O_1 Outcome		O_2 Outcome

In some cases, psychologists may evaluate the effectiveness of a treatment or intervention which has been implemented by a business or community organization (e.g. hospital, school, law enforcement, government agency). For example, a Psychologist who specializes in Gerontology (i.e. the study of the ageing process) is interested in studying the effectiveness of a "pet therapy" program in reducing depression in nursing home residents. A local nursing home has recently implemented a "pet therapy" program for its residents. Community volunteers bring dogs and cats to the nursing home once a week and let each resident who participates in the "pet therapy" program choose a dog or cat to spend some quality time with. The nursing home believes that the "pet therapy" program will be effective in decreasing the level of depression experienced by the residents who participate in the program. In order to study the effectiveness of the program, the Psychologist goes to the nurse in charge of patient care at the nursing home and asks her to provide the results of the most recent depression screening conducted on each resident prior to the "pet therapy" program being implemented. Scores on the depression screening range from 0–10 (i.e. scores of 6 or higher indicate the presence of clinical depression). The Psychologist uses this data to compute an average depression score for residents who participated in the "pet therapy" program (i.e. "experimental group") and an average depression score for residents who chose not to take part in the program (i.e. "control group"). After the "pet therapy" program has been in effect for 3 months, all residents undergo a new depression screening. The Psychologist uses the data from this new depression screening to once again compute an average depression score for each of the two groups.

Now, let's take a look at some possible outcomes for the Psychologist's study. In the graphs below, data for residents who participated in the "pet therapy" program are represented by the letter **E** (i.e. "experimental group") and data for residents who chose not to participate in the "pet therapy" program are represented by the letter **C** (i.e. "control group").

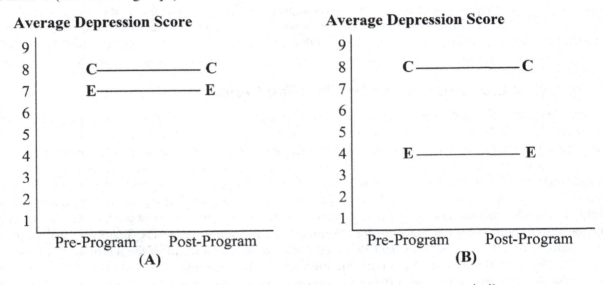

For the first set of results, in graph (**A**) the average depression scores were similar across groups prior to the start of the "pet therapy" program (i.e. Control $M = 8$; Experimental $M = 7$) and remained unchanged after the program had been in effect for 3 months. Neither group had experienced any change in their average depression scores over time. In graph (**B**) there was a larger difference in average depression scores across groups prior to the start of the "pet therapy" program (i.e. Control $M = 8$; Experimental $M = 4$) and this difference remained after the program had been in effect for 3 months. Neither group experienced a change in their average depression score over time. For the data presented in graphs (**A**) and (**B**), the Psychologist could conclude the "pet therapy" program was not effective in reducing depression.

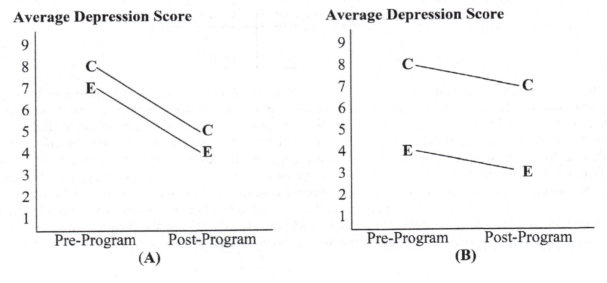

For the second set of results, in graph (**A**) average depression scores were similar across groups prior to the start of the "pet therapy" program (i.e. Control $M = 8$; Experimental $M = 7$) and remained similar after the program was in effect for 3 months (Control $M = 5$; Experimental $M = 4$). Both the groups experienced a 3-point decrease in their average depression scores over time. In graph (**B**) there was a larger difference in average depression scores across groups prior to the start of the "pet therapy" program (i.e. Control $M = 8$; Experimental $M = 4$) and this larger difference remained after the "pet therapy" program had been in effect for 3 months (i.e. Control $M = 7$; Experimental $M = 3$). Both groups experienced a 1-point drop in their average depression scores over time. In each of these cases, since both of the groups experienced a similar decrease in their average depression scores, there was likely some uncontrolled factor in the nursing home environment that led to a similar decrease in depression for all residents (e.g. improvement in the food, improvement in patient care, increase in social activities). For the data presented in graphs (**A**) and (**B**), the Psychologist could conclude that the "pet therapy" program was not effective in reducing depression.[13,15]

Average Depression Score

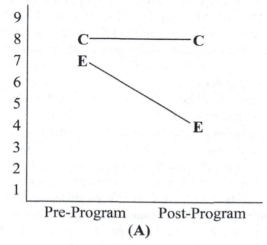

(**A**)

Average Depression Score

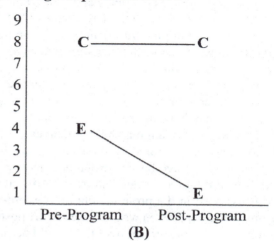

(**B**)

For the third set of results, in graph (**A**) the average depression score was similar across groups prior to the start of the "pet therapy" program (i.e. Control $M = 8$; Experimental $M = 7$). After the program had been in effect for 3 months, however, there was a 4 point difference in the average depression scores of the groups (i.e. Control $M = 8$; Experimental $M = 4$). While there was no change in the average depression score of the "control group" over time, there was a 3-point decrease in the average depression score of the "experimental group" (i.e. the "pet therapy" group). In graph (**B**) there was a larger difference in the average depression scores of the groups prior to the start of the "pet therapy" program (i.e. Control $M = 8$; Experimental $M = 4$) and this difference grew even larger after the program had been in effect for 3 months (i.e. Control $M = 8$; Experimental $M = 1$). While no change occurred in the average depression score of the "control group," there was a 3-point decrease in the average depression score of the "experimental group" (i.e. the "pet therapy" group). In each of these cases, those residents who participated in the "pet therapy" program experienced a 3-point decrease in their average depression score. Based on the results, can the Psychologist conclude that the "pet therapy" program was effective in reducing depression in nursing home residents? The answer is "maybe!"[2,13,15,18]

To conclude that the "pet therapy" program was the cause of the decrease in depression, the Psychologist would have to rule out the effects of any potential "threats to internal validity" that could provide an alternative explanation for the decrease in depression. One such "threat" is that of "selection."[2,3,8] While the difference in the average depression scores of the two groups after the "pet therapy" program had been in effect for 3 months might have been due to the effect of the "pet therapy" program, it may also be due to a difference in the average depression scores of the two groups that already existed at the start of the study. Remember the Psychologist did not randomly assign residents to groups. The residents were assigned to groups based on their decision as to whether they would participate in the "pet therapy" program. Those residents who decided to participate in the program were assigned to the "experimental group" and those who chose not to participate were assigned to the "control group." By not using random assignment, the Psychologist had no assurance the two groups would have equivalent levels of depression prior to the start of the "pet therapy" program. In graph (**A**) the threat of "selection" is minimal. The two groups had very similar average depression scores (i.e. Control $M = 8$; Experimental $M = 7$) prior to the start of the "pet therapy" program. By comparison, in graph (**B**) the threat of "selection" is much larger. There was a large difference between the average depression scores of the groups prior to the start of the "pet therapy" program (i.e. Control $M = 8$; Experimental $M = 4$). The large difference in average depression scores across groups during the pre-intervention phase of the study could be an indication there are additional uncontrolled differences that exist between the groups. These uncontrolled differences may have had an influence on current levels of depression and could continue to have an influence on the levels of depression experienced by the two groups during the post-intervention phase of the study.

In addition to "selection," there are additional factors that pose a potential "threat" to the internal validity of the Psychologist's study. First, there may have been events which occurred during the study that had a greater impact on the level of depression experienced by residents in the "pet therapy" program (i.e. "differential history").[2,9,13] For example, the residents in the "pet therapy" program may have had an increased number of people who visited them in the nursing home during the study, while the number of visitors for residents who did not participate in the program remained unchanged. This increase in the number of visitors could perhaps account for the decrease in depression among the residents in the "pet therapy" program. Second, residents in the "pet therapy" program may have experienced a greater level of meaningful change during the study (i.e. "differential maturation").[2,3,13] For example, the health of residents who took part in the "pet therapy" program may have improved during the study while the health of residents who chose not to take part in the "pet therapy" program may have remained unchanged during the course of the study. An improvement in health could perhaps account for the decrease in depression among the residents in the "pet therapy" program. Finally, there may have been a difference between the groups with respect to the number of residents who passed away during the research study (i.e. "differential attrition").[2,13] As a result, the residents whose depression was assessed in the pre-intervention (i.e. pre-test) phase of the study may have been different from the residents whose depression was assessed in the post-intervention (i.e. post-test) phase of the study. A change in the composition of the groups over time could perhaps account for the decrease in depression among residents in the "pet therapy" program. While the Psychologist would be more confident concluding the "pet therapy" program caused a decrease in depression on nursing home residents based on the results shown in graph (**A**) due to being able to rule out the effect of "selection," the extent to which she can also rule out the effects of these additional "threats to internal validity" would ultimately determine her level of confidence in making a causal statement about the effectiveness of the "pet therapy" program. Although the "Non-Equivalent Control Group Pre-Test/Post-Test" design mirrors that of a "true experiment," the lack of random assignment makes it more vulnerable to several "threats to internal validity." As a result, causal statements about the effectiveness of a treatment should be made with caution.

In some cases, psychologists may evaluate the effect of an unplanned event that occurs within society. For example, a Community Psychologist is interested in evaluating the effect of a Mayor's decision to decrease the budget of her town's fire department on the time it takes the fire department to respond to a fire in the town (i.e. Town A). Residents of the town, as well as members of the fire department, have expressed concern that a decrease in the fire department's budget will significantly increase the fire department's response time to fires resulting in a loss of property, and potentially a loss of lives. To evaluate whether the Mayor's cutting of the fire department's budget significantly increased response time, she first meets with the Chief of the town's fire department and has him provide her with the department's response time for each fire they responded to in the month prior to the Mayor's budget cut and in the month following the Mayor's budget cut. She uses the data provided by the Chief to compute the fire department's average response time to a fire both before and after the Mayor's budget cut. For a comparison group (i.e. "control group"), she selects a fire department in a neighboring town (i.e. Town B) whose budget had not been cut by the town's Mayor. She meets with the Chief of the town's fire department and has him provide her with the department's response time for each of the fires the department responded to in the month prior to the Mayor of Town A's decision to cut the budget of her town's fire department and in the month after the Mayor of Town A's decision to cut the budget of her town's fire department. She uses the data provided by the Chief to compute the fire department's average response time to a fire both before and after the Mayor of Town A's decision to cut the budget of her town's fire department.

Below are three graphs representing possible outcomes for the Psychologist's study of fire department "response time." In the graphs below, the data for the average response time of the fire department in Town A that experienced a budget cut is represented by the letter **E** (i.e. "experimental group"). Data for the average response time of the fire department in Town B that did not experience a budget cut is represented by the letter **C** (i.e. "control group").

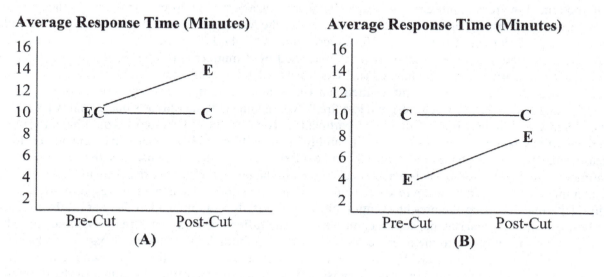

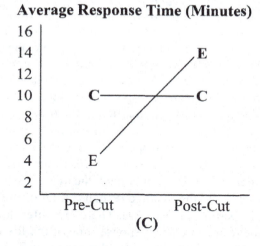

In looking at the results presented in graph (**A**) the average response time was identical in the two fire departments in the month prior to the Mayor of Town A's decision to cut the budget of her fire department (i.e. Control $M = 10$; Experimental $M = 10$). Following the budget cut, the average response time of the fire department in Town A increased by 4 minutes. In Town B, the average response time of the fire department was unchanged (i.e. Control $M = 10$; Experimental $M = 14$). Based on the results, it would appear that the Mayor's budget cut resulted in a 4 minute increase in the average amount of time it takes for the fire department in Town A to respond to a fire.[13,18] To conclude that the Mayor's budget cut was the cause of the increase in response time of the fire department in Town A, the Psychologist would have to rule out the effects of potential "threats to internal validity" that could provide an alternative explanation for the increase in the average response time. Given that both fire departments had identical response times during the pre-intervention (i.e. pre-test) phase of the study, the Psychologist could rule out "selection" as a serious threat to the internal validity of the study.

The most likely "threat" to the internal validity of the study would be that of "differential history."[2,9,13] There may have been an event that took place in Town A during the study (other than the cut in the fire department's budget) which had a negative effect on the average response time of the Town A fire department. For example, there may have been construction projects going on in Town A during the course of the research study that made it more difficult for the fire department to respond to fires. The extent to which the Psychologist is able to rule out the potential effects of "differential history" will determine her level of confidence in concluding that the Mayor's budget cut was responsible for the increase in average response time for the fire department in Town A.

In looking at the results presented in graph (**B**), there was a 6-minute difference in the average response time across the two fire departments in the month prior to the Mayor of Town A's decision to cut the budget of her fire department (i.e. Control $M = 10$; Experimental $M = 4$). Following the budget cut, the average response time of the fire department in Town A increased by 4 minutes. In Town B, the average response time of the fire department was unchanged (i.e. Control $M = 10$; Experimental $M = 8$). Based on the results, it would appear the Mayor's budget cut resulted in a 4-minute increase in the average amount of time it takes for the fire department in Town A to respond to a fire.[18] To conclude that the Mayor's budget cut was the cause of the increase in response time of the fire department in Town A, the Psychologist would have to rule out the effects of any potential "threats to internal validity" that could provide an alternative explanation for the increase in the average response time. Given the large difference in average response time between the two fire departments prior to the Mayor of Town A's decision to cut the budget of her fire department, "selection" is a potential threat to the validity of the research study.[2,8,12] The large difference in average response times across the fire departments during the pre-intervention phase of the study is an indication there are differences that exist between the fire departments which contributed to the difference in average response time and which might continue to contribute to the average response times exhibited by the two fire departments during the post-intervention phase of the study. Without measuring additional characteristics of the two fire departments that may influence response time, the Psychologist will be unable to determine the extent of the differences that exist between the fire departments. The most likely "threat" to the internal validity of the research study would be that of "differential regression."[2,13,18] Prior to the Mayor of Town A's decision to cut the budget of her fire department, the fire department in Town A had an extremely fast average response time of 4 minutes. Over time, it is possible the average response time regressed (i.e. increased) to a more average response time (i.e. 8 minutes) resulting in an average response time that was more comparable to that of Town B's department. This can make it appear that the increase in average response time for Town A's fire department was due to the budget cut, when it was actually due to a natural "regression to the mean."

In looking at the results presented in graph (**C**), in the month prior to the Mayor of Town A's decision to cut the budget of her fire department, the average response time of the Town A fire department was 6 minutes quicker than the fire department in Town B (i.e. Control $M = 10$; Experimental $M = 4$). Following the Mayor of Town A's decision to cut the budget of her fire department, the average response time of the fire department in Town A increased by 10 minutes while the average response time of the fire department in Town B was unchanged (i.e. Control M = 10; Experimental M = 14). Therefore, after the Mayor of Town A's decision to cut the budget of her fire department, the average response time of the fire department in Town A was now 4 minutes slower than the average response time of the fire department in Town B! Whenever the relative positions of the "experimental group" and "control group" in the pre-intervention phase of the study are reversed in the post-intervention phase of the study, this is known as a "cross-over" pattern.[18] In the Community Psychologist's study, Town A's fire department had a faster average response time than the Town B fire department during the pre-intervention phase of the study. (However, in the post-intervention phase of the study a "cross-over" occurred so that the Town A fire department now had a slower average response time than the fire department in Town B). A "cross-over" pattern is considered strong evidence the treatment or intervention had an effect on the outcome measure (i.e. the Mayor of Town A's budget cut had a strong negative influence on the average response time of her fire department).[18] There is one potential "threat" to the validity of the Psychologist's study that would need to be taken into consideration. That specific "threat" would be "participant bias." It's possible that members of the fire department in Town A purposely slowed down their average response time in the month following the Mayor's budget cut! By showing the Mayor the dangers associated with her decision to cut the budget of the fire department (i.e. increased response time, increased potential loss of property and life), they may have hoped to be able to convince her to reverse her decision and restore the fire department's budget. The extent to which the Psychologist is able to rule out the effects of "participant bias" (perhaps through confidential interviews with members of the fire department in Town A) will determine her level of confidence in concluding the budget cut was responsible for the increase in average response time for the fire department in Town A.

Non-Equivalent Control Group Interrupted Time Series Design

The "Non-Equivalent Control Group Interrupted Time Series" design is created by the addition of a "control group" to the "Interrupted Time Series" pre-experimental research design. This design is also referred to as a "Multiple Time Series" design.[3,13] In the "Non-Equivalent Control Group Interrupted Time Series" design, two groups of participants are assessed on an outcome measure multiple times (O_1, O_2, O_3) during the pre-intervention phase of the study. One of the groups (i.e. "experimental group") is then exposed to a treatment or intervention (X). The second group acts as a "control group" and is not exposed to the treatment or intervention. Both groups are then assessed on the outcome measure multiple times during the post-intervention phase of the study (O_4, O_5, O_6).[2,5,6] In the "Non-Equivalent Control Group Interrupted Time Series" design, the participants are not randomly assigned to groups. Instead, participants are assigned to groups based on a preexisting characteristic or membership in pre-existing groups. Because random assignment is not used to assign the participants to groups, there is no assurance the "experimental group" and "control group" are equivalent.[2,5,6] The "Non-Equivalent Control Group Interrupted Time Series" design is an improvement over the "Interrupted Time Series" research design due to the inclusion of the "control group."[1,2,6] This allows psychologists to determine if short-term and long-term changes in the outcome measure for a group would have occurred, even without the group being exposed to the treatment or intervention.[1,11] The "Non-Equivalent Control Group Interrupted Time Series" design is shown below.

O_1 Pre-Test	O_2 Pre-Test	O_3 Pre-Test	X Treatment	O_4 Post-Test	O_5 Post-Test	O_6 Post-Test
O_1 Pre-Test	O_2 Pre-Test	O_3 Pre-Test		O_4 Post-Test	O_5 Post-Test	O_6 Post-Test

To illustrate how a psychologist would use a "Non-Equivalent Control Group Interrupted Time Series" design to conduct a research study, let's assume a Sports Psychologist is interested in studying whether hiring a new coach in the middle of a bad season has a positive effect on the performance of a professional sports team. For his study, he selects an NBA team that is having a terrible season and has recently hired a new head coach. The main reason behind the team's terrible season is the large number of turnovers the players typically have during games. These turnovers have lead to points for their opponents, and losses for the team. In order to study the effect of hiring a new coach on the performance of the team, the Psychologist examines the number of turnovers the team had in each of its games played during the 6 weeks prior to hiring the new coach. He uses this data to compute an average number of turnovers per game for each of the 6 weeks prior to the hiring of the new coach. He then examines the number of turnovers the team had in each of its games during the 6 weeks following the hiring of the new coach. He uses this data to compute an average number of turnovers per game for each of the 6 weeks after the hiring of the new coach. As a control group, he selects another NBA team (i.e. Team B) who is having an equally terrible season, but which has not hired a new head coach. He examines the number of turnovers the team had in each of its games played during the 6 weeks prior to Team A's hiring a new coach and in each of its games played during the 6 weeks after Team A's hiring of a new coach. He uses this data to compute an average number of turnovers per game by Team B for each of the 6 weeks before, and each of the 6 weeks after, Team A's hiring of a new coach. The data for the Sports Psychologist's study appears following.

Average # of Turnovers per Game

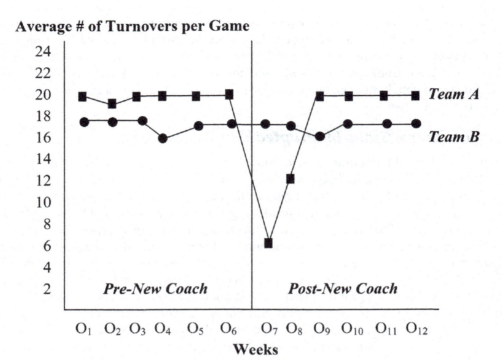

In looking at the results, during the pre-intervention (i.e. pre-test) phase of the study, the average number of turnovers per game was similar across the two NBA teams. In the week after hiring a new coach, the average number of turnovers per game for Team A dropped dramatically (O_6 $M = 20$ turnovers; O_7 $M = 6$ turnovers). During this same time period, the average number of turnovers per game committed by Team B (who had not hired a new coach) was unchanged (O_6 $M = 17$ turnovers; O_7 $M = 17$ turnovers). Based on these results, it would appear the hiring of a new coach led to a significant improvement in the performance of Team A. To conclude that the hiring of a new coach was responsible for the improvement in the performance of Team A, the Sports Psychologist would have to also rule out the effects of any potential "threats to internal validity" that could provide an alternative explanation for the decrease in the average number of turnovers committed by Team A. The Sports Psychologists can rule out several of the potential "threats" if assessments of the outcome measure (i.e. average number of turnovers per game) for the two groups remain stable across multiple measurements during the pre-intervention phase of the study. If the assessments of the outcome measure remain stable over time, it would indicate the participants in the two groups are not changing at a different rate over time (i.e. "differential maturation"),[2,3,13] the scores of the two groups on the outcome measure are not deviating from one another in a meaningful way as the groups are repeatedly assessed on the outcome measure (i.e. "differential testing")[2,13] and the scores of the "experimental group" on the outcome measure are not naturally "drifting" toward an average level of performance over time (i.e. "differential regression").[2,13,18] Since average number of turnovers was similar between Team A and Team B throughout the pre-intervention phase of the study, the Sports Psychologists could also rule out "selection"[2,8,12] as a major "threat."

While the hiring of a new coach may have resulted in a short-term improvement in the performance of Team A, was Team A able to sustain its improved level of performance over the long-term? In looking at the results of the study, the answer is "no!" Since the "Non-Equivalent Control Group Interrupted Time Series" design contains multiple assessments of the outcome measure (i.e. average number of turnovers per game) during the post-intervention phase of the study, it allows psychologists to assess both the short-term and long-term effects of a treatment or intervention.[1,11] We can see in the second week after hiring a new coach, the average number of turnovers committed by Team A began to increase (O_7 $M = 6$ turnovers; O_8 $M = 12$ turnovers). By the third week after hiring a new coach, the average number of turnovers per game for Team A had increased to pre-intervention levels and remained at this level throughout the duration of the 6 week post-intervention phase of the study (O_9, O_{10}, O_{11}, O_{12} $M = 20$ turnovers). Clearly, the hiring of a new coach did not result in a long-term improvement in the performance of Team A. So, if there was only a short-term improvement in the performance of Team A, is there an alternate explanation for that short-term improvement other than the hiring of the new coach? Perhaps "differential history"[2,9,13] is a "threat" to the internal validity of the study. There is the possibility that an event occurred during the week following the hiring of the new coach which contributed to the short-term improvement in the performance of Team A (e.g. a player who had been out injured, returned to the starting lineup). This "event" may not have occurred during the remaining 5 weeks of the post-intervention phase of the study (e.g. the player who had returned to the team's starting lineup may have reinjured himself leaving him unable to play). The extent to which the Sports Psychologist can rule out "differential history" as a potential "threat" to the validity of the study will determine whether he can conclude the short-term improvement in the performance of Team A was due to the hiring of the new coach.

As a second example of how psychologists might use a "Non-Equivalent Control Group Interrupted Time Series" design to conduct a research study, let's assume that an Educational Psychologist is interested in examining the effect of a new law on school attendance at a local high school. Recently, in response to the rising number of students at the high school who are missing more than 50 days of school during the school year (i.e. more than 25% of the school year!), the county passed a new law which established that parents of a child who misses 25 or more days of school during a school year can be sent to jail to serve a 100 day jail sentence and be required to pay a $500 fine! The county believes this new law will be effective in increasing the attendance of the students at the high school. To test the effectiveness of the new law in increasing attendance at the high school, the Educational Psychologist meets with the Principal of the high school (i.e. School A) and asks her to provide him with the percentage of students who attended school each day during the 4 weeks prior to the new law being put into effect and the 4 weeks following the new law being put into effect. He uses the data to compute an average daily attendance rate (%) at the high school for each of the 4 weeks prior to the new law being put into effect and each of the 4 weeks after the new law was put into effect. For a "control group," he selects a high school in a neighboring county (i.e. School B) which has not passed a similar "parent imprisonment" law. He meets with the Principal of his "control" high school and he has the Principal provide him with the percentage of students who attended school each day during the 4 weeks prior to the date when the new law went into effect within the county where School A is located and during the 4 weeks after the date when the new law went into effect in the county where School A is located. He uses this data to compute an average daily attendance rate (%) for School B for each of the 4 weeks prior to the date when the new law was put into effect in the county where School A is located and for each of the 4 weeks after the date when the new law was put into effect in the county where School A is located. The data for the Educational Psychologist's study of high school attendance appears below.

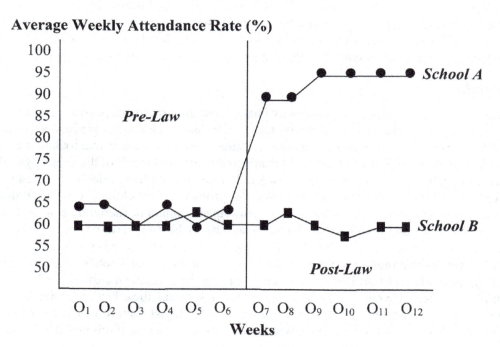

In looking at the results, during the pre-intervention (i.e. pre-test) phase of the study the average weekly attendance rate (%) was similar across the two high schools. Both high schools reported a 60–65% average weekly attendance rate in the weeks prior to the new law being put into effect in the county where School A is located (O_1, O_2, O_3, O_4, O_5, O_6). In the week after the new law went into effect in the county where School A is located (O_7), the average weekly attendance rate at School A increased to 90%! During this same time period, the average weekly attendance rate at School B was unchanged (i.e. 60%). Based on these results, it would appear the new law was effective in increasing the attendance of high school students at School A. To conclude the new law was responsible for the increased attendance at School A, the Educational Psychologist would have to rule out the effects of any potential "threats to internal validity" that could provide an alternative explanation for the increase in attendance at School A. Since the average weekly attendance rates (%) of the two high schools were consistent throughout the pre-intervention phase of the research study, the Psychologist could rule out "differential maturation, testing, instrumentation, and regression" as potential threats to the internal validity of the study. He could also rule out "selection" as a major threat, since the average weekly attendance rates (%) at the two schools were very similar throughout the pre-intervention phase of the study.

While the new law may have resulted in a short-term increase in attendance at School A, was School A able to sustain its increased level of attendance over the long-term? In looking at the results of the study, the answer is definitely "yes!" Given that the "Non-Equivalent Control Group Interrupted Time Series" design contains multiple assessments of the outcome measure (i.e. average weekly attendance rate) during the post-intervention phase of the study, it allows psychologists to assess both the short-term and long-term effects of a treatment or intervention. We can see in the second week after the new law was put into effect (O_8), the average weekly attendance rate (%) at School A remained at 90%. By the third week after the new law had been put into effect, the average weekly attendance rate (%) at School A had risen to 95% and would remain at this level throughout the duration of the 6-week post-intervention phase of the study (O_9, O_{10}, O_{11}, O_{12}). Clearly, the new law was effective in producing a long-term increase in the attendance at School A. Given that: (a) the increase in average weekly attendance rate occurred immediately after the new law was put into effect, (b) the increase in average weekly attendance rate was maintained throughout the post-intervention phase, and (c) the Psychologist could rule out multiple "threats to internal validity," the Educational Psychologist would likely conclude with a high level of confidence that the increase in the average weekly attendance rate (%) at School A was the result of the new law being put into effect.

Some quasi-experimental designs do not contain a "true independent variable."[3,5,8] A "true independent variable" is one which can be manipulated (i.e. controlled) by psychologists and which allows for the random assignment of participants to different levels of the variable (i.e. conditions). In some cases, psychologists are interested in studying variables that cannot be manipulated (or are unethical to manipulate)[4] and which do not allow for the random assignment of participants to the different levels of the variable (i.e. conditions).[4,5,8] Subject variables and natural treatment variables are examples of such variables.

Subject Variables

"Subject variables" are demographic or personality characteristics participants possess prior to taking part in a research study (e.g. gender, age, race, personality trait).[4,5,6] When psychologists are interested in studying the effect of a subject variable on one or more outcome measures, they are unable to manipulate (i.e. "control") the subject variable or to randomly assign their participants to the different levels of the subject variable (i.e. conditions). Therefore, subject variables are not considered "true independent variables." Instead, subject variables are referred to as "quasi-independent variables." The problem for psychologists when studying the effect of a "quasi-independent variable," is that because the participants cannot be randomly assigned to the different levels of the variable (i.e. conditions), psychologists would be unable to determine whether the groups of participants are equivalent on all factors other than the subject variable (i.e. quasi-independent variable). These uncontrolled differences that may exist between the groups would provide a potential alternative explanation in the event there is an observed difference between groups on the outcome measure(s).[4,6,8]

For example, a Military Psychologist may be interested in studying the effect of soldier gender on military marksmanship. The independent variable in the Military Psychologist's study would be soldier gender and the dependent variable (i.e. outcome measure) would be the score on a test of military marksmanship. Soldier gender is a "subject variable," rather than a "true independent variable" because the Military Psychologist is unable to manipulate soldier gender and unable to randomly assign participants (i.e. soldiers) to the groups (i.e. conditions). Rather, the soldiers are assigned to groups (i.e. conditions) based on the gender they bring with them when they join the military. Soldier gender must therefore be considered a "quasi-independent variable." Since the soldiers in her study were not randomly assigned to groups, the Military Psychologist would be unable to determine whether the groups of male and female soldiers are equivalent on all factors other than gender. These uncontrolled differences which may exist between the groups of soldiers would provide an alternative explanation in the event there was a difference in the average marksmanship score observed across the groups of male and female soldiers. If the Military Psychologist is unable to rule out these alternative explanations for a difference in average marksmanship scores across groups, she would have to be cautious in making any causal statements about the effect of soldier gender on military marksmanship.

As a second example, assume that a Personality Psychologist is interested in studying whether introverts or extroverts have a better sense of humor. The independent variable in the Personality Psychologist's study would be introversion/extroversion status and the dependent variable would be the score on a measure of sense of humor. Introversion/extroversion status is a "subject variable" rather than a "true independent variable" because the Psychologist is unable to manipulate introversion/extroversion status, and is unable to randomly assign participants to groups (i.e. conditions). Rather, participants are assigned to groups (i.e. conditions) based on whether they were an introvert or an extrovert prior to taking part in the study. Introversion/extroversion status must therefore be considered a "quasi-independent variable." Because the participants in her study were not randomly assigned to groups, the Personality Psychologist would be unable to determine whether the groups of introverts and extroverts are equivalent on all factors other than introversion/extroversion status. These uncontrolled differences that may exist between the groups would provide an alternative explanation in the event there was an observed difference in the average sense of humor scores across the groups of introverts and extroverts. If the Psychologist is unable to rule out alternative explanations for a difference in average sense of humor scores across groups, she would have to be cautious in making a causal statement about the effect of introversion/extroversion status on sense of humor.

Natural Treatment Variables

"Natural treatment variables" are life experiences that participants possess prior to taking part in a research study (e.g. getting divorced, being fired, serving in the military).[4,5,15] When psychologists are interested in studying the effects of a natural treatment variable (i.e. quasi-independent variable) on one or more outcome measures, they are unable to manipulate (i.e. "control") the natural treatment variable and the participants cannot be randomly assigned to the different levels of the variable (i.e. conditions). Therefore, natural treatment variables are not considered "true independent variables." Instead, natural treatment variables are referred to as "quasi-independent variables." As was the case with "subject variables," since participants cannot be randomly assigned to different levels of the variable (i.e. conditions), psychologists would be unable to determine whether the groups of participants are equivalent on all factors other than the natural treatment variable (i.e. quasi-independent variable). The uncontrolled differences that may exist between the groups would provide a potential alternative explanation in the event there is an observed difference between groups on the outcome measure(s).[4,6,8]

For example, a Parapsychologist may be interested in studying the effect of having a "near-death experience" (NDE) on psychological health. In the Parapsychologist's study, NDE status would be the independent variable and scores on a measure of psychological health would be the dependent variable. However, NDE status would not be considered a "true independent variable" because the Parapsychologist would be unable to manipulate NDE status (and it would be unethical to do so), or randomly assign participants to the different levels of the variable (i.e. conditions). Rather, participants would be assigned to groups (i.e. conditions) based on whether they had an NDE prior to taking part in the research study. NDE status is therefore an example of a natural treatment variable and would be considered a "quasi-independent variable." Since participant NDE status is a "quasi-independent variable," and participants cannot be randomly assigned to groups (i.e. conditions), the Parapsychologist would be unable to determine whether the groups of individuals who have or have not had an NDE are equivalent on all factors other than NDE status. These uncontrolled differences that may exist between the groups provide an alternative explanation in the event there is a difference in the average psychological health scores observed between the groups of individuals who have or have not had a NDE. If the Parapsychologist is unable to rule out these alternative explanations for a difference in average psychological health scores across groups, he would have to be cautious in making any causal statements about the effect of having an NDE on psychological health.

As a second example, assume that a Counseling Psychologist is interested in studying the effect of parental divorce during childhood on attitudes toward marriage in adulthood. In the Counseling Psychologist's study, parental divorce status would be the independent variable and attitudes toward marriage would be the dependent variable. However, parental divorce status would not be considered a "true independent variable" because the Counseling Psychologist would be unable to manipulate parental divorce status (and it would be unethical to do so), or randomly assign participants to the different levels of the variable (i.e. conditions). Rather, the participants would be assigned to groups (i.e. conditions) based on whether their parents had divorced during their childhood prior to taking part in the research study. Parental divorce status is therefore an example of a natural treatment variable and is considered a "quasi-independent variable." Since parental divorce status is a "quasi-independent variable," and the participants cannot be randomly assigned to groups (i.e. conditions), the Counseling Psychologist would be unable to determine whether the groups of individuals whose parents did, or did not, divorce during their childhoods are equivalent on all factors other than parental divorce status. These uncontrolled differences that may exist between groups would provide an alternative explanation in the event there is a difference in average attitude toward marriage scores observed between the groups of individuals whose parents did, or did not, get a divorce during their childhoods. If the Counseling Psychologist is unable to rule out these alternative explanations for a difference in average attitude toward marriage scores across groups, she must be cautious in making any causal statements about the effect of parental divorce during childhood on attitudes toward marriage in adulthood.

Conclusion

There are several strengths associated with "quasi-experimental" research. First, quasi-experimental research allows psychologists to study variables of interest within applied settings outside of the controlled environment of the laboratory.[2,3,6] Second, quasi-experimental research allows psychologists to conduct research in settings where situational, methodological, and/or ethical constraints prevent them from conducting a true experiment.[2,4] Third, quasi-experimental research allows psychologists to study the effect of a subject or natural treatment variable they are unable to manipulate (i.e. control), and which does not allow for participants to be randomly assigned to the different levels of the variable (i.e. conditions).[3,4,5] Fourth, quasi-experimental research allows psychologists to study the effect of a treatment or intervention which has been designed and/or implemented by another person or social entity (e.g. organizations, businesses, schools, health care facilities, community or governmental agencies), and which is currently in progress.[2,3,10] Finally, quasi-experimental research allows psychologists to study the short-term and long-term effects of both anticipated (i.e. passage of a law, planned community intervention) and unanticipated events (e.g. natural disaster, unanticipated life experiences) on members of a community. [1,4,11]

Like the "true experiment," the goal of a quasi-experimental study is to determine if an independent variable (i.e. treatment or intervention) has a causal effect on one or more dependent variables (i.e. outcome measures). However, "quasi-experimental" research designs lack one or more elements of a "true experiment" (e.g. control group,[1,5] random assignment of participants to groups (or conditions),[1,3,7] manipulation of a "true independent variable,"[3,5,8] control over factors in the experimental environment[2,3,4]) that make these research designs more vulnerable to several potential "threats to internal validity" (e.g. history, selection, attrition, instrumentation, testing, maturation). When psychologists are unable to rule out the effects of these potential "threats to internal validity," they become alternative explanations for observed differences found between the "experimental" and "control" groups on the outcome measures. If alternative explanations for the results are present, psychologists must use caution in making a causal statement about the effect of the treatment or intervention on the outcome measure(s).[6,9,10]

EXERCISE 10A

Analysis of "Pre-Experimental" Designs

When psychologists face situational, methodological, and ethical constraints that prevent them from using an experimental research design, they often use "quasi-experimental" designs to answer their research questions. Some quasi-experimental designs contain no control group and are known as "pre-experimental" designs. The "pre-experimental" designs most commonly used by psychologists are: (a) the One Group Post-Test Only design, (b) the One Group Pre-Test/Post-Test design, and (c) the Interrupted Time Series design. Below are the descriptions of 6 research studies in which a psychologist has used a "pre-experimental" design. For each research study, please: **(a)** identify the "pre-experimental" design being used by the psychologist, **(b)** decide if the psychologist's conclusion is justified (provide a rationale for your decision), and **(c)** describe how the psychologist could improve the design to be more confident in his/her conclusion.

01. A Clinical Psychologist has designed a therapy program to reduce the fear of flying. To test the effectiveness of his program, he places an ad in the paper to recruit individuals who are afraid to fly on a plane to take part in his study. He enrolls the first 10 people who respond to his ad in his study. He has each of his 10 participants complete a test that measures the intensity of his/her fear of flying. Scores on the test range from 0–100. The average fear of flying score for his 10 participants was $M = 98$. He then has his participants complete his 6-month therapy program. At the end of the 6-month program, he has each of his participants again complete the test that measures the intensity of his/her fear of flying. The average fear of flying score for his 10 participants after completing the therapy program was $M = 78$. He concludes that his therapy program is effective in reducing the fear of flying.

Design =

Is the Psychologist's conclusion justified by the results of the study?
YES   NO
Rationale:

What modifications should the Psychologist make to his design to be more confident in the validity of his conclusion?

02. The Chair of a Psychology Department needs to know whether the training program used by the Department to train its Graduate students to be Teaching Assistants (TA's) is producing TA's who are high-quality teachers. To examine the effectiveness of the training program, the Chair conducts classroom observations for 10 TA's who recently completed the training program. During each classroom observation, he uses a 10-point rating scale (1 = Terrible Teaching; 10 = Terrific Teaching) to rate the quality of the teaching displayed by each TA. After completing his classroom observations, he computes an average quality rating for the 10 TA's he observed in the classroom. He finds that the average quality rating is $M = 8.8$. The Chair concludes the Department's training program is effective in producing TA's who are high-quality teachers.

Design =

Is the Chair's conclusion justified by the results of the study?

YES   NO

Rationale:

What modifications should the Chair make to his design to be more confident in the validity of his conclusion?

03. Recently, a local restaurant added several new healthy, low-fat lunch and dinner options to its menu. A Consumer Psychologist wants to know if the new healthier menu has led to an increase in the number of customers who eat at the restaurant. To examine the effect of the new healthier menu, the Consumer Psychologist has the restaurant owner provide him with the number of customers who ate at the restaurant for each of the 7 days before the change to the healthier menu and for each of the 7 days following the change to the healthier menu. The data for the Consumer Psychologist's study appears below. Based on these results, the Consumer Psychologist concludes that the restaurant's change to a healthier menu caused an increase in the number of customers who eat at the restaurant.

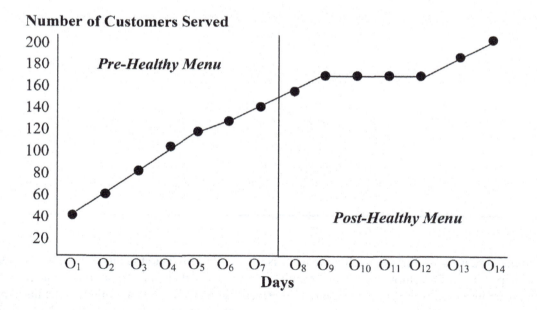

Design =

Is the Psychologist's conclusion justified by the results of the study?

YES   NO

Rationale:

What modifications should the Psychologist make to his design to be more confident in the validity of his conclusion?

---

04. One of the hardest tasks for a pre-school teacher is to get all of his/her students to lie down and fall asleep during nap time. A Developmental Psychologist hypothesizes that playing soothing music in the classroom during nap time will help the students fall asleep faster. To test her hypothesis, she has a pre-school teacher select a school day and record the amount of time it takes each of her 15 students to fall asleep during nap time. Her students fell asleep in an average of $M = 28$ minutes. The next day, the Psychologist has the pre-school teacher play soothing music in the classroom during nap time and record the amount of time it takes each of her students to fall asleep. Her students fell asleep in an average of $M = 21$ minutes. The Developmental Psychologist concludes that playing soothing music during nap time will make students in pre-school fall asleep faster.

Design =

Is the Psychologist's conclusion justified by the results of the study?

YES   NO

Rationale:

What modifications should the Psychologist make to her design to be more confident in the validity of her conclusion?

---

05. A Counseling Psychologist has developed a new group-based therapy program designed to help men cope with the grief associated with the death of a spouse. To test the effectiveness of his new group-based therapy program, he has 8 men who recently experienced the death of a spouse participate in his program. Before beginning the group-based therapy program, he has each of the 8 men rate the intensity of the grief he has experienced due to the death of his spouse during each of the 3 previous weeks. The men use a 10-point rating scale (1 = I experienced minimal grief due to the death of my spouse; 10 = I experienced a debilitating level of grief due to the death of my spouse). The Counseling Psychologist uses this data to compute an average level of grief experienced by the 8 men during each of the 3 previous weeks. He then has the 8 men complete his therapy program. At the end of the program, he has each of the men rate the intensity of the grief he has experienced due to the death of his spouse for each of the 3 weeks following his completion of the therapy program. The men use the same 10-point scale to provide their ratings. The Counseling Psychologist uses this data to compute an average level of grief experienced by the 8 men during each of the 3 weeks following their completion of the therapy program. The data for the Psychologist's study appears below. Based on these results, the Counseling Psychologist concludes that his new group-based therapy program is effective in decreasing the intensity of the grief experienced by men following the death of a spouse.

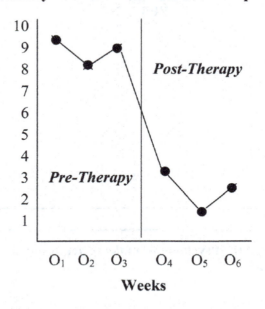

Intensity of Grief Due to Death of a Spouse

Weeks

Design =

Is the Psychologist's conclusion justified by the results of the study?
YES   NO
Rationale:

What modifications should the Psychologist make to his design to be more confident in the validity of his conclusion?

06. A Cognitive Psychologist hypothesizes that learning to play a musical instrument increases intelligence. To test her hypothesis, she administers an IQ test to 20 students who play a musical instrument in the band at a local high school. A score of 100 on the test represents an average level of intelligence. She finds the average IQ score for the 20 students who play a musical instrument in the band is $M = 118$ (an above average level of intelligence). The Cognitive Psychologist concludes that learning to play a musical instrument does indeed increase intelligence.

Design =

Is the Psychologist's conclusion justified by the results of the study?

YES   NO

Rationale:

What modifications should the Psychologist make to her design to be more confident in the validity of her conclusion?

EXERCISE 10B

Analysis of "Quasi-Experimental" Designs

Unlike "pre-experimental" designs which do not contain a control group, there are some "quasi-experimental" designs that do contain a control group. The "quasi-experimental" designs that contain a control group most commonly used by psychologists are: (a) the Non-Equivalent Control Group Post-Test Only design, (b) the Non-Equivalent Pre-Test/Post-Test design, and (c) the Non-Equivalent Control Group Interrupted Time Series design. Below are descriptions of 6 research studies in which a psychologist is using a "quasi-experimental" design which contains a control group. For each study, please: **(a)** identify the "quasi-experimental" design that is being used by the psychologist, **(b)** decide if the conclusion drawn by the psychologist is justified and provide a rationale for your decision, and **(c)** describe how the psychologist could improve the design to be more confident in his/her conclusion.

01. A Social Psychologist wants to know if there is any truth to the saying, "absence makes the heart grow fonder." The Psychologist goes to an airport and finds 10 men who are waiting for their girlfriends to return home. Their girlfriends have been "absent" for a week while away on vacation. He asks each of the 10 men to rate how fond they are of their girlfriends using a 10-point rating scale (1 = I feel very little love for my girlfriend; 10 = I am truly and hopelessly in love with my girlfriend). He finds the average "fondness" rating for these 10 men is $M = 8.2$. For a control group, he finds 10 other men in the airport whose girlfriends have been in town all week and have not been "absent." He asks each of the 10 men to rate how fond they are of their girlfriends using the same 10-point scale. He finds the average "fondness" rating for these 10 men is $M = 7.2$. He concludes that absence truly does make the heart grow fonder.

Design =

Is the Psychologist's conclusion justified by the results of the study?

YES   NO

Rationale:

What modifications should the Psychologist make to his design to be more confident in the validity of his conclusion?

02. A Political Psychologist is interested in the effect of a "sex scandal" on voter approval for a political candidate (i.e. Candidate A). She examines the results of political polls which have measured the % of likely voters who give Candidate A a high approval rating. Specifically, she records the poll results for Candidate A for the 4 weeks prior to the public learning about his involvement in a "sex scandal," and for the 4 weeks after news of the "sex scandal" was made public (i.e. experimental group). For a control group, she selects another candidate (i.e. Candidate B) competing in the same election, who had similar "pre-scandal" approval ratings and who has had no involvement in a "sex scandal." She records the poll results for Candidate B for the 4 weeks prior to the public learning about Candidate A's involvement in a "sex scandal," and for the 4 weeks after the news of Candidate A's involvement in a "sex scandal" was made public. The results of the Political Psychologist's study appear below. The Psychologist concludes the "sex scandal" had a negative impact on the voter approval ratings of the political candidate (i.e. Candidate A).

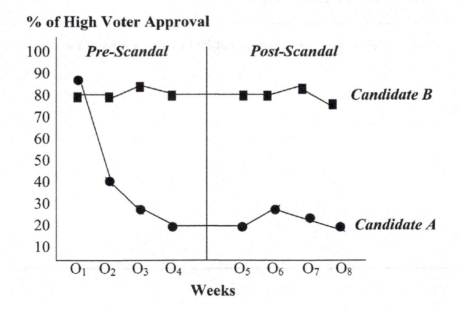

Design =

Is the Psychologist's conclusion justified by the results of the study?

YES   NO

Rationale:

What modifications should the Psychologist make to her design to be more confident in the validity of her conclusion?

03. An Educational Psychologist wants to determine whether children who attend pre-school are more prepared for kindergarten than children who do not attend pre-school. She begins her study by going to a local elementary school on the day parents are signing their children up for pre-school. She finds 10 parents willing to have their children complete a test designed to assess their readiness for kindergarten (i.e. experimental group). Scores on the test range from 0–10 (a higher score indicates greater readiness for kindergarten). She uses the scores to compute an average "readiness" score for the 10 children. For a control group, she goes to a local park and finds 10 parents whose children will not be attending pre-school and who are willing to have their children complete the same test of kindergarten readiness. She uses the scores to compute an average "readiness" score for these 10 children. She then waits for the 10 children enrolled in pre-school to complete their year of pre-school. At the end of the year, she has each of the 20 children once again complete the kindergarten readiness test. She uses the scores to compute average readiness scores for the 10 children who completed a year of pre-school and the 10 children who did not attend pre-school. The results of the Psychologist's study appear below. She concludes that children who attend pre-school are more prepared (i.e. "ready") for kindergarten than children who do not attend pre-school.

Average Kindergarten Readiness Score

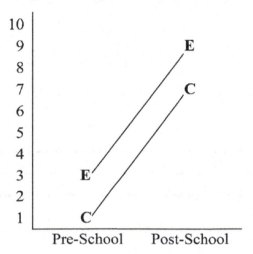

Design =

Is the Psychologist's conclusion justified by the results of the study?
YES   NO
Rationale:

What modifications should the Psychologist make to her design to be more confident in the validity of her conclusion?

---

04. A CEO has grown concerned with the way her younger managers are treating older workers. She hires a Psychologist with an interest in gerontology (the study of the ageing process) to develop an educational program to teach younger managers to have a more positive attitude toward older workers. The Psychologist selects 8 managers who work in Sales and another 8 managers who work in Marketing to take part in her study. She begins by having each of the managers complete an instrument designed to assess their attitude toward older workers. Scores on the test range from 0-40 (a higher score indicates a more positive attitude toward older workers). She uses the test scores to compute average attitude scores for the managers who work in Sales and the managers who work in Marketing. She then has the 8 managers who work in Sales complete an educational program designed to teach them to have a more positive attitude toward older workers (i.e. experimental group). After the managers have completed her program, she once again has each of the 16 managers complete the instrument designed to assess their attitude toward older workers. She uses the test scores to compute average attitude scores for the managers who work in Sales and the managers who work in Marketing (i.e. control group). The results of the Psychologist's study appear below. The Psychologist concludes her program is effective in teaching younger managers to have a more positive attitude toward older workers.

Average Attitude Toward Older Workers

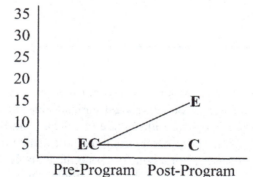

Pre-Program   Post-Program

Design =

Is the Psychologist's conclusion justified by the results of the study?

YES   NO

Rationale:

What modifications should the Psychologist make to her design to be more confident in the validity of her conclusion?

---

05. A Psychiatrist is interested in studying whether a new anti-depressant is effective in reducing depression. He begins his study by having each of his 10 newest patients rate the depression they have experienced during the past 3 months using a 10-point rating scale (1 = I have had only mild depression; 10 = I have had severe depression). He uses these ratings to compute an average depression rating for his 10 newest patients for each of the past 3 months. For a control group, he calls 10 people who are on a waiting list to get an appointment to see him. He has each of these 10 people rate the depression they have experienced during the past 3 months using the same 10-point rating scale. He uses these ratings to compute an average depression rating for the 10 people on the waiting list for each of the past 3 months. Then, he has his 10 patients take the new anti-depressant for a period of 3 months. At the end of the 3 months, he has each of his 10 patients rate the depression they experienced during each of the 3 months they were taking the new anti-depressant. He also calls the 10 people on the waiting list and has each of the people rate the depression they experienced during each of the 3 months the Psychiatrist's patients were taking the new anti-depressant. He uses these ratings to compute average depression ratings for the 10 patients and the 10 people on the waiting list for each of the 3 months the Psychiatrist's patients were taking the new anti-depressant. The results of the Psychiatrist's research study appear below. The Psychiatrist concludes the new anti-depressant is effective in reducing depression.

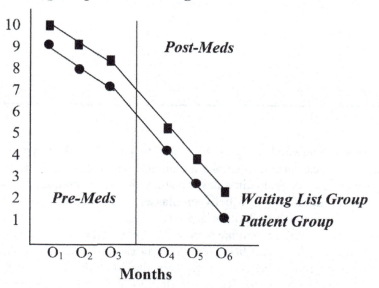

Average Depression Rating

Post-Meds

Pre-Meds

Waiting List Group

Patient Group

O_1 O_2 O_3 O_4 O_5 O_6

Months

Design =

Is the Psychiatrist's conclusion justified by the results of the study?

YES   NO

Rationale:

What modifications should the Psychiatrist make to his design to be more confident in the validity of his conclusion?

06. A Psychology professor interested in hypnosis wants to know whether hypnotizing people and giving them a post-hypnotic suggestion not to smoke a cigarette when they feel the urge to smoke, can reduce the number of cigarettes they consume in a day. To study this research question, the Psychologist recruits 20 college students who are smoking in between classes to participate in his study. He has each of the 20 college students undergo a 1 hour hypnosis session. While each student is hypnotized, he gives him/her a post-hypnotic suggestion not to smoke a cigarette the next day when he/she feels the urge to smoke. A few days later, he asks each student how many cigarettes he/she had smoked the day after being hypnotized. He finds the average number of cigarettes for the 20 students is $M = 8$. For a control group, he asks 20 students who are enrolled in his Research Methods class, and who smoke, to tell him how many cigarettes each of them had smoked the previous day. He finds the average number of cigarettes for these 20 students is $M = 15$. He concludes hypnotizing individuals and giving them a post-hypnotic suggestion not to smoke a cigarette when they feel the urge to smoke, is effective in decreasing the number of cigarettes smokers consume in a day.

Design =

Is the Professor's conclusion justified by the results of the study?

YES   NO

Rationale:

What modifications should the Professor make to his design to be more confident in the validity of his conclusion?

EXERCISE 10C

True vs. Quasi Independent Variables

A "true" independent variable is a variable which can be manipulated (i.e. controlled) by psychologists and which allows for the random assignment of participants to the different levels of the variable (i.e. conditions). In some cases, psychologists are interested in studying variables that cannot be manipulated (or which are unethical to manipulate) and which do not allow for the random assignment of participants to different levels of the variable. Such variables are referred to as "quasi" independent variables. Below are descriptions of 7 research studies. For each of the research studies, please: **(a)** determine whether the Psychologist is examining a true or quasi independent variable (subject or natural treatment) and provide a rationale for your decision and **(b)** describe the types of variables the Psychologist would need to control or account for in order to conclude the independent variable was responsible for any observed differences between the groups on the dependent variable.

01. A Psychologist is interested in studying the impact of having a heart attack on the "fear of death." He has 25 individuals who have had a heart attack, and who are in the cardiac care unit at a local hospital, complete an instrument designed to measure their fear of death. For a control group, he has 25 individuals from the local community who have not had a heart attack complete the fear of death instrument. He then compares average fear of death scores across groups to determine if individuals who have had a heart attack are significantly more afraid of death than individuals who have not had a heart attack.

What is the independent variable?	
What is the dependent variable?	
What type of independent variable is being studied?	True Quasi
If you selected Quasi, what type of Quasi IV?	Subject Natural Treatment

How did you decide whether a True or Quasi IV is being studied?

If you selected True IV, what are 2 factors the Psychologist must control to ensure the IV was the cause of any difference observed between groups on the dependent variable?
1. _____
2. _____
If you selected Quasi IV, what are 2 additional differences that may exist between the groups that may account for a difference between the groups on the dependent variable?
1. _____
2. _____

02. A Psychologist is interested in studying the effect of sleep deprivation on pilot performance. He randomly selects 30 pilots from an airline for his study. He then randomly assigns pilots to groups so that 10 pilots are deprived of sleep for 24 hours, 10 pilots are deprived of sleep for 48 hours, and 10 pilots are deprived of sleep for 72 hours. He then has each pilot take a 1 hour performance test in a flight simulator. Finally, he compares the average performance scores across groups to determine if the amount of sleep deprivation produced a significant difference in pilot performance.

What is the independent variable?	
What is the dependent variable?	
What type of independent variable is being studied?	True Quasi
If you selected Quasi, what type of Quasi IV?	Subject Natural Treatment

How did you decide whether a True or Quasi IV is being studied?
If you selected True IV, what are 2 factors the Psychologist must control to ensure the IV was the cause of any difference observed between groups on the dependent variable?
1. _____
2. _____

If you selected Quasi IV, what are 2 additional differences that may exist between the groups that may account for a difference between the groups on the dependent variable?
1. _____
2. _____

03. An Industrial-Organizational Psychologist is interested in studying the impact of having a visible tattoo on getting hired for a job. He goes to a local tattoo parlor and finds 10 people with a visible tattoo who are currently looking for work. He asks each of the 10 people how many jobs they had applied for in the last month and not been hired. For a control group, he goes to the local employment office and finds 10 people who are currently looking for work and who do not have a visible tattoo. He asks each of these 10 people how many jobs they had applied for in the last month and not been hired. He then compares the average number of job rejections across groups to determine if people who have a visible tattoo are rejected by a significantly higher number of employers than people who do not have a visible tattoo.

What is the independent variable?	
What is the dependent variable?	
What type of independent variable is being studied?	True Quasi
If you selected Quasi, what type of Quasi IV?	Subject Natural Treatment

How did you decide whether a True or Quasi IV is being studied?

If you selected True IV, what are 2 factors the Psychologist must control to ensure the IV was the cause of any difference observed between groups on the dependent variable?
1. _____
2. _____

If you selected Quasi IV, what are 2 additional differences that may exist between the groups that may account for a difference between the groups on the dependent variable?
1. _____
2. _____

04. A Political Psychologist is interested in studying how people of different ages feel about the job performance of Barack Obama; the current President of the United States. Specifically, he wants to know how individuals between the ages of 20–29, 30–39, 40–49, and 50 or older feel about President Obama's job performance. He recruits 10 people between the ages of 20–29 at a local college, 10 people between the ages of 30–39 at a local fast food restaurant, 10 people between the ages of 40–49 at a local movie theater, and 10 people age 50 or older from a local community center. He asks each of the 40 individuals to rate the performance of President Obama on a 10-point rating scale (1 = His job performance has been terrible; 10 = His job performance has been excellent). He then compares the average performance ratings across groups to determine whether age had a significant effect on perceptions of President Obama's job performance.

What is the independent variable?	
What is the dependent variable?	
What type of independent variable is being studied?	True Quasi
If you selected Quasi, what type of Quasi IV?	Subject Natural Treatment

How did you decide whether a True or Quasi IV is being studied?
If you selected True IV, what are 2 factors the Psychologist must control to ensure the IV was the cause of any difference observed between groups on the dependent variable?
1. _____   2. _____
If you selected Quasi IV, what are 2 additional differences that may exist between the groups that may account for a difference between the groups on the dependent variable?
1. _____   2. _____

05. A fast-food restaurant chain has hired a Consumer Psychologist to conduct a research study to determine whether customers prefer the restaurant's salty, high calorie french fries or its low salt, low calorie french fries. The Psychologist randomly selects 50 customers to take part in the study. She then randomly assigns customers to groups so that 25 customers eat the salty, high calorie french fries and 25 customers eat the low salt, low calorie french fries. She then has all the customers rate the taste of the french fries they were assigned to eat on a 10-point rating scale (1 = these french fries are nasty! 10 = these french fries are great!). She then compares the average taste ratings across groups to determine which french fries received a significantly higher rating from customers.

What is the independent variable?	
What is the dependent variable?	
What type of independent variable is being studied?	True Quasi
If you selected Quasi, what type of Quasi IV?	Subject Natural Treatment

How did you decide whether a True or Quasi IV is being studied?
If you selected True IV, what are 2 factors the Psychologist must control to ensure the IV was the cause of any difference observed between groups on the dependent variable?
1. _____
2. _____
If you selected Quasi IV, what are 2 additional differences that may exist between the groups that may account for a difference between the groups on the dependent variable?
1. _____
2. _____

06. A Psychology Professor is interested in studying the effect of personality on physical health. Specifically, she wants to know if there is a significant difference in the physical health of individuals who are "optimists" (i.e. individuals who approach life with a positive state of mind) or "pessimists" (i.e. individuals who approach life with a negative state of mind). She begins by recruiting college students to take a personality test. She identifies the first 10 students classified as "optimists" and the first 10 students classified as "pessimists" on the basis of their scores on the personality test. She then has each of the 20 students take part in a physical exam conducted by a team of medical doctors. The doctors assign each student a health score that could range from 1 (Extremely Unhealthy) to 10 (Extremely Healthy). She then compares the average physical health scores across groups to see if there is a significant difference in the physical health of "optimists" and "pessimists."

What is the independent variable?	
What is the dependent variable?	
What type of independent variable is being studied?	True Quasi
If you selected Quasi, what type of Quasi IV?	Subject Natural Treatment

How did you decide whether a True or Quasi IV is being studied?

If you selected True IV, what are 2 factors the Professor must control to ensure the IV was the cause of any difference observed between groups on the dependent variable?

1. _____

2. _____

If you selected Quasi IV, what are 2 additional differences that may exist between the groups that may account for a difference between the groups on the dependent variable?

1. _____

2. _____

07. A Forensic Psychologist wants to know if serving on a jury affects the level of confidence people have in the accuracy of the decisions made by juries about the innocence or guilt of defendants. At the conclusion of a jury trial in her local community, she approaches the 10 members of the jury and asks each of them to rate the confidence they have in the accuracy of the decisions made by juries using a 10-point rating scale (1 = I have minimal confidence in the accuracy of the decisions made by juries; 10 = I have total confidence in the accuracy of the decisions made by juries). For a control group, she goes to the coffee shop across the street from the courthouse and finds 10 people who have never served on a jury. She asks each of them to rate the confidence they have in the accuracy of the decisions made by juries using the same 10-point rating scale. Finally, she compares the average confidence ratings across groups to determine whether serving on a jury had a significant effect on the level of confidence people have in the accuracy of the decisions made by juries.

What is the independent variable?	
What is the dependent variable?	
What type of independent variable is being studied?	True Quasi
If you selected Quasi, what type of Quasi IV?	Subject Natural Treatment

How did you decide whether a True or Quasi IV is being studied?
If you selected True IV, what are 2 factors the Psychologist must control to ensure the IV was the cause of any difference observed between groups on the dependent variable?
1. _____
2. _____
If you selected Quasi IV, what are 2 additional differences that may exist between the groups that may account for a difference between the groups on the dependent variable?
1. _____
2. _____

References

1. Cozby, P. C., & Bates, S. C. (2011). *Methods in behavioral research* (11th ed.). New York, NY: McGraw-Hill Publishers.

2. Passer, M. W. (2013). *Research methods: Concepts and connections*. New York, NY: Worth Publishers.

3. Ray, W. J. (2011). *Methods: Towards a science of behavior and experience* (10th ed.). Belmont, CA: Wadsworth/Cengage Learning.

4. Kantowitz, B. H., Roediger, H. L., & Elmes, D. G. (2014). *Experimental psychology* (10th ed.). Stamford, CT: Cengage Learning.

5. Jackson, S. L. (2014). *Research methods: A modular approach* (3rd ed.). Stamford, CT: Cengage Learning.

6. Bordens, K. S., & Abbot, B. B. (2011). *Research design and methods: A process approach* (8th ed.). Boston, MA: McGraw-Hill Publishers.

7. Harris, A. D., McGregor, J. C., Perencevich, E. N., Furuno, J. P., Zhu, J., Peterson, D. E., & Finkelstein, J. (2006). The use and interpretation of quasi-experimental studies in medical informatics. *Journal of the American Medical Informatics Association, 13*(1), 16–23.

8. Beins, B. C. (2012). *Research methods: A tool for life* (3rd ed.). Boston, MA: Pearson Publishers.

9. Leary, M. R. (2007). *Introduction to behavioral research methods* (5th ed.). Boston, MA: Pearson/Allyn & Bacon.

10. Bradley, K. (2009). Quasi-experimental research. *Education.com*. Retrieved from http://www.education.com/reference/article/quasiexperimental-research/

11. ALLPsych Online. (2011). Research methods: Experimental designs. *ALLPsych.com*. Retrieved from http://allpsych.com/researchmethods/experimentaldesign.html

12. Rosnow, R. L., & Rosenthal, R. (2012). *Beginning behavioral research: A conceptual primer* (7th ed.). Boston, MA: Pearson Publishers.

13. Fife-Schaw, C. (2012). Quasi-experimental designs. In G. M. Breakwell, J. A. Smith, & D. B. Wright (Eds.) *Research Methods in Psychology* (4th ed.; pp. 75–92). Thousand Oaks, CA: Sage Publications.

14. Robson, L. S., Shannon, H. S., Goldenhar, L. M., & Hale, A. R. (2001). Quasi-experimental and experimental designs. *Guide to Evaluating the Effectiveness of Strategies for Preventing Work Injury* (pp. 29–42). Cincinnati, OH: National Institute for Occupational Safety and Health (NIOSH). Retrieved from http://www.cdc.gov/niosh/docs/2001-119/

15. Smith, R. A., & Davis, S. F. (2012). *The psychologist as detective: An introduction to conducting research in psychology* (6th ed.). Boston, MA: Pearson Publishers.

16. Evans, A. N., & Rooney, B. F. (2007). *Methods in psychological research*. Thousand Oaks, CA: Sage Publications.

17. Price, P., & Oswald, K. (2008). Quasi-experiments. *Research Methods for Dummies*. Retrieved from http://psych.csufresno.edu/psy144/Content/Design/Nonexperimental/quasi.html

18. Trochim, W. M. (2006). The nonequivalent groups design. *The Research Methods Knowledge Base* (2nd ed.). Retrieved from http://www.socialresearchmethods.net/kb/quasnegd.php

MODULE
11

Survey Research

Psychologists conduct research to answer important questions. There are a variety of research methods that psychologists can use to find the answers to their questions. Included among these methods is survey research. In survey research, psychologists select a sample of individuals from a population of interest and ask these individuals to provide responses to a set of predetermined questions.[1,2,3] Through their responses to these questions, the members of the research sample provide psychologists with information regarding behavior, values, attitudes, beliefs, life experiences, knowledge, motivations, emotions, interests, as well as demographic characteristics.[1,2,4] Psychologists can then analyze the information provided by members of the research sample and use this information to answer questions about a population of interest.[3,4,5]

In survey research, since psychologists attempt to answer questions about a population of interest based on information provided by a sample of individuals drawn from that population, it is important that the sample of individuals surveyed possess the following characteristics. First, the sample must be "representative" of the population of interest (i.e. possess characteristics that mirror those found in the population). The more "representative" the sample, the more likely the sample is to yield information that will generalize to the much larger population.[1,2,3] Second, the sample should yield information that is reliable and accurately reflects the true characteristics of the sample (i.e. and by association the true characteristics of the population of interest).[6] Third, members of the sample should be "randomly selected" from the population of interest. Random selection ensures that all members of the population have an equal opportunity to be selected for inclusion in the research sample.[4,7,8] Fourth, members of the sample should be selected from the population of interest in an "unbiased" manner.[4,9] Psychologists must not allow their biases to influence the selection of sample members (e.g. purposefully selecting only those members of a population of interest who are likely to provide responses that will support a specific research hypothesis or a desired study outcome). Finally, the research sample must be "sufficient in size" to detect meaningful relationships that exist between variables of interest, significant differences between groups within the population, and significant changes in members of the population that result from exposure to a treatment, intervention, or personal experience.[1,3,4]

Psychologists can use the information gathered through survey research for a variety of purposes. These purposes may include: (a) the creation of a detailed, descriptive profile of the characteristics of a population of interest,[2,8,10] (b) identification of meaningful trends occurring between different points in time within a population,[1,2,9] (c) analysis of the relationships which exist between variables of interest and the nature of these relationships,[1,2] (d) identification of the similarities and differences that exist between the different subgroups within a population,[2,11] (e) the prediction of future behavior and/or social outcomes,[4,12] (f) the testing of specific research hypotheses and/or theories,[2,10] (g) the assessment of attitudes toward important social issues that exist within a population,[3,9,12] (h) the evaluation of the effectiveness of organizations that provide services to the members of a population (e.g. schools; health care organizations; social services; law enforcement; utilities),[1,2] and (i) the evaluation of how satisfied the members of a population are with the products they buy and the quality of service they receive as consumers.[8,12] This list illustrates the numerous ways in which psychologists can use the information gathered through survey research to achieve a variety of research goals and objectives. Clearly, survey research provides psychologists with a tool they can use to answer a wide range of questions they have about human behavior.

Types of Surveys Used By Psychologists

In survey research, there are a variety of methods psychologists can use to ask members of a population specific questions of interest. These methods can be classified into 3 general categories: (a) paper-and-pencil surveys, (b) interviews, and (c) electronic surveys.

Paper-and-Pencil Surveys

One method psychologists can use to survey the members of a population of interest is to provide them with a paper-and-pencil survey (i.e. questionnaire) that contains specific questions of interest. The 3 types of paper-and-pencil surveys commonly used by psychologists are mail surveys, in-person surveys, and drop-off surveys. When conducting a *"mail survey,"*[2,3,4] the psychologists will initially send members of the research sample a paper-and-pencil copy of the survey accompanied by a letter of introduction which explains: (a) who is conducting the study, (b) why the study is being conducted, and (c) the amount of time they have to complete the survey and to mail it back to the psychologists conducting the study.[3,4,13] After some time has passed, psychologists will then send out a follow-up letter which reminds sample members about the survey they received in the mail and once again invites them to complete the survey and return it by the specified deadline.[3,4,13] Finally, as the deadline for completing the survey approaches, psychologists will send out a second wave of surveys. This second wave of surveys provides those members of the research sample who may have lost, misplaced, forgotten, and/or thrown away the first copy of the survey they received in the mail with a final opportunity to participate in the research study.[3,4,11]

There are several strengths associated with a mail survey. First, they are an inexpensive way to collect information from a large number of population members.[1,2] Second, members of the research sample can complete the survey at their own pace in the comfort of their homes.[4,8,14] Third, members of the research sample may be more willing to answer questions of a personal and/or sensitive nature that they might not be willing to answer in a more personal face-to-face or telephone interview.[2,8,14] Fourth, mail surveys provide psychologists with an opportunity to access and collect information from members of the population in geographic locations that fall outside the area their resources would normally allow them to access in person.[3,13] Finally, the mail survey eliminates the potential for experimenter bias to influence survey responses because members of the research sample have no direct interaction with the psychologists conducting the research study.[14]

There are also several potential weaknesses associated with the mail survey. First, low response rates are common for surveys conducted via the mail.[2,3,13,14] Second, when conducting mail surveys, psychologists must be patient as it can take some time for a sufficient number of surveys to be returned to allow for a meaningful analysis of survey responses. Third, for a mail survey to acquire information that can be used to answer questions about a population of interest, members of the research sample must have the reading, language, and cognitive abilities to be able to complete the survey accurately and without assistance.[2,8] Finally, the members of the research sample motivated enough to complete and return the survey may differ in meaningful ways from those members of the research sample who choose not to complete and return the survey. This would raise serious concerns regarding the extent to which the research sample is representative of the larger population.[3,4,15]

Some paper-and-pencil surveys are administered directly to the members of a population of interest and are known as *"in-person surveys."*[1,4,8] In some cases, the survey is administered to one member of the research sample at a time (i.e. individual administration). In other cases, the survey is administered to groups of sample members (i.e. group administration).[8,16] In either case, the members of the research sample are brought to a specified location and receive a paper-and-pencil copy of the survey directly from the psychologists who are conducting the research study. Members of the research sample complete the survey in the presence of the psychologists and return the survey directly to them when they have finished providing their responses to the questions contained in the survey.

Administering a paper-and-pencil survey directly to the members of the research sample has several advantages. First, psychologists are able to collect information from members of the population quickly.[1,4,8] Unlike a mail survey, psychologists do not have to wait for members of the research sample to return their completed surveys at some later point in time. Second, since members of the research sample complete the survey in the presence of the psychologists who are conducting the research study, they can receive assistance if they encounter any difficulties in reading, comprehending, or interpreting the questions they are asked on the survey.[1,8,16] Finally, the psychologists conducting the research study can observe the members of the research sample as they complete the survey. This allows them to assess the amount of time it took members of the research sample to complete the survey, whether or not they read all questions thoroughly before providing their responses, and their level of interest and/or effort throughout the survey process.

There are also several potential disadvantages associated with administering a paper-and-pencil survey directly to the members of the research sample. First, the loss of anonymity may make members of the research sample hesitant to provide information on the survey; especially when the information is personal and/or sensitive in nature.[4,17] Second, since the members of the research sample complete the survey in the presence of the psychologists who are conducting the research study, there is a possibility the psychologist's presence and/or behavior could influence the manner in which sample members respond on the survey (e.g. the psychologists could make comments in the presence of the members of the research sample that would encourage them to respond in such a way as to help them achieve their desired research outcome). Finally, when completing a survey in a group setting, the dynamics occurring within the group (e.g. levels of compliance, commitment, responsiveness) may influence (positively or negatively) the level of effort and commitment displayed by the individual members of the research sample during the survey process.[4,17]

The third type of paper-and-pencil survey known as a *"drop off survey,"*[16,17] combines some of the elements of both the mail survey and the in-person survey. In a drop-off survey, individuals receive a paper-and-pencil survey directly from the psychologists conducting the research study. When studying members of a community, psychologists will personally deliver the paper-and-pencil surveys to their homes.[16,17] When studying an organization, psychologists will personally deliver paper-and-pencil surveys to employees at their places of employment.[17] The survey recipients are then given the opportunity to complete the survey on their own time and at their own pace. Survey recipients are given the contact information for the psychologists conducting the study in the event they have questions regarding the survey or need assistance in completing the survey. When they have completed their surveys, sample members can: (a) mail the survey back to the psychologists at a specified address, (b) drop the survey off directly to the psychologists at a specified location, (c) drop the survey off at a secure collection site (e.g. "drop box") where it will be picked up by psychologists at a later point in time for analysis, or (d) give the survey directly to the psychologists when they return to their homes or places of employment to pick up the completed surveys.[17] The multiple drop off options allow members of the research sample to return their completed surveys in the manner that is most convenient and which makes them the most comfortable. The availability of multiple drop off options is likely to increase the response rate for the survey.[16,17]

Interviews

Rather than collect information via a paper-and-pencil survey, psychologists can collect information about a population of interest by having members of the research sample take part in an interview. During the interview, individual members of the research sample are asked to provide verbal responses to a series of predetermined questions that are posed to them by a trained interviewer. When conducting survey research, psychologists use multiple types of interviews including face-to-face interviews, telephone interviews, focus group interviews, and computer-assisted interviewing. In a *"face-to-face interview,"* members of the research sample take part in a one-on-one interview with a trained interviewer. The interviewer, who may or may not be one of the psychologists who are conducting the research study, asks the members of the research sample to answer the same set of predetermined questions and records their responses to these questions (e.g. video, audio, written notes) for later quantitative or qualitative analysis.[1,2,3]

The main strengths of the face-to-face interview arise from the relationships that develop between the interviewer and individual members of the research sample. When an interviewer is able to establish a rapport with sample members and can gain their trust, a face-to-face interview can yield open, honest, and in-depth responses to the questions contained on the survey. Sample members are also more likely to be willing to disclose information of a personal and/or sensitive nature to an interviewer they trust and feel comfortable talking with.[1,2,8] In addition, in face-to-face interviews, there is an opportunity for the trained interviewer to ask follow-up questions if they need additional information or need to clarify a response provided by a sample member.[3,8] A face-to-face interview has the potential to be a natural, lively discussion between two people who feel comfortable with one another; an experience that can be far more enjoyable than the impersonal experience of completing a paper-and-pencil survey by oneself.

The face-to-face interview also has several potential weaknesses that psychologists need to consider. First, face-to-face interviewing can be expensive and time-consuming depending on the number of interviews that are conducted.[1,3,13] Second, sample members may be hesitant to disclose personal information for fear that their responses are being "judged" by the interviewer (i.e. evaluation apprehension).[2,3,11] Third, characteristics of the interviewer may influence the amount and type of information members of the research sample are willing to disclose about themselves to an interviewer[2,3,4] (e.g. male sample members may feel uncomfortable responding to questions of a sensitive nature when they are posed to them by a female interviewer). Finally, face-to-face interviews are subject to interviewer bias[1,3,4,13] (e.g. interviewers may pose questions differently to different individuals or pose questions in a way that increases the likelihood of eliciting the desired responses from sample members) and experimenter bias (e.g. psychologists conducting the research study interpret interview responses provided by members of the research sample in a way that increases the likelihood of supporting a favored hypothesis or achieving a desired study outcome).[1,4]

A second type of interview that can be used by psychologists to collect information from the members of a population of interest is the *"telephone interview."* In a telephone interview study, each member of the research sample receives a telephone call from a trained interviewer (who may or may not be one of the psychologists conducting the study). During the interview, the trained interviewer reads a set of predetermined questions and records the responses to these questions.[1,3,4] An important decision that psychologists must make when conducting a telephone interview study is how they will determine which members of a population will be selected for inclusion in the research sample and take part in a telephone interview. There are 2 approaches that are commonly used by psychologists to select the members of their research sample. These 2 approaches are: (a) random selection from a membership list and (b) random digit dialing.

For some populations of interest, there is publicly available information that can be used by psychologists to acquire the names and contact information for all members of a population.[18] For example: (a) an Experimental Psychologist interested in studying the methods Psychology professors are using to teach a course in Research Methods could access the websites of all the Universities in her state and use University and Departmental directories to acquire the names and contact information for all the Psychology professors in the state who teach a course in Research Methods, (b) a Political Psychologist interested in studying the views of politicians toward important issues facing the residents of his state could acquire the names and contact information for all members of the House of Representatives and Senate from the Office of the Governor, and (c) an Educational Psychologist interested in studying the attitudes of school principals toward year-round schooling could acquire the names and contact information for all school principals within her county from the Board of Education. Once psychologists have acquired the membership list for their population of interest, they will then randomly select the desired number of population members for inclusion in their research sample. Those individuals selected for inclusion in the research sample will then receive a telephone call from a trained interviewer in which they will be invited to take part in a telephone interview.

In "random digit dialing,"[2,3,4] psychologists first select the geographic areas within which they want to conduct their telephone interview study. Next, they randomly select a sample of area codes from these geographic areas. Then, they determine how many telephone interviews they would like to conduct within each of the randomly selected area codes. Finally, they use a random numbers table or a computer-based random numbers generator to generate a list of the desired number of telephone numbers within each of the randomly selected area codes (e.g. 500 randomly generated telephone numbers within the 518 and 914 area codes). Those individuals associated with the randomly generated telephone numbers are then selected for inclusion in the research sample and will receive a telephone call from a trained interviewer in which they will be invited to take part in a telephone interview. During these telephone interviews, the interviewer reads a predetermined set of questions to the individuals and then records the responses to these questions. But why don't psychologists simply get access to telephone books for their randomly selected area codes and select a random sample of telephone numbers from these phone books? The answer is that randomly selecting telephone numbers from a phone book can be problematic since some members of the population (i.e. individuals living within the randomly selected area codes) have unlisted landline and/or mobile phone numbers and can't be selected for inclusion in the research sample. The process of random digit dialing, by being able to generate all possible telephone numbers within selected area codes, ensures that all members of selected area code populations who own a phone (i.e. listed and unlisted landline and mobile phones) have an equal opportunity to be selected for inclusion in the research sample.[2,3,4]

There are several advantages to using telephone interviews to acquire information from the members of a population. First, since most individuals own a telephone, psychologists have access to a large percentage of the members of a population.[11,13,14] Second, telephone interviews allow psychologists to access members of a population residing in distant geographic locations.[8] Third, since telephone interviews are often short in length (i.e. 10–20 minutes), large numbers of interviews can be conducted over a short period of time.[3,8] Fourth, interviews that are conducted by telephone provide psychologists with immediate feedback from the members of the research sample. Fifth, in telephone interviews there is an opportunity for the interviewer to ask probing, follow-up, and clarification questions to get the most accurate information from members of the research sample.[2,3,14] Finally, a trained interviewer has the ability to encourage individuals who were prepared to decline the invitation to take part in a phone interview to consent to participate in the research study.[6,9] This will increase the response rate and potentially increase the extent to which the research sample is representative of the population.

There are also several potential disadvantages associated with the telephone interview. First, there are some members of populations of interest who do not own a landline telephone and cannot be selected for inclusion in the research sample.[2,3,8,9] This can be problematic if the individuals who don't own a landline phone would have provided different responses from the individuals who do own landline phones. This can raise questions about the representativeness of the research sample. Second, telephone interviews may be perceived by sample members as an intrusion into their personal lives.[3,4,8,13] To protect their privacy, the members of the research sample may screen telephone calls or refuse to answer telephone calls from unknown numbers (i.e. such as the unknown number of the psychologists conducting the study). Third, individuals may be distracted by people and activities occurring in their homes during a telephone interview (e.g. children, conversations, televisions) which could affect their level of attention to interview questions. Fourth, there are some members of a population of interest who have busy schedules or who have non-traditional work schedules who may be very difficult to reach by telephone during normal calling times.[6,8,11] Fifth, since psychologists try to limit the length of telephone interviews, this places restrictions on the types of questions interviewers can ask.[3,8,16] Sixth, as in the face-to-face interview, responses provided by sample members are likely to be influenced by the relationship they develop with the interviewer.[3] Finally, it is easier for members of the research sample to end a telephone interview by hanging up the phone than it is to end a face-to-face interview being conducted in the physical presence of an interviewer.[3,8,9]

The main weaknesses of both the face-to-face and telephone interview is the potential for the responses of the members of the research sample to be influenced by: (a) the relationship that develops between the interviewer and the interviewee and (b) bias introduced by the manner in which the interviewer asks questions, elicits responses, interprets responses, and conducts the interview. One way of addressing these weaknesses is to completely remove interviewers from the interview process. This can be done through the use of an interviewing technique known as the *"computer-assisted web interview."*[17,18,20] In a computer-assisted web interview, members of a population of interest use a computer to type in responses to a series of interview questions rather than providing verbal responses to questions posed by trained interviewers. To conduct a computer-assisted self interview study, psychologists create a set of interview questions and post them to an online location that can be accessed by the members of the population of interest (via a personal or public computer). When members of the population access the interview questions, they first read a letter of introduction[18] explaining: (a) who is conducting the study, (b) why the research study is being conducted, (c) the safeguards established to ensure their anonymity and the confidentiality of the responses they provide, and (d) the date after which they will no longer be able to access the interview questions. Once they begin the study, they are guided through the interview process by a series of instructional pages that provide answers to the more common questions they might have while completing the interview. In addition, they can access help menus if additional questions arise.[18] Error messages will appear on their computer screens in the event they make an error when typing in a response to an interview question or attempting to navigate their way through the interview. When they have completed the interview, they are provided with instructions as to how to submit their completed interview responses. The entire interview process is completed without any interaction between members of the population of interest and the psychologists conducting the research study.[17,18,20]

The main strength of the computer-assisted self-interview is the anonymity it provides to the members of a population of interest who take part in the interview process.[17] By allowing the population members to remain anonymous, a computer-assisted self-interview may increase the likelihood that population members will provide honest responses to the interview questions and be willing to respond to questions of a personal and/or sensitive nature. Furthermore, population members no longer have to fear how their responses to interview questions might be "judged" or evaluated by an interviewer.[17,20] The computer-assisted self-interview can be less expensive than a face-to-face or phone interview since no financial resources need to be devoted to employing or training interviewers.[17,18] Computer-assisted self-interview programs can be designed in such a way that they save psychologists time during the data entry and data analysis phases of their research studies by allowing them to download the interview responses in a format that can be immediately used to conduct various quantitative or qualitative analyses.[17,18,20] Finally, by being able to post the interview questions on an online site that can be accessed by individuals located throughout the world, psychologists who conduct a computer-assisted self-interview study can acquire large research samples and gather a large amount of information they can use to answer questions about a population of interest.[20]

While the computer-assisted self-interview does provide some advantages over the face-to-face interview and telephone interview, there are some potential weaknesses associated with this type of interview. For instance, the individuals who participate in a computer-assisted self-interview study are more likely to be the members of a population who have more technological knowledge and experience. If these individuals differ in meaningful ways from those members of the population who lack technological knowledge or expertise, this could raise questions about the extent to which the research sample is representative of the population.[18,20] In addition, there is the possibility that members of the research sample could encounter: (a) technical difficulties or (b) have difficulty reading, comprehending, or interpreting the meaning of interview questions when completing a computer-assisted self-interview. Since there is no interviewer available to provide assistance to the members of the research sample, they must rely on the instructions and help provided by the computer-based interviewing program. If the instructions or help provided by the program are not sufficient, members of the research sample are likely to exit the interview and drop out of the research study.[18,20] As the rate of "drop outs" increases, the response rate for the interview will decrease, which in turn, can influence the extent to which the research sample is representative of the population of interest.

While both face-to-face interviews and telephone interviews with individual population members are conducted by a trained interviewer, psychologists can conduct *"focus groups"*[1,8,13] run by a trained moderator if they are interested in interviewing a group of population members. When psychologists conduct a focus group, they bring together a group of individuals who are all members of a population of interest. The individuals in the group may have been randomly selected from the population or they may be those members of a population who were willing to volunteer to participate in the focus group. When the focus group has been assembled, a trained moderator (who may be or may not be one of the psychologists conducting the research study) will ask the group to respond to a series of predetermined questions.[1,13] What follows is an open and interactive discussion in which all members of the group are encouraged to provide their individual responses to the questions being asked by the moderator. Members of the group are encouraged to talk with one another and build upon each other's responses to questions. As the group members provide their responses, the moderator can ask additional probing questions, ask for clarification of responses, and ask additional questions that were not on the original list of questions if the group discussion proceeds in an interesting or unanticipated direction that may provide information of value to the psychologists conducting the research study.[8,21] Throughout the focus group, the moderator and/or a team of trained note-takers attempt to create a written summary of group member's responses to the moderator's questions that can be analyzed at a later point in time by the psychologists conducting the study.[8,16] In the written summary, group members are not identified by name nor linked in any identifiable way with their responses.

There are several reasons why psychologists use focus groups to gather information from the members of a population of interest. First, focus groups can be very effective in generating a large number of ideas or responses to specific questions of interest.[8,16,21] Second, the interaction and the free and open exchange of ideas among focus group members can often lead to creative responses to interview questions that may not have been generated by individuals interviewed individually.[1,8,21] Third, focus groups produce immediate feedback that can be used to answer questions about the larger population of interest. Fourth, during a focus group, the members of a population of interest have an opportunity to share and compare their opinions, experiences, and responses to specific interview questions with one another within a controlled and supportive environment.[21] This type of environment is likely to enhance the quality, depth, and honesty of the information provided by the members of the group. Finally, the quality and research value of the information produced by a focus group can be enhanced by an effective moderator.[1,8,21] An effective moderator will keep members of the group focused on the specific questions of interest and can use follow-up and clarification questions to gather information that is pertinent to the specific questions psychologists are attempting to answer about a population of interest.

There are also several reasons why psychologists must carefully consider whether a focus group is the most effective method of interviewing for gathering the information they seek from the members of a population of interest. First, since most focus groups are typically small in size (5–10 participants), there is a potential that the members of the focus group are not representative of the population from which they were selected. In addition, there is the potential the interview responses provided by the focus group members will not generalize to the larger population of interest.[1,21] Second, the quality of the information generated by a focus group is highly dependent on the quality of the focus group moderator.[8] If the moderator is ineffective, members of a focus group may spend a large amount of their time discussing irrelevant topics and ultimately provide information that is of little value to the research study. Third, there is a potential for focus group discussions to be dominated by a small number of group members whose responses may not be reflective of the views of the larger group.[1,8,21] Fourth, not all members of a population are well suited to participate in a focus group. Individuals who are shy, non-assertive, or who do not feel comfortable answering questions of a personal and/ or sensitive nature in a group would not be comfortable or effective in a focus group setting.[21] Finally, the responses provided to the open-ended questions asked during a focus group can be difficult to analyze and require psychologists to be knowledgeable in the area of qualitative analysis.[1,8]

Electronic Surveys

With the on-going technological advances occurring within society, it is not surprising that psychologists have begun using this technology as a tool for conducting different types of research including survey research.[5] Through use of the current technology, psychologists can survey the members of a population of interest through a variety of "electronic media." Examples of the "electronic media" that have been used by psychologists to conduct survey research include the Internet and personal electronic communication devices owned by members of the population of interest (e.g. personal computers, cell phones, tablet devices).[1,3,4]

When psychologists use the Internet to conduct survey research, they create a survey and post it to an online web location that can be accessed by the members of a population of interest. Some psychologists post their survey to web locations operated by companies that specialize in the administration of online surveys (e.g. SurveyMonkey; eSurveyPro; SurveyGizmo).[5] Some psychologists post their surveys on their personal web pages or the web pages of the companies they are affiliated with (e.g. organizations, colleges/universities, agencies).[4] Some psychologists obtain permission to post their survey on the websites of organizations (e.g. community groups, professional societies) that members of the population of interest are affiliated with.[1,3,4] Finally, with the recent rise in the use of social media, some psychologists post links to their surveys on social media sites frequented by members of the population of interest.[1,2,] When the population members are connected to the Internet and access these various web locations, they will have the opportunity to access the survey and take part in the research study.

Psychologists can also provide the members of the population of interest access to their survey through the personal electronic devices they own. By obtaining the e-mail addresses of population members, psychologists can send an e-mail message that contains a link to the survey that they can then access through their personal computers, cell phones or tablet devices.[1,4] In some cases, e-mail addresses of population members are publicly available and can be acquired at no cost to the psychologists who are conducting the research study.[18] In other cases, the e-mail addresses of population members are not publicly available and may need to be purchased from organizations who make this contact information available to researchers (e.g. employers who provide researchers with access to employee contact information, professional associations who provide researchers access to the contact information of its membership, businesses who provide researchers access to the contact information of their customers).[18]

Once population members have gained access to the survey via the Internet or through their personal electronic devices (e.g. personal computers, cell phones, tablet devices), they will follow the same process used in a computer-assisted web-interview. Participants will first read a letter of introduction explaining: (a) who is conducting the survey, (b) the purpose of the survey, (c) the safeguards put in place to protect their anonymity and the confidentiality of the responses they provide, and (d) the deadline for submitting the survey. After they have provided consent to participate in the study, population members will follow the instructions provided by the survey program to successfully complete the survey. Throughout the survey, help menus are available if population members have specific questions they need answered in order to complete the survey. When they have completed the survey, the survey program will provide instructions as to how to submit the completed survey. The entire process is completed without any interaction between population members and the psychologists conducting the research study. It is up to population members to independently navigate their way through the survey program and to successfully complete the survey.[2,5,17]

There are several advantages associated with electronic surveys. First, electronic surveys allow psychologists to gather information from the members of a population of interest who are located throughout the world.[3,4,5] Electronic surveys have eliminated geographic barriers faced by survey researchers before the emergence of the Internet. Second, population members can be given access to an electronic survey and return their completed surveys at high rates of speed.[1,4,5] This can reduce the amount of time it takes for psychologists to collect the information they need to answer questions about a population of interest. Third, electronic surveys offer psychologists an inexpensive way to collect information from a large number of members of a population of interest.[5,17,22] Fourth, if proper safeguards are put in place to protect the anonymity of population members and the confidentiality of their survey responses, electronic surveys can gather honest, in-depth, and valuable information from the members of a population; even in response to survey questions of a personal or sensitive nature.[18,23] Finally, psychologists can download responses from an electronic survey directly into computer programs designed specifically for the purpose of conducting statistical analyses on research data (e.g. SPSS; SAS; EXCEL).[5,17,18,22] This can save psychologists a significant amount of time and resources they normally have to devote to the data entry phase of their research.

There are also several potential weaknesses associated with the electronic survey. First, not all members of a population have access to the Internet or personal electronic devices.[3,4,18] As a result, individuals from lower economic groups, older individuals, and individuals living in rural areas may be underrepresented in research samples of psychologists conducting web-based survey research.[5,23] Individuals who lack technological knowledge or who do not use technology in their lives are also likely to be under-represented in electronic survey studies.[18] Second, given the recent incidents of security breaches involving electronic data stored by retailers, financial institutions, insurance agencies, and government agencies, population members may be wary of providing information via an electronic survey for fear that their anonymity and confidentiality will be compromised.[18,23] Third, it is easier for the members of the research sample to end their involvement in an electronic survey study (i.e. logging off Internet, deleting e-mail containing the link to the survey) than it is to drop out of a survey study being conducted in the physical presence of an interviewer. Finally, when psychologists conduct an electronic survey study in which survey respondents remain anonymous, they can never be 100% sure who is actually completing the surveys.[1,3,22,23] As a result, psychologists may be unaware they are answering questions about a population of interest based on data provided by individuals who are not even population members.

As the members of a society consume the various goods and services available to them, the companies and business establishments who manufacture, sell, and provide these goods and services are interested in assessing consumers' satisfaction toward the goods and services they consume. Consumer survey research provides an excellent perspective into the world of survey research given that psychologists who conduct consumer survey research rely on multiple survey methods including paper-and-pencil surveys, interviews, and electronic surveys. Psychologists who conduct consumer survey research design, administer, and analyze surveys and interviews that fall into 2 general categories: (a) point-of-purchase surveys and (b) post-purchase surveys.

Point-of-purchase surveys are designed to collect information from consumers as they purchase a product or receive a service.[24,25] Some *"point-of-purchase surveys"* are administered in the form of a paper-and-pencil survey. For example, when consumers dine at a restaurant, they may be asked by their server to fill out a customer comment card on which they provide written comments describing their satisfaction with their meals and the customer service they received. Some point-of-purchase surveys are administered in the form of an interview. As an example, a sales manager at a car dealership could interview a customer who just purchased a new car for his family to assess the customer's satisfaction with the salesperson who sold him the car and the amount of money he received for his trade-in. As another example, a grocery store manager could conduct an *"intercept interview"*[17,24,25] with a customer shopping in the store. In an *"intercept interview,"* the store manager would wait for a customer to select an item from the store shelves and place it in his/her shopping cart. The store manager would then "intercept" the customer in the aisle of the store and conduct an interview to determine why the customer made the decision to purchase the product he/she chose. Finally, some point-of-purchase surveys are administered in the form of electronic surveys. For example, a customer who has just purchased an engagement ring at a jewelry store could be asked by a store manager to sit down at an *"in-store kiosk"*[16] and complete an online survey in which he evaluates his shopping experience at the store.

Post-purchase surveys are designed to assess consumers' satisfaction with the products they purchased and the services they received at some later point in time.[26] Some post-purchase surveys are administered in the form of a paper-and-pencil survey. For example, a woman who was treated in a hospital's emergency room after suffering a heart attack could receive a paper-and-pencil *"customer satisfaction survey"* in the mail which would provide her the opportunity to tell the hospital how satisfied she was with the care she received. Some post-purchase surveys are administered in the form of a telephone interview.[26] For example, after a man buys a new lawnmower from a home improvement store, a representative of the store may call the man and invite him to participate in a telephone interview in which he will be asked questions about his satisfaction with the performance of his new mower. Finally, some post-purchase surveys are administered in the form of an electronic survey. Access to an electronic survey can be provided to consumers via product receipts, labels applied to product packaging, or e-mail messages sent to consumers' personal computers, cell phones, and tablet devices.[26] For example, after attending a national research conference, a psychologist may be sent an e-mail message from the hotel where he stayed during the conference containing a link to an online survey. By accessing the online survey, the psychologist could provide the hotel with feedback regarding the quality of its rooms, fitness facility, and spa.

Clearly, psychologists who conduct consumer survey research must be able to conduct a variety of different types of surveys. They must also have the ability to weigh the strengths and weaknesses associated with different types of surveys in order to determine the types of surveys that will: (a) provide organizations with the information they need to develop better products and provide higher quality services to their customers and (b) generate a high rate of responses from consumers. To increase the response rates for both point-of-purchase surveys and post-purchase surveys, consumers may be offered incentives (e.g. store coupons, gift cards, entrance into raffles for a variety of prizes) in exchange for their participation in the survey process.[26] For businesses and organizations whose survival depends on the satisfaction of their customers, the cost of these financial incentives are a small price to pay for the knowledge they stand to gain with respect to (a) the behavior and decision-making processes of consumers and (b) consumer perceptions of various product features and dimensions of customer service.

Types of Survey Questions

When psychologists conduct survey research, they use many different types of questions to gather information from the members of a population of interest. The different question types can be classified into 2 categories: (a) open-ended questions and (b) close-ended questions.

Open-Ended Questions

An open-ended question has two general characteristics. First, there are no restrictions on how the individual completing the survey responds to the questions. Second, individuals completing the survey must provide an in-depth response to the question.[1,2,3] This in-depth response could be in the form of a list, several sentences, or even an essay length response. A one-word response, or a response containing only a few words, will not adequately answer the question. Below are some examples of open-ended questions.

Question 1: How did you and your wife first meet?

Question 2: How did you feel when you found out you were going to be a father?

Question 3: What can society do to prevent teen substance use?

Question 4: Tell me about a decision you made during your life that you would change if you could go back in time?

Close-Ended Questions

A close-ended question provides the individual completing the survey with a set of potential response options from which he/she must choose the response (or responses) that, from his/her individual perspective, best answers the question.[1,2,3] There are a variety of close-ended question types that psychologists can use to gather information from the members of a population of interest.

Some close-ended questions are designed to have the individuals completing the survey describe themselves and their lives. *Demographic questions*[1,4,22] ask the individuals completing a survey to describe their personal characteristics (e.g. sex, race). *Psychographic questions*[27] ask the individuals completing the survey to describe their lifestyles and the events in their lives that have shaped who they are as individuals (e.g. interests, group memberships, life experiences). Examples of demographic and psychographic questions appear below.

Demographic:	What is your current marital status?
	How old are you?
	What is the highest level of education you have completed?
Psychographic:	Have you ever been convicted of a crime?
	What are your favorite things to do in your free time?
	What types of jobs have you had during your life?

Some close-ended questions provide the individuals completing the survey with a limited number of response options from which they must choose the one response that best answers the question. A *dichotomous question*[16,22,28] provides individuals completing the survey with only 2 possible response options. Some common response options for dichotomous questions include yes/no, agree/disagree, and true/false response options. A *multiple choice question*[2,27] provides individuals completing the survey with 3 or more possible response options. Some examples of dichotomous and multiple choice questions appear below.

Dichotomous Question	**Multiple Choice Question (Single Response)**
Do you believe in ghosts?	Which of the following vegetables would you least like to eat?
(a) Yes (b) No	(a) Lettuce (d) Cucumbers (b) Carrots (e) Cauliflower (c) Broccoli

There are also multiple choice questions which allow individuals to select more than one response option when answering a question. In these *multiple choice questions*,[2,16] individuals completing the survey are provided with 3 or more possible response options from which they can choose as many response options as are applicable for them to answer the question. An example of this type of multiple choice question appears below.

Multiple Choice Question (Multiple Responses Allowed)

What aspects of your life are you satisfied with? (Check all that apply)

(a) My Marriage   (d) My Job   (g) My Health
(b) My Appearance   (e) My Car   (h) My Energy Level
(c) My Faith   (f) My House   (i) My Golf Game

There are some close-ended questions in which the individuals completing the survey are asked to place a set of response options into a rank-ordered list. In these *ranking questions*,[2,16,27] individuals completing the survey will read a set of response options and then rank the response options on the basis of perceived importance or personal preference. An example of a ranking question appears below.

Ranking Question

Below is a list of factors people consider when buying a new car. How would you rank the importance of these factors if you were buying a car? (1 = Most Important Factor; 5 = Least Important Factor).

Rank	Factor	Rank	Factor
_____	Price of the Car	_____	Stereo System
_____	Color of the Car	_____	Gas Mileage
_____	Safety Features		

There are some close-ended questions in which the individuals completing the survey are asked to provide a numerical rating that represents their answer to the question. In these *rating scale questions*,[1,4] individuals completing the survey read each question and then use a specific rating scale provided by the survey designer to provide their numerical rating. These rating scale questions are often used by psychologists to assess population members' attitudes and feelings (and the intensity of these attitudes/feelings) toward a specific question or statement.

Some rating scale questions require individuals completing a survey to use a Likert-scale to provide their numerical rating. A *Likert-scale*[2,3,4] is a 5-point rating scale with descriptive labels at each point along the scale and equal units of measurement between the points along the scale. An example of a rating scale question that uses a Likert-scale appears below.

Rating Scale Question (Likert-scale)

Most teens will drink alcohol before graduating from High School.

1 = Strongly Disagree
2 = Disagree
3 = Neither Disagree/Nor Agree
4 = Agree
5 = Strongly Agree

Some rating scale questions require the individuals completing the survey to use a scale known as a *semantic differential scale* to provide their numerical rating. A semantic differential scale is a 7-point rating scale in which the anchor points on the scale are: (a) bipolar adjectives or (b) contrasting statements.[1,3,16,27] The semantic differential scale has equal units of measurement between the points along the scale. Some examples of rating scale questions that use a semantic differential scale appear below.

Rating Scale Question (Semantic Differential scale)

If asked to describe my coworkers, I would say they are......

Unintelligent 1 2 3 4 5 6 7 Intelligent

Unmotivated 1 2 3 4 5 6 7 Motivated

Some rating scale questions require the individuals completing the survey to use a Stapel scale to provide their numerical ratings. A *Stapel scale*[27] is a 10-point scale with values of –5 and +5 at the anchor points on the scale. There is no 0 value (i.e. no neutral value) on the scale. Where the 0 value would be located is a single adjective or a short statement which describes a characteristic of the target (e.g. person, product/service, situation) being evaluated by the survey question. The positive values on the Stapel scale indicate a greater amount of the characteristic while negative values on the scale indicate a lesser amount of the characteristic. Some examples of rating scale questions that use a Stapel scale appear below.

Rating Scale Question (Stapel scale)

How did our customer service employees handle your customer complaint?

–5 –4 –3 –2 –1 Accurately +1 +2 +3 +4 +5

–5 –4 –3 –2 –1 Courteously +1 +2 +3 +4 +5

There are some close-ended questions in which the individuals completing the survey are provided with a series of response options and are then required to divide 100 points or 100% up among these response options on the basis of their perceived importance or personal preference. These types of questions are known as *continuous sum questions*.[27] They are called continuous sum questions because as the individuals completing the survey assign different point values (or % values) to the response options, a running total (or sum) is computed. When all the response options have been assigned a point (or %) value, the total sum of the points (or %) must equal 100. An example of a continuous sum question appears below.

Continuous Sum Question

As a Professor of Psychology, what percentage of your time would you like to devote to each of these activities during the upcoming Fall semester?

% of time	Activity
_____	Teaching & Advising
_____	Research & Scholarly Activity
_____	University & Community Service
100%	

There are some close-ended questions in which the individuals completing the survey are presented with a series of response options and are asked to indicate which response option they most prefer. Rather than evaluating the response options as a group, they are presented with the response options in pairs. For each *paired comparison*,[15] they indicate which of the 2 response options they prefer. They continue this process until they have evaluated all possible pairs of response options. An example of a paired comparisons questions appears below.

Paired Comparisons Question

For each pair of restaurants below, which restaurant has the best french fries?

McDonald's or Burger King   Wendy's or Burger King
McDonald's or Wendy's   Wendy's or Arby's
McDonald's or Arby's   Arby's or Burger King

There are some close-ended questions designed to determine if individuals completing the survey have the knowledge and/or experience to answer a subsequent question on the survey. These questions are known as *filter or contingency questions*.[16,28] Based on the response to the filter or contingency question, the individuals completing the survey will either answer or bypass the subsequent survey question. An example of a filter or contingency question appears below.

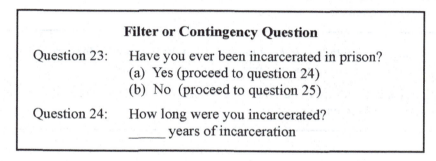

Filter or Contingency Question

Question 23:   Have you ever been incarcerated in prison?
                (a) Yes (proceed to question 24)
                (b) No (proceed to question 25)

Question 24:   How long were you incarcerated?
                _____ years of incarceration

Finally, there are some close-ended questions in which the individuals completing the survey are presented with response options that are images, symbols, and/or pictures rather than verbal descriptions and numerical rating scales. These *non-verbal questions*[1,3] are typically used to allow children, individuals with communication difficulties, and/or individuals with minimal reading skills to respond to survey questions. A non-verbal question appears below.

Non-Verbal Question

Tell me how much you like your teacher?

☺   ☺☺   ☺☺☺   ☺☺☺☺
A   B   C   D

Poorly Structured and Poorly Written Survey Questions

When psychologists develop a survey, they write a variety of types of questions to gather information from the members of a population of interest. The quality of the questions will have a major influence on the quality of the information gathered from the population members. If a survey question is poorly structured and/or poorly written, it can produce responses that can lead psychologists to make inaccurate conclusions about a population of interest. In the table below, you will find a list of different types of poorly structured and/or poorly worded questions which psychologists should attempt to avoid including on a research survey.

Types of Poorly Structured and Poorly Written Survey Questions

1. Questions that use "overly complex language," jargon, or terminology[1,4,8,19,22]

   Example: "Are Psychotherapeutic interventions effective in alleviating the symptomology of a depressive mood state?" (complex language)

   The same question could be asked using much simpler language:

   Example: "Is psychotherapy effective in reducing depression?"

2. Questions that are "leading" (i.e. suggest a desired answer respondents are to give)[2,3,14,30]

   Example: "Over 90% of psychologists now use Cognitive-Behavioral Therapy to treat depression." Do you agree or disagree that Cognitive-Behavioral Therapy is the most effective therapeutic treatment for depression?

3. Questions that are "loaded" (i.e. contain strong emotional words that are designed to make respondents select a response option based on their emotions)[1,2,5,8,28,29]

   Example: "Are you willing to quit smoking in order to avoid the painful death that individuals who die from lung cancer experience?"

---

4. Questions that use "culturally insensitive language" (i.e. reinforce social stereotypes)[6,11]

Example: "What percentage of your state's population consists of old, colored, and handicapped people?"

5. Questions that have "non-mutually exclusive response options" (i.e. a respondent's desired answer falls in more than one of the available response options)[11,30]

Example: "How long do you think a couple should be engaged before they get married?"

(a) 1–6 months   (d) 18–24 months
(b) 6–12 months   (e) 24 months or more
(c) 12–18 months

6. Questions that have "non-exhaustive response options" (i.e. there is not a response option available for every response participants could make to the question)[11,14,29,30]

Example: "How many children do you have?"

(a) 1 child   (d) 4 children
(b) 2 children   (e) 5 children
(c) 3 children

There is no response option available to respondents who have 0 children or who have more than 5 children.

7. Questions that are "double-barreled" (i.e. ask about 2 topics in a single question)[1,2,3,4,8,29,30]

Example: "How long has it been since you had an eye examine and your teeth cleaned?"

8. Questions that contain a "double negative" (i.e. contain 2 negatives which cancel each other out and create a positive statement)[2,3,8,14]

Example: "I believe when you see someone that needs help you should not do nothing." This statement would imply that if you see someone who needs help you should do something (take positive action).

9. Questions that use too many "acronyms" or acronyms respondents are unfamiliar with[11]

Example: "When you ask someone to send information to your computer, do you prefer they send the information as a PDF, JPEG, RTF, GIF, or ZIP file?"

10. Questions that are "vague" (i.e. don't provide sufficient information to respond)[1,3,4,13,22,29]

Example: "What did you think of the comment the boss made during the meeting?" To answer the question, the respondents would need to know what comment from which meeting they were evaluating.

11. Questions that have "built-in assumptions" (i.e. assume the respondent has had a specific experience that will allow him/her to respond to the question)[3,22,29]

   Example: "How would you compare the quality of Stephen King's current novel with the novel he published last year?" This question has the "built-in assumption" that the respondents have read the novel Stephen King published the previous year.

12. Questions respondents are "unlikely to know" due to the specificity of the question or to a lack of access to the thoughts of others[5,6,22,29]

   Example: "How many times in your life have you said "I love you" to your spouse?"

13. Questions that are overly personal or threatening to the respondents[3,4,5,6]

   Example: "Can you describe what happened when you were sexually assaulted?"

14. Questions that include the words "always" and "never" in their structure[3]

   Example: "My coworkers are always willing to put in extra effort to get the job done."

Surveys as a Method of Research

Survey research is a popular method of research for psychologists interested in learning about, and answering questions about, a population of interest. There are several reasons for the popularity of survey research among psychologists. These reasons include: (a) surveys can be developed quickly and with limited resources, (b) surveys can be a cost-effective way to gather information from a large number of members of a population, (c) surveys allow psychologists to gather information from all the members of a population, regardless of where they are located geographically, (d) surveys can be used for a variety of research purposes including describing the characteristics of a population, assessing the relationships that exist between variables, and evaluating the behavior and attitudes of the members of a population of interest, and (e) surveys can be designed in a number of different formats (e.g. paper-and-pencil, interviews, electronic surveys) which gives psychologists the flexibility to conduct survey research in the manner that gives them the best opportunity to collect the information they need to answer questions about a population of interest.

Although survey research is a popular method of research among psychologists, there are characteristics of survey research that can potentially lead to erroneous conclusions being drawn about a population of interest. First, the data gathered in survey research is self-report data. The quality of the information gathered through survey research is therefore reliant on the willingness of members of a population to provide honest, reliable, and potentially personal and/or sensitive information about themselves. Second, the quality of the data gathered during survey research is influenced by the extent to which all members of a population of interest have an equal chance to be selected for inclusion in a research sample. Third, the quality of data gathered during survey research is influenced by the extent to which the research sample is representative of the larger population of interest. Finally, the quality of data gathered during survey research is influenced by the response rate to the survey and the characteristics of those members of the population of interest who do not respond to the survey. Together, these factors influence the extent to which the information supplied by the members of the research sample will generalize to the larger population of interest.

EXERCISE 11A

Selecting an Appropriate Survey Methodology

There are a variety of different types of surveys psychologists can design and administer to gather information from the members of a population of interest. The main challenge faced by psychologists is to select a survey method that: (a) encourages population members to provide honest, accurate, reliable, and potentially personal and/or sensitive information about themselves and (b) provides the best opportunity to collect information from the research sample necessary to answer questions about the larger population of interest. Below are 10 scenarios describing research questions that psychologists would like to answer by conducting survey research. For each of the 10 scenarios, please select the 1 survey method from the list below that you feel would provide the best survey methodology to answer the research question and provide your rationale for your choice in the space provided.

Mail Survey	Focus Group
In-Person Survey (Individual)	Point-of-Purchase Survey
In-Person Survey (Group)	Point-of-Purchase Interview
Drop-Off Survey	Post-Purchase Survey
Face-to-Face Interview	Post-Purchase Interview
Telephone Interview	Internet Survey
Computer-Assisted Web-Interview	

01. A Clinical Psychologist is interested in learning if men and women cope differently with the loss of a child. What method of survey research will allow the Clinical Psychologist to best answer her research question? Why?

Method =

Rationale:

02. An Industrial-Organizational Psychologist is interested in learning from employees whether the management of the mine where they work encourages them to bypass safety procedures to increase the amount of coal that is mined. What method of survey research will allow the Industrial-Organizational Psychologist to best answer his research question? Why?

Method =

Rationale:

03. The Chair of the Psychology Department at a small liberal-arts college is interested in finding out from former students how well their undergraduate degree in Psychology prepared them for a job in the mental health field. What method of survey research will allow the Chair of the Psychology Department to best answer his research question? Why?

Method =

Rationale:

04. A Consumer Psychologist is hired by a local restaurant known for the 40 varieties of hot dogs it serves. The restaurant is interested in learning whether customers like or hate its new "fat free hot dog." What method of survey research will allow the Consumer Psychologist to best answer the restaurant's research question? Why?

Method =

Rationale:

05. A Political Psychologist is hired by a politician to determine whether she is likely to win her upcoming election. Specifically, she wants the Political Psychologist to ask a representative sample of 500 "likely voters" how they plan to vote in the election. Which method of survey research will allow the Political Psychologist to best answer the politician's question? Why?

Method =

Rationale:

06. A Governor is considering whether to sign legislation legalizing same-sex marriage in his state. To help him make his decision, his office hires a Social Psychologist to assess how the residents of his state feel about same-sex marriage. What method of survey research will allow the Social Psychologist to best answer the Governor's question? Why?

Method = [   ]

Rationale:

07. A School Psychologist is interested in learning from students what types of bullying and harassment students experience in the area high schools. What method of survey research will allow the School Psychologist to best answer his research question? Why?

Method = [   ]

Rationale:

08. For the first time in 50 years, there is a surplus in the budget of a large city. The Mayor of the city hires a Community Psychologist to learn from city residents what they would like her to do with the money to improve quality of life in the city. What method of survey research will allow the Community Psychologist to best answer the Mayor's question? Why?

Method =

Rationale:

09. A Sports Psychologist is interested in learning from the coaches of professional sports teams (i.e. basketball, baseball, football, hockey) whether they are aware of athletes on their teams who are currently taking steroids to improve their athletic performance. Which method of survey research will allow the Sports Psychologist to best answer her question? Why?

Method =

Rationale:

10. A Health Psychologist is interested in learning whether there are common demographic and psychographic (i.e. lifestyle) characteristics among "vegetarians." He would like to study a representative sample of 1,000 "vegetarians." Which method of survey research will allow the Health Psychologist to best answer his research question? Why?

Method =

Rationale:

EXERCISE 11B

Identifying Different Types of Survey Questions

When psychologists conduct survey research, they use a variety of question types to gather information from the members of a population of interest. Below are 25 examples of questions that might appear on surveys developed by psychologists who are conducting survey research. For each example, please identify the type of survey question being illustrated from the list below and write your response in the space provided.

Continuous Sum   Multiple Choice (Single Response)   Paired Comparisons
Dichotomous   Multiple Choice (Multiple Response)   Rank Order
Filter/Contingency   Non-Verbal   Semantic Differential
Likert-Scale   Open-Ended   Stapel Scale

01.

> **For each pair of sports below, which sport is the most exciting to watch?**
>
> Boxing or Basketball   Boxing or Tennis   Basketball or Tennis
> Boxing or Footbal   Basketball or Football   Football or Tennis

       Question Type = _____

02.

> **Men are more likely than women to cheat on their spouses?**
>
>   1 = Strongly Disagree
>   2 = Disagree
>   3 = Neither Disagree/Nor Agree
>   4 = Agree
>   5 = Strongly Agree

       Question Type = _____

03.

> **How do you feel about the crime rate in your community?**
>
> Encouraged   1   2   3   4   5   6   7   Discouraged

       Question Type = _____

04.

> Describe the time in your life when you felt the most depressed. What were the circumstances that led to your feelings of depression?

Question Type = _____

05.

> Have you ever driven a motor vehicle under the influence?
>
> (a) No
> (b) Yes
>
> If yes, what substance had you consumed before driving?
>
> (a) Alcohol   (d) Marijuana
> (b) Cocaine   (e) Methamphetamine
> (c) Heroin

Question Type = _____

06.

> Spanking is the best form of discipline for a parent to use.
>
> (a) Agree
> (b) Disagree

Question Type = _____

07.

> Below is a list of physical features that men and women look at when evaluating someone's physical attractiveness. How important are each of these features to you when you evaluate someone's physical attractiveness? (1 = Most Important Feature; 6 = Least Important Feature).
>
> | Rank | Feature | Rank | Feature |
> |------|---------|------|---------|
> | _____ | Hair Color | _____ | Chest |
> | _____ | Eyes | _____ | Legs |
> | _____ | Face | _____ | Buttocks |

Question Type = _____

08.

> **Which of the following college majors is most valuable in today's job market?**
>
> (a) History   (c) English   (e) Psychology   (g) Nursing
> (b) Marketing   (d) Engineering   (f) Philosophy   (h) Mathematics

Question Type = _____

09.

> **As a single mother, what percentage of your time do you devote to each of these activities during a typical week?**
>
> | % of time | Activity |
> |---|---|
> | ____ | Cooking meals |
> | ____ | Cleaning the house |
> | ____ | Transporting my child to activities |
> | ____ | Working at my job |
> | ____ | Sleeping |
> | ____ | Playing with my child |
> | ____ | Dating |
> | **100%** | |

Question Type = _____

10.

> **For each pair of U.S. Presidents below, who was the better President?**
>
> Washington or Lincoln   Lincoln or Kennedy
> Washington or Kennedy   Lincoln or Obama
> Washington or Obama   Kennedy or Obama

Question Type = _____

11.

> **How do you feel about your purchase of a hybrid vehicle?**
>
> Best Decision   1   2   3   4   5   6   7   Worst Decision
> I ever made   I ever made

Question Type = _____

12.

> **Which of the following activities would you like to do before your die?**
> **(Select all that apply)**
>
> (a) Climb a mountain
> (b) Go on an African Safari
> (c) Go bungee jumping
> (d) See the Grand Canyon
> (e) Play golf at St. Andrews
>
> (f) Renew my wedding vows
> (g) Buy an expensive sports car
> (h) Dance at my children's weddings
> (i) Write a novel
> (j) Learn to fly a plane

Question Type = _____

13.

> **In my opinion, the keynote speaker at the Psychology conference was......**
>
> −5 −4 −3 −2 −1 Inspiring +1 +2 +3 +4 +5

Question Type = _____

14.

> **How often do you talk on your cell phone each day?**

Question Type = _____

15.

> **Which of the following activities would you recommend as the most fun activity**
> **for a couple going out on their first date?**
>
> (a) Going to a movie
> (b) Going to a concert
> (c) Going out to dinner
>
> (d) Going to a bar
> (e) Going on a picnic

Question Type = _____

16.

I am the type of person who enjoys being the center of attention.

(a) True
(b) False

Question Type = _____

17.

Did you vote in the most recent presidential election?

(a) No
(b) Yes

If yes, what political party's candidate did you vote for?

(a) Democrat   (d) Green
(b) Libertarian   (e) Independent
(c) Republican   (f) Other

Question Type = _____

18.

When my boss told me that I was being fired, it was..........

–5   –4   –3   –2   –1   Surprising   +1   +2   +3   +4   +5

Question Type = _____

19.

Below are factors that contribute to college failure. If you were given 100 points to divide among the factors (the more points you assign to a factor the more you feel it contributes to failure), how many points would you assign to each factor below?

% of time	Failure factors
_____	Alcohol/Substance Use
_____	Not attending class
_____	Not studying
_____	Low academic ability
_____	No desire to be in college
_____	Homesickness
100%	

Question Type = _____

20.

> **Where do you see yourself 10 years from now? What will you be doing, what will your life be like, and how will your life be different from your current life?**

Question Type = _____

21.

> **How likely is it that scientists will find evidence of intelligent life some-where in the universe within the next 10 years?**
>
> | 1 | 2 | 3 | 4 | 5 |
> |---|---|---|---|---|
> | Extremely Unlikely | Unlikely | Unsure | Likely | Extremely Likely |

Question Type = _____

22.

> Below is a list of some of the most prestigious colleges and universities in the United States. How would you personally rank these colleges and universities based on their level of prestige? (1 = Most Prestigious; 6 = Least Prestigious)
>
> | Rank | Institution | Rank | Institution |
> |------|-------------|------|-------------|
> | _____ | Ohio University | _____ | Marshall University |
> | _____ | SUNY at Oswego | _____ | Plymouth State College |
> | _____ | Dartmouth College | _____ | Harvard University |

Question Type = _____

23.

> **Which of the following types of exercise do you engage in on a regular basis?**
>
> **(Select all that apply)**
>
> | (a) Running | (d) Weight Lifting | (g) Kick Boxing |
> |-------------|--------------------|-----------------|
> | (b) Walking | (e) Yoga | (h) Playing Golf |
> | (c) Playing Tennis | (f) Zumba | (i) Bike Riding |

Question Type = _____

24.

> **What is your gender?**
>
> (a) Male
> (b) Female

Question Type = _____

25.

> **What person has had the greatest positive impact on your life? In what ways did this person impact your life in a positive way?**

Question Type = _____

EXERCISE 11C

Poorly Structured and Poorly Worded Survey Questions

When psychologists conduct survey research, they write a variety of question types to gather information from the members of a population of interest. Below are 25 examples of poorly structured and poorly worded questions that might appear on the surveys developed by psychologists conducting survey research. For each example, please identify the type of poorly structured or poorly worded survey question being illustrated from the list below and write your response in the space provided.

Complex Language	Double-Barreled	Built-In Assumptions
Leading	Double Negatives	Unlikely to Know
Loaded	Acronyms	Overly Personal/Invasive
Culturally Insensitive	Vague	Always/Never
Non-Mutually Exclusive Response Options	Non-Exhaustive Response Options	

01. After you graduate from college, would you prefer to take a managerial job that would require you to move or a non-managerial job that would not require you to move?

> **Poor Question Type =**

02. There is nothing I hate more than when children (i.e. rug rats, ankle biters, snot monsters, spawn, booger eaters, poop factories) sit next to me on an airplane.

> **Poor Question Type =**

03. Would you be willing to pay $100 for a bottle of our miraculous, incredible, phenomenal, and unbelievable advanced formula skin care cream that will make you look young again?

> **Poor Question Type =**

04. When it comes to explaining human behavior, I believe psychologists don't know nothing.

> **Poor Question Type =**

05. In your opinion, how likely is it that the woman who committed that crime last year will be found guilty by a jury of her peers?

> **Poor Question Type =**

06. How many hours of studying did you do from the time you first entered college as an undergraduate Psychology major until the time you earned your Ph.D. in Psychology?

> **Poor Question Type =**

07. Low carb diets have one of the lowest rates of success for people trying to lose weight. When you begin your summer diet so that you can fit into your new bathing suit, how likely are you to go on a low carb diet?

> **Poor Question Type =**

08. What was going through the minds of management when you and your fellow employees voted to officially go on strike?

> **Poor Question Type =**

09. How many minutes does it take you to make your morning commute to work?

   (a) 15–30 minutes   (d) 60–75 minutes
   (b) 30–45 minutes   (e) 75 minutes or more
   (c) 45–60 minutes

> **Poor Question Type =**

10. Can you describe the sexual positions you are your partner most enjoy as a couple?

> **Poor Question Type =**

11. In my opinion, the southern United States will continue to live in the past because of all the country bumpkins, good ol' boys, and hillbillies that live in these states.

> **Poor Question Type =**

12. Are professional athletes from the NFL, NBA, NHL, MLB, or PGA more likely to get arrested for DUI during their professional sports careers?

> **Poor Question Type =**

13. When it comes to the world of Internet dating, I believe that people are never who they claim to be in their dating profiles.

> **Poor Question Type =**

14. In your opinion, is the position of CEO, CIO, CFO, or CLO most important to the level of success achieved by an organization?

> **Poor Question Type =**

15. How would you rate the job being done by the current Chief of Police in your town in the "war on drugs" compared to the former Chief of Police whom she replaced?

> **Poor Question Type =**

16. Would you support the Board of Education's decision to cut funding for the music and sports programs at the local high schools?

> **Poor Question Type =**

17. How many pounds of garbage that eventually ended up in a landfill did you and your family produce in the last 12 months?

> **Poor Question Type =**

18. How many hours a day do you let your children use technology (e.g. cell phones, iPads, iPods, computers, tablet devices)?

(a) 1 hour a day	(d) 4 hours a day
(b) 2 hours a day	(e) 5 hours a day
(c) 3 hours a day	

> **Poor Question Type =**

19. During the course of your lifetime, have you ever had thoughts of committing suicide?

> **Poor Question Type =**

20. When you eat our new 8-cheese pizza, to what extent does it cause the neurotransmitters in your brain to flood into the synaptic gaps, bind to the awaiting receptor sites, and elicit a sensation that your brain interprets as a pleasurable level of arousal?

> **Poor Question Type =**

21. In my opinion, the members of Congress shouldn't do nothing about the gun ownership laws as they currently exist in the United States.

> **Poor Question Type =**

22. How many animals would someone have to have living in her home for you to consider her to be an "animal hoarder"?

    (a) 1–5 animals   (d) 15–20 animals
    (b) 5–10 animals   (e) 20 animals or more
    (c) 10–15 animals

> **Poor Question Type =**

23. Are you willing to support President Obama's health care program (i.e. Obama-Care) so that millions of Americans will not suffer horrible deaths due to a lack of health care?

> **Poor Question Type =**

24. Most people have no memories of their childhood before the age of 2. Do you have any childhood memories of your life between birth and 2 years of age?

> **Poor Question Type =**

25. In your opinion, if employees in the United States were paid fairly for the work they do, what should the minimum wage be in the United States?

    (a) $5 per hour   (d) $10 per hour
    (b) $7 per hour   (e) $12 per hour
    (c) $9 per hour

> **Poor Question Type =**

References

1. Cozby, P. C., & Bates, S. C. (2011). *Methods in behavioral research* (11th ed.). New York, NY: McGraw-Hill Publishers.

2. Passer, M. W. (2013). *Research methods: Concepts and connections.* New York, NY: Worth Publishers.

3. Ray, W. J. (2011). *Methods: Towards a science of behavior and experience* (10th ed.). Belmont, CA: Wadsworth/Cengage Learning.

4. Bordens, K. S., & Abbot, B. B. (2011). *Research design and methods: A process approach* (8th ed.). Boston, MA: McGraw-Hill Publishers.

5. Beins, B. C. (2012). *Research methods: A tool for life* (3rd ed.). Boston, MA: Pearson Publishers.

6. American Association for Public Opinion Research. (2006). *Best practices for survey and public opinion research.* Retrieved from http://www.aapor.org/Best_Practices.htm

7. Maclin, M. K., & Solso, R. L. (2007). *Experimental psychology: A case approach* (8th ed.). Boston, MA: Pearson/Allyn & Bacon.

8. Evans, A. N., & Rooney, B. F. (2007). *Methods in psychological research.* Thousand Oaks, CA: Sage Publications.

9. Rosnow, R. L., & Rosenthal, R. (2012). *Beginning behavioral research: A conceptual primer* (7th ed.). Boston, MA: Pearson Publishers.

10. Kantowitz, B. H., Roediger, H. L., & Elmes, D. G. (2014). *Experimental psychology* (10th ed.). Stamford, CT: Cengage Learning.

11. Check, J., & Schutt, R. K. (2011). Survey research. *In Research methods in education* (pp. 159–186). Thousand Oaks, CA: Sage Publications.

12. Neill, J. (2014). Survey research and design in psychology. *Slideshare.net.* Retrieved from http://www.slideshare.net/jtneill/introduction-to-survey-research

13. Smith, R. A., & Davis, S. F. (2012). *The psychologist as detective: An introduction to conducting research in psychology* (6th ed.). Boston, MA: Pearson Publishers.

14. Jackson, S. L. (2014). *Research methods: A modular approach* (3rd ed.). Stamford, CT: Cengage Learning.

15. Muchinsky, P. M. (2011). *Psychology applied to work* (10th ed.). Summerfield, NC: Hypergraphic Press.

16. Trochim, W. M. (2006). Types of surveys. *The Research Methods Knowledge Base* (2nd ed.). Retrieved from http://www.socialresearchmethods.net/kb/survtype.php

17. Burns, A., & Bush, R. F. (2003). Survey data collection methods. *In Marketing Research: Online Research Applications* (4th ed.; pp. 236–267). Upper Saddle River, NJ: Pearson/Prentice Hall Publishers.

18. Schonlau, M., Fricker, R. D., & Elliott, M. N. (2002). *Conducting research via e-mail and the web.* Santa Monica, CA: RAND Corporation.

19. Survey Expression. (2013). Computer-assisted web interviewing (CAWI). *SurveyExpression.Com.* Retrieved from http://www.surveyexpression.com/surveys/survey-articles/Computer-assisted-web-interviewing-cawi/

20. DJS Research, Ltd. (n.d.). What are CAPI, CATI, and CAWI? *MarketResearchWorld.Net.* Retrieved from http://www.marketresearchworld.net/content/view/2114/78/

21. Franz, N. K. (2011). The unfocused focus group: Benefit or bane? *The Qualitative Report, 16*(5), 1380–1388.

22. Leary, M. R. (2007). *Introduction to behavioral research methods* (5th ed.). Boston, MA: Pearson/ Allyn & Bacon.

23. Parsons, C. (2007). Web-based surveys: Best practices based on the research literature. *Visitor Studies, 10*(1), 13–33.

24. Integrated Research Associates. (2014). Point of purchase interviews. *IntegratedResearch.Com.* Retrieved from http://www.integratedresearch.com/techniques/pointofpurchaseintercept.htm

25. Brown, N. (2013). Customer intercepts: The solution to quiet consumer feedback. *ICC Decision Services.* Retrieved from http://www.iccds.com/customer-intercepts-the-solution-to-quiet-consumer-feedback/

26. Integrated Research Associates. (2014). Post-purchase surveys. *IntegratedResearch.Com.* Retrieved from http://www.integratedresearch.com/techniques/postpurchasesurveys.htm

27. Battey, K. (n.d.). Survey questions and answer types. *QuestionPro.Com.* Retrieved from http:// www.questionpro.com/a/showArticle.do?articleID=survey-questions

28. Trochim, W. M. (2006). Types of questions. *The Research Methods Knowledge Base* (2nd ed.). Retrieved from http://www.socialresearchmethods.net/kb/questype.php

29. Trochim, W. M. (2006). Question content. *The Research Methods Knowledge Base* (2nd ed.). Retrieved from http://www.socialresearchmethods.net/kb/quescont.php

30. Smith, S. (2013). Survey questions 101: Do you make any of these 7 question writing Mistakes? *Qualtrics.Com.* Retrieved from http://www.qualtrics.com/blog/writing-survey-questions/

MODULE 12

Observational Research

Throughout our lives, we are constantly observing the world around us. We observe the individual differences and common qualities in the people we meet during the course of our daily lives. We observe the positive and negative changes that occur within the environments in which we live and the events (e.g. economic, political, environmental, social) that lead to these changes. We observe the positive impact people have on their environments through their innovation and their concern for others and the negative impact people have on their environments through their greed, self-centeredness, and their introduction of negative elements into their environments (e.g. crime, drugs). We can also observe how people display the positive and negative sides of human behavior in response to the events occurring within their environments.

While we are observing our world, the world is also observing us. We are observed by the people we live with, work with, and socialize with. There are also times we are unaware we are being observed by the people around us. We are observed by law enforcement to ensure we are living within the rules of society. We are observed by cameras and surveillance equipment as we frequent the schools, businesses, hospitals, financial institutions, and government agencies in our communities. We are also observed electronically through our credit card purchases and our activities on the Internet. We can also be observed through the information about ourselves that we make publicly available through social media.[1,2,3,4]

Clearly, the world is full of interesting things for psychologists to observe. To acquire a more thorough understanding of the world around them, psychologists will employ a variety of observational research strategies. Before examining these observational research strategies, we will first look at the different types of observation that may be used by psychologists when they observe the interactions between both human and non-human subjects and their environments.

Types of Observation

When psychologists conduct an observational research study, there are a variety of types of observation they may use to observe the world around them. These types of observation that may be used by psychologists vary on 7 key dimensions. These 7 key dimensions are: (a) direct vs. indirect, (b) participant vs. non-participant, (c) structured vs. unstructured, (d) controlled vs. uncontrolled, (e) disguised vs. undisguised, (f) natural vs. artificial, as well as (g) quantitative vs. qualitative observation.

Direct vs. Indirect Observation

When psychologists use "direct" observation, they are physically present when the behavior of interest is occurring and actively involved in observing the behavior as it occurs.[5] For example, if a psychologist interested in animal behavior conducts a study to determine whether laboratory rats raised in isolation will be aggressive when they are placed in the same cage, the psychologist will be physically present in the lab when the rats are placed in a cage together and will directly observe whether aggressive behavior is displayed by one or more of the rats. When psychologists use "indirect" observation, they are not physically present when the behavior of interest occurs.[2,5] In some instances, they rely on the observations of others. For example, psychologists may rely on the observations of trained observers who are part of their research staff or "informants" from the community when studying the behaviors of interest.[6,7] Other times, psychologists must search the environment for clues that allow them to draw inferences about a behavior of interest that occurred in their absence.[8,9] As an example, a Developmental Psychologist may be interested in studying the types of activities pre-school-age children prefer to do while at school. While she may not be physically present during the school day when the children are in their classrooms, by observing the condition of the classrooms after the children have left for the day, she can draw some inferences as to the activities the children preferred to do while they were at school.

Participant vs. Non-Participant Observation

When "participant" observation is used by psychologists, they begin by selecting a group they are interested in studying. Next, they take all the necessary actions to become a member of this group. They do not, however, disclose the fact that they are actually psychologists conducting research on the behavior of the group. Once they are accepted as a member of the group, they become an active participant in the activities of the group and observe the group's behavior while engaged in these activities.[10,11,12] For example, a Sports Psychologist could volunteer to become a coach of a little league baseball team. In his position as coach, he could then observe the behavior of the parents of his players to study the types of poor sportsmanship they exhibit while watching their children play baseball. Through the use of "participant" observation, psychologists can get an "insider's view"[7,8,13] of a group's behavior. When psychologists use "non-participant" observation, they observe the behavior of a group without becoming a member of the group and without interacting with the members of the group.[5,7,9] They are a detached observer of the group's behavior. For example, an Experimental Psychologist interested in studying if there is any truth to the common belief that "dog owners and their dogs look like one another" could observe a group of dog owners and their dogs as they play at a dog park. The Experimental Psychologist would observe the group from a distance and would not enter the dog park nor interact with any of the dog owners or their dogs while she was observing the group. Through the use of "non-participant" observation, psychologists are able to get an "outsider's view" of a group's behavior.

Structured vs. Unstructured Observation

In "structured" observation, psychologists observe a specific behavior (or set of behaviors), under specific conditions, during a specific time period, at specific time intervals.[5,8,10] The goal of structured observation is to observe and record the frequency, intensity, and/or duration of a specific behavior (or set of behaviors) at specified time intervals (e.g. every 5 minutes) throughout the observation period.[11,14,15] As an example, assume that a Counseling Psychologist is interested in studying the behavior of married couples while they are receiving marriage counseling. She first videotapes her counseling sessions with a sample of 20 married couples. She could then observe each of the videotapes and record the number of times the members of each couple insult, compliment, and/or affectionately touch one another during 5 minute time intervals throughout their one-hour counseling sessions. When psychologists use "unstructured" observation, they are more flexible in their observations of a behavior (or set of behaviors) of interest. Rather than observing the frequency, intensity, or duration of a specific, predetermined behavior (or set of behaviors) during predetermined time intervals, psychologists take a more global perspective and attempt to observe as many aspects of a behavior (or set of behaviors) and the environment in which the behavior (or set of behaviors) occurs as is possible.[5,10,16] The goal of unstructured observation is to identify potential patterns of behavior that can then be examined in greater detail through structured observation of the behavior (or set of behaviors). As an example, assume a Consumer Psychologist is interested in observing consumer behavior during a post-Thanksgiving, "Black Friday" sale at a large retail store. Rather than developing a predetermined list of consumer behaviors that he will observe at specific points in time during the sale, he decides to simply wait until the doors of the store are opened at midnight on "Black Friday," and observe as many aspects of consumer behavior as he possibly can as they naturally occur throughout the store. From his observations, he hopes to be able to identify patterns of consumer behavior the store can use to develop procedures that can be implemented to make the "Black Friday" sale a more enjoyable experience for consumers.

Controlled vs. Uncontrolled Observation

In "controlled" observation, psychologists control one or more characteristics of an environment in which a behavior (or set of behaviors) will be observed. Specifically, psychologists will manipulate one or more characteristics of an environment and will then observe how participants behave under these controlled conditions.[17] For example, a Military Psychologist could control one or more of the characteristics of a combat situation (e.g. terrain, enemy troop size, nature of the combat mission, time allotted to complete the mission) that a platoon of marines will encounter during a training exercise and then observe how the marines perform under these controlled combat conditions. When psychologists use "uncontrolled" observation, they observe a behavior (or set of behaviors) within the context of an environment they have not manipulated or influenced in any way.[17] For example, assume that a Psychology professor is interested in studying the different ways college students attempt to cheat while taking tests in his Research Methods course. Rather than manipulating one or more characteristics of the test environment (e.g. leaving the answer key to the test on his desk while he leaves the room for 15 minutes to use the restroom), she would simply observe her student's behavior, looking for signs of attempts to cheat while they are taking their Research Methods exam under normal test conditions.

Disguised vs. Undisguised Observation

In "disguised" observation (i.e. unobtrusive, covert, or concealed observation), participants in a research study are unaware their behavior is being observed.[6,7] Psychologists can conduct "disguised" observation by: (a) disguising their true identity while in the environment they are observing,[13] (b) concealing audio/video recording equipment participants are unaware is recording their behavior,[8,10] or (c) observing participants from a concealed vantage point within the research environment.[6,10] For example, a Forensic Psychologist could conceal his presence behind a one-way mirror while observing the behavior of suspected criminals to study the effectiveness of various interrogation techniques in securing a confession to a crime. In "undisguised" observation (i.e. obtrusive, overt, and/or non-concealed observation),[6,7] participants are aware their behavior is being observed. There is no attempt on the part of psychologists to conceal the fact they are observing the behavior of participants. For example, a Psychology professor in charge of training the new teaching assistants (TAs) to teach an Introductory Psychology course will conduct classroom observations in order to evaluate their effectiveness in the classroom. During his classroom observations, the TAs are fully aware of his presence and are aware that the purpose of his presence is to evaluate their teaching.

Natural vs. Artificial Observation

When psychologists use "natural" observation, they observe behavior as it occurs within an actual real-world setting. The goal of natural observation is to observe real people doing what they normally do under normal conditions.[6,7,8] For example, an Industrial-Organizational Psychologist could observe employees as they perform their actual jobs on an assembly line to study the extent to which employees are following safety procedures they were taught during an organizational safety training program. In "artificial" observation[6,8] (which is also known as "contrived" observation), psychologists observe behavior in an artificial setting that has been designed to mirror the characteristics of a real-world setting. For example, assume an Engineering Psychologist is interested in studying the ability of pilots to operate an airplane equipped with a new cockpit design. Rather than have pilots fly (and potentially crash) an actual airplane equipped with the new cockpit design, he could instead develop a "simulated" airplane cockpit in a laboratory setting. He could then observe the performance of pilots in the simulated cockpit to see how they are likely to perform if they were flying an actual airplane equipped with the new cockpit design.

Quantitative vs. Qualitative Observation

In "quantitative" observation, psychologists use quantitative (i.e. numerical) values and statistical analyses of quantitative data to summarize their observations. Psychologists may count the number of times a behavior (or set of behaviors) occurs or use various measurement instruments to assess the amount, duration, and/or intensity of a behavior (or set of behaviors) they are observing. They may also describe the environment in which their behavior of interest is occurring in quantitative terms.[7,8,11] For example, a Health Psychologist interested in studying the world of "competitive eating," could observe a group of "competitive eaters" while they compete in the Nathan's Hot Dog Eating Championship.[18] She could summarize her observations of the "competitive eaters" by: (a) counting the total number of hot dogs that were consumed during the event, (b) computing the average number of hot dogs consumed per minute by the champion, and (c) computing the percentage of "competitive eaters" who experienced a "reversal of fortune" (i.e. throwing up the hot dogs) during the event. When psychologists use "qualitative" observation, they summarize their observations by providing a rich and detailed description of the behavior (or set of behaviors) they have observed.[7,8,11] They also rely on their senses rather than measurement instruments to describe (rather than measure) the "qualities" of the behavior (or set of behaviors) they are observing. They will also describe the "qualities" of the environment in which the behavior (or set of behaviors) of interest occurs. As an example, a Political Psychologist could attend the national convention of the Democratic Party and observe the behavior of the delegates during the convention. He could describe their reactions toward the speeches of the speakers at the convention and their level of enthusiasm throughout the convention. He could also describe different qualities of the environment inside the convention hall (e.g. Is there a mood of confidence or fear inside the convention hall about the upcoming election? Does the convention feel like a party or a business meeting? Is there a sense of unity or division within the convention hall?).

Observational Research Methods

There are a variety of research methods available to psychologists who are interested in conducting an observational research study. These methods of research allow psychologists to: (a) study on-going behavior or past behavior that has been videotaped or documented in the form of archival records, (b) conduct a long-term, detailed study of an individual, group, organization, or event possessing a unique trait, quality, characteristic, or historical significance, or (c) study a behavior (or set of behaviors) through observing the impact of the behavior (or set of behaviors) on the environment in which it occurred. The methods of research that are commonly used by psychologists when conducting an observational research study are: (a) naturalistic observation, (b) systematic observation, (c) participant observation, (d) the case study, (e) archival research, and (f) physical trace research.

Naturalistic Observation

When psychologists engage in "naturalistic observation," they observe behavior as it naturally occurs. To observe naturally occurring behavior, psychologists observe behavior that occurs outside of the confines of a controlled, artificial laboratory setting. They make no attempt to alter, control, or manipulate the environment in which the behavior of interest occurs. They do not interact with human or non-human participants in the environment in which the behavior of interest occurs.[10,14,19] They take actions necessary to ensure participants are unaware that their behavior is being observed (e.g. hidden recording devices, observing from a concealed vantage point). The primary goal of naturalistic observation is to observe how both human and/or non-human participants behave within their natural environments.

When psychologists engage in "naturalistic observation," they are not in a "hypothesis testing" mindset.[7,13] They are not entering the environment with the goal of answering specific research questions about a specific behavior (or specific set of behaviors). Rather, they enter the environment in an "information gathering" mindset. They will observe as many aspects of the environment as possible and describe their observations in as much detail as possible. They will take note of behaviors or events that may seem trivial at the time, but which upon later analysis, may represent important information about a behavior of interest.[7] They will attempt to describe what they observe at a level of detail that would provide someone who had not been physically present with a clear picture of what was observed.[10,11,13] If the nature of the environment will not allow a psychologist to record written notes of their observations without the participants becoming aware their behavior is being observed, they will dictate observations into a digital recorder that can be easily concealed.[8,10,11] While observing the environment, psychologists will not attempt to interpret what they are observing. The interpretation of their observations occurs after they have left the environment.[11,12,14] After they have left the environment, psychologists will analyze their field notes and video recordings that have been collected. They then attempt to identify potential patterns of behavior and common "themes" that emerge from the field notes of multiple observers.[7,13] These potential behavioral patterns and common "themes" are then used by psychologists to generate research questions that can be examined through further observation or through more controlled, experimental research.

There are three main strengths associated with "naturalistic observation." First, it allows psychologists to observe behavior as it naturally occurs.[8,12,13] Second, it is a method of research that reduces "reactivity" (i.e. changing one's natural behavior as a result of the knowledge that one's behavior is being observed) among participants.[8,10,19] Third, it is a method of research that allows psychologists to collect large amounts of information that can then be used to further their understanding of behavior. There are also three main weaknesses associated with naturalistic observation. First, it can be a time-consuming process requiring many hours in the field (which can include hours of time in which nothing of interest is observed).[10,11,19] Second, the timing of the observation can have a significant influence on what is observed.[19] Two different individuals can, potentially, observe dramatically different behavior if they observe the same environment but at different times. Third, there are important ethical concerns with observing people without their knowledge. The main concern is whether naturalistic observation violates people's right to privacy.[8,15,16] To address this concern, psychologists can limit their naturalistic observation to behavior that occurs in public locations where there is no expectation of privacy.[16] An additional concern is since participants are unaware they are being observed, they typically will not provide informed consent nor be debriefed at the conclusion of the observation period. To address these concerns, psychologists who use naturalistic observation will not manipulate the environment they are observing in any way that might influence or alter the behavior of participants, or place participants at a level of risk that is higher than what is normally present in that environment.[16]

Systematic Observation

Systematic observation varies from naturalistic observation in several important ways. First, rather than taking a global perspective and attempting to observe as many aspects of the environment as possible, psychologists will instead focus observations on a specific behavior (or set of behaviors).[8,10] Second, rather than approaching the environment to be observed in an "information gathering" mindset, psychologists approach the environment in a "hypothesis testing" mindset.[7,8] The primary goal is to observe behavior in a systematic manner and collect observational data that can be used to test specific research hypotheses. Third, rather than summarizing their observations of an environment in a "qualitative" manner (i.e. describing the various "qualities" of an environment), psychologists will summarize their observations in a "quantitative" manner[7,10] (i.e. measuring the quantity and/or duration of events that occur within an environment). Fourth, while naturalistic observation occurs in real-world settings, systematic observation can be used by psychologists in both real-world and laboratory settings.[6,8,10] Fifth, while psychologists do not manipulate and/or control an environment they are observing when conducting naturalistic observation, psychologists using systematic observation will sometimes manipulate or control characteristics of an environment and observe how different individuals respond.[8,10,19] For example, a psychologist interested in studying how individuals respond to frustration could manipulate the mechanisms on a snack machine so that it takes people's money without dispensing their snacks. He could then observe their behavior and record the number of times various behaviors are exhibited in response to the frustration of getting "ripped off" by the snack machine. Finally, rather than using a notebook or an audio recorder to record observations of an environment, psychologists will instead use a coding system to code what they observe into predefined categories of behavior.[10,14,19,20]

To create a coding system that allows observers to easily categorize their observations into different categories of behavior, the behaviors to be observed during the study must first be clearly defined. When defining their behaviors of interest, psychologists will typically consult the research literature to see how other researchers have defined these behaviors and determine whether there are definitions for these behaviors that have been accepted as the "standard" by the scientific community.[16,19] By using accepted definitions for behaviors of interest, psychologists will be able to directly compare the results of their research with the results of research being conducted by other psychologists studying the same behaviors. After defining their behaviors of interest, psychologists must then decide whether observers will observe the frequency, duration, and/or intensity of behavior and whether they will be asked to summarize their observations at the end of the observation period or at various predetermined intervals of time throughout the observation period (e.g. every 5 minutes).[11,15,16] The observers should then receive training with the coding system. The training ensures that all of the observers have a common understanding of how the behaviors of interest are defined and can reliably apply these definitions when asked to observe actual behavior.[13,15,16] Since the observations made by psychologists in systematic observation are quantitative in nature, the reliability of raters (i.e. inter-rater reliability) can be evaluated during training.[7,8,11] When the observers are able to achieve an acceptable level of reliability, psychologists can then allow them to observe behavior under research conditions.

There are several strengths associated with "systematic observation." These strengths include the focused observation of a specific behavior (or set of behaviors), the development of an objective coding system for observers, and the ability to assess the reliability of the observers both during their initial training and after observing behavior under research conditions. There are, however, two potential weaknesses associated with systematic observation psychologists must be aware of if they are considering using this method of observation. These two potential weaknesses are known as "observer bias" and "observer drift." Observer "bias" occurs when an observer, rather than objectively coding behavior as it is observed, codes behavior in a "biased" manner to support a specific research hypothesis.[11,16] Observer "drift" occurs when, over time, the observers' mental definitions of the behaviors of interest change or "drift" from definitions that were established at the start of the study. This in turn, results in a change in how behavior is being coded throughout the course of the study and a reduction in the reliability of observations both within and across observers.[16] To reduce the potential for "observer drift," the length of the observation period can be shortened for observers to help them maintain focus and consistency. Psychologists can also require observers to review the established definitions for the behaviors of interest throughout the study and especially before each period of observation.

Participant Observation

When psychologists engage in "participant observation," they join a group they are interested in studying in an effort to gain an "insider's perspective" on the behavior of the group.[8,12] They are especially interested in studying the behaviors of a group or the characteristics of an environment that are normally not observed by the general public. There are two different levels of "participant" observation that psychologists can use to study a group's behavior. These two levels are known as "full participant observation" and "partial participant observation." In "full participant observation," psychologists become an active member of the group they are interested in studying and will take part in all activities that are associated with being a member of the group.[20] They do not, however, disclose to members of the group that they are psychologists who have concealed their true identities in order to study the behavior of the group.[8,13] By concealing their true identity, psychologists hope to observe natural behavior by eliminating "reactivity"[10,11] (i.e. altering one's behavior in response to knowledge that one's behavior is being observed) among group members. A challenge faced by psychologists who engage in "full participant observation" is how to record observations without being discovered by members of the group.[11,19] To address this challenge, some psychologists use hidden audio and/or video recording devices to record behavior while in the presence of the group, while other psychologists observe the behavior of the group and will then record their observations at a later point in time when they are no longer in the presence of the group.

In "partial participant observation," psychologists approach a group of interest and will disclose that they are psychologists who are interested in studying the behavior of the group.[20] If the group agrees to allow psychologists to observe their behavior and agrees to give them access to the day-to-day activities of the group, psychologists will then have to decide how they will deal with the strong potential for "reactivity" among group members since they are fully aware psychologists will be observing their behavior. There are two methods psychologists will use to minimize the potential for participant reactivity. In method one, while psychologists inform the group they will be observing their behavior, they either: (a) do not disclose the specific behavior (or set of behaviors) they will be observing, or in some instances will (b) mislead the group as to the specific behavior (or set of behaviors) they will be observing.[8,20] This method is an example of "partial participant observation" because although psychologists do not conceal their identities to the group, they do conceal the true purpose of the observation. In method two, psychologists will spend a lot of time in the presence of the group with the hope that over time, members of the group will get so used to their presence they will forget that they are psychologists rather than a normal part of the group. This method is an example of "partial participant observation" because although psychologists do not conceal their identities to the group, they rely on members of the group "habituating" to their presence over time, thus allowing them to observe the behavior of the group while "hiding in plain sight."[7,10,11]

There are two main strengths associated with "participant observation." First, it allows psychologists to study naturally occurring behavior under normal conditions.[11,12,19] Second, it allows psychologists to observe the private behaviors of a group that can't be examined through other methods of research.[19,20] For example, in a "full participant observation" study, a team of Forensic Psychologists may enter a prison disguised in the role of new prison inmates in order to study the gang activity and drug trafficking that occurs in the prison. In a "partial participant observation" study, a team of Health Psychologists may inform the staff at a psychiatric hospital they are there to observe how the staff administers medications to patients, when they are actually there to observe whether there is any evidence of abuse of patients by hospital staff. In both of these examples, "participant observation" would allow psychologists to observe behaviors that those outside of these environments would be unaware are occurring.

There are also several challenges associated with "participant observation." First, it may take a long time to gain access to a group of interest. In fact, there is no guarantee psychologists will be accepted as a member of a group they are interested in studying.[11,12] Second, if they are able to gain membership to their group of interest, there is a possibility over time that they will begin to develop relationships with members of the group. When this occurs, the potential exists for psychologists to begin to lose their "objectivity" [6,7] when evaluating the behavior of the group members (i.e. objective observations of group members as "strangers" are replaced over time by subjective observations of group members as "friends"). Third, if they can gain membership to their group of interest, psychologists must be aware that their own behavior has the potential to alter the normal behavior that occurs within the group and that their observations may no longer be an accurate reflection of typical group behavior.[6,11] Fourth, in a "full participant observation" study, psychologists can find themselves facing dangerous situations if the group discovers their true identities and learns that they have been observing and studying the group's behavior. Fifth, as with "naturalistic observation," there are ethical concerns with observing people without their awareness, or as is the case in "partial participant observation," deceiving people as to the true purpose of one's observation.[7,8,11] To address these concerns, psychologists typically conduct a "participant observation" study after having considered the range of available research methods and made a determination that participant observation is the method of research that will allow them to observe the specific behavior (or set of behaviors) they need to observe. Finally, in a participant observation study, psychologists may observe or be asked to engage in behaviors that are illegal (e.g. criminal activity) and/or unethical (e.g. deceptive and/or discriminatory business practices) to maintain their membership in the group they are observing. To prepare for these possibilities, psychologists must develop an "exit strategy" for how they will extract themselves from the group prior to beginning a "participant observation" study and consider what course of action they will take in the event they observe various forms of criminal or unethical behavior.

Case Study

A "case study" is an in-depth, observational study of an individual, group, event, or organization.[10,14] To conduct a case study, psychologists must first select a "subject" for study. Psychologists use several criteria to select the individual, group, event, or organization that will serve as the "subject" for their case study. Some psychologists select the "outliers" of society for study (e.g. subjects whose characteristics, circumstances, or experiences are atypical and represent the extremes of the human experience).[6] Some psychologists select subjects based on their historical significance, their role in producing societal change, their potential to lead to advancements in science, medicine, education, and business, or their potential to advance our understanding of behavior as individuals, or as a society.[7] Some psychologists select subjects that have received extensive media coverage (i.e. television, print, social) and are of interest to society, while others select subjects that have been ignored, overlooked, or forgotten by society. Finally, some psychologists select subjects based on the influential role these subjects played in their own personal lives (e.g. people and events that shaped who they are as individuals and the lives of the people in the communities in which they have lived).

After selecting the individual, group, event, or organization that will be the "subject" of their case study, psychologists must decide which methods of research they will utilize to study their subject. Two of the defining features of the case study are the use of multiple methods of research and the analysis of multiple types of information.[8] In case studies, psychologists will typically analyze a combination of qualitative and quantitative information.[6,8] When conducting a case study, psychologists may use multiple methods of observation. For example, they may observe their subject in-person or observe video recordings of their subject. They may also use participant observation in order to get an insider's perspective on their subject. In addition to observation, psychologists may also conduct interviews with individuals who have a personal knowledge of their subject.[6,8] They will also examine archival records pertaining to their subject. Examples of archival records may include historical documents, government records, financial records, newspaper articles, photographs, employment records, educational records, criminal records, military service records, birth/marriage/death certificates, and public information that is stored on social media websites.[11,12] At the conclusion of the case study, psychologists produce a detailed and comprehensive narrative account of their "subject." In addition to the detailed narrative, they may also discuss potential causal factors that may explain their subject, identify additional research questions or hypotheses that could be examined through further research, and discuss the extent to which the results of their case study support those of prior research on the subject or support the predictions of a relevant theory.[6,8,16]

After selecting the methods of research they will use to study their subject, psychologists must then decide if they will use a "prospective" or "retrospective" approach when conducting their case study. When psychologists conduct a "prospective" case study, they select a subject for study and then follow this subject over time and evaluate the outcomes experienced by their subject.[7] For example, a Political Psychologist could select a controversial politician elected to his first term in Congress as the subject of her case study. She would then observe all aspects of the politician's life and his work performance (e.g. voting record, political speeches, committee activities, bills introduced) throughout his first term in office and ultimately observe the outcome of the politician's first term in office (e.g. he becomes a transformative political figure, he is a 1-term failure, he is forced to leave office after a political/personal scandal). While observing the politician throughout his first term in Congress, she would examine the personal, social, political, and global factors that shape the course of his life and career and ultimately lead to the outcome he experiences at the end of his first term. As a second example, a Developmental Psychologist could select a child with a rare developmental disability as his subject for case study. He would then observe all aspects of the child's development and ultimately observe the developmental milestones achieved by the child at age 3. While observing the child's development, he would examine the influence of parental involvement, social support (e.g. family, friends, community), and early intervention services on the developmental milestones achieved by the child at age 3.

When psychologists conduct a "retrospective" case study, they select a subject based on an outcome associated with the subject and then take a look "back in time" to identify the factors that contributed to the outcome.[7] For example, an Industrial-Organizational Psychologist could select a company that went out of business as the subject of his case study. He would then take a look back at the company's history to identify internal (e.g. employee, management, product quality) and external factors (e.g. economy, legislation, competition) that may have contributed to the failure of the company. As a second example, a Forensic Psychologist could select a mass murderer as the subject of her case study. Specifically, she could select an individual who has committed a mass shooting in the workplace. She would then take a look back at all aspects of the individual's life (e.g. medical history, family environment, education, personal relationships, employment history, life stresses/conflicts, psychological history) in an effort to identify the potential causal factors involved in the individual's decision to go to his place of employment and commit mass murder.

There are three main strengths associated with the "case study." First, the depth at which psychologists study their subject (i.e. individual, group, event, organization) surpasses most other methods of research.[10,11,14] At the conclusion of a case study, psychologists have studied their subject from multiple perspectives and have analyzed all the available and relevant information that is necessary to prepare a detailed review of their subject. Second, psychologists can conduct a case study on individuals, groups, events, and organizations. Third, psychologists use the case study to examine the "extremes" of society (i.e. rare, unusual, atypical individuals). By studying the "extremes" within our society, psychologists hope to expand their current understanding of the range of the human experience and to use this knowledge to make advances in fields such as science, medicine, education, and business that are applicable to all members of society.[7,8,13]

There are also some weaknesses and challenges associated with the case study method. First, the case study has the potential to be a time-consuming method of research. Psychologists who elect to use the case study method should be prepared to commit months, and in some cases, years of their lives, to studying their subject of interest. Second, since case studies often focus on the more unique individuals, groups, events, or organizations in society, it is unlikely that the results of a case study will generalize beyond the case itself.[8,12,16] Third, because the case study does not involve manipulation of variables under highly controlled conditions, it is more difficult for psychologists to identify the causal factors that explain the subject of their case study than is the case in experimental methods of research.[8,11,14] Fourth, because psychologists conducting a case study spend a large amount of time immersed in the study of their subject, over time, they may begin to develop an emotional connection to the subject that can lead to a loss of objectivity when they are observing their subject or evaluating information related to their subject. Finally, there is the potential for observer bias in the case study method. If psychologists have a specific research hypothesis they would like to see supported by the results of the case study, this could influence their observations of their subject, as well as their analysis of information related to the subject.[10,16,20] Either intentional or unintentionally, psychologists' observations, interpretations, and analyses may be biased in the direction of supporting the favored outcome.

Archival Research

In "archival research," rather than collecting their own research data, psychologists study existing sources of data, documents, and/or records.[10,14,19] Psychologists can use archival research to conduct exploratory studies or test specific research hypotheses.[11] The data, documents, and/or records studied by psychologists during archival research were collected and archived by individuals, groups, or organizations for purposes other than the psychologists' research.[12,16,19] During archival research, psychologists will study "paper archives" (i.e. written and printed materials), "electronic archives" (i.e. information stored in electronic formats),[7,12,20] and both public and private sources of existing data, documents, and/or records.[9]

Public data, documents, and/or records are those that are available and accessible to the public. Archival information considered "public" includes information collected and archived by: (a) government agencies, (b) law enforcement and courts of law, (c) businesses and industry, (d) community and human service agencies, (e) health care organizations, (f) school systems and institutions of higher education, (g) research organizations, (h) libraries, and (i) the television and print media.[9,11] This archival information is available for research purposes and it provides the public with a record of the activities of public organizations, agencies, and institutions. Archival information considered "public" is not protected by any confidentiality agreements or privacy laws and does not require special permission to access. Private data, documents, and/or records by comparison are those for which there is restricted access to the information.[9,11] Archival data, documents, and/or records that are considered "private" include information of a highly personal and/or sensitive nature (e.g. medical, financial, legal information) collected by organizations that have the responsibility of maintaining the information, protecting the privacy of individuals who supplied the information, and protecting the confidentiality of the data. Psychologists who are interested in studying archival data, documents, and/or records considered "private" will have to obtain special permission to access the information.

Once psychologists have gained access to the archival data, documents, and/or records they are interested in studying, they will typically have to use a variety of analyses to interpret the information and test research hypotheses.[21] In some instances, the archival information will be quantitative in nature and psychologists can perform multiple statistical analyses on the data.[20] For example, an Industrial-Organizational Psychologist could study quantitative information in the personnel records of a manufacturing organization (e.g. number of absences, yearly salaries, performance evaluation scores) and use this data to test hypotheses about employee behavior. In other instances, the archival information is qualitative in nature and will require psychologists to conduct a variety of qualitative analyses on the material.[20] For example, a Political Psychologist could study the speeches of our U.S. Presidents and conduct a qualitative analysis of the content of these speeches to determine whether there is a difference in the tone, language, and/or themes in the speeches made by our most effective and least effective Presidents. It should be noted that the quantitative or qualitative information psychologists need to test research hypotheses may not always be directly accessible in archived materials. In such instances, psychologists may have to recode or transform the information found in the archive into a format that will then allow them to conduct the appropriate quantitative or qualitative analyses to test their research hypotheses.

There are several strengths associated with "archival research." First, because the data, documents, and/or records of interest have already been collected, psychologists do not have to devote time and resources toward collecting the information themselves.[10] Second, archives often contain data that will allow psychologists to conduct a variety of different types of research including cross-sectional studies (i.e. a comparison of multiple groups at a single point in time), longitudinal studies (i.e. the comparison of a single group at multiple points in time), and inter-generational studies (i.e. the comparison of groups who represent different generations).[7] Third, psychologists can conduct archival research for a variety of purposes which include pilot studies, exploratory studies, testing specific research hypotheses, and studying changes occurring within society over time.[7] Fourth, archival sources often contain a large volume of information which exceeds what psychologists could collect given their available resources.[7,12,19] Fifth, archival sources may contain international and/or cross-cultural data, documents, and/or records that can be expensive and time-consuming for psychologists to acquire. Finally, organizations reluctant to have their daily operations disrupted by psychologists conducting a research study, may still be willing to allow psychologists to study existing sources of data, documents, and/or records that have been collected and archived by the organization.

There are also several challenges associated with "archival research." First, because the data, documents, and/or records of interest were collected and archived by someone other than the psychologists conducting the study, there is always a concern about the quality and accuracy of the archived information.[7,9,12] In many instances, it may be impossible for psychologists to determine whether an error was made when the information was entered into the archive. For example, if a Health Psychologist was studying archived medical records, it would be impossible for him to know whether a patient's blood pressure truly was 120/85 on May 27, 1978, unless he also had access to the physician's original report for the physical exam where this blood pressure value was recorded. It is possible that the true blood pressure reading was actually 150/95, but an error occurred when the blood pressure value was entered into the medical records. Second, there is the potential for "selective deposit" to occur in archival research. Selective deposit refers to the process whereby personal biases influence the information that is placed into (or excluded) from an archive.[9,11,12] For example, individuals who believe the events of 9/11 were an act of terrorism would be likely to archive different information about the event than individuals who believe the events of 9/11 were orchestrated by individuals within the United States government. Third, there is a potential for "selective survival" to occur in archival research. Selective survival refers to cases when desired information in an archive is missing or incomplete.[9,12,16] In some instances, information may be missing because it has been lost, destroyed, or it has physically deteriorated over time.[10] In other instances, the information may be missing as a result of limits placed on the amount of time the records are maintained. The records may have been destroyed once time had expired. The information may also be missing simply because no record was ever entered into an archive. Finally, there may be inconsistencies over time in the manner in which information is collected and archived. These inconsistencies may prevent psychologists from studying changes occurring in a population over time if the information has not been collected and archived in a similar manner at multiple points in time.[9]

Physical Trace Research

When psychologists conduct "physical trace research," they study the observable, physical evidence (i.e. "physical traces") that is left behind following the interactions that occur between both humans and animals and their environments.[8,9,22] Much like the evidence that is left behind at a crime scene (e.g. fingerprints, blood, DNA) can be used by law enforcement to make inferences about the nature of a crime, physical trace evidence that is observed in an environment can be used by psychologists to make inferences about the nature of the human and animal behavior that occurs within that environment.[8,11,14] In addition to physical traces left in our physical world, psychologists are also interested in studying "electronic traces" left in the "online" world (e.g. e-mails, tweets, texts, social media postings). When evaluating the physical traces left in the physical or online worlds, psychologists use both quantitative and qualitative methods of analysis to draw inferences about the behaviors that produced the physical traces. The types of evidence psychologists evaluate when conducting physical trace research is typically categorized in relation to two key dimensions: (a) accretion vs. erosion and (b) use traces vs. products.

Accretion refers to physical traces that build up over time in an environment due to both human and animal behavior.[9,11,14,23] Examples of accretion due to human behavior may include garbage, graffiti, and pollution. Accretion due to the behavior of animals would include tracks, nets, hives, dams, scat droppings, and remnants of meals (e.g. bones, hair, feathers). In all these examples, humans and animals have added something to their environments, that when observed, could be used to make inferences about the human or animal behavior that created the physical trace. By contrast, erosion refers to physical traces left in an environment when the behavior of humans or animals cause parts of an environment to be worn down or diminished.[9,22,23] Erosion caused by the behavior of humans may include wear patterns on hardwood floors, faded letters on the keys of a computer keyboard, and worn patches on a pair of jeans. Examples of erosion caused by behavior of animals may include game trails worn into a forest floor, wooden beams in a home eaten away by termites, and chewed vegetables in a farmer's field or a family garden. In these examples, the behavior of both humans and animals can be inferred through observation of things within their environments they have consumed, diminished, or caused to wear away.

Use traces refer to physical traces that indicate the level of use or non-use of items within an environment.[22] In some instances, psychologists will observe use traces without manipulating the environment in any way. These traces are referred to as "natural use" traces.[9] For example, a Psychology professor could observe the wear pattern on the seats or ink stains on the surface of the desks in a college classroom to determine where students typically sit when taking a course in the classroom. In other instances, psychologists manipulate an element of an environment and then observe how this manipulation affects the use or non-use of items within that environment. These traces are referred to as "controlled use" traces.[9] For example, a Consumer Psychologist hired to save a restaurant money by reducing the number of napkins customers use, could place a sign in the restaurant which says, "To reduce the cost of doing business, we ask that customers use only 1 napkin during their meals." At the end of the business day, after all customers have left the restaurant, the Consumer Psychologist can then observe and count the actual number of napkins customers used and determine whether napkin use by customers decreased as a result of her posting the sign in the restaurant.

Products refer to the things (i.e. "artifacts") that are produced by a culture which can be observed to make inferences about the culture that produced the artifacts.[8,9] Examples of cultural artifacts could include written materials (e.g. books, documents, speeches), works of art, music, inventions, new technologies, entertainment (e.g. plays, movies, television shows), architectural achievements, monuments, and symbols. Products also refer to things that people buy, own, and use as a means of self-expression.[22] Through observing how people use products to express who they are to the world, psychologists hope to be able to make inferences about their behavior and various aspects of their lives. For example, a Community Psychologist who observes the brands of clothing people wear, the types of cars they drive, the homes they live in, and the schools their children attend may be able to draw inferences about people's socioeconomic status, occupation, as well as other behaviors and/or attitudes (e.g. political views, attitudes toward social issues) associated with level of income.

There are several strengths associated with "physical trace research." First, there is no shortage of physical trace evidence for psychologists to study.[22,23] Physical traces of human and animal behavior can be found in all environments in which they live. Second, the study of trace evidence allows psychologists to study the impact of the "real world" behavior of humans and animals on an environment.[22,23] Finally, "reactivity" (i.e. altering one's behavior in response to the knowledge one's behavior is being observed) is less of a concern in physical trace research than in other forms of observational research. Why? Because the physical traces of behavior left behind by both humans and animals are often studied only after the source of the physical trace has left the environment.[9,22]

There are also several challenges associated with "physical trace research." First, not all human and animal behaviors leave behind a physical trace.[8] For example, a conversation among two people walking in the park is unlikely to leave behind a physical trace. However, if the same two people were to have a conversation via their cell phones, there will be an "electronic trace" of the conversation left behind. Second, some physical traces are not permanent, and if they are not observed quickly enough, they will disappear and be unavailable for scientific study[9,22] (e.g. researchers who believe in the existence of cryptids (i.e. undiscovered creatures inhabiting the Earth) may be unable to study reported footprints of a "bigfoot" after a rainstorm washes away the prints or the tracks of a "yeti" (i.e. abominable snowman) after an avalanche covers up the reported tracks under 30 feet of snow). Third, when the behaviors of humans or animals leave behind physical traces, the more recent physical traces can destroy or "erase" physical traces that were left behind at an earlier point in time.[9,22] Finally, there may be multiple inferences that can be made from the same physical trace.[9,23] As an example, assume that a Sports Psychologist is interested in studying the level of use a public golf course receives in a typical day. To study the "level of use," he arrives at the course at the end of the day after all golfers have left the course and counts the number of divots in the fairways of the golf course. He observes 1,000 divots in the fairways. What will he infer from these 1,000 divots? Did 100 golfers each make 10 divots during their rounds or did 1 really bad golfer make all 1,000 divots during his round? In this case, the same physical traces (i.e. 1,000 divots) could lead to multiple inferences about the behavior that left behind these traces without the availability of additional information.

Observation as a Method of Research

Observation, when done properly, can be one of the most powerful tools available to psychologists conducting research on the behavior of both humans and animals. Through the process of observation, psychologists can observe behavior as it occurs within both natural and controlled contexts.[7,8] Rather than speculating about what people might do, or asking people what they think they would do, psychologists can directly observe what people actually do when in a specific setting or situation. There are numerous types of observation that can be used in a research context. This provides psychologists the flexibility to study a wide range of behaviors; some of which may not be able to be studied through more controlled, experimental methods of research. For observation to be an effective research tool, psychologists must be willing to do the following: (a) spend a large amount of time in the field or laboratory observing behavior,[10,11] (b) clearly define the behaviors of interest so there is no ambiguity as to what has been observed during the course of a study,[6,11,16] (c) undergo training to become a better observer in order to ensure that observations of behavior are reliable, (d) not allow personal biases, knowledge of the desired results, or subjectivity to diminish the objectivity of one's observations,[6,7,8] (e) create a detailed, accurate record of observations (e.g. written notes, coding sheets, video/audio),[8,10,11] and (f) adhere to the ethical principles established for conducting observational research.[8,15,16] If psychologists are willing to commit to these actions, observation will provide them with the tool they need to develop a greater understanding of the human and animal behavior occurring in the world around them.

EXERCISE 12A

What Type of Observation Are Psychologists Using?

There are a variety of observational research methods that can be used by psychologists to study both humans and animals within natural and controlled environments. Through the use of these various observational research methods, psychologists can study the behavior, archived information, and physical traces associated with individuals, groups, organizations, cultures, and society as a whole. Below are 25 scenarios describing observational research studies conducted by psychologists with expertise in different disciplines within the field of psychology. For each scenario, use the list of observational research methods presented below, to identify the type of observational research study being conducted and place your answer in the space provided.

Naturalistic Observation	Systematic Observation
Participant Observation	Case Study
Archival Research	Physical Trace Research

01. A Military Psychologist studying soldier perceptions of the different wars that have occurred during our nation's history, visits museums throughout the world and studies collections of letters written by soldiers and sent home to their families during the Civil War, World War I, and the Vietnam War. He analyzes the content of the letters to determine whether there are differences in how soldiers described their experiences during the different wars.

> **Method =**

02. To study the attention span of his students, a Psychology professor places a hidden camera in his classroom and records the behavior of his students during a 1-hour lecture. After the class ends, he goes back to his office and watches the videotape. He divides the lecture into 5-minute segments and then records the number of students who are awake, taking notes, and whose eyes were tracking his movement during each five-minute segment of his lecture.

> **Method =**

03. A Consumer Psychologist has been hired to evaluate customers' satisfaction with the food at a fast food restaurant. Rather than asking customers to complete a food satisfaction survey, he instead observes the amount and types of food customers leave on their plates when their dishes are removed from their tables and returned to the kitchen area to be washed.

> **Method =**

04. To study how people prepare for an impending snowstorm, a psychologist walks around a grocery store and observes the types of items customers are stocking up on 24 hours before the approach of a large winter snowstorm.

> **Method =**

05. To study the amount and types of bullying behavior that occurs among middle school and high school students, a psychologist assumes the role of a school bus driver and observes the bullying behavior that occurs on the school bus everyday while driving his bus route.

> **Method =**

06. A Media Psychologist interested in the master of horror, Stephen King, studies all available information about King's childhood, reads all of his books, reads the transcripts of all of his interviews, and conducts interviews with people who know him. He then writes a book in which he describes the factors he believes led to King becoming the master of horror.

> **Method =**

07. A Counseling Psychologist studying whether there is a difference in the intensity of the emotional reaction of men and women to the loss of a spouse, observes the number of tissues left in his wastebasket at the end of a therapy session by each of his male and female clients who have recently lost a spouse.

> **Method =**

08. To observe whether school-age children are eating a well-balanced meal for lunch, a Health Psychologist places hidden cameras in several school cafeterias and observes the nutritional characteristics of the foods students buy for their lunches.

> **Method =**

09. To learn more about the homeless community in his city, a Social Psychologist assumes the role of an individual who is homeless and lives among the homeless for one month. During this time, he observes what daily life is like for the members of the homeless community and the methods of coping people use to address the challenges associated with being homeless.

> **Method =**

10. A Physiological Psychologist is conducting a research study to try to determine why a man has been struck by lightning 26 times during his life! He has reviewed the medical records for all 35 years of the man's life, conducted extensive tests of the man's physiology, spoken with the man's family to learn when the lightning strikes began, and interviewed witnesses to the lightning strikes. He plans to publish an article that details the man's life and presents his observations and conclusions in a scientific journal.

> **Method =**

11. A School Psychologist has been asked by a school principal to determine whether the school needs to increase its special education budget in the coming years. To answer this question, the psychologist accesses the school's student records system and finds out the number of special education students who were enrolled at the school each year over the last decade. She notices an upward trend in the data and recommends to the principal that she increase the special education budget in the coming years.

> **Method =**

12. To study whether there is a difference in the amount of profanity used by male and female comedians, an Experimental Psychologist attends a comedy festival and observes the 10-minute comedy routines of several male and female comedians. He divides each of the 10-minute comedy routines into 2-minute segments and counts the number of profane words used by male and female comedians during each 2-minute segment of their routines.

> **Method =**

13. After a "wrongful death" lawsuit had been filed against the surgeons at the hospital where she worked, a Research Psychologist accessed the hospital's patient records for the last 3 years to find out how many patients had died from complications following surgery during each of the last 3 years. She discovered the number of patient deaths had more than tripled over the last 3 years and recommended the hospital hire the best attorney it could find.

> **Method =**

14. After hearing horror stories about the long lines at the local Department of Motor Vehicles, a Psychologist goes to the DMV, and for one hour, observes people standing in line waiting for assistance. Every 15 minutes, he records the number of people who complain about the long lines, yell at a DMV employee, or get tired of standing in line and storm out.

> **Method =**

15. A Cultural Psychologist observes how people from different cultures express their cultural identities through their language, food, clothing, and music as he observes the city's annual international street festival from the window of his apartment, high above the festival.

> **Method =**

16. A Psychologist interested in determining whether the legendary cryptid (i.e. undiscovered creature) known as "El Chupacabra" (i.e. the "goat sucker") exists, observes the bite marks on the bodies of goats found near locations where there have been Chupacabra sightings to see whether the bite patterns match those of any known creatures.

> **Method =**

17. After reading a newspaper article about a construction worker who suffered an injury to his brain that had never been seen before in medical history, a Biopsychologist began a detailed study of the man's case. He studied the details of the accident, all of the information in the man's medical files, the results of tests conducted to assess the man's brain functions, and he even talked with members of the construction crew who witnessed the accident. After reviewing all the available information in the case, the Biopsychologist spoke at a national research conference and presented a summary of the man's case and offered some potential explanations for how the man was able to survive his unique brain injury.

> **Method =**

18. To study the quality of care animals who live in zoos receive when they are not on display to the public, a team of psychologists applied for jobs at several zoos around the country. The jobs required the team of psychologists to clean and/or do maintenance work on the animal cages and enclosures at the various zoos. Once they were hired, they were able to observe the quality of care the animals received after the public had left the zoos each day.

> **Method =**

19. A Psychologist with expertise in city planning and traffic control was hired by city planners to study how dangerous the 5 main intersections within the city were for drivers. The next day, she went to each of the 5 intersections and observed the amount of broken glass, pieces of damaged metal, and skid marks from tires at each of the intersections. She then used her observations to provide the city planners with a rank ordering of the 5 intersections from the most dangerous intersection (Rank 1) to the least dangerous intersection (Rank 5).

> **Method =**

20. A Community Psychologist is interested in learning whether his neighbor is selling drugs. To find out, he observes his neighbor, and the people who visit his neighbor, every day for a month while taking his dog for its daily walks around the neighborhood.

> **Method =**

21. To determine if the military should increase its recruiting efforts, a Military Psychologist examined military records and recorded the number of new enlistments that occurred each year during the last 10 years to see whether there is a downward trend in enlistments.

> **Method =**

22. A Psychologist interested in "conspiracy theories" studied all the evidence associated with the J.F.K. assassination (e.g. Zapruder film, Warren Commission report, CIA, FBI, Secret Service files) and even visited the Dallas Book Depository and infamous "grassy knoll." After reviewing all the available evidence, he wrote the definitive book on the subject in which he concludes the assassination was the result of the actions of a lone gunman.

> **Method =**

23. To determine whether employees are able to maintain a consistent work pace throughout the course of a day, an Industrial-Organizational Psychologist observed employees sorting mail at a U.S. Postal Service distribution center. She records the number of letters each employee sorts every half-hour throughout their 8-hour shift.

> **Method =**

24. To determine how widespread the growing drug problem is in his hometown, a Psychologist assumes the role of an individual who wants to buy drugs. She observes how long it takes to find someone willing to sell her drugs in different areas of town and the types of people who are selling drugs in her hometown.

> **Method =**

25. To study how people establish boundaries of "personal space," a Psychologist on vacation at the beach, conceals himself under the boardwalk and observes how people on the beach use their towels, chairs, umbrellas, and coolers to display to others on the beach which piece of the beach they have claimed as their own private space.

> **Method =**

EXERCISE 12B

Participant Observation:
Studying Behavior from the Inside

Participant observation is a method of observation that allows psychologists to observe and study behavior that is normally not visible to the general public. Psychologists gain access to the behavior of interest by becoming a member of a group or by assuming roles that provide them with the opportunity to observe the behavior of interest. While participant observation can provide psychologists with a valuable "inside perspective" on behavior, it can also place them in situations that present a high degree of risk and significant ethical challenges. Below is a list of 4 behaviors psychologists could study through participant observation. Please select *1* behavior you would be interested in observing and then answer the questions that follow to describe how you would conduct a participant observation study of your chosen behavior of interest.

Behavior 1: Bullying of high school students

Behavior 2: Discrimination against minority customers at a clothing store

Behavior 3: Physical and verbal abuse of children at a child care center

Behavior 4: Treatment of a gay athlete in a professional sports locker room

Which behavior would you be most interested in observing and studying?

01. Identify *3* "roles" you could assume to study your behavior of interest. Which "role" would provide you with the most informative information about your behavior of interest? Provide a rationale for your choice of "role."

Role 1 = _____

Role 2 = _____

Role 3 = _____

Most Informative "Role":

02. What actions would you need to take in order to place yourself in a position to observe your behavior of interest (e.g. what would you have to do to join a group or to gain access to the setting in which your behavior of interest occurs)?

To be able to observe my behavior of interest, I would need to......

---

03. Once you have gained access to the setting in which your behavior of interest occurs, what are *3* specific behaviors you would want to observe while in that setting? Provide a rationale for the *3* behaviors you would choose to observe.

Behavior 1 = _____

Behavior 2 = _____

Behavior 3 = _____

Rationale:

---

04. Which of the following strategies would be the most effective way for you to create an accurate record of your observations and avoid having your true identity revealed to the individuals whose behavior you are observing? Provide a rationale for your strategy.

☐	Write Detailed Notes While in the Field
☐	Placing Hidden Recording Devices in the Field
☐	Placing Hidden Recording Devices on Your Body
☐	Writing Detailed Notes After Leaving the Field

Rationale for your choice of strategy:

05. What risks would you face if your true identity were discovered by the individuals whose behavior you were observing?

The risks I would face would be.......

06. If you were asked to engage in a behavior that was illegal, or which posed a risk of harm or injury to those individuals who you are observing, what would you do? Why?

> ☐ I would end my research study immediately and leave the situation
>
> ☐ I would consult other psychologists to get advice on whether I should end my research study or maintain my "role" and continue the study
>
> ☐ I would make up an excuse so I could maintain my "role" and avoid having to engage in the behavior and continue my research study
>
> ☐ I would engage in the behavior so that I could strengthen my "role" and continue my research study
>
> **Rationale:**

07. At the conclusion of your study, what "cover story" would you create to extract yourself from the situation without raising suspicion from those whose behavior you observed?

> **My "cover story" would be.......**

08. If during the course of your research study, you observed behavior that was illegal, posed a risk of harm or injury, or caused harm or injury to the individuals that you were observing, which of the following *best* represents what you would do with this information at the end of your study? Provide a rationale for your selection.

	I would give the information to the police (with the names of those involved)
	I would give the information to the police (without names of those involved)
	I would give the information to the school, store, child care center, or sports team (with the names of those involved) and let them handle it internally
	I would give the information to the school, store, child care center, or sports team (without names of those involved) and let them handle it internally
	I would give the information to the media (with the names of those involved)
	I would give the information to the media (without names of those involved)
	I would publish a research article (with the names of those involved)
	I would publish a research article (without names of those involved)
	I would lock all of the information away in a secure file cabinet and forget that I ever conducted the study and the behavior I observed
	I would not disclose the information to anyone. I would protect the privacy of those I observed and protect the confidentiality of their behavior.

Rationale:

EXERCISE 12C

Studying Behavior and the Physical Traces They Leave Behind

When psychologists conduct "physical trace research," they study the physical and/or electronic traces that are left behind in an environment by the behaviors of both humans and animals. These physical and electronic traces include accretion traces (i.e. traces that build up over time), erosion traces (i.e. wearing down of the environment), use traces (i.e. use or non-use of items in an environment), and products (i.e. artifacts we create and possessions we own as a means of self-expression). Through the analysis of these physical traces, psychologists attempt to make inferences about the behavior that left behind the trace in the environment. Below are 10 scenarios describing physical trace research being conducted by psychologists. For each of the scenarios, please identify *3* physical and/or electronic traces the psychologists could use to study the behavior of interest.

01. A Clinical Psychologist receives a call from the parents of a teenage boy who are concerned their son is suicidal. They asked the Clinical Psychologist to come to their home when their son is at school and observe their son's room for any signs he may be suicidal. What are *3* physical traces that would lead the Clinical Psychologist to infer their son is/is not suicidal?

> Physical Trace 1 = _____
>
> Physical Trace 2 = _____
>
> Physical Trace 3 = _____

02. A Research Psychologist is hired by an insurance company to help reduce the number of their customers who are robbed while on vacation. The Research Psychologist wants to determine how criminals know when a family is away on vacation. What are *3* physical traces that would lead a criminal to infer a family is/is not away on vacation?

> Physical Trace 1 = _____
>
> Physical Trace 2 = _____
>
> Physical Trace 3 = _____

03. A Counseling Psychologist and his wife go to the home of their new neighbors to welcome them to the neighborhood. They are invited in by their neighbors for a cup of coffee. While they wait for the coffee to be ready, their neighbors take them on a tour of their home. What are *3* physical traces that would lead the Counseling Psychologist to infer that his neighbor's marriage is/is not headed for divorce?

Physical Trace 1 = _____

Physical Trace 2 = _____

Physical Trace 3 = _____

04. An Industrial-Organizational Psychologist has been hired by an organization to determine the level of commitment employees have toward the organization. They do not, however, want employees to know the Industrial-Organizational Psychologist is studying their level of organizational commitment. What are *3* physical traces that would lead the Industrial-Organizational Psychologist to infer employees are/are not committed to the organization?

Physical Trace 1 = _____

Physical Trace 2 = _____

Physical Trace 3 = _____

05. A Military Psychologist wants to have sufficient psychological services available to soldiers when they return to base following the various conflicts that occur during a war. The more intense the conflict, the more services he wants to be available. If the Military Psychologist is given photographs taken at the scene of a conflict, what are *3* physical traces that could be used by the Military Psychologist to infer the intensity level of the conflict?

Physical Trace 1 = _____

Physical Trace 2 = _____

Physical Trace 3 = _____

06. An Engineering Psychologist is given the task of identifying which features of a company's new line of cars are of most interest to consumers. The company does not, however, want consumers to know their interests are being studied. The Engineering Psychologist goes to a dealership that sells the new line of cars after the lot closes. What are *3* physical traces the Psychologist can use to infer which features are of most interest to consumers?

Physical Trace 1 = _____

Physical Trace 2 = _____

Physical Trace 3 = _____

07. A Community Psychologist has been hired by the Mayor of a large city after the Mayor read an editorial in the local paper which expressed the opinion there was growing racial tension in his city. The Mayor wants the Community Psychologist to determine whether the opinion in the editorial is accurate. What are *3* physical traces that can be used by the Community Psychologist to infer that there is/is not growing racial tension within the city?

> **Physical Trace 1 =** _____
>
> **Physical Trace 2 =** _____
>
> **Physical Trace 3 =** _____

08. An Environmental Psychologist has been hired by the Manager at a local mall to identify the restaurant in the mall Food Court that is the most popular. To conduct the study without the awareness of mall customers, the Manager gives the Environmental Psychologist access to Food Court after the mall has closed. What are *3* physical traces that could be used by the Environmental Psychologist to infer which restaurant is the most popular?

> **Physical Trace 1 =** _____
>
> **Physical Trace 2 =** _____
>
> **Physical Trace 3 =** _____

09. A Health Psychologist is hired to design a new fitness center. His first task is to decide what equipment he needs for the new center. To help him decide, he visits a nearby facility and is given a tour of the facility after it closes for the evening. What are *3* physical traces that can be used by the Psychologist to infer which pieces of fitness equipment are the most popular?

> **Physical Trace 1 =** _____
>
> **Physical Trace 2 =** _____
>
> **Physical Trace 3 =** _____

10. A Psychologist with expertise in animal behavior is hired by a zoo to evaluate how its animals are adapting to the cages and enclosures at the zoo. She tours the zoo after it closes and observes the various cages and enclosures. What are *3* physical traces that could be used by the Psychologist to infer how the animals are/are not adapting to their cages and enclosures at the zoo?

> **Physical Trace 1 =** _____
>
> **Physical Trace 2 =** _____
>
> **Physical Trace 3 =** _____

PART B

Select *3* of the 10 scenarios and describe how the physical traces of behavior you identified could be interpreted by the Psychologists in such a way that the inferences they make are inaccurate.

Scenario 1	Suicidal Intentions		Scenario 6	Car Features	
Scenario 2	Robbed on Vacation		Scenario 7	Racial Tension	
Scenario 3	Marital Stability		Scenario 8	Popular Restaurant	
Scenario 4	Work Commitment		Scenario 9	Fitness Equipment	
Scenario 5	Conflict Intensity		Scenario 10	Zoo Enclosures	

Scenario # and Title:

How might the physical traces of behavior you identified be interpreted by the Psychologist in such a way that the inferences he/she makes about behavior are inaccurate?

_____

_____

_____

_____

_____

Scenario # and Title:

How might the physical traces of behavior you identified be interpreted by the Psychologist in such a way that the inferences he/she makes about behavior are inaccurate?

_____

_____

_____

_____

_____

Scenario # and Title:

How might the physical traces of behavior you identified be interpreted by the Psychologist in such a way that the inferences he/she makes about behavior are inaccurate?

_____

_____

_____

_____

_____

References

1. Johnson, A. (2013). Surveillance society: 7 ways you're being watched, and didn't know it. *CTV News.* Retrieved from http://www.ctvnews.ca/sci-tech/surveillance-society-7-ways-you-re-being-watched-and-didn-t-know-it-1.1337075

2. Von Drehle, D. (2013). The surveillance state. *Time.* Retrieved from http://nation.time.com/20013/08/01/the-surveillance-society/

3. Bennett, S. (2012). With social media you're always being watched so ask yourself...Should I post this? *Media Bistro: All Twitter.* Retrieved from http://www.mediabistro.com/alltwitter/should-i-post-this_b28545

4. Irby, K., Watkins, A., Graff, T., & Thibodeaux, K. (2103). All the ways you're being watched. *MSN News.* Retrieved from http://news.msn.com/us/all-the-ways-youre-being-watched

5. Singh, K. J. (2013). What are the types of observation? *Total MBA Guide.* Retrieved from http://www.mbaofficial.com/mba-courses/research-methodology/what-are-the-types-of-observation/

6. Leary, M. R. (2007). *Introduction to behavioral research methods* (5th ed.). Boston, MA: Pearson/Allyn & Bacon.

7. Cozby, P. C., & Bates, S. C. (2011). *Methods in behavioral research* (11th ed.). New York, NY: McGraw-Hill Publishers.

8. Passer, M. W. (2013). *Research methods: Concepts and connections.* New York, NY: Worth Publishers.

9. Schweigert, W. A. (2012). *Research methods in psychology: A handbook* (3rd ed.). Long Grove, IL: Waveland Press.

10. Jackson, S. L. (2014). *Research methods: A modular approach* (3rd ed.). Stamford, CT: Cengage Learning.

11. Bordens, K. S., & Abbot, B. B. (2011). *Research design and methods: A process approach* (8th ed.). Boston, MA: McGraw-Hill Publishers.

12. Smith, R. A., & Davis, S. F. (2012). *The psychologist as detective: An introduction to conducting research in psychology* (6th ed.). Boston, MA: Pearson Publishers.

13. Ray, W. J. (2011). *Methods: Towards a science of behavior and experience* (10th ed.). Belmont, CA: Wadsworth/Cengage Learning.

14. Kantowitz, B. H., Roediger, H. L., & Elmes, D. G. (2014). *Experimental psychology* (10th ed.). Stamford, CT: Cengage Learning.

15. Maclin, M. K., & Solso, R. L. (2007). *Experimental psychology: A case approach* (8th ed.). Boston, MA: Pearson/Allyn & Bacon.

16. Beins, B. C. (2012). *Research methods: A tool for life* (3rd ed.). Boston, MA: Pearson Publishers.

17. Dewey, R. A. (2007). Observational research. *Psychology: An Introduction.* Retrieved from http://www.intropsych.com/ch01_psychology_and_science/observational_research.html

18. Nathan's Famous, Inc. (2014). International hot dog eating championship. *Nathan's Famous.Com.* Retrieved from http://nathansfamous.com/index.php/hot-dog-eating-contest

19. Evans, A. N., & Rooney, B. F. (2007). *Methods in psychological research.* Thousand Oaks, CA: Sage Publications.

20. Rosnow, R. L., & Rosenthal, R. (2012). *Beginning behavioral research: A conceptual primer* (7th ed.). Boston, MA: Pearson Publishers.

21. Price, P., & Oswald, K. (2008). Observational research. *Research Methods for Dummies.* Retrieved from http://psych.csufresno.edu/psy144/Content/Design/Nonexperimental/observation.html

22. Sommer, B. A. (2006). *Physical trace measures.* Retrieved from http://psychology.ucdavis.edu/faculty_sites/sommerb/sommerdemo/traces/intro.htm

23. Zeisel, J. (1984). Observing physical traces. *In Inquiry by design: Tools for environment-behavior research* (pp. 89–110). Cambridge, UK: Cambridge University Press.

MODULE
13

Correlational Research

When psychologists conduct research, they attempt to describe, predict, explain, and/or modify behavior and mental processes. In order to predict, explain, and/or modify behavior and mental processes, psychologists must possess a thorough understanding of the relationships that exist among both individual and environmental variables and the behaviors and mental processes of interest. To acquire a thorough understanding of the relationships that exist among variables as they naturally occur in the world around them, psychologists engage in a method of research known as correlational research.[1,2,3]

Correlational research provides psychologists with a valuable tool that can be used for a variety of research purposes. First, correlational research can be used to examine the strength (i.e. size), form (i.e. linear, non-linear), and direction (i.e. direct, inverse) of the relationship that exists between two variables of interest.[1,2,3] Second, if a meaningful relationship exists between two variables, psychologists can use the values on one of the variables to make predictions about values on the second variable[2,4,5] (e.g. if there is a meaningful relationship between study time and exam performance, psychologists could use the number of hours students studied to predict their scores on the final exam in their college Research Methods course). Third, correlational research can be used by psychologists to assess the reliability of the measurement instruments (e.g. tests, scales, raters, observers) they use when conducting research.[6,7,8] Reliable instruments produce scores, ratings, or observations that are consistent (i.e. highly and positively correlated) across time, test administrations, and raters/observers. Fourth, correlational research can be used by psychologists to assess the validity of a measurement instrument[6,7,8] (i.e. does the instrument measure what it's intended to measure?). If a measurement instrument is valid, it will produce scores that are highly and positively correlated with: (a) other instruments that measure the same construct and (b) instruments that measure related constructs (e.g. for a job satisfaction measure created by an Industrial-Organizational Psychologist to be considered a valid measure, it must produce scores that correlate strongly and positively with scores on other existing measures of job satisfaction as well as measures of constructs related to job satisfaction (e.g. organizational citizenship, absenteeism, turnover). Finally, correlational research can be used by psychologists to verify or falsify the relationships between variables predicted by a psychological theory. If the predicted relationships between variables are not verified, psychologists will have evidence that the theory needs further modification and development.[2,3,9]

Conducting Correlational Research

When conducting a correlational research study, psychologists must first select the two variables they are interested in studying.[1,2,3] The goal of the study is to then determine the nature of the relationship that exists between these two variables. Psychologists must then determine how they will measure their two variables of interest. By consulting existing research literature, psychologists can examine: (a) the methods used by other psychologists to measure the variables of interest, (b) the methods of measurement that have been demonstrated to be reliable and valid ways to measure the variables of interest, and (c) the methods of measurement that have gained acceptance among both scientists and practitioners working in research and applied settings. If the variables of interest have not received any prior research attention, psychologists will have to develop methods of measurement for their variables of interest and establish the reliability and validity of these methods before they can be used to collect data in a correlational research study. Once psychologists have selected and/or developed their methods of measurement, they will then use these methods to measure their variables of interest. An important feature of a correlational research study is that the two variables of interest are measured as they naturally occur. There is no attempt on the part of the psychologists conducting the study to manipulate any elements of the environment in which the variables of interest are measured.[10,11,12] After they have collected data on their variables of interest, psychologists will compute a statistic known as a "correlation coefficient"[1,2,11] and create a graph known as a "scatterplot"[8,10,13] to help them draw conclusions about the: (a) strength, (b) direction, and (c) form of the relationship between the variables.

Strength of a Relationship

To measure the "strength" of the relationship between two variables, psychologists will compute a statistic known as a correlation coefficient. The letter "r" is used to represent a correlation coefficient. Correlation coefficients can range in value from .00 (i.e. indicating the absence of a systematic relationship between variables) to 1.00 (i.e. indicating the presence of a perfect systematic relationship between variables).[1,2,5] The greater the absolute size of the correlation coefficient value: (a) the stronger the relationship between two variables and (b) the more likely psychologists can use the values of one variable (X) to make accurate predictions about the values of a second variable (Y).[2,4,5] While there are many rules of thumb for evaluating the strength of the relationship that exists between variables based on the size of the correlation coefficient, we will use Cohen's (1988)[2,14] criteria to determine whether the relationship between two variables is considered weak, moderate, or strong.

Relationship Strength	Correlation Coefficient (r)
Weak	.10–.29
Moderate	.30–.49
Strong	.50–1.00

Direction of a Relationship

When a correlation coefficient is computed, the value may be positive or negative. A positive correlation coefficient indicates there is a positive (i.e. direct) relationship between the variables. A positive correlation coefficient indicates the values of the variables increase or decrease in direct relationship to one another (i.e. as the value of variable X increases, the value of variable Y also increases; as the value of variable X decreases, the value of variable Y also decreases).[2,3,8] For example, we would expect to find a positive correlation exists between the variables of physical attractiveness and number of telephone numbers received at a single's bar (i.e. as physical attractiveness increases, the number of telephone numbers received would also increase; as physical attractiveness decreases, the number of telephone numbers received would also decrease). A negative correlation coefficient indicates the values of the variables increase or decrease in an inverse relationship to one another (i.e. as the value of variable X increases, the value of variable Y decreases; as the value of variable X decreases, the value of variable Y increases).[2,3,8] As an example, we would expect to find a negative correlation between the variables of job stress and job satisfaction (i.e. as level of job stress increases, job satisfaction would decrease; as level of job stress decreases; job satisfaction would increase). Because correlation coefficient values can be positive or negative, the true range of potential correlation coefficient values is −1.00 to +1.00.[7,8,9]

Form of a Relationship

A correlation coefficient measures the extent to which there is a linear (i.e. straight line) relationship between two variables. The greater the size of the correlation coefficient, the more linear the relationship between variables. A correlation coefficient of 1.00 would indicate there is a perfect linear relationship between two variables (i.e. an increase in the value of variable X is accompanied by a similar increase in the value of variable Y).[1,2,8]

   To illustrate the strength, direction, and form of the relationship that exists between two variables, psychologists can create a graph known as a "scatterplot." In a "scatterplot," variable X is placed on the horizontal axis and variable Y is placed on the vertical access. The pair of X and Y values for each member of the research sample is then plotted on the "scatterplot." The completed "scatterplot" provides psychologists with a visual representation of the relationship that exists between two variables.[8,10,13] The strength of the relationship can be evaluated by observing the extent to which the "scatterplot" displays a "linear" (i.e. straight line) relationship between the variables. The higher the correlation coefficient, the more "linear" the relationship will appear on the "scatterplot." The direction of the relationship can be evaluated by observing the type of pattern formed by the data points on the "scatterplot." When a correlation coefficient is positive (i.e. as X increases, Y increases; as X decreases, Y decreases), the pattern formed by the data points will extend from the lower left portion of the "scatterplot" up to the upper right portion of the "scatterplot."[2,3,8] Below are a set of "scatterplots" illustrating positive correlations of various strengths between two variables. Notice how: (a) the relationship between the two variables becomes more linear, and (b) the pattern of the data points more clearly assumes the classic lower left to upper right pattern characteristic of a positive correlation as the strength of the relationship increases.

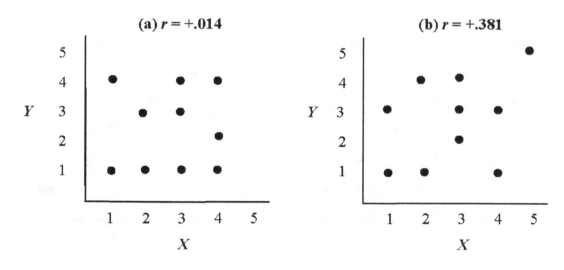

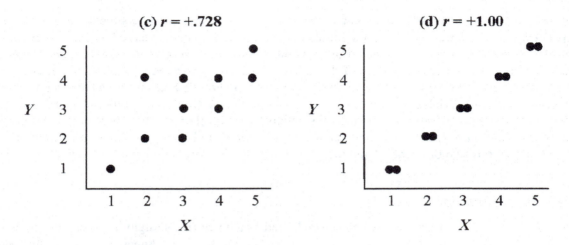

When the value of a correlation coefficient is negative (i.e. as X increases, Y decreases; as X decreases, Y increases), the pattern formed by the data points will extend from the upper left portion of the "scatterplot" to the lower right portion of the "scatterplot."[2,3,8] Below are a set of "scatterplots" illustrating negative correlations of various strengths.

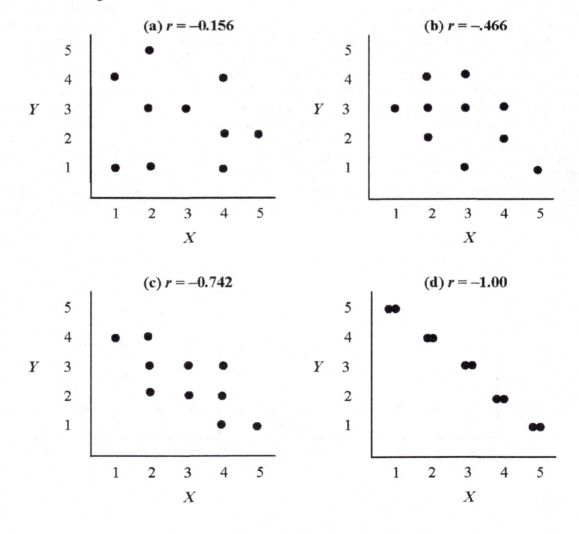

Psychologists also use "scatterplots" to detect the presence of a non-linear relationship between two variables that is known as a "curvilinear" relationship.[1,2,10] When a "curvilinear" relationship exists between two variables, the pattern formed by the data points will assume a "U-shaped" or an "Inverted-U-shaped" form. The presence of a "curvilinear" relationship can be overlooked by psychologists who compute a correlation coefficient to assess the relationship between two variables but who fail to also create a "scatterplot" of the relationship. How can a "curvilinear" relationship be overlooked by psychologists? Given that a correlation coefficient measures the degree to which a "linear" (i.e. straight line) relationship exists between variables, when a "curvilinear" (i.e. non-linear) relationship is present, the computed correlation value will be small in size. Psychologists may interpret this small correlation coefficient as indicating there is a weak relationship between the variables that does not warrant further attention. However, if psychologists were to create a "scatterplot" of the relationship, they would see that there actually was a systematic relationship between the two variables; just not a linear relationship. Therefore, when doing correlational research, it is important psychologists assess the relationship between two variables both statistically and graphically to draw the most accurate conclusions about the nature of the relationship that exists between variables.[2,10,11] Below are scatterplots representing a "curvilinear" relationship between two variables. Note how: (a) the correlation coefficients in both cases are small in size, (b) the "curvilinear" relationships can assume either a "U-shaped" or "Inverted-U-shaped" pattern, and (c) the "curvilinear" relationships reveal important information about the nature of the relationships that exist between the variables.

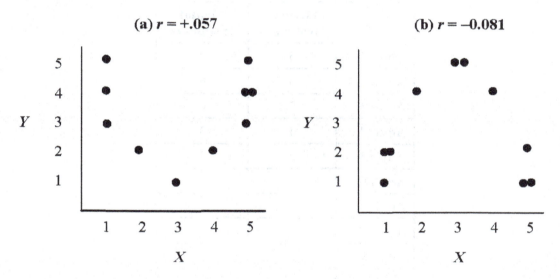

To illustrate how psychologists interpret a "curvilinear" relationship between variables, let's assume that in "scatterplot" **(a)** above that variable X is the number of siblings and variable Y is the average number of arguments per day with one's siblings. The correlation coefficient value ($r = +.057$) could be interpreted as indicating that there is a negligible relationship between the two variables. However, the "curvilinear" relationship illustrated by the "scatterplot" of the relationship would indicate people who have a small ($X = 1$) or large ($X = 5$) number of siblings are likely to have more daily arguments with their siblings than people with a moderate ($X = 3$) number of siblings. Why? Perhaps people argue more when they have only one sibling because they resent having to share the attention of mom and dad with the "other kid in the house" and argue more when they have 5 siblings because with 5 siblings in the house it simply provides more opportunities to argue with someone!

Now let's assume that in "scatterplot" **(b)** that variable X is physical attractiveness and variable Y is the number of people who ask you to dance at a party. The correlation coefficient value ($r = -.081$) could be interpreted as indicating that there is a negligible relationship between the two variables. However, the curvilinear relationship illustrated by the "scatterplot" of the relationship would indicate people who are of moderate attractiveness ($X = 3$) are likely to get asked to dance by more people at a party than people who are of lower attractiveness (X =1) or highly attractive (X = 5). Why? Perhaps people don't want to dance at a party with people who are unattractive and they are too intimidated to ask highly attractive people to dance!

Examples of Correlational Research

To illustrate the steps involved in conducting a correlational research study, let's assume that a Health Psychologist is interested in studying the relationship that exists between 2 health-related variables: (a) perception of current physical health and (b) perception of current mental health. The Health Psychologist consults the research literature and finds a pair of 7-point rating scales that have been shown to be reliable and valid measures of health-related perceptions and which are recognized as effective measures by psychologists conducting health-related research and working as practitioners within health-care settings. The Health Psychologist then selects a random sample of n = 10 adults from the local community for inclusion in her research sample. She then has each of the n = 10 adults in her research sample provide ratings of current physical health and current mental health using the 7-point rating scales selected for the study (i.e. higher ratings indicating better physical and mental health). The ratings provided by members of the Health Psychologist's research sample appear below.

	Physical Health (X)	Mental Health (Y)
Adult 1	3	2
Adult 2	5	6
Adult 3	7	6
Adult 4	4	3
Adult 5	2	2
Adult 6	6	6
Adult 7	5	5
Adult 8	3	4
Adult 9	6	5
Adult 10	4	4

The Health Psychologist will then compute a statistic known as a correlation coefficient to determine the strength (i.e. size) of the relationship that exists between perceptions of physical and mental health for the members of her research sample. The statistic the Health Psychologist will use to compute her correlation coefficient is known as Pearson's r (i.e. the Pearson product moment correlation coefficient).[8,9,13] The formula for Pearson's r appears below.

$$r = \frac{\sum XY - \frac{(\Sigma X)(\Sigma Y)}{n}}{\sqrt{\left(\Sigma X^2 - \frac{(\Sigma X)^2}{n}\right)\left(\Sigma Y^2 - \frac{(\Sigma Y)^2}{n}\right)}}$$

To compute Pearson's r, the Health Psychologist will first label one of her variables X (perception of physical health) and one of her variables Y (perception of mental health). She will then compute a value for each of the individual terms in the Pearson's r formula. Below are two tables. The first table describes how the Health Psychologist will compute each of these values and the second contains the actual values for each individual term in the Pearson's r formula.[8]

ΣXY	Multiply the X and Y values for each sample member and then sum the XY values
ΣX	Add up the X values for all members of the research sample
ΣY	Add up the Y values for all members of the research sample
ΣX^2	Square the X value for each sample member and then sum the X^2 values
ΣY^2	Square the Y value for each sample member and then sum the Y^2 values

	Physical Health (X)	Mental Health (Y)	XY	X^2	Y^2
Adult 1	3	2	6	9	4
Adult 2	5	6	30	25	36
Adult 3	7	6	42	49	36
Adult 4	4	3	12	16	9
Adult 5	2	2	4	4	4
Adult 6	6	6	36	36	36
Adult 7	5	5	25	25	25
Adult 8	3	4	12	9	16
Adult 9	6	5	30	36	25
Adult 10	4	4	16	16	16
	$\Sigma X = 45$	$\Sigma Y = 43$	$\Sigma XY = 213$	$\Sigma X^2 = 225$	$\Sigma Y^2 = 207$

The Health Psychologist will then enter each of these values into the Pearson's r formula (shown below). She will then compute the value of the correlation coefficient that will allow her to determine the strength (i.e. size) and the direction (i.e. direct, inverse) of the relationship that exists between perceptions of physical and mental health for members of her research sample.

$$r = \frac{213 - \dfrac{(45)(43)}{10}}{\sqrt{\left(225 - \dfrac{(45)^2}{10}\right)\left(207 - \dfrac{(43)^2}{10}\right)}} = +.87$$

In addition to using the Pearson's *r* formula to compute her correlation coefficient, she will also create a "scatterplot" of the relationship between the perceptions of physical and mental health for the members of her research sample. Her "scatterplot" appears below.

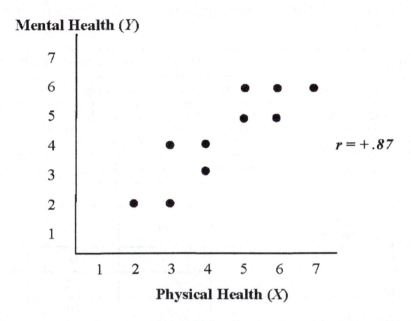

Based on her correlation coefficient ($r = +.87$), the Health Psychologist can conclude there is a strong, positive correlation between perceptions of physical health and mental health among the members of her sample. The "strength" of the correlation can be seen in the strong "linear" nature of the relationship illustrated in the scatterplot (i.e. the data points form a pattern that closely approximates a straight line). To further examine the "strength" of the relationship, the Health Psychologist can calculate a statistic known as r^2 (i.e. "coefficient of determination"). The r^2 statistic would tell the Health Psychologist what percentage of the variability in variable *Y* can be accounted for by the variability in variable *X* (i.e. and conversely what percentage of the variability in variable *X* can be accounted for by variability in variable *Y*).[2,8,11] In other words, what percentage of the variability in variable *Y* can be accounted for by knowing the value of variable *X* (i.e. and conversely, what percentage of the variability in variable *X* can be accounted for by knowing the value of variable *Y*). As the value of r^2 increases (and the "strength" of the relationship between variables *X* and *Y* increases), we can: (a) account for a greater percentage of the variability and (b) make more accurate predictions about the value of one variable knowing the value of the second variable. The r^2 statistic is calculated by simply squaring the calculated *r* value (i.e. correlation coefficient). For the Health Psychologist's study, the value of r^2 would be $(+.87)^2 = .76$. This r^2 value would tell the Health Psychologist she can account for 76% of the variability in variable *Y* (perception of one's mental health) by knowing the value of variable *X* (perception of one's physical health). Conversely, she can account for 76% of the variability in variable *X* (perception of one's physical health) by knowing the value of variable *Y* (perception of one's mental health).

The "positive" direction of the relationship is evident in the way the pattern formed by the data points moves from the lower left portion of the "scatterplot" to the upper right portion of the "scatterplot"; a pattern that is characteristic of a positive correlation. The "positive" direction of the relationship also indicates that there is a direct relationship between the two variables. As perceptions of physical health increase (become more positive), perceptions of mental health also increase (become more positive).

But can the Health Psychologist conclude that an increase in perceptions of physical health (*X*) causes an increase in perceptions of mental health (*Y*)? Unfortunately, the answer to that question is no. There are 3 reasons why psychologists are unable to make a causal statement about the relationship between two variables in a correlational research study. First, in order to make a causal statement about the relationship between 2 variables, psychologists must conduct an experimental research study.[2,3,4] In an experimental study, psychologists: (a) systematically manipulate an independent variable, (b) eliminate all extraneous and/or confounding variables, (c) measure a dependent variable to assess the effect of the independent variable, and (d) control all other factors within the experimental environment to ensure that the independent variable is the only factor that could be the cause of an observed change in the dependent variable. It is this systematic manipulation and high degree of control that allows psychologists to be able to make a causal statement about the relationship between two variables (i.e. independent and dependent variables). In a correlational study, there is no systematic manipulation of variables nor a high degree of control. Psychologists simply measure two naturally-occurring variables.[10,11,12] As a result, while there may be a causal relationship between the variables, the conditions necessary to make a causal statement about that relationship are not present in a correlational research study. This fact is best captured by the classic phrase associated with correlation research, "correlation does not imply causation." [2,3,12]

The second reason why psychologists are unable to make a causal statement about the relationship between two variables is that in some instances, it may be unclear how to interpret the direction of the relationship between the two variables.[4,5,10] If a significant relationship is found to exist between variable X and variable Y, it is possible that variable X causes a change in variable Y. However, it is equally possible that variable Y causes a change in variable X. For example, if a significant relationship is found between depression and weight, it is possible that level of depression (X) causes a change in weight (Y). However, it could also be the case that weight (Y) causes a change in level of depression (X). In the correlational study conducted by the Health Psychologist, it could be the case that perceptions of one's physical health (X) could cause a change in perception of one's mental health (Y). However, it could also be the case that perception of one's mental health (Y) could cause a change in perception of one's physical health (X). A correlational research study does not provide psychologists with sufficient information to determine the true direction of the relationship that exists between variables. When the problem of "directionality" arises, psychologists have to conduct additional statistical analyses or conduct additional experimental tests of their two variables to determine which directional interpretation (i.e. X causes Y vs. Y causes X) has greater empirical support.

The problem of "directionality" is not an issue in all correlational research studies. In some instances, the direction of the relationship between two variables can only be interpreted in one direction. For example, let's assume a Counseling Psychologist who specializes in marital therapy finds a significant relationship between months of cohabitation before marriage (X) and years of marriage before divorce (Y) in a sample of his clients. In interpreting this relationship, it is possible variable X causes a change in variable Y (i.e. months of cohabitation before marriage could cause a change in years of marriage before divorce). It would not be possible, however, for variable Y to cause a change in variable X (i.e. years of marriage before divorce could not cause a change in months of cohabitation before marriage). As a second example, assume that a Developmental Psychologist finds a significant relationship between the number of siblings (X) and language skills (Y) in a sample of 3-year-old children. In interpreting this relationship, while it is possible variable X causes a change in variable Y (i.e. the number of siblings could cause a change in language skills in 3-year-old children), it would not be possible, however, for language skills in 3-year-old children to cause a change in the number of siblings).

There is a third reason why psychologists are unable to make a causal statement about the relationship between two variables. In some instances, although there is a significant correlation between two variables, there is no causal relationship between them (i.e. variable X does not cause changes in variable Y; variable Y does not cause changes in variable X). However, there is an unidentified variable known as a "3rd variable," which causes changes in both variable X and Y. The effects of the "3rd variable" makes it appear as though variable X and variable Y are causally related to one another.[3,4,5] In the Health Psychologist's correlational study, it is possible there is no causal relationship between perceptions of one's physical and mental health. There may be a 3rd variable which causes a change in perceptions of both physical and mental health that makes it appear that perceptions of one's physical and mental health are causally related to one another. Since there was a positive relationship between perceptions of physical and mental health in the Health Psychologist's study ($r = +.87$), a potential 3rd variable would have to cause variables X and Y to both increase or both decrease at the same time. Potential 3rd variables could include: (a) level of income, (b) marital satisfaction, and (c) level of exercise. A high level of income, a satisfying marriage, or a high level of exercise could cause an increase (i.e. or improvement) in perceptions of both physical and mental health. A low level of income, an unsatisfying marriage, or a low level of exercise could cause a decrease (i.e. or decline) in perceptions of both physical and mental health. The simultaneous change in variables X and Y caused by a 3rd variable can give the appearance that there is a causal relationship between variables X and Y when no causal relationship actually exists. The potential effect of these "3rd variables" is illustrated below.[2]

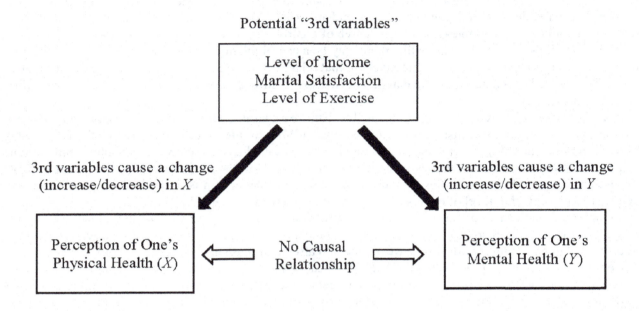

Potential "3rd variables"

Level of Income
Marital Satisfaction
Level of Exercise

3rd variables cause a change
(increase/decrease) in X

3rd variables cause a change
(increase/decrease) in Y

Perception of One's
Physical Health (X)

No Causal
Relationship

Perception of One's
Mental Health (Y)

If the relationship between perceptions of physical health and mental health in the Health Psychologist's study had been negative, a potential 3rd variable would have to be able to cause one variable to increase and the second variable to decrease at the same time (i.e. as variable X increases, variable Y decreases; as variable X decreases, variable Y increases). For the Health Psychologist's study, potential "3rd variables" could include: (1) age and (2) number of children. An increase in age could cause perceptions of physical health to decline (i.e. due to the negative health effects associated with ageing) but cause perceptions of mental health to increase (i.e. due to having more experience coping with the pressures of life). An increase in number of children could cause perceptions of physical health to increase (i.e. due to the increased activity required to keep up with a large number of children) but cause perceptions of mental health to decrease (i.e. due to the increase in parental stress associated with raising a large number of children).

As a second example of correlational research, let's assume an Industrial-Organizational Psychologist is interested in studying the relationship between 2 dimensions of life satisfaction: (a) satisfaction with one's work life and (b) satisfaction with one's family life. He consults the research literature and finds a life satisfaction scale that contains a 10-item subscale measuring satisfaction with one's work life and another 10-item subscale measuring satisfaction with one's family life. Both subscales have been used in prior life satisfaction research and have been used by practitioners working in both therapeutic and business settings. The Industrial-Organizational Psychologist then selects a random sample of n = 10 employees who work at businesses within the local community for inclusion in his research sample. He then has each of the employees in his research sample complete the life satisfaction scale and he records each employee's scores on the satisfaction with one's work life subscale and the satisfaction with one's family life subscale (i.e. Higher ratings indicating higher levels of satisfaction). The subscale scores for each of the n = 10 employees in his research sample appear below.

	Work Satisfaction (X)	Family Satisfaction (Y)
Employee 1	3	6
Employee 2	9	8
Employee 3	5	10
Employee 4	7	4
Employee 5	10	4
Employee 6	2	10
Employee 7	5	5
Employee 8	7	2
Employee 9	9	6
Employee 10	6	7

The Industrial-Organizational Psychologist will then compute a Pearson's r correlation coefficient to determine the strength (i.e. size) of the relationship that exists between satisfaction with one's work life and family life for the members of his research sample. In the table below are the values for each of the individual terms in the Pearson's r formula.[8]

	Work Satisfaction (X)	Family Satisfaction (Y)	XY	X²	Y²
Employee 1	3	6	18	9	36
Employee 2	9	8	72	81	64
Employee 3	5	10	50	25	100
Employee 4	7	4	28	49	16
Employee 5	10	4	40	100	16
Employee 6	2	10	20	4	100
Employee 7	5	5	25	25	25
Employee 8	7	2	14	49	4
Employee 9	9	6	54	81	36
Employee 10	6	7	42	36	49
	$\Sigma X = 63$	$\Sigma Y = 62$	$\Sigma XY = 363$	$\Sigma X^2 = 459$	$\Sigma Y^2 = 446$

The Industrial-Organizational Psychologist will then enter each of these values into the Pearson's r formula (shown below). He will then compute a correlation coefficient that he will use to determine the strength (i.e. size) and the direction (i.e. direct, inverse) of the relationship between satisfaction with one's work life and family life for the members of his research sample.

$$r = \frac{363 - \frac{(63)(62)}{10}}{\sqrt{\left(459 - \frac{(63)^2}{10}\right)\left(446 - \frac{(62)^2}{10}\right)}} = -.45$$

In addition to using the Pearson's r formula to compute his correlation coefficient, he will also create a "scatterplot" of the relationship between satisfaction with one's work life and one's family life for the members of his research sample. His "scatterplot" appears below.

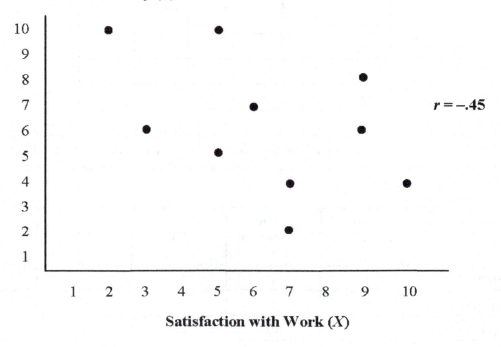

Satisfaction with Family (Y)

Satisfaction with Work (X)

Based on his correlation coefficient ($r = -.45$), the Industrial-Organizational Psychologist can conclude that there is a moderate, negative correlation between satisfaction with one's work life and family life among the members of his research sample. The "strength" of the correlation can be seen in the moderate linear nature of the relationship (i.e. data points line up in a manner that only moderately approximates a straight line). If the Industrial-Organizational Psychologist computes the value for the r^2 statistic $(-.45)^2$, he would arrive at a value of .20. This r^2 value would tell the Industrial-Organizational Psychologist that he can account for only 20% of the variability in variable Y (satisfaction with one's family life) by knowing the value of variable X (satisfaction with one's work life). Conversely, he can account for only 20% of the variability in variable X (satisfaction with one's work life) by knowing the value of variable Y (satisfaction with one's family life).

The "negative" direction of the relationship is evident in the way the pattern formed by the data points moves from the upper left portion of the "scatterplot" to the lower right portion of the "scatterplot"; a pattern characteristic of a negative correlation. The "negative" direction of the relationship also indicates that there is an inverse relationship between the two variables. As satisfaction with one's work life increases (becomes more positive), satisfaction with one's family life decreases (becomes more negative).

But can the Industrial-Organizational Psychologist conclude there is a causal relationship between satisfaction with one's work life and family life? Since he has conducted a correlational research study, the answer is no. Although he can conclude that his two variables are related to one another (i.e. a moderate, negative correlation), he cannot make a causal statement about the relationship that exists between the two variables (i.e. correlation does not imply causation).[2,3,12] He will also face a "directionality" problem when attempting to interpret the relationship that exists between the two variables. While it is possible that satisfaction with one's work life could cause a change in satisfaction with one's family life (i.e. variable X causes a change in variable Y), it is also possible that satisfaction with one's family life could cause a change in satisfaction with one's work life (i.e. variable Y causes a change in variable X). Finally, there could be a "3rd variable" that could account for the relationship between the two variables. Since the correlation between the two variables was negative, the 3rd variable would have to cause an increase in one variable while causing a decrease in the second variable at the same time. As an example, the availability of overtime could be a potential 3rd variable. An increase in availability of overtime could cause an increase in satisfaction with one's work life (i.e. due to the opportunity to earn more money), but cause a decrease in satisfaction with one's family life (i.e. due to the amount of time spent away from one's family).

Conclusion

Correlational research provides psychologists with a means of evaluating the strength (i.e. size), form (i.e. linear, non-linear), and direction (i.e. positive, negative, curvilinear) of the relationship that exists between two variables of interest.[1,2,3] Psychologists can use correlational research to achieve a variety of research goals including: (a) making accurate predictions about variables of interest, (b) assessing the reliability and validity of measurement instruments (e.g. tests; rating scales; raters/observers), and (c) testing predictions that are derived from different psychological theories.[2,6,7,8,9] However, due to limitations associated with correlational research (e.g. lack of experimental control/manipulation; directionality, 3rd variables), psychologists must use caution when attempting to draw causal conclusions about relationships that exists between variables of interest.[2,4,5]

EXERCISE 13A

Interpreting Relationships Between Variables

To examine the strength, form, and direction of the relationship between two variables, psychologists will calculate a statistic known as a "correlation coefficient" and create a graphical representation of the relationship known as a "scatterplot." Below are "correlation coefficients" and "scatterplots" for 6 different correlational studies. For each of the studies: **(a)** determine the strength (i.e. negligible, weak, moderate, strong), form (i.e. non-linear, linear, curvilinear), and direction (i.e. positive, negative) of the relationship, **(b)** determine the percentage of variable Y that can be accounted for by knowing the value of variable X, and **(c)** determine if psychologists will face a "directionality" problem when attempting to interpret the relationship.

01. An Educational Psychologist examined the relationship between high school student's level of self-confidence (X) and academic performance (Y).

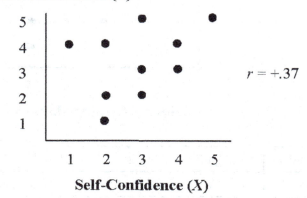

Strength	Negligible	Weak	Moderate	Strong
Form	Non-Linear		Linear	Curvilinear
Direction	Positive		Neutral	Negative

What % of academic performance (Y) can be accounted for by self-confidence (X)?	

What do the correlation coefficient and scatterplot reveal about the relationship between self-confidence (X) and academic performance (Y)?	
Does the psychologist face a directionality problem when interpreting the relationship between self-confidence (X) and academic performance (Y)? Explain.	
Can the psychologist conclude that a lack of self-confidence is the cause of poor academic performance among high school students? Explain.	

02. An Experimental Psychologist examined the relationship between critical thinking skills (X) and belief in paranormal phenomena (Y).

Belief in Paranormal (Y)

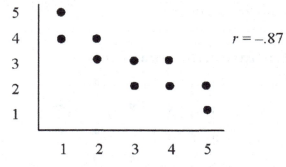

$r = -.87$

Critical Thinking Skills (X)

Strength	Negligible	Weak	Moderate	Strong
Form	Non-Linear	Linear	Curvilinear	
Direction	Positive	Neutral	Negative	

What % of paranormal belief (Y) can be accounted for by critical thinking skills (X)?	
What do the value of the correlation coefficient and scatterplot reveal about the relationship between critical thinking skills (X) and paranormal belief (Y)?	

Does the psychologist face a directionality problem when interpreting the relationship between critical thinking skills (X) and the belief in the paranormal (Y)? Explain.	
Can the psychologist conclude that belief in paranormal phenomena is caused by a lack of critical thinking skills? Explain.	

03. A Psychologist interested in the study of religiosity examined the relationship between belief in the afterlife (X) and fear of death (Y).

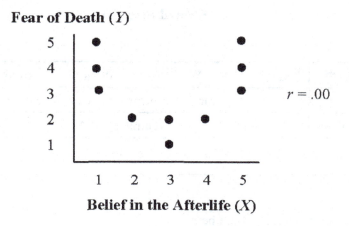

Fear of Death (Y)

$r = .00$

Belief in the Afterlife (X)

Strength	Negligible	Weak	Moderate	Strong
Form	Non-Linear	Linear	Curvilinear	
Direction	Positive	Neutral	Negative	

What % of fear of death (Y) can be accounted for by belief in the afterlife (X)?	
What does the value of the correlation coefficient reveal about the relationship between belief in the afterlife (X) and fear of death (Y)?	
What does the scatterplot reveal about the relationship between belief in the afterlife (X) and fear of death (Y)?	
How would you interpret the relationship between belief in the afterlife (X) and fear of death (Y)?	

04. A Sports Psychologist examined the relationship between crowd size (X) and athletic performance (Y) among professional tennis players.

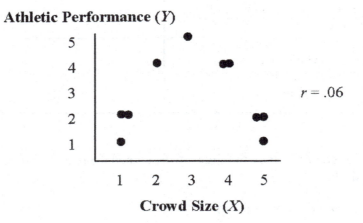

$r = .06$

Strength	Negligible		Weak	Moderate	Strong
Form		Non-Linear	Linear	Curvilinear	
Direction		Positive	Neutral	Negative	

What % of athletic performance (Y) can be accounted for by crowd size (X)?	
What does the value of the correlation coefficient reveal about the relationship between crowd size (X) and athletic performance (Y)?	
What does the scatterplot reveal about the relationship between crowd size (X) and athletic performance (Y)?	
How would you interpret the relationship between crowd size (X) and athletic performance (Y) among tennis players?	

05. An Industrial-Organizational Psychologist examined the relationship between applicant's job interview scores (X) and future job performance (Y).

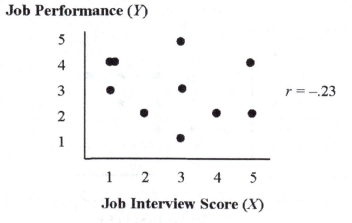

Job Performance (Y)

$r = -.23$

Job Interview Score (X)

Strength	Negligible	Weak	Moderate	Strong
Form		Non-Linear	Linear	Curvilinear
Direction		Positive	Neutral	Negative

What % of job performance (Y) can be accounted for by interview score (X)?	
What do the correlation coefficient and scatter-plot reveal about the relationship between job interview score (X) and job performance (Y)?	
Does the psychologist face a directionality problem when interpreting the relationship between job interview score (X) and job per-formance (Y)? Explain.	
How successful will the company be in select-ing high performing employees based on job interview scores? Explain.	

06. A Military Psychologist examined the relationship between physical fitness level (X) and performance during combat (Y) among military personnel.

Combat Performance (Y)

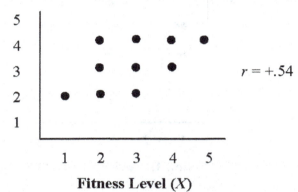

$r = +.54$

Fitness Level (X)

Strength	Negligible	Weak	Moderate	Strong
Form	Non-Linear		Linear	Curvilinear
Direction	Positive		Neutral	Negative

What % of combat performance (Y) can be accounted for by fitness level (X)?	
What do the correlation coefficient and scatterplot reveal about the relationship between fitness level (X) and combat performance (Y)?	
Does the psychologist face a directionality problem when interpreting the relationship between fitness level (X) and combat performance (Y)? Explain.	
Can the military conclude that a lack of physical fitness among military personnel is the cause of combat failure during times when our country is at war?	

EXERCISE 13B

Calculating and Interpreting Pearson's *r*

To assess the relationship that exists between two variables of interest, psychologists will calculate a statistic known as a "correlation coefficient" and create a graphical representation of the relationship known as a "scatterplot." A common statistical formula used by psychologists to calculate the correlation between two variables is Pearson's *r* (i.e. the Pearson product moment correlation coefficient). Below are two correlational research studies conducted by psychologists interested in assessing the relationship between two variables of interest. For each correlational study: **(a)** compute a correlation coefficient using the Pearson's *r* formula, **(b)** create a graphical representation of the relationship that exists between the 2 variables by creating a "scatterplot," and **(c)** interpret what the correlation coefficient and the scatterplot reveal about the relationship that exists between the two variables of interest.

Correlational Study #1

A Media Psychologist is interested in studying consumer attitudes toward a new horror movie. Specifically, he wants to know whether there is a relationship between consumers' level of excitement about going to see the movie (*X*) and the extent to which they enjoyed the movie (*Y*). He goes to a local movie theater and waits for a showing of the movie to end. As the crowd files out of the theater, he approaches a random sample of n = 10 movie patrons and asks each of them: (a) how much they were looking forward to seeing the movie (1 = I was a little excited to see the movie; 7 = I couldn't wait to see the movie) and (b) how much they ultimately enjoyed the movie (1 = I was disappointed with the movie; 7 = I though the movie was spectacular). The ratings provided by the n = 10 movie patrons appear below.

	Excitement Level (*X*)	Enjoyment Level (*Y*)
Patron 1	5	5
Patron 2	2	4
Patron 3	7	3
Patron 4	4	6
Patron 5	3	5
Patron 6	6	4
Patron 7	5	5
Patron 8	1	3
Patron 9	4	6
Patron 10	2	4

Please compute the value for each of the individual terms found in the Pearson's r formula.

	Excitement Level (X)	Enjoyment Level (Y)	XY	X^2	Y^2
Patron 1	5	5			
Patron 2	2	4			
Patron 3	7	3			
Patron 4	4	6			
Patron 5	3	5			
Patron 6	6	4			
Patron 7	5	5			
Patron 8	1	3			
Patron 9	4	6			
Patron 10	2	4			
	$\Sigma X =$	$\Sigma Y =$	$\Sigma XY =$	$\Sigma X^2 =$	$\Sigma Y^2 =$

Using the formula below, please compute the value for Pearson's r
(Show your work in the space provided)

$$r = \frac{\sum XY - \frac{(\Sigma X)(\Sigma Y)}{n}}{\sqrt{\left(\Sigma X^2 - \frac{(\Sigma X)^2}{n}\right)\left(\Sigma Y^2 - \frac{(\Sigma Y)^2}{n}\right)}}$$

Create a "scatterplot" to illustrate the relationship that exists between level of excitement (*X*) and level of enjoyment (*Y*)

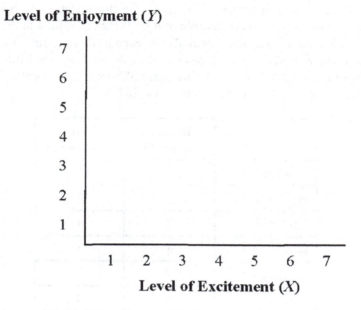

Level of Enjoyment (*Y*)

Level of Excitement (*X*)

Based on your Pearson's *r* value and your "scatterplot" of the relationship between level of excitement (*X*) and level of enjoyment (*Y*), what can the Media Psychologist conclude about the relationship that exists between his two variables of interest?

What percentage of the variability in enjoyment (*Y*) can the Media Psychologist account for by knowing the level of excitement (*X*)? (Show your work)

Study #2

A Social Psychologist is interested in whether there is a relationship between the sense of humor of men (X) and the sense of humor of the women they marry (Y). To answer this question the Social Psychologist goes to a local auto parts store and randomly selects a sample of n = 10 men shopping at the store who are wearing a wedding ring. She approaches the 10 married men and asks each of them to rate: (a) his own sense of humor and (b) his wife's sense of humor. The Social Psychologist asks each married man to provide his sense of humor ratings using a 7-point rating scale (1 = Terrible sense of humor; 7 = Great sense of humor). The sense of humor ratings provided by the n = 10 married men appear below.

	Husband Humor (X)	Wife Humor (Y)
Husband 1	6	7
Husband 2	2	2
Husband 3	4	4
Husband 4	4	5
Husband 5	7	5
Husband 6	6	4
Husband 7	1	3
Husband 8	3	5
Husband 9	7	7
Husband 10	5	6

Please compute the value for each of the individual terms found in the Pearson's r formula.

	Husband Humor (X)	Wife Humor (Y)	XY	X^2	Y^2
Husband 1	6	7			
Husband 2	2	2			
Husband 3	4	4			
Husband 4	4	5			
Husband 5	7	5			
Husband 6	6	4			
Husband 7	1	3			
Husband 8	3	5			
Husband 9	7	7			
Husband 10	5	6			
	$\Sigma X =$	$\Sigma Y =$	$\Sigma XY =$	$\Sigma X^2 =$	$\Sigma Y^2 =$

Using the formula below, please compute the value for Pearson's *r*
(Show your work in the space provided)

$$r = \frac{\sum XY - \frac{(\Sigma X)(\Sigma Y)}{n}}{\sqrt{\left(\Sigma X^2 - \frac{(\Sigma X)^2}{n}\right)\left(\Sigma Y^2 - \frac{(\Sigma Y)^2}{n}\right)}}$$

Create a "scatterplot" to illustrate the relationship that exists between husband sense of humor (*X*) and wife sense of humor (*Y*)

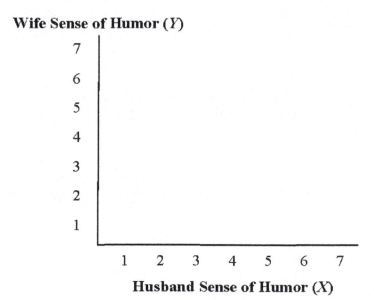

Wife Sense of Humor (*Y*)

Husband Sense of Humor (*X*)

Based on your Pearson's r value and your "scatterplot" of the relationship between husband sense of humor (X) and wife sense of humor (Y), what can the Social Psychologist conclude about the relationship that exists between her two variables of interest?

What percentage of the variability in wife sense of of humor (Y) can the Social Psychologist account for by knowing husband sense of humor (X)? (Show your work)

EXERCISE 13C

Correlation and "3rd Variables"

In some correlational studies, there may be no causal relationship between two variables (e.g. variable X does not cause a change in variable Y). However, there may be a "3rd variable" that causes a change in both variables X and Y. When the correlation between variables X and Y is positive, a 3rd variable would cause variables X and Y to increase or decrease at the same time (e.g. as X decreases, Y decreases). When the correlation between the two variables is negative, a 3rd variable would cause one of the variables to increase and the second variable to decrease (e.g. as X increases, Y decreases). The simultaneous change in variables X and Y caused by the "3rd variable" increases the strength of the relationship between the two variables. This can give the appearance there is a causal relationship between variables X and Y when no causal relationship actually exists. Below are descriptions of the results of correlational research studies. For each of the 13 studies: **(a)** identify a "3rd variable" that could account for the relationship between the variables, and **(b)** provide a rationale for the "3rd variable" you select.

01. As the number of doctors on duty in a hospital's emergency room (X) increases, the number of patient deaths in the hospital's emergency room (Y) increases.

3rd Variable =
Rationale?

02. As the price of a gallon of gas (X) increases in the southern United States, the amount of tourism revenue generated by these states (Y) increases.

3rd Variable =
Rationale?

03. As employee hair length (X) increases, the yearly salary they are paid by an employer (Y) decreases.

3rd Variable =
Rationale?

04. As the number of toys children are bought by their parents (X) increases, the number of tantrums the children throw (Y) increases.

3rd Variable =
Rationale?

05. As the rate of new home sales in the United States (X) increases, the rate of unemployment in the U.S. (Y) decreases.

3rd Variable =
Rationale?

06. As the amount of money spent annually on teen drug prevention programs in the United States (X) increases, the rate of teen deaths due to drug overdose in the U.S. (Y) increases.

3rd Variable =
Rationale?

07. As the amount of life insurance individuals purchase (X) increases, their life expectancy (Y) decreases.

3rd Variable =
Rationale?

08. As condom sales in the United States (X) increases, the rate of teen pregnancy in the U.S. (Y) increases.

3rd Variable =
Rationale?

09. As the number of bathing suits sold in the United States (X) decreases, the number of people admitted to psychiatric hospitals for depression in the U.S. (Y) increases.

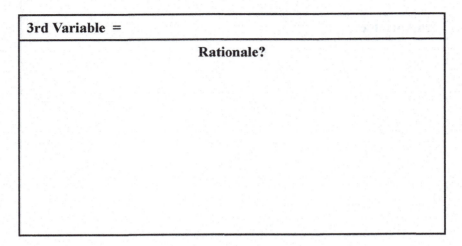

3rd Variable =
Rationale?

10. As the number of people who own a gun in the United States (X) increases, the rate of violent crime in the U.S. (Y) increases.

3rd Variable =
Rationale?

11. As the number of people attending church in the United States (X) increases, the amount of money donated to charitable organizations in the U.S. (Y) decreases.

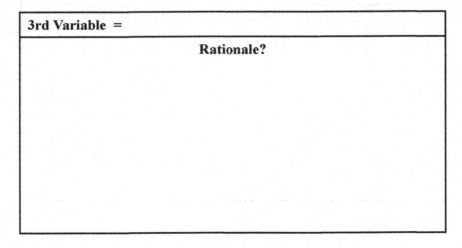

3rd Variable =
Rationale?

12. As the number of different women a man dates increases (X), the likelihood he will ever get married (Y) decreases.

3rd Variable =
Rationale?

13. As the average number of hours of television watched per day in the United States (X) increases, the rate of heart-attack related deaths in the U.S. (Y) increases.

3rd Variable =
Rationale?

References

1. Cozby, P. C., & Bates, S. C. (2011). *Methods in behavioral research* (11th ed.). New York, NY: McGraw-Hill Publishers.

2. Passer, M. W. (2013). *Research methods: Concepts and connections*. New York, NY: Worth Publishers.

3. Ray, W. J. (2011). *Methods: Towards a science of behavior and experience* (10th ed.). Belmont, CA: Wadsworth/Cengage Learning.

4. Bordens, K. S., & Abbot, B. B. (2011). *Research design and methods: A process approach* (8th ed.). Boston, MA: McGraw-Hill Publishers.

5. Beins, B. C. (2012). *Research methods: A tool for life* (3rd ed.). Boston, MA: Pearson Publishers.

6. Levy, P. E. (2012). *Industrial-organizational psychology: Understanding the workplace (*4th ed.). New York, NY: Worth Publishers.

7. Muchinsky, P. M. (2011). *Psychology applied to work* (10th ed.). Summerfield, NC: Hypergraphic Press.

8. Gravetter, F. J., & Wallnau, L. B. (2012). *Statistics for the behavioral sciences* (9th ed.). Belmont, CA: Wadsworth-Cengage Learning.

9. Kantowitz, B. H., Roediger, H. L., & Elmes, D. G. (2014). *Experimental psychology* (10th ed.). Stamford, CT: Cengage Learning.

10. Jackson, S. L. (2014). *Research methods: A modular approach* (3rd ed.). Stamford, CT: Cengage Learning.

11. Leary, M. R. (2007). *Introduction to behavioral research methods* (5th ed.). Boston, MA: Pearson/ Allyn & Bacon.

12. Smith, R. A., & Davis, S. F. (2012). *The psychologist as detective: An introduction to conducting research in psychology* (6th ed.). Boston, MA: Pearson Publishers.

13. Rosnow, R. L., & Rosenthal, R. (2012). *Beginning behavioral research: A conceptual primer* (7th ed.). Boston, MA: Pearson Publishers.

14. Cohen, J. (1988). *Statistical power analysis for the behavioral sciences* (2nd ed.). Hillsdale, New Jersey: Lawrence Erlbaum Associates.

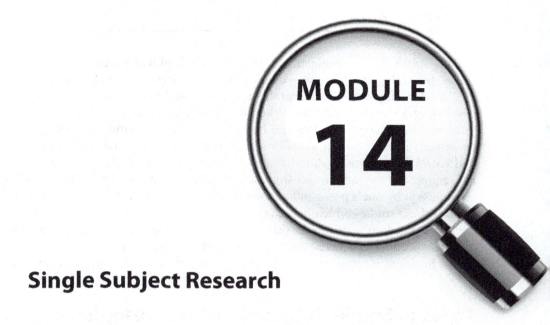

MODULE
14

Single Subject Research

When we think about psychological research, we typically think about research in which psychologists acquire a representative sample from a population of interest and randomly assign the members of the research sample to groups. Each group is exposed to a different level of an independent variable and measured on a dependent variable. An average score on the dependent variable is computed for each group and a statistical analysis is performed to determine if there is a significant difference between the groups caused by the effect of the independent variable.[1,2,3] While many psychologists elect to investigate the effect of independent variables on the behavior of groups of individuals, some psychologists take a different approach to psychological research and examine the effect of an independent variable on the behavior of a single subject.[1,2,4] While this "single subject" is typically a single individual (or a single animal), psychologists may also study larger social entities such as a single family, business, organization (e.g. school, agency, department), or community.[4] This type of psychological research is referred to as "single subject research,"[1,2,5] "small n research,"[2,3,6] or "N = 1 research."[2,7]

Single-subject research provides psychologists with a tool for achieving a primary goal of psychological research: modifying behavior. Psychologists can use single-subject research for a variety of purposes including: (a) investigating the effectiveness of an intervention (e.g. therapy, medical treatment, educational program, behavior modification program) in modifying a specific targeted behavior in a single subject,[1,8,9] (b) investigating the individual differences that occur in response to an intervention,[8,9,10] (c) investigating the extent to which the effect of an intervention will generalize beyond a single subject,[2,4,5] (d) investigating long-term effects of an intervention through repeated measurement of a targeted behavior over time,[2,7,9] and (e) investigating how an intervention can be best tailored to an individual's unique circumstances to achieve the desired modification (i.e. increase, decrease) of a targeted behavior.[2,4,10]

In some single-subject research studies, the goal is to investigate the effectiveness of an intervention in increasing a targeted behavior. When the "single subject" is an individual, these studies typically focus on interventions designed to increase behaviors that are healthy, adaptive, and appropriate for one's age or situation.[3,4,9] The goal of these studies is to improve well-being and the ability to change one's behavior to meet the expectations of society. When the "single-subject" is a larger unit of society such as an organization (e.g. business, school, hospital), these studies typically focus on interventions designed to increase behaviors related to performance, efficiency, and service.[11] The goal of these studies are to improve organizational performance and the ability of an organization to meet the needs of its consumers, and to adapt to changes (e.g. economic, social, technological) that may occur in the environment in which it operates.

In other single-subject research studies, the goal is to investigate the effectiveness of an intervention in decreasing a targeted behavior. When the "single subject" is an individual, these studies typically focus on interventions designed to decrease behaviors that are harmful, socially unacceptable, maladaptive, or inappropriate for one's age or situation.[3,4,5,9] The goal of these studies is to improve an individual's well-being and social acceptance by diminishing behaviors that can lead to physical harm to oneself or others, punitive consequences (e.g. suspension from school, trouble with the law, loss of employment, loss of relationships), or exclusion by one's peers and/or society. When the "single subject" is a larger unit of society such as a community, these studies typically focus on interventions designed to decrease behaviors that are contributing to a decline in the quality of life for the members of the community[1,5] (e.g. crime, drug use, litter, pollution, racial tension, speeding, distracted driving). The goal of these studies is to increase the safety, prosperity, reputation, and/or health of a community by decreasing the behaviors that serve as barriers to achieving these goals.

Types of Single-Subject Research Designs

There are multiple research designs that can be used by psychologists to conduct a single-subject research study. Three single-subject research designs commonly used by psychologists are the: (a) baseline design, (b) multiple baseline design, and (c) alternating treatment design.

The Baseline Design

The simplest form of the "baseline design" is known as an "AB design."[2,3,7,9] In an **"AB design,"** "A" refers to a "baseline phase." During the "baseline phase," psychologists will: (a) take repeated measurements of the target behavior as it naturally occurs and without any intervention, (b) plot these measurements on a graph to create a visual record of the rate of occurrence of the target behavior, and (c) continue to measure the target behavior until a stable pattern of behavior is observed.[1,2] A "baseline phase" in a single-subject research study is the equivalent to the "control group condition" in an experimental design. Both represent the measurement of a target behavior in the absence of any treatment or intervention. In order to be able to study the effectiveness of an intervention in modifying a target behavior, it is critical that psychologists establish a stable baseline measure of the target behavior before the intervention can be introduced.[2,5,9] Therefore, psychologists need to establish a "stability criteria"[2] that they will use to determine when they have acquired a stable baseline measure of the target behavior (e.g. an equal occurrence of the target behavior for three consecutive days). Psychologists must also be prepared and willing to extend to length of the "baseline phase" until they have achieved a stable baseline measure of behavior.[2]

To illustrate the process of establishing a stable baseline measure of a target behavior, let's assume that a distraught father has approached a psychologist for help. The father tells the psychologist his daughter has become terribly rude and everything that comes out of her mouth is a rude comment. Her rudeness has become so bad she has been suspended from school, she is constantly grounded at home, and she has lost all her friends. The father tells the psychologist he and his wife have tried everything to stop their daughter from being so rude. The psychologist agrees to help the father and tells him that he will use a single-subject research design to try to modify his daughter's behavior and reduce the number of rude comments she makes. He tells the father that the first phase of the study will be to establish a baseline measure of his daughter's rudeness. He tells the father he wants him to count the number of rude comments his daughter makes for each of the next 5 days and to plot his measurements on a graph. He tells the father not to make any changes in his daughter's life during these 5 days in order to get a measure of his daughter's rudeness as it naturally occurs and to not introduce any confounding factors into the study. The father's graph of his daughter's behavior appears following.

# of Rude Comments

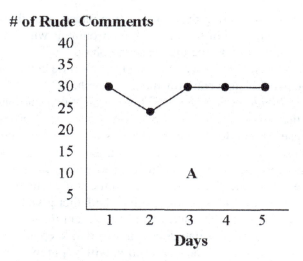

Days

In looking at the number of rude comments made by the daughter during the "baseline phase" of the study, the psychologist has acquired a stable measure of the daughter's rudeness. In the last three days of the "baseline phase," the daughter's rude behavior stabilized at a rate of 30 rude comments per day. Had the baseline not stabilized after 5 days, the psychologist would have asked the father to continue measuring the number of rude comments made per day by his daughter until the baseline became stable.[2,5]

While the psychologist was able to acquire a stable baseline in his "rudeness" study, this does not always occur in single-subject research. In some instances, psychologists are unable to acquire a stable baseline. In other instances, psychologists acquire a type of baseline known as a "drifting baseline."[2] A "drifting baseline" is one in which the measurements of a target behavior during the "baseline phase" of a single-subject research study progressively increase or decrease over the course of the "baseline phase." For example, let's assume that the father's graph of the number of rude comments made by his daughter during the "baseline phase" of the study had appeared as shown below.

# of Rude Comments

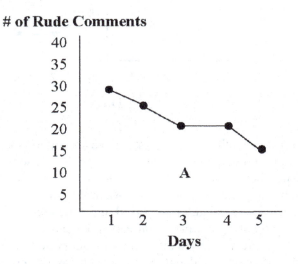

Days

Notice in the graph how the daughter's rudeness progressively decreases over the course of the 5-day "baseline phase." This is an example of a "drifting baseline" (i.e. the target behavior is "drifting" downward and declining during the baseline phase). When psychologists acquire a "drifting baseline," it presents them with two significant problems. First, since no intervention is occurring during the "baseline phase," the increase or decrease in the target behavior occurring throughout the "baseline phase" is being caused by some uncontrolled factor within the research environment.[2] Second, if the intervention is put into effect and an increase or decrease in target behavior is observed, psychologists will be unable to determine whether the increase or decrease in target behavior during the "intervention phase" was due to: (a) the effect of the intervention or (b) an uncontrolled factor within the research environment which had already caused the target behavior to begin to increase or decrease during the "baseline phase."[2,3,7,10]

Having established a stable baseline measure of the daughter's rude behavior during the "baseline phase" of the study, the father and the psychologist can now move on to phase "B" of the "AB design." Phase "B" in an "AB design" is known as the "intervention phase."[1,2] During the "intervention phase," the intervention (i.e. treatment) is introduced and the target behavior is repeatedly measured over the course of the "intervention phase." The "intervention phase" in single-subject research is equivalent to the "experimental group condition" in an experimental design. Both represent the measurement of a target behavior while a treatment or intervention is in effect. The psychologist has decided to use a monetary intervention to modify the daughter's rude behavior. Based on the results of the "baseline phase" of the study which revealed that the daughter typically made 30 rude comments per day, the psychologist has the father give her $30 each morning during the "intervention phase." Every time his daughter makes a rude comment throughout the day, she must return $1 back to her father. At the end of each day, his daughter is allowed to keep all the money she has left from the $30 she received at the beginning of the day. The intervention will be put in effect for 5 days. Each day during the 5-day "intervention phase," the father will once again count the number of rude comments made by his daughter and record his measurements on a graph. The father's graph of the number of rude comments made by his daughter during the 5-day "intervention phase" appears below.

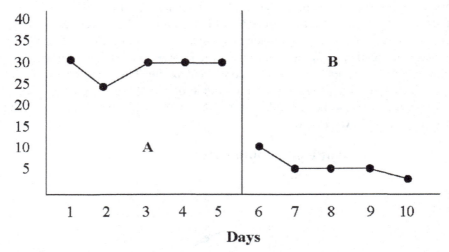

Looking at the graph, it appears that the psychologist's monetary intervention has been successful in modifying the daughter's behavior and reducing her rudeness. During the "baseline phase" of the study when no intervention was in effect, the number of rude comments made by the daughter stabilized at 30 rude comments per day. By comparison, during the "intervention phase" when the monetary intervention was in effect, the number of rude comments made by the daughter stabilized at 5 rude comments per day. Had the number of rude comments made per day by the daughter not stabilized at the end of the 5 day "intervention phase," the psychologists would have kept the intervention in effect for a longer period of time and had the father continue to measure the number of rude comments his daughter made each day during the "intervention phase" until a stable measure of behavior was acquired. Since the psychologist has acquired stable measures of the daughter's rudeness in both the "baseline" and "intervention" phases, and the only difference that exists between the "baseline" and "intervention" phases is whether the intervention is in effect, the psychologist would likely attribute the change (i.e. decrease) in the daughter's rudeness across phases of the study to the effect of the monetary intervention.

Now, let's take a look at what the results of the study would have looked like had the psychologist acquired a "drifting baseline"[2] rather than a stable baseline. In the graph following, the "drifting baseline" discussed earlier in the module has been substituted for the psychologist's stable baseline in phase "A" (i.e. "baseline phase") of the study.

# of Rude Comments

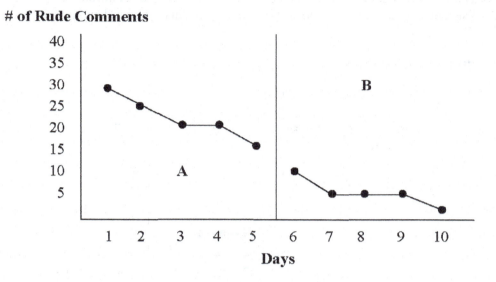

Notice how with the "drifting baseline" we have no stable measure of behavior during the "baseline phase" of the research study. If we were asked how many rude comments the daughter typically makes in a day, we would be unable to provide a reliable number due to the variability in the number of rude comments that she made per day during the 5-day "baseline phase." This is problematic because to evaluate the effectiveness of the intervention we need a stable measure of the target behavior from the "baseline phase" that we can then compare to a stable measure of the target behavior from the "intervention phase." In addition, when we analyze the decrease in the number of rude comments made by the daughter during the "intervention phase," it is unclear whether this decrease in rudeness: (a) is due to the effect of the intervention or (b) is simply an extension of a decline in the daughter's rudeness that was caused by some uncontrolled factor that began during the "baseline phase" of the study.[3,7,10] A lack of a stable baseline measure of the target behavior prevents psychologists from having a high level of confidence in conclusions they draw about the effectiveness of an intervention in modifying behavior.

But even if psychologists have acquired a stable measure of a target behavior during both the "baseline" and "intervention" phases of a single-subject research study, can they confidently conclude that the change in behavior across phases of the study are caused by the intervention in an "AB design"? Unfortunately, the answer to that question is "no." The reason why is that in addition to the intervention, there may be additional factors within the research environment that also change over time as the subject takes part in the "baseline" and "intervention" phases of the study.[7,9,10] These factors include events occurring outside of the research study (i.e. history),[1,2,4] and changes in the physical, psychological, or emotional state of the subject (i.e. maturation)[1,2,4] that can cause a change in a subject's behavior over the course of the research study. As a result, the observed change in behavior during the "intervention phase" may be due to the intervention or the effect of a confounding variable. To determine whether the intervention is responsible for the change in behavior, the psychologist needs to remove the intervention and see if the change in behavior that occurred during the "intervention phase" disappears when the intervention is no longer in effect. This would require a psychologist to use an "ABA research design."[1,6,8]

In an **"ABA design,"** after an initial "baseline phase" (A$_1$) and "intervention phase" (B) have been completed, a second "baseline phase" (A$_2$) will be conducted in which the intervention is removed and repeated measurements of the target behavior are collected.[1,3,6,7] This process is often referred to as a "return to baseline."[7,8] In the "rudeness" study, during the second "baseline phase," the psychologist would have the father end the monetary intervention for the next 5 days (i.e. the daughter would no longer have the opportunity to earn money by reducing the number of rude comments she makes). During this 5-day period, the psychologist would have the father count the number of rude comments made by his daughter each day and plot these measurements on a graph. Once again, he would tell the father not to make any changes in his daughter's life during the 5 days in order to get a stable measure of his daughter's rudeness as it naturally occurs and to not introduce any confounding factors into the study. The father's graph of the number of rude comments made by his daughter during the second 5-day "baseline phase" appears below.

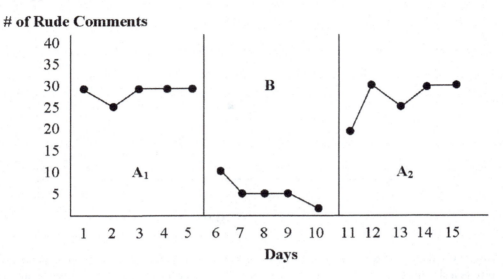

Notice in the graph how the number of rude comments made per day by the daughter during the second "baseline phase" (A_2) increased when the monetary intervention was removed. In addition, notice how the number of rude comments the daughter made per day during the second "baseline phase" (A_2) is comparable to the number of rude comments she made per day during the initial "baseline phase" (A_1). When this occurs, the initial "baseline" is said to have been "recovered."[2] It also establishes the reliability of the initial baseline measure of the target behavior (i.e. number of rude comments).[2,4] Given that the daughter's rudeness decreased when the intervention was in effect and increased back to pre-intervention level when the intervention was no longer in effect, the psychologist would now be more confident in concluding that the decrease in rudeness during the "intervention phase" was due to the effect of the intervention.

But how would the psychologist have interpreted the results of the study if the initial "baseline" level of rudeness had not been "recovered" during the second "baseline phase" of the study? Specifically, how would the psychologist have interpreted the results of the study if the father's graph of the number of rude comments his daughter made during the second "baseline phase" of the study had appeared as shown below?

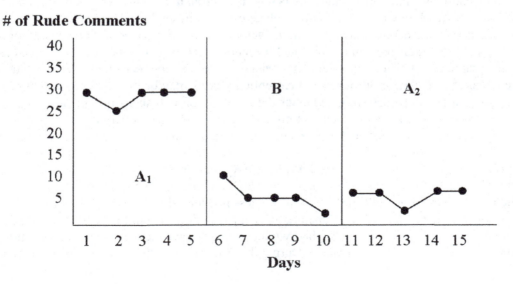

Notice in the graph how the number of rude comments made per day by the daughter during the second "baseline phase" (A_2) remains at a level that is comparable to what occurred during the "intervention phase" (B). Furthermore, notice how the number of rude comments made per day by the daughter during the second "baseline phase" (A_2) is not comparable to the number of rude comments she made per day during the initial "baseline phase" (A_1) of the study. Therefore, the initial "baseline" level of rudeness (A_1) has not been "recovered."[2] The problem that arises when the initial "baseline" level of the target behavior is not "recovered" is that the results of the study are open to multiple interpretations. On one hand, the results could indicate the intervention was not the cause of the decrease in the number of rude comments the daughter made per day during the "intervention phase." The decrease in the number of rude comments may have been caused by a factor other than the intervention that is still affecting the daughter's behavior during the second "baseline phase."[2,4,8] On the other hand, the results could indicate the intervention was responsible for the decrease in the number of rude comments during the "intervention phase" and this decrease in rudeness is being reinforced by some new factor during the second "baseline phase."[4] For example, someone in the daughter's life (e.g. a friend, family member, acquaintance) may have noticed the decrease in the number of rude comments she was making during the 5-day "intervention phase" and complimented her on this change in behavior. This recognition of the change in her behavior by others may have motivated her to maintain her decreased number of rude comments per day during the second "baseline phase" of the study after the intervention was no longer in effect.

Unfortunately, when the initial "baseline" level of a target behavior is not "recovered," and the results are open to multiple interpretations, the single-subject research design does not allow psychologists to determine with a high level of confidence which interpretation is correct. For this reason, when an intervention is likely to have an irreversible effect on a subject and the initial "baseline" level of a target behavior is unlikely to be "recovered," an "ABA design" is not recommended.[3,4,8] This is often the case in single-subject research studies where the intervention being studied is designed to modify behavior by increasing knowledge, skills, abilities, and/or experience of a subject.[2,7] Since a subject is unlikely to "unlearn" the knowledge, skills, abilities and/or experience acquired during the "intervention phase," the effect of the intervention is likely to be irreversible, and it is unlikely that behavior will return to the initial "baseline" level when the intervention is withdrawn. In such cases, the "ABA design" is not a recommended strategy for assessing the effectiveness of the intervention in modifying behavior.

In addition to potentially being unable to "recover" the initial "baseline" level of a target behavior, the "ABA design" also presents a potential ethical dilemma for psychologists. This ethical dilemma arises when a positive behavioral change occurs during the "intervention phase" (e.g. increase in a healthy, adaptive behavior; decrease in an unhealthy, maladaptive behavior). In order to determine if the positive behavioral change was due to the effect of the intervention, psychologists would have to conduct a second "baseline phase" in order to determine whether the behavior returns to the initial "baseline" level when the intervention is withdrawn. But a "return to baseline"[7,8] would mean that a subject's behavior would return to the less healthy and maladaptive level that existed before the introduction of the intervention.[1,2,9] When faced with this ethical dilemma, psychologists have two options. Option 1 would be to introduce a second "baseline phase" to assess the effectiveness of the intervention, knowing the subject's behavior may return to a less healthy or maladaptive level. Option 2 would be to not introduce a second "baseline phase," but instead continue the "intervention phase" where the subject's behavior is at a healthy, adaptive level.[6,7,9] Psychologists who select Option 2 know that as a result of their decision, they will be unable to determine whether the positive change in behavior was due to the effect of the intervention. The level of risk to the subject (e.g. physical, psychological, social) associated with a "return to baseline" will often play a significant role in the decisions made by psychologists who are facing this ethical dilemma.

The psychologist's "rudeness" study provides an illustration of this ethical dilemma. In the "intervention phase" of the study, the number of rude comments the daughter made per day decreased to a healthier, adaptive level compared to her behavior during the initial "baseline phase." In response to this positive, behavioral change, the psychologist would have to decide if he will: (a) introduce a second "baseline phase" to determine if the reduction in the number of rude comments made by the daughter was due to the effect of the monetary intervention while knowing that the daughter's level of rudeness could return to the unhealthy, maladaptive level that caused her father to seek his assistance or (b) not introduce a second "baseline phase," but instead continue the "intervention phase" where the daughter's rudeness is at a healthy, adaptive level knowing that he will be unable to determine whether the positive change in the daughter's behavior was due to the effect of the intervention. The level of risk to the daughter (e.g. social, physical, psychological) associated with a "return to baseline" would have a strong influence on how the psychologist responds to this ethical dilemma.

When psychologists use an "ABA design" and are able to "recover" the initial "baseline" level of a target behavior, they can collect additional evidence to support the effectiveness of the intervention by adding an additional "intervention phase" to their design and transforming their "ABA design" into an "ABAB design." In an ***ABAB design,*** after an initial "baseline phase" (A_1), an initial "intervention phase" (B_1), and a second "baseline phase" (A_2), psychologists will conduct a second "intervention phase" (B_2) in which the intervention is reintroduced, and then repeated measurements of the target behavior are collected.[1,2,4,5] In the "rudeness" study, during the second "intervention phase," the psychologist would have the father reinstate the intervention for 5 days (i.e. the daughter would once again have the opportunity to earn money by reducing the number of rude comments she makes). During this 5-day period, the psychologist would have the father count the number of rude comments made by his daughter each day and plot his measurements on a graph. He would tell the father not to make any changes in his daughter's life during the 5 days in order to get a stable measure of his daughter's rudeness as it naturally occurs and to not introduce any confounding factors into the study. The father's graph of the number of rude comments made by his daughter during the second 5-day "intervention phase" appears below.

# of Rude Comments

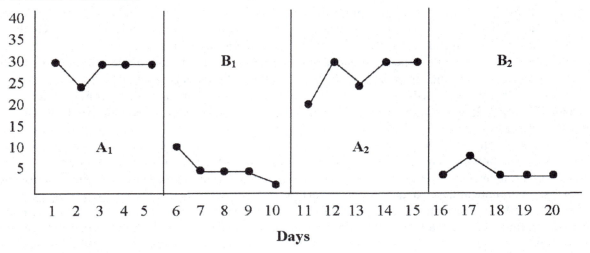

Notice in the graph how the number of rude comments made per day by the daughter during the second "intervention phase" (B_2) decreased when the intervention was reintroduced. Also, notice how the number of rude comments made per day by the daughter during the second "intervention phase" (B_2) is comparable to the number of rude comments that she made per day during the initial "intervention phase" of the study (B_1). Therefore, the initial "intervention" level of the target behavior has been "recovered."[2] In addition, notice how the number of rude comments made per day by the daughter decreases when the intervention is in effect (i.e. B_1 and B_2 "intervention phases") and increases whenever the intervention is not in effect (i.e. A_1 and A_2 "baseline phases"). Finally, you should notice how the number of rude comments made per day by the daughter during the second "baseline" and "intervention" phases of the study (i.e. A_2 and B_2) replicate the number of rude comments made per day by the daughter in the initial "baseline" and "intervention" phases of the study (i.e. A_1 and B_1). In sum, the results of the psychologist's "ABAB design" allow him to confidently conclude that his monetary intervention was effective in modifying the daughter's behavior and decreasing the number of rude comments the daughter made per day; a result for which her father will be eternally grateful!

Multiple Baseline Designs

When psychologists want to conduct a single-subject study to test the effectiveness of an intervention and they believe: (a) the intervention is likely to have an irreversible effect on a subject, (b) the initial "baseline" level of a target behavior is unlikely to be "recovered" during a second "baseline phase," and (c) that it would be unethical to return a subject to baseline after the "intervention phase," their design of choice should be the "multiple baseline design."[1,2,4] The *"multiple baseline design"* is used by psychologists to demonstrate that an intervention is effective in modifying a target behavior across multiple subjects, multiple settings, or multiple behaviors.

Multiple Baseline Design (Multiple Subjects)

To determine whether an intervention is effective across multiple subjects, psychologists will begin by taking repeated measurements of a target behavior for multiple subjects to establish an initial "baseline" measure of behavior for each subject. Each subject will then be exposed to the intervention at a different point in time, and repeated measurements of the target behavior will once again be taken. If the intervention is effective in modifying a target behavior, a change in behavior will be observed immediately after each of the subjects has been exposed to the intervention and the behavioral change will be maintained throughout the "intervention phase."[6,9,10] Unlike the traditional "AB design" whose results can be influenced by uncontrolled factors within the research environment that change over time as the subject takes part in the "baseline" and "intervention" phases of the research study, the "multiple baseline design" allows psychologists to rule out such uncontrolled factors as a potential cause of observed changes in the target behavior.[1,2,5] How? By exposing subjects to the intervention at different points in time (rather than at one point in time as is done in the traditional "AB design"), psychologists can rule out uncontrolled factors which change over the phases of the study as potential causes of a change in behavior if all the subjects experience a similar change in behavior immediately following the introduction of the intervention.

To illustrate how a psychologist would conduct a "multiple baseline design" study with multiple subjects, let's assume a School Psychologist has developed a program designed to teach high school students anger management skills. The School Psychologist wants to determine if her program will be effective in modifying the behavior of aggressive high school students and decrease the number of fights these students are involved in each week at school. To conduct her study, she recruits three high school students who the principal identified as having a history of being involved in a high number of fights every week at school. She observes the three students at school for several weeks and counts the number of fights each of the students is involved in each week and records her measurements on a graph. She then introduces her intervention (i.e. anger management program) to each of the students. She has Student #1 take part in her anger management program after observing his behavior for 4 weeks. She has Student #2 take part in her anger management program after observing his behavior for 8 weeks. She has Student #3 take part in her anger management program after observing his behavior for 12 weeks. During the "intervention phase" of her study, the School Psychologist would continue to observe the three students at school and count the number of fights each of the students are involved in each week and record her measurements on her graph. The total duration of the School Psychologist's study will be 16 weeks. The results of the School Psychologist's study appear following.

# of School Fights

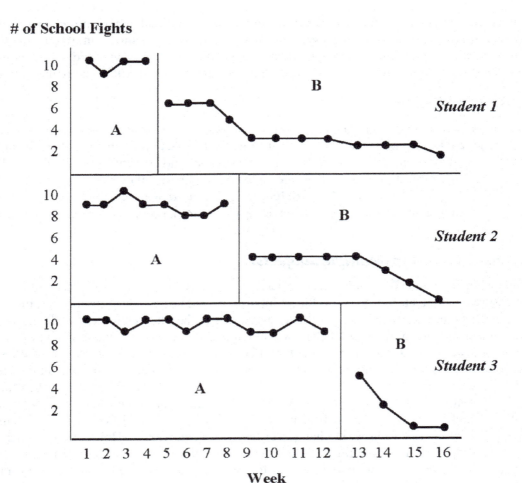

In looking at the School Psychologist's data, we can see that the number of fights each of the three students was involved in each week at school decreased immediately after taking part in the School Psychologist's anger management program. In addition, the decline in the number of fights was maintained by all three of the students throughout the "intervention phase." Based on the results of her research study, the School Psychologist could confidently conclude that: (a) her anger management program was effective in modifying the behavior of aggressive high school students and decreasing the number of fights the students were involved in each week at school, and (b) the positive effect of her anger management program was shown to generalize across multiple students.

Multiple Baseline Design (Multiple Settings)

To determine whether an intervention is effective in modifying a target behavior across multiple settings, psychologists begin by taking repeated measurements of a target behavior for a single subject in multiple settings to establish an initial "baseline" measure of the target behavior in each setting. The subject is then exposed to the intervention in each setting at a different point in time and repeated measurements of the target behavior are again taken. If the intervention is effective in modifying a target behavior across multiple settings, a change in the subject's behavior will be observed across each setting immediately after the subject has been exposed to the intervention and this behavioral change will be maintained during the "intervention phase."[1,2,6,10]

To illustrate how a psychologist would conduct a "multiple baseline design" study across multiple settings, let's assume a Developmental Psychologist has developed a program designed to reduce tantrums in young children. He wants to determine if his program will be effective in reducing the tantrums of a 4-year-old child who, according to both her parents, is having several tantrums each day at home and at school. He begins by observing the 4-year-old child at home and at school for several days. He counts the number of tantrums the child has each day at home and at school and records his measurements on a graph. He then exposes the child to his anti-tantrum program (i.e. intervention) in each setting, at different points in time. He introduces his intervention program at school after observing the child's behavior for five days. He introduces his intervention program in the home after observing the child's behavior for eight days. During the "intervention phase" of his study, the Developmental Psychologist will continue to observe the child's behavior at home and at school and count the number of tantrums the child has in each setting. He will again record his measurements on his graph. The results of the Developmental Psychologist's study appear below.

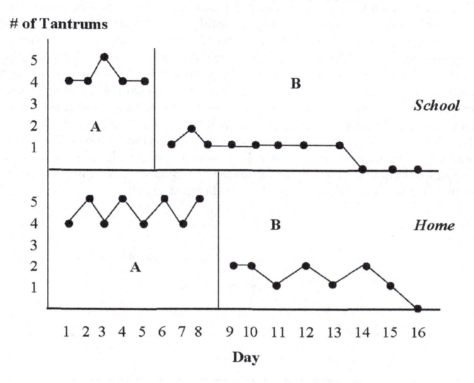

In looking at the Developmental Psychologist's data, we can see the number of tantrums the child had each day at school and at home decreased immediately after the child was exposed to the anti-tantrum program. In addition, the decline in the number of tantrums at school and at home was maintained by the child throughout the "intervention phase." Based on the results of his study, the Developmental Psychologist could confidently conclude that: (a) his anti-tantrum program was effective in modifying the child's behavior and decreasing the number of tantrums the child had each day at school and in the home, and (b) the positive effect of his anti-tantrum program generalized across multiple settings.

Multiple Baseline Design (Multiple Behaviors)

To determine whether an intervention is effective in modifying multiple target behaviors in a single subject, psychologists would begin by taking repeated measurements of the target behaviors in order to establish an initial "baseline" measure for each of the target behaviors. The intervention is then introduced at different points in time to determine whether it is effective in modifying each of the target behaviors. During the "intervention phase" of the study, psychologists would once again take repeated measurements of the multiple target behaviors. If the intervention is effective in modifying the multiple target behaviors, a change in each of the subject's target behaviors will be observed immediately after the subject has been exposed to the intervention and these behavioral changes will be maintained throughout the "intervention phase."[1,4,5,6]

To illustrate how a psychologist would conduct a "multiple baseline design" study for the purpose of determining whether an intervention is effective in modifying multiple behaviors in a single subject, let's assume that a Personality Psychologist has developed a program designed to help individuals overcome shyness. Specifically, the program is designed to help extremely shy individuals acquire the skills they need to be able to engage in a conversation with someone they have just met. These skills include maintaining: (a) proper eye contact, (b) appropriate volume of one's voice, and (c) a confident body posture during a conversation. She begins by placing an ad in the local paper to recruit an individual who suffers from extreme shyness to participate in her study. A college-age female agrees to participate in the study. The Personality Psychologist takes her subject to a local mall and has her subject attempt to engage in 1-minute conversations with people in the mall whom the subject has never met. During these 1-minute conversations, the Personality Psychologist observes the amount of time (i.e. # of seconds) the subject maintains proper eye contact, keeps her voice at an appropriate conversational volume, and displays a body posture that signals confidence, and records her measurements on a graph. After observing her subject engage in three, 1-minute conversations, the Personality Psychologist exposes the subject to the portion of her program designed to improve an individual's skill in maintaining proper eye contact during a conversation. She then exposes her subject to the portion of her program that is designed to improve an individual's skill in keeping their voice at an appropriate conversational volume during a conversation after observing her subject engage in six, 1-minute conversations. Finally, she exposes her subject to the portion of her program that is designed to improve an individual's ability to maintain a confident body posture during a conversation after observing her subject engage in eleven, 1-minute conversations. During the "intervention phase" of her study, the Personality Psychologist will continue to observe the amount of proper eye contact, appropriate conversational volume, and confident posture her subject displays while attempting to engage in 1-minute conversations. The results of the Personality Psychologist's study appear in the graph below.

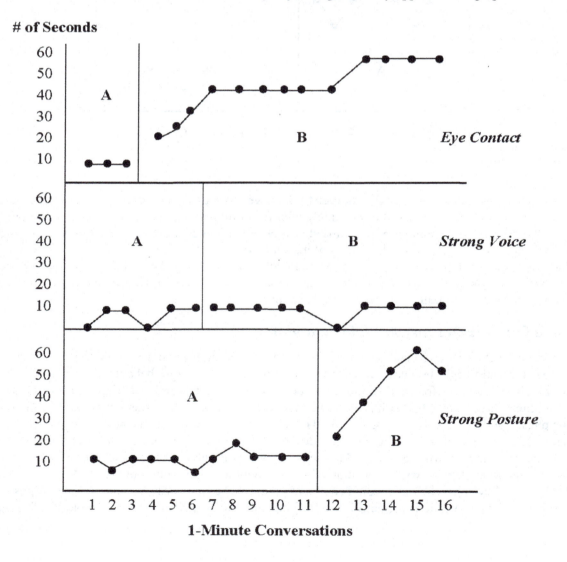

In looking at the Personality Psychologist's data, we can see that the amount of time the subject maintained proper eye contact and a confident posture while engaging in conversations with people whom they have never met both increased immediately after the introduction of the intervention. In addition, the increase in eye contact and confident posture were maintained by the subject throughout the "intervention phase." On the other hand, the amount of time that the subject maintained an appropriate conversational volume remained unchanged immediately after the intervention was introduced. In addition, the amount of appropriate conversational volume displayed by the subject remained unchanged throughout the "intervention phase." In response to her program's inability to increase the amount of time the subject maintained an appropriate conversational volume, the psychologist is likely to: (a) examine the portion of her program that is designed to enhance this behavior to explore why it may have been ineffective in changing this behavior, (b) examine additional factors that were present in the research environment during the study to determine whether any of these factors could have specifically caused the conversational volume behavior to remain unchanged by the intervention, and (c) conduct additional "multiple baseline design" studies with additional extremely shy subjects in order to determine the extent to which the results of her study generalize across multiple subjects.

Alternating Treatments Design

While most single-subject research studies examine the effectiveness of a single intervention in modifying a target behavior of a single subject, there are also single-subject research studies in which psychologists examine the effectiveness of two (or more) interventions in modifying a target behavior in a single subject. Single-subject research studies that examine the effectiveness of two (or more) interventions often use a research design referred to as an *"alternating treatments design."*[10,12,13] In some "alternating treatment design" studies, psychologists compare a target behavior when an intervention is in effect versus when an intervention is not in effect (i.e. treatment vs. no treatment).[11,12] In other "alternating treatment design" studies, psychologists compare a target behavior when intervention A is in effect versus when intervention B is in effect (i.e. treatment vs. treatment).[9,12,13] Let's see how psychologists use an "alternating treatment design" to study the effectiveness of two (or more) interventions in modifying a target behavior.

To study the effectiveness of two (or more) treatments in modifying a target behavior, psychologists would begin by taking repeated measurements of the target behavior while there are no interventions in effect. This would establish a "baseline" measure of the target behavior. Psychologists would then decide how many "treatment sessions" they will have in their study (i.e. how many times will the subject be exposed to each of the interventions during the study). The subject would then be exposed to each intervention an equivalent number of times and in a randomized order across treatment sessions.[3,12,13] During each treatment session (i.e. when an intervention is in effect), psychologists will once again measure the target behavior and plot these measurements on their graph. When creating their graph, psychologists plot the data for each intervention separately.[12,13] This allows psychologists to compare the effectiveness of the two (or more) interventions in modifying the target behavior through a visual inspection of their graph. The intervention which produces the greatest positive change in the target behavior (i.e. increase of a healthy, adaptive behavior; decrease of an unhealthy, maladaptive behavior) would be considered the most effective of the interventions.[13]

To illustrate how a psychologist could use an "alternating treatments design" to study the effectiveness of two or more interventions in modifying a target behavior in a single subject, let's assume that an Industrial-Organizational Psychologist has been hired by an organization's CEO to help the organization address its current absenteeism problem. Over the last year, the average percentage of the organization's employees who call off work each day has reached 25%! With a quarter of its workforce calling off work each day, the organization has been unable to meet the needs of its customers. The Industrial-Organizational Psychologist decides to use an "alternating treatments design" to conduct his single-subject research study. The organization will serve as the "single subject" in his research study.[2]

To begin, the Industrial-Organizational Psychologist first measures the percentage of the organization's employees who call off work each day for 1 week (i.e. 5 work days), and he plots these measurements on a graph. He uses these measurements to establish his "baseline" measure of employee absenteeism. He then decides that he will expose the employees to two intervention programs designed to reduce employee absenteeism over the next two weeks (i.e. 10 work days). He will expose the employees to each intervention for

5 days and employees will be exposed to the two interventions in a randomized order during the 10 day "intervention phase" of the study. When employees are exposed to intervention A, all employees who show up for work on that day will have their names entered into a raffle for a $25 gift card that can be used at area stores and restaurants. When employees are exposed to intervention B, all employees who show up for work on that day will be given a $10 coupon they can use to buy lunch in the company cafeteria. Prior to the start of the "intervention phase" of the study, the CEO sends all employees a memo in which he describes the two interventions that will be implemented during the next two weeks (i.e. 10 work days) and provides a schedule of the days on which each of the interventions will be implemented. Intervention A (i.e. gift card raffle) will be implemented on days 2, 5, 7, 8, and 10 of the "intervention phase." Intervention B (i.e. free lunch coupon) will be implemented on days 1, 3, 4, 6, and 9 of the "intervention phase." Since the employees know on which days each of the interventions will be implemented, the Industrial-Organizational Psychologist will be able to determine which intervention is more effective in encouraging employees to come to work by measuring the rate of absenteeism on the days each of the interventions is implemented. During the "intervention phase," the Industrial-Organizational Psychologist will once again measure the percentage of employees who call off work each day and plot these measurements on his graph. He will plot the data for each intervention separately so he will be able to identify which of the interventions was more effective in reducing employee absenteeism through a visual inspection of his graph. The results of the Industrial-Organizational Psychologist's study appear below.

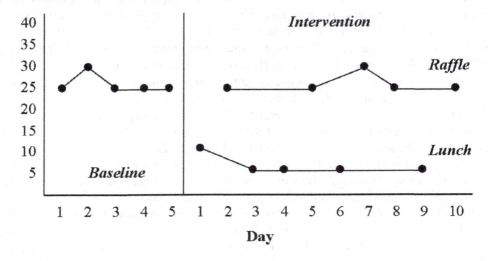

In looking at the Industrial-Organizational Psychologist's data, it is clear intervention B (i.e. free lunch coupon) was more effective than intervention A (i.e. gift card raffle) in reducing the percentage of employees calling off work each day. On the days when intervention B was in effect, the percentage of employees calling off work fell well below the current rate of 25%. By comparison, on those days when intervention A was in effect, the percentage of employees who called off work remained at the current rate of 25%. Based on these results, if the organization provides a free lunch to all employees who come to work, a higher percentage of the employees will show up to work each day which will allow the organization to better meet the needs of its customers. If the money saved by reducing absenteeism exceeds the money needed to provide employees who come to work each day with a free lunch, the organization will have identified a cost-effective intervention that will be effective in addressing their current absenteeism problem.

Strengths of Single-Subject Research

Single-subject research has several strengths that make it an attractive method of research for psychologists. First, single-subject research allows psychologists to draw a causal conclusion about the effectiveness of an intervention based on the results of a single subject[2,10] and examine the generalizability of the results through replicating the study with a small number of additional subjects.[1,2,5] Second, unlike research studies that examine the effectiveness of an intervention by comparing the average levels of behavior across large groups of subjects, single-subject research allows psychologists to see how behavior of individual subjects is affected by an intervention.[1,2,4] Third, psychologists can use single-subject research to study individuals who exhibit behaviors that are atypical, are living with rare physical or psychological conditions, or have unique life experiences.[4,8,11] Fourth, by taking multiple measurements of behavior over time, psychologists can use single-subject research to examine short-term and long-term effects of an intervention.[4,9] Fifth, psychologists can use single-subject research to study the effectiveness of an intervention in modifying behavior of both individuals and larger social units (e.g. organizations, businesses, communities).[4] Sixth, single-subject research provides psychologists with a considerable amount of flexibility. Psychologists can tailor an intervention to an individual's life circumstances rather than having to present a standard intervention to all subjects.[4,8,10] In addition, as psychologists monitor the results of a single-subject study they can make modifications to the intervention and assess its effect by adding additional "baseline" and "intervention phases" to their study. Finally, psychologists can use results of single-subject research to generate additional hypotheses about potential strategies for modifying behavior which can be tested through additional single-subject research or through more experimental methods.[8,9]

Limitations of Single-Subject Research

Single-subject research also has some limitations that psychologists need to consider before making it their design of choice. First, the results of a single-subject research study may have limited generalizability.[2,10,11] An intervention that is effective in changing the behavior of a single subject may not produce an effect that generalizes across different subjects, behaviors, and/or settings. Second, single-subject research can be a time-consuming process.[2,8] In order to test the effectiveness of an intervention in changing a behavior, psychologists must first acquire a stable "baseline" measure of the behavior before the intervention can be introduced. For some behaviors, it can take an extended period of time before psychologists acquire a stable baseline. For some behaviors, psychologists may never be able to acquire a stable baseline. Third, since psychologists take multiple measurements of a subject's behavior during single-subject research, there is the potential for the results of a single-subject research study to be affected by "subject reactivity" (i.e. a subject changes his/her behavior as a result of being aware that his/her behavior is being observed). Fourth, since single-subject research involves measurement of the change in a behavior over time, its results are susceptible to the effects of uncontrolled factors within both the subject (e.g. maturation) and the experimental environment (e.g. history) that change over time.[1,2,4] Fifth, single-subject studies may present psychologists with an ethical dilemma.[1,2,9] In order to determine whether an intervention is responsible for an observed change in behavior, the intervention must be withdrawn to see if a subject's behavior reverts to a "baseline" level. At this point in the study, psychologists must decide if the benefits of withdrawing the intervention (i.e. determining whether the intervention is the cause of the behavioral change) outweigh the risks to the subject associated with withdrawing the potentially beneficial intervention (i.e. the potential return to a less healthy, maladaptive "baseline" level of behavior). Sixth, psychologists do not often rely on advanced statistical analyses when interpreting the results of a single-subject research study. Instead, they typically rely on a more subjective interpretation of the graphical representation of the change in a behavior that occurs during the "baseline" and "intervention" phases of the study.[3,4,8] Finally, when psychologists conduct a single-subject research study, it is obvious to them when their subject is in a "baseline" or "intervention" phase. As a result of this knowledge, there is a potential for "experimenter bias" to influence the results of a single-subject research study.[9] How? By knowing when the subject is in a "baseline" or "intervention" phase, and by knowing the research hypothesis under investigation, psychologists conducting a single-subject research study may allow bias to enter into their measurements of the target behavior in order to ensure the intervention produces the desired change in the target behavior (e.g. increase of a healthy, adaptive behavior; decrease of an unhealthy, maladaptive behavior).

EXERCISE 14A

Analysis of a Baseline Design

The "baseline design" is used by psychologists to demonstrate an intervention is effective in modifying a target behavior in a single subject. Below you will find a description of a single-subject research study in which a Clinical Psychologist is using a "baseline design" to modify the compulsive gambling behavior of a male client and decrease the number of hours he spends each day on Internet gambling sites. Please read the description of the study below and provide your analysis of its methodology and results by answering the questions that follow the description of the study in the spaces provided.

The Study

A Clinical Psychologist has a male client who is a compulsive gambler. His client has told him that he is currently spending 18–20 hours a day on Internet gambling sites. As a result, he has lost his marriage, his job, and his life savings. The Clinical Psychologist has decided to conduct a single-subject research study with his client and to use a "baseline design" to test the effectiveness of a therapeutic intervention in modifying his client's behavior and decreasing the number of hours he spends each day on Internet gambling sites.

To begin his study, the Clinical Psychologist monitors the Internet activity of his client and records the number of hours his client spends on Internet gambling sites each day for 1 week (i.e. 7 days) and plots these measurements on a graph. He uses these measurements to establish a "baseline" measure of the number of hours his client spends each day on Internet gambling sites. He then exposes his client to a therapeutic intervention designed to reduce his impulse to gamble each day for 1 week (i.e. 7 days). During the "intervention phase" of the study, he continues to monitor the Internet activity of his client and records the number of hours his client spends on Internet gambling sites. He once again plots the measurements on his graph. The results of the Clinical Psychologist's study of his client's compulsive gambling appear below.

of Hours of Internet Gambling

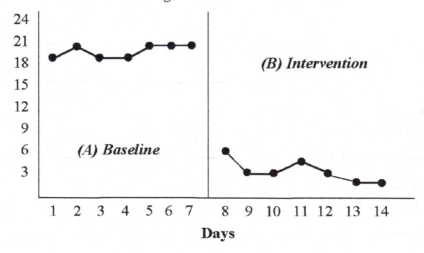

01. Based on the results of the Clinical Psychologist's study, has his therapeutic intervention been effective in modifying his client's behavior and reducing the number of hours his client spent each day on Internet gambling sites?

Effective? ☐ Yes ☐ No

Rationale:

02. Based on the results of his study, can the Clinical Psychologist conclude that his therapeutic intervention was the cause of the reduction in the number of hours his client spent each day on Internet gambling sites? If you answer "No," what are two alternative explanations that could account for the change in his client's gambling behavior?

Cause? ☐ Yes ☐ No

Rationale:

Alternative Explanation 1	
Alternative Explanation 2	

03. How could the Clinical Psychologist modify his research design to be more confident that his therapeutic intervention was the cause of the reduction in the number of hours his client spent each day on Internet gambling sites?

Design Modification?

04. The Clinical Psychologist is considering adding an additional "baseline" phase to his research study (i.e. transform his "AB design" to an "ABA design"). What would you tell the Clinical Psychologist are the "pros" and "cons" of adding an additional "baseline" phase?

"Pros" of additional baseline phase	
"Cons" of additional baseline phase	

05. Imagine that you are the Clinical Psychologist conducting this research study. Would you add an additional "baseline" phase to your research design?

Additional "Baseline" Phase? ☐ Yes   ☐ No
Rationale:

06. Assume that the Clinical Psychologist does add an additional "baseline" phase to his research design. Based on the results, can the Clinical Psychologist now conclude that his therapeutic intervention was the cause of the reduction in the number of hours his client spent each day on Internet gambling sites?

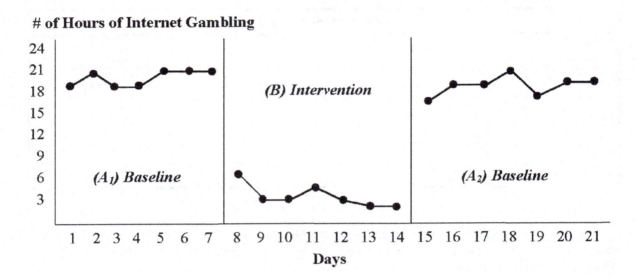

# of Hours of Internet Gambling

Cause? ☐ Yes   ☐ No

Rationale:

07. What additional modifications could the Clinical Psychologist make to his research design to allow him to more confidently conclude that his therapeutic intervention was the cause of the reduction in the number of hours his client spent each day on Internet gambling sites?

Additional Modifications?

EXERCISE 14B

Analysis of a Multiple Baseline Design

The "multiple baseline design" is used by psychologists to demonstrate an intervention is effective in modifying a target behavior across multiple subjects, settings or behaviors. Below is a description of a single-subject research study in which a Sports Psychologist is using a multiple baseline design to modify the putting of three professional golfers and decrease the total number of putts each of the professional golfers takes during a round of golf. Please read the description of the study and provide your analysis of its methodology and results by answering the questions that follow the description of the study in the spaces provided.

The Study

A Sports Psychologist has developed a new training program designed to improve the putting performance of professional golfers. Her new program is designed to improve putting by teaching professional golfers to use a combination of "positive visual imagery" (i.e. if you see a putt going in the hole, the more likely it will) and "muscle relaxation" (i.e. if you can reduce the tension in your muscles, the more likely you will produce a smooth and effective putting stoke). The Sports Psychologist is currently preparing to test the effectiveness of her new program on a small number of professional golfers. Her plan is to have three professional golfers complete her new training program, observe their putting performances during professional golf tournaments, and assess whether her training program is effective in decreasing the number of putts each of the three professional golfers takes during a typical round of golf.

To begin her research study, the Sports Psychologist recruits three professional golfers who have been having trouble making putts during recent golf tournaments to participate in her research study. She then observes the putting behavior of these three professional golfers during professional golf tournaments and counts the total number of putts each golfer takes during each round of golf and plots her measurements for each professional golfer on a graph. She uses these measurements to establish a "baseline" measure of the number of putts each golfer takes during a typical round of tournament golf. She then has the three professional golfers complete her new training program after completing a different number of rounds of tournament golf. Professional golfer A completes the Sports Psychologist's new training program after completing 6 rounds of tournament golf. Professional golfer B completes the training program after completing 9 rounds of tournament golf. Finally, Professional golfer C completes the training program after having completed 13 rounds of tournament golf. During the "intervention phase" of her research study, the Sports Psychologist continues to observe the putting of the three professional golfers during professional golf tournaments and counts the total number of putts each golfer takes during each round of golf. She once again plots her putting measurements for each professional golfer on her graph. The graph containing the data for the Sports Psychologist's "multiple baseline design" study of the putting performance of her three professional golfers appears on the following page.

# of Putts Per Round

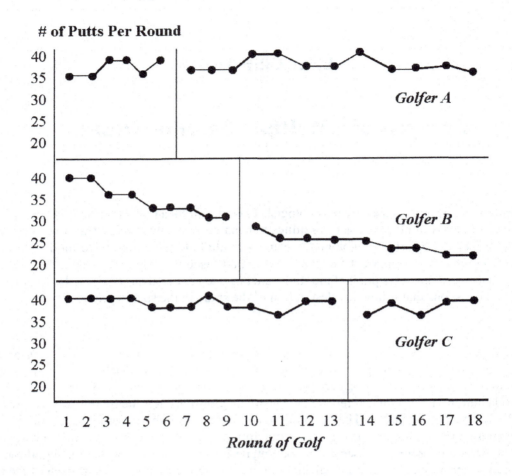

Round of Golf

01. Based on the results of the Sports Psychologist's study, how effective was her new training program in decreasing the number of putts taken during a round of tournament golf for each of the three professional golfers in her research study?

	Effectiveness of Training Program
Professional Golfer A	
Professional Golfer B	
Professional Golfer C	

02. Based on the results of the Sports Psychologist's study, has her new training program been effective in modifying the putting of the three professional golfers and reducing the number of putts taken during a round of tournament golf for all three professional golfers?

Effective? ☐ Yes   ☐ No

Rationale:

03. For which professional golfer was the Sports Psychologist's training program most effective?

Golfer A ☐   Golfer B ☐   Golfer C ☐

While the change in this professional golfer's putting may have been due to the effect of the Sports Psychologist's new training program, what are two alternative explanations that could account for the positive change in this professional golfer's putting performance?

Alternative Explanation 1	
Alternative Explanation 2	

04. What changes would you make to the Sports Psychologist's study to eliminate the alternative explanations and conduct a more valid assessment of the program's effectiveness?

Recommended Changes:

05. Based on the results of the Sports Psychologist's study, what would you recommend her next course of action should be? Provide a rationale for your course of action.

	Market her training program to professional golfers as an effective method for improving putting performance
	Market her training program to professional golfers as a method that will improve the putting performance of 1 in 3 professional golfers
	Conduct additional research on the three professional golfers who took part in her study to see what individual differences in the golfers could have had an influence on the effectiveness of the program
	Repeat her study with another sample of three professional golfers to see if the results replicate those found in her first study
	Redesign or modify her training program to make it more effective and test the new program's effectiveness on a new sample of professional golfers
	Conclude that her training program is not effective and begin designing a new program to improve the putting of professional golfers

Rationale:

EXERCISE 14C

Analysis of an Alternating Treatments Design

Psychologists who want to examine the effectiveness of two (or more) interventions in modifying a target behavior in a single subject often use a single-subject research design known as an "alternating treatments design." Below is a description of a single-subject research study in which a Counseling Psychologist is attempting to use an "alternating treatments design" to try to save a couple's marriage. Please read the description of the study and then provide your analysis of the study's methodology and results by answering the questions that follow the description of the study in the spaces provided.

The Study

A Counseling Psychologist has a female client who is concerned about her marriage. Her husband is spending so much time at work that he spends only 5–10 minutes a day with his kids. As a result, all of the childcare responsibilities have fallen on her shoulders and the kids have no relationship with their father. If her husband does not change his behavior, she is prepared to file for a divorce. The Counseling Psychologist tells her that he is going to conduct a single-subject research study with her husband as the "subject" and use an "alternating treatments design" to test the effectiveness of three interventions in modifying her husband's behavior, and increasing the amount of time he spends at home with his kids.

To begin the study, the Counseling Psychologist has his client measure the amount of time her husband spends with his kids each day for 1 week (i.e. 5 work days) and he plots these measurements on a graph. He uses these measurements to establish a "baseline" measure of the amount of time the husband spends with his kids each day. He then exposes the husband to each of the interventions for 1 week (i.e. 5 work days). Prior to introducing each of the interventions, the Counseling Psychologist sits down with the husband and explains to him exactly what will occur during each intervention and that each intervention will last for 1 week (i.e. 5 work days). During the first week of the research study (i.e. days 1–5) he exposes the husband to intervention A. When intervention A is in effect, for each day the husband does not spend at least 30 minutes at home with his kids, he has to buy each of his three kids a $25 toy. During the second week of the research study (i.e. days 6–10), he exposes the husband to intervention B. When intervention B is in effect, each day the husband does not spend at least 30 minutes with his kids, he has to do all the laundry, wash all the dishes, and put the kids to bed while his wife gets the night off from any household responsibilities. Finally, during the third week of the research study (i.e. days 11–15), he exposes the husband to intervention C. When intervention C is in effect, for each day the husband does not spend at least 30 minutes with his kids, his wife will withhold affection, touch, and physical intimacy from her husband. During the "intervention phases" of the research study, the Counseling Psychologist has his client measure the amount of time her husband spends with his kids each day and he plots these measurements on his graph. He plots the data separately for each of the three interventions so that he will be able to identify which of the interventions was more effective in increasing the amount of time the husband spends with his kids though a quick visual inspection of his graph. The results of the Counseling Psychologist's study appear on the following page.

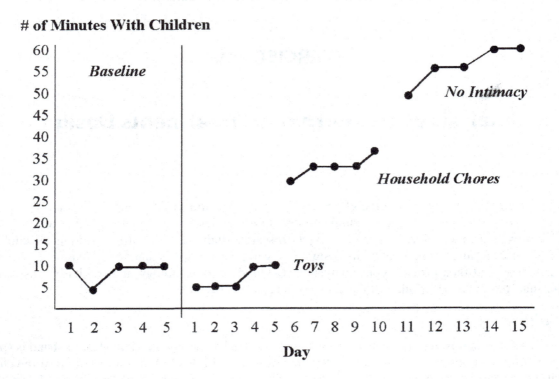

# of Minutes With Children

01. Based on the results of the Counseling Psychologist's study, how effective were each of the interventions in increasing the amount of time the husband spent each day with his kids?

	Effectiveness of Intervention
Intervention A (i.e. Toys)	
Intervention B (i.e. Chores)	
Intervention C (i.e. Intimacy)	

02. Which of the Counseling Psychologist's interventions appears to have been most effective in increasing the amount of time the husband spent each day with his kids?

Most Effective?	

03. While change in the husband's behavior may have been due to the Counseling Psychologist's interventions, what are **three (3)** alternative explanations that could account for the change in the amount of time the husband spent each day with his kids?

Alternative Explanation 1	
Alternative Explanation 2	
Alternative Explanation 3	

04. After reviewing the methodology he used to conduct his study, the Counseling Psychologist realized there was a flaw in his methodology that could have influenced the results of his study. What is the flaw in the Counseling Psychologist's methodology?

Design Flaw?

05. How would you redesign the Counseling Psychologist's study to: **(a)** eliminate the alternative explanations you identified, **(b)** remove the methodological flaw in the Psychologist's design, and **(c)** conduct a more valid assessment of the effectiveness of the interventions in modifying the husband's behavior and increasing the amount of time he spends each day with his kids?

Redesigned Methodology

References

1. Cozby, P. C., & Bates, S. C. (2011). *Methods in behavioral research* (11th ed.). New York, NY: McGraw-Hill Publishers.

2. Bordens, K. S., & Abbot, B. B. (2011). *Research design and methods: A process approach* (8th ed.). Boston, MA: McGraw-Hill Publishers.

3. Kantowitz, B. H., Roediger, H. L., & Elmes, D. G. (2014). *Experimental psychology* (10th ed.). Stamford, CT: Cengage Learning.

4. Passer, M. W. (2013). *Research methods: Concepts and connections*. New York, NY: Worth Publishers.

5. Ray, W. J. (2011). *Methods: Towards a science of behavior and experience* (10th ed.). Belmont, CA: Wadsworth/Cengage Learning.

6. Jackson, S. L. (2014). *Research methods: A modular approach* (3rd ed.). Stamford, CT: Cengage Learning.

7. Smith, R. A., & Davis, S. F. (2012). *The psychologist as detective: An introduction to conducting research in psychology* (6th ed.). Boston, MA: Pearson Publishers.

8. Beins, B. C. (2012). *Research methods: A tool for life* (3rd ed.). Boston, MA: Pearson Publishers.

9. Rizvi, S. L., & Nock, M. K. (2008). Single-case experimental designs for the evaluation of treatments for self-injurious and suicidal behaviors. *Suicide and Life Threatening Behavior, 38*(5), 498–510.

10. Evans, A. N., & Rooney, B. F. (2007). *Methods in psychological research*. Thousand Oaks, CA: Sage Publications.

11. Leary, M. R. (2007). *Introduction to behavioral research methods* (5th ed.). Boston, MA: Pearson/ Allyn & Bacon.

12. Barlow, D. H., & Hayes, S. C. (1979). Alternating treatments design: One strategy for comparing the effects of two treatments in a single subject. *Journal of Applied Behavior Analysis, 12*(2), 199–210.

13. The Wing Institute. (n.d.). Single-subject design examples. *WingInstitute.Org*. Retrieved from http://winginstitute.org/Graphs/Mindmap/Single-Subject-Design-Examples/